A STUDY IN TRADE-CYCLE HISTORY

A STUDY IN
TRADE-CYCLE HISTORY

ECONOMIC FLUCTUATIONS IN
GREAT BRITAIN
1833–1842

BY

R. C. O. MATTHEWS

Fellow of St John's College, Cambridge
Lecturer in Economics in the University of Cambridge

CAMBRIDGE
AT THE UNIVERSITY PRESS
1954

PUBLISHED BY
THE SYNDICS OF THE CAMBRIDGE UNIVERSITY PRESS
London Office: Bentley House, N.W. I
American Branch: New York
Agents for Canada, India, and Pakistan: Macmillan

Printed in Great Britain at the University Press, Cambridge
(Brooke Crutchley, University Printer)

CONTENTS

CONTENTS

LIST OF TABLES

LIST OF CHARTS

PREFACE

THE method of inquiry exemplified by the present work is only one of a number of ways in which empirical research on the trade cycle may be carried out. By subjecting a single brief period to close study, we are enabled to do as full justice as the evidence permits to the complexity of the fluctuations experienced, and to avoid the dangers of over-simplification which are liable to result from attempts to impose too uniform a pattern on the history of fluctuations in different periods. On the other hand, an inquiry along the present lines does not by itself permit us to assess the place of the fluctuations studied in the longer-run evolution of the national economy nor to discern changes in the cyclical process itself over time. Extended comparisons of the 1830's with other periods are accordingly not entered into in the following pages. I hope, however, that the reader will consider that I have provided material from which such comparisons may usefully be made.

The general line of approach adopted is 'quantitative-historical'. I have endeavoured to make full use of such statistics as are available, including both continuous series and more isolated indicators, but have not engaged in elaborate econometric manipulation which the uneven coverage and unreliability of the figures would render inappropriate. At the same time I have drawn largely on 'literary' sources. The amount of material available for the study of so remote a period is, of course, lamentably inadequate when compared with that available for the study of the trade cycle in more modern times. In particular, statistics on the volume of production are extremely defective, and no amount of future research is likely to succeed in making them otherwise. But our sources are capable of telling us a good deal—more, perhaps, than has always been realised. Moreover, it cannot be said that the material relevant for the study of the trade cycle in the earlier part of the nineteenth century is yet anything like exhausted. It has repeatedly been brought home to me in the course of my work that the historian of the trade cycle should ideally make himself expert on all aspects of the economy he is concerned with; no branch of economic history is irrelevant. In practice, of course, this is an unattainable ideal, and I have had for the most part to rely on the more readily accessible sources. When further specialised studies, based on business records and similar sources, dealing with such subjects as the organisation of trade and payments between Britain and her various overseas markets and the evolution of particular industries and regions, have been made by scholars aware of the cyclical problem, the task of the student of trade-cycle history will be substantially lightened, and his chances of arriving at true and valuable conclusions will be correspondingly enhanced.

It remains for me to express my thanks to those who have assisted me by their advice and suggestions. I am indebted to Professor W. W. Rostow for what I have learnt from his published writings and from discussion with him on nineteenth-century trade cycles generally, and also for calling my attention to a number of sources of information which I should otherwise have overlooked. Professor A. H. Imlah's work on import statistics forms the basis of much of what is said in Chapters III, VI and VII, and my thanks are due to him for allowing me to use certain calculations of his which have not been published. The typescript has been read through by Professor J. R. Hicks, Professor Sir Dennis Robertson and Mr A. J. Youngson Brown, all of whom have assisted me greatly by their constructive suggestions and by enabling me to eliminate a number of errors and obscurities that were present in the original draft. In addition, I have had the benefit of the advice and encouragement of Professor Hicks throughout the period while the book has been in preparation. Mr D. M. Joslin read an earlier version of the chapter on banking and favoured me with many useful comments and criticisms, and a like service was rendered by Mr F. Thistlethwaite in connection with the chapter on America. At an earlier stage of my work I received some valuable suggestions from Mr C. N. Ward-Perkins, particularly on the subject of railways. None of the above-mentioned persons is, of course, in any way responsible for the views I have expressed or for any errors of fact or of logic which may remain.

R. C. O. MATTHEWS

CAMBRIDGE

November 1952

CHAPTER I

INTRODUCTION

1. THE PROBLEM TO BE STUDIED

THE purpose of this study is to describe and to attempt to explain the course of short-period fluctuations in the economy of Great Britain between the years 1833 and 1842. Many of the questions we shall seek to answer are such as must be answered by any student of business cycles, whatever country or period he is concerned with. What were the magnitudes that fluctuated: real income, production, employment, prices, profits, or all of these? Were the fluctuations that took place of similar character and timing in different sectors of the economy? What were the main factors contributing to changes in the level of effective demand and in the productive capacity from which that demand was met? A particular question affecting our period concerns the double-headed appearance of the cycle: some students have discerned two peaks of business activity, 1836 and 1839 (or 1840).[1] Were these two peaks of the same nature? Is it legitimate to describe one of them as the major peak and the other in some sense subordinate?

In endeavouring to answer these and other questions, our aim will not be to test any particular theoretical model of the trade cycle, but rather to see what explanation or explanations are suggested by the facts themselves. The pattern of events that will emerge from our inquiry is a complicated one, and in a number of respects does not exactly conform to the normal idea of what happens during business cycles. What we seek to apply in analysis of these events is theory rather than *a* theory.

The arrangement of the following chapters is by subject, not chronological. Chapters II–VII deal with different aspects of Britain's balance of overseas trade, the topic on which the statistical material at our disposal is most ample, and contain also a sketch of the fluctuations taking place contemporaneously in the United States. This extended treatment of Britain's international economic relationships is necessary in view of the large place occupied by foreign trade in the British economy and of the magnitude of the fluctuations that occurred on both sides of the balance of payments, though it will appear in the upshot that the impact of foreign influence on the course of the cycle in this country, while by no means unimportant, was somewhat less great than might perhaps at first sight have been expected. Chapters VIII, IX and X are concerned with the cyclical experience of certain leading industries which between them accounted for a large proportion of that part of the national income which was most liable to short-period fluctuations. Chapter XI discusses movements in the sphere of money and banking, while in the concluding chapter an attempt is made to assess the relative importance in shaping the cyclical process as a whole of the

[1] Cf. Sir William Beveridge, 'The trade cycle in Britain before 1850', *Oxford Economic Papers* (1940), pp. 78, 83–4; W. W. Rostow, *British Economy of the Nineteenth Century* (1948), p. 33. On the other hand, W. L. Thorp, *Business Annals* (1926), p. 160, classifies 1838, 1839, 1840, 1841 and 1842 all as depression years.

various factors that have previously been discussed. The non-chronological method of presentation that has been adopted is not without its disadvantages, but it appeared to be on the whole the most suitable for the purpose in hand. It is hoped that the disadvantages involved are to some extent overcome by the chronological survey and summary which is given in Chapter XII.

2. An Outline of the Cycle

It may be of assistance to the reader unfamiliar with the details of nineteenth-century trade-cycle history if an outline survey of the pattern of fluctuations in our period is here given to precede the fuller analysis of later chapters. The reader might also with advantage cast his eye at this stage over our charts depicting the movement of some of the more important variables which we shall be considering. It should be emphasised that the account given below is intended only as a rough guide, and many of the statements made in it will require to be expanded and qualified as we proceed.

The boom that culminated in the celebrated crisis of December 1825 was followed by seven years of predominantly dull trade. Minor fluctuations took place during these years, and at some times, for instance, in 1828 and in the first half of 1831, trade was relatively prosperous. But there was no full recovery and nothing that could be described as a boom. 1832 was not a good year for trade, but in 1833 there was a fairly marked revival. Recovery proceeded steadily but unspectacularly until about half-way through 1835, when a more violent upward tendency began to be felt. The boom reached its peak in spring 1836, by when a 'mania' was diagnosed in certain fields of activity. In the latter part of 1836 there was a slight fall in prices and in the more speculative manifestations of the boom, and in 1837—a year of financial panic in the United States—the recession became sharp. The next year there was a recovery, and the state of trade was felt to be sound but unexciting. 1839 was a year of conflicting tendencies; for several important statistical series it marked a peak nearly as high as that of 1836, but it none the less witnessed considerable distress in a number of industries, and it was also a year of very high food prices and corn imports and of an alarming drain of gold from the Bank of England. 1840 was more quiescent; business was said to be generally unprofitable, but production for the most part remained high. In 1841, however, recession moved into depression, and in 1842 into deep depression. This year was the hungriest of the 'hungry forties' in Great Britain. There is no doubt that distress was exceptionally acute. In 1842 our chronicle ends, for the recovery which came in 1843 was unmistakable, even though it did not immediately lift the economy to any very high level of activity.

3. The Structure of the Economy

In the following pages many of the magnitudes with which we shall be dealing will be expressed in money terms, and it would therefore be of assistance in getting them into the right perspective if we had a figure for the total value of the national income with which to compare them. Calculation of the movement of the national income between different years is out of the question for a period for which wage statistics are scanty and income-tax figures non-existent; but we can perhaps get some indication of the order of magnitude involved, first by comparing the average level of money wage rates and earnings and the size of the population in our period with the corresponding figures for later periods for which national income estimates have been made and rest on a tolerably sure foundation, and secondly by using the various rough estimates that are available on the value or volume of production in particular industries and the number of persons employed in them.

The conclusion to which calculations of this sort appear to point is that the national income of Great Britain in this period averaged somewhere about £400 million per annum. Of this total the contribution of agriculture may be taken as in the region of £150 million and that of all branches of manufacturing as exceeding £100 million, but probably falling somewhat short of that of agriculture. The most important of the categories which together went to make up the remaining £100–150 million were building, shipping, mining and the service and distributive trades, including domestic service. These figures are of course approximate in the highest degree, but they are perhaps not too misleading to serve for purposes of comparison. It may be observed that on the present reckoning exports comprised about an eighth of the national income.

Table 1. *Occupational distribution of the population of Great Britain in 1841*

	Thousands	
Farmers and others engaged in agriculture	1,499	
Domestic servants	1,165	
Textile operatives	800	
In cotton industry		378
In woollen and worsted industries		167
Builders*	353	
Seamen	248	
Tailors, dressmakers and milliners	233	
Boot and shoe makers	215	
Bakers, butchers, grocers and tavern-keepers	209	
Professional and other educated persons	206	
Miners	194	
General labourers	386	
Persons of independent means	511	
Total enumerated	7,660	
Residue (dependants, etc.)	10,996	
Total population	18,656	

* Viz. bricklayers, carpenters, masons, painters, glaziers, plumbers, plasterers and slaters.

Some further idea of the structure of the economy may be obtained from the particulars of occupational distribution of the population given in the Census of 1841 and summarised in Table 1. These figures are useful and interesting, but it would be a mistake to suppose that they necessarily provide a measure of the proportional contribution to the *national income* of the respective occupational and industrial divisions distinguished, since the ratio of the amount of labour employed to the amount of land and capital employed varied greatly between industries. The value of output per worker was, for example, doubtless a great deal lower in domestic service and in the distributive trades than it was in

3

agriculture or in the textile industries. For this reason—as well as because the less capitalistic trades contributed less proportionately to fluctuations in the national income than they did to the average level of the national income—it is a less serious omission than might be supposed that we shall be able to find little to say about the impact of the cycle upon several of the occupational groups which appear most prominently in Table 1, and instead will be dealing at greater length with such industries as iron and shipbuilding, in which the number of men employed was comparatively small. On the other hand, it will be important to bear in mind throughout the following chapters the very large numbers of people who can have felt only at several removes the impact of the fluctuations with which we shall be concerned.

CHAPTER II

THE BALANCE OF PAYMENTS:
SOME GENERAL CONSIDERATIONS

IT will be convenient in this chapter to deal briefly with a certain number of general points concerning the balance of payments before proceeding to the more detailed discussion of different categories of imports and exports in the ensuing chapters.

1. THE EFFECT OF BALANCE-OF-PAYMENTS MOVEMENTS ON THE LEVEL OF INCOMES

A favourable or unfavourable movement in the balance of payments (the argument applies symmetrically to each) is likely to influence effective demand in two distinct ways.

The first is that which we shall describe as the monetary effect. Under the monetary institutions prevalent in the period under review, a favourable balance of payments led to an inflow of specie which increased the Bank of England's reserve and so tended to reduce the market rate of discount. Similarly, an unfavourable balance tended to lead to stringency in the money market. It will be seen in Chapter XI that the relationship between the level of the Bank of England's reserve and the market rate of discount was extremely close—so close that a statement of the connection between the two scarcely needs to be qualified by *ceteris paribus*. Finally, a rise or fall in discount rates, carrying with it a shift in the structure of interest rates generally, was likely in turn to depress or stimulate trade, although for this period, as for more modern times, the strength of this influence and hence the importance of the monetary effect in general is difficult to assess.

The second way in which the balance of payments is likely to affect the level of activity is that which we shall term the direct effect.[1] Exports taken by themselves are a source of purchasing power to those engaged in the export industries, without providing any corresponding supply of goods for consumption in the exporting country. Consumption of imports, on the other hand, constitutes a diversion of the purchasing power of the nationals of a country away from its own products. Imports represent a leakage from the circular flow of incomes, that is to say, and exports represent an injection into it. Therefore if, for example, exports are higher in year II than in year I, and if imports are the same in the two years or do not rise to the same extent as exports, income and activity will, *ceteris paribus*, tend to rise in year II above the level obtaining in year I, even if the rate of interest is unaffected.[2]

---

[1] The term is chosen merely for convenience, and it is not intended to imply that the monetary effect, by contrast, is necessarily to be considered recondite or unimportant.

[2] For a further discussion of some of the theoretical issues involved here, see pp. 99–101.

2. The Overall Balance of Payments and the Income Balance

Both the direct effect and the monetary effect are of importance in our period. But it is necessary to call attention to an important difference in their respective manners of operation.

The state of the foreign exchanges and of the gold reserve—the significant factors from the point of view of the monetary effect—are the resultant of all items entering into a country's balance of payments, both on current account and on capital account. In reckoning the direction and magnitude of the direct effect, on the other hand, it is necessary to abstract from capital transactions. For example, an increase in capital export (purchase of foreign securities as contrasted with purchase of foreign goods or services) does not represent any subtraction from aggregate expenditure out of income on home-produced goods (unless it is accompanied by an increase in the propensity to save). It is therefore possible if, for example, there is a rise in capital export accompanied by an improvement in the balance of *trade*, for the direct effect to move favourably, although the trend in the balance of *payments* in aggregate (and hence in the monetary effect) is neutral or even adverse. The only way in which capital export as such might operate to depress incomes is through making finance less readily available for purposes of home investment. This less availability of finance would result in an increase in interest rates, or else might manifest itself in a variety of other forms of a less easily ascertainable character. In the absence of specific information on these, we are obliged to limit our attention to interest-rate movements, which brings us back to the monetary effect. We shall designate as the 'income balance' the balance between the various items in the overall balance of payments that are relevant for the direct effect.

In practice the statistics for our period do not enable us to distinguish with any confidence between current and capital transactions. The movement of the Bank of England's gold reserve gives some indication of the state of the balance of payments. It is not a perfect indication, since the amount of gold in circulation within the country was subject to variation; but it is usually possible to take account of this roughly, so that as a measure of the balance-of-payments position the movement of the Bank's reserve is more or less adequate. But we are not able to calculate the balance of trade with any certainty, for reasons that will be explained presently, and invisible items on current account present an even greater difficulty. We therefore have to rely on qualitative evidence—which as far as capital movements are concerned is fairly ample—and on miscellaneous scattered statistical indications.

But purchase of foreign securities is not the only complication. Equally important are the difficulties arising out of inventory accumulations of exports and imports. In estimating the direct effect on incomes of movements in exports and imports, we are interested in the *consumption* of imports, not the amount currently being brought into the country, and in the *production* of exports, not the amount currently being sold abroad. This requires a little elucidation.

If merchants import more foreign goods than are currently being drawn into consumption, the increase in their inventory holding will normally be financed out of their own capital or by borrowing in the money market. This gives rise to deflationary consequences only, if at all, through raising the rate of interest or

6

otherwise tightening the terms of credit. There will be no diversion of expenditure away from home-produced goods until the imports actually come to be sold to the ultimate consumer (who in the case of imported raw materials may, of course, be a business firm). A similar result holds in the case of exports. The labour and raw materials employed in the manufacture of exported goods have to be paid for immediately, whether the goods are sold or not. If sales are delayed, borrowing or drawing on capital will have to be resorted to in the meanwhile.

Now it so happens that for our period this difficulty occasions little trouble on the side of exports, but requires great attention in the case of imports. The figures we have for exports are of 'declared value', that is to say, what the exporter said that the goods were worth at the time when they left the country. There is no reason to suppose that goods destined for foreign markets were often kept in stock in Britain for any length of time, and presumably the value declared corresponded roughly to the cost, including a margin of profit for the manufacturer. Fluctuations in inventory holdings *abroad* are irrelevant for the present purpose, and the declared value of exports may therefore be taken as a fair measure of the income generated by production of exports within the year in question.

In the case of imports we have no proper figures for values at all, since the returns in the Trade and Navigation Accounts relate to 'Official' values, which were based on conventional prices. The same is true of re-exports. Resort must therefore be had to estimates which, though probably accurate enough for a general picture, are of necessity imperfect. But not merely is the accuracy of the results open to question; they are also subject to the difficulty just discussed arising out of inventory movements. There is reason to suppose that fluctuations in the stocks of imported goods held in this country were by no means unimportant, and this has to be borne in mind in assessing the effect on incomes of changes recorded in the value of imports. This point will be further discussed in Chapter III.

In so far as we are interested in the monetary effect, the interpretation of the statistics is also not without its complications. Whether the declared value of exports for any year represents the amount of foreign exchange actually earned in that year by exports depends on whether the goods sent commanded a market immediately and fetched as good a price as was hoped, and also on the length of credit allowed and on whether the risk bearer was the British export merchant or the foreign import merchant. Similarly, the value of imports brought into the country in a given year probably represents more or less the value of foreign exchange required for the purchase of imported goods in that year, but need not do so exactly if payment was delayed or if the foreign exporter continued to bear the risk of a tardy sale or a fall in prices after the merchandise had been shipped to England. These difficulties in the interpretation of the statistics are not easy to take account of, but they will be touched upon again in Chapter VII. In Chapters III–VI we shall be mainly concerned with those aspects of imports and exports that are relevant for the direct effect.

3. IMPORTS AND PRICES

Fluctuations in prices require to be considered in close conjunction with the behaviour of the foreign trade balance, especially with the behaviour of imports. The reason for this lies in the nature of the statistics at our disposal. On some commodity prices very little statistical material exists. This applies particularly to the prices of manufactures. A few series of prices of manufactured goods do exist, but the great bulk of the prices which can be traced in detail—i.e. quarterly or monthly—are those of primary products. It is therefore inevitable that the general price indices that have been constructed for this period, such as Silberling's,[1] should be heavily weighted with primary product prices. One important class of such commodities for which prices are known is made up of the produce of home agriculture, such as wheat, beef and butter. A very large proportion of the remainder consists of imported goods. Of the thirty-five commodities on which Silberling's index is based, twenty-three were entirely or mainly derived from overseas sources. These include cotton imported from the United States, colonial produce (sugar, tea, coffee, indigo) and the produce of southern Europe and the Mediterranean (silk, wool and a large variety of dyestuffs and other minor articles). It was such commodities as these that men like Tooke had in mind when they talked of the movement of 'prices', and it was these commodities whose prices interested the merchants and the readers of the city articles in the contemporary press.

It is for this reason that it is necessary to discuss the behaviour of 'prices', as commonly understood and measured, in conjunction with the behaviour of imports. The prices of agricultural products depended very much on harvest fluctuations, and these in turn were closely associated with the volume of corn imports. The price movements of other imported goods depended largely on the relationship between the volume currently imported and the volume currently being taken into consumption. For example, the great fall registered by the Silberling price index in 1837 was largely the result of the exaggeratedly high prices that had been reached by imported commodities in 1836 because of the need to increase inventories.[2] Similarly, the rise in prices in 1839 seems to have been mostly confined to the prices of corn and of imported primary products, and home manufactures were scarcely affected except in so far as they incorporated raw materials whose prices had risen.[3] The behaviour of Silberling's price index therefore requires to be understood very much otherwise than would be the case if the prices of British manufactures had been what was mainly involved. The movements of the prices of the articles in the categories mentioned will accordingly be discussed along with the behaviour of imports in Chapters III and IV.

In the next four chapters imports and exports are each treated in two parts. Corn imports require to be discussed separately from other imports on account of their dependence on the arbitrary factor of harvest fluctuations and a number of other special considerations. Exports to the United States followed different lines from exports to other markets because in no other part of the world were there endogenous cycles of similar magnitude in economic activity and hence in demand for imports. The net direct effect exercised by foreign trade as a whole on the level of incomes in each year of the period will be assessed in Chapter VII, where we shall also discuss international capital movements and the monetary effect of fluctuations in Britain's overall balance of payments.

---

[1] See Chart 3 and p. 26.   [2] See p. 19.   [3] See p. 74.

CHAPTER III

IMPORTS OF COMMODITIES OTHER THAN CORN

1. INTRODUCTION

SOME of the main questions arising in connection with imports other than corn have already been sketched. It is convenient, as has been explained, to discuss imports closely in conjunction with price movements, since imported commodities dominate the price indices commonly used. Another important point already mentioned is the need to distinguish as far as possible between the volume of goods imported into the country in a given year and the volume actually taken into consumption, the difference between the two being due not merely to re-exports, fluctuations in which were mostly fairly small, but also to fluctuations in the level of stocks. If we are trying to measure the direct effect on incomes of changes in expenditure on imports from one year to another, what is relevant is not the value of the goods brought into the country but the value of imported goods actually consumed. On the other hand, it is the value of goods imported which is relevant for analysis of the overall balance of payments and of the behaviour of the foreign exchanges—assuming, as it is apparently correct to do, that payment to the foreign supplier was usually made soon after the goods had been brought into the country[1]—and it is also the value of the goods imported which is relevant in estimating the effect of economic fluctuations in this country on the purchasing power of overseas producers. As will be seen in Chapter VI, this had much importance in determining the course of our exports. It is for this latter reason that our treatment of imports precedes our treatment of exports, notwithstanding that exports have been commonly given more attention in the study of the trade cycle in Great Britain.

2. THE STATISTICAL MATERIAL

Before proceeding to an analysis of these matters, a little should be said on the nature of the statistical material available. The bulk of this material is very great, but the form in which it exists is inconvenient. We shall deal briefly in turn with the evidence relating to (a) volume: (i) of imports, (ii) of imports taken into consumption; (b) prices; (c) values.

Volume of imports. The Parliamentary Papers contain statistics on volume of imports in two forms. The first are the so-called Official Values, given for individual commodities and for imports as a whole, computed on the basis of current quantities and conventional prices (namely, the prices supposedly prevailing in 1694). In addition to these, the Trade and Navigation Accounts include statements of quantities of individual goods imported, measured in the appropriate physical units. The great advantage of the Official values is that they are readily

---

[1] Corn was probably to some extent an exception on account of the special speculative element involved in the holding of corn in bond. See p. 40, n. 1. On the system of payment and credit in the import trades generally, see Sir John Clapham, *Economic History of Modern Britain* (1930 edition), I, pp. 254–62.

additive between different commodities. The aggregate Official value figures for imports and for re-exports are shown in Chart 1.[1] Unfortunately, the valuations used in arriving at the Official values of imports differed in important respects from those used in arriving at the Official value of re-exports, so the latter cannot be simply deducted from the former to show net imports. On the same Chart 1 are therefore also shown the estimates of the value of *net* imports at

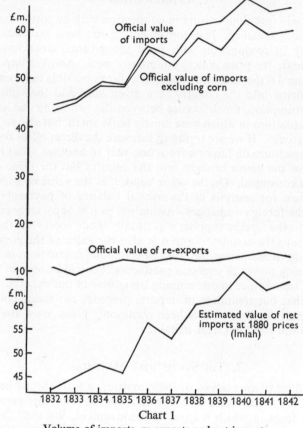

Chart 1

Volume of imports, re-exports and net imports

1880 prices reached by Professor A. H. Imlah from a full reworking of the whole material.[2] A comparison of the behaviour of this series with that of the Official value series for imports and for re-exports suggests that the shortcomings of the Official series as indices of quantity are not unduly serious, despite the remoteness of the base year and certain other anomalies in the manner in which they were calculated.[3]

[1] The figures on which Charts 1, 2, 3 and 4 are based are given at the end of this chapter.
[2] A. H. Imlah, 'Terms of trade of the United Kingdom, 1798–1913', *Journal of Economic History* (1950), pp. 170–94.
[3] For the details of the Official valuation system, see *Accounts and Papers*, 1849, L, pp. 429–43. (N.B. References to Parliamentary Papers will be given throughout by session, volume and page of volume, or, in the case of evidence before Select Committees, by question numbers.)

Volume of imports taken into consumption. By this is meant quantities taken out of bond and paid duty in each year. Here no Official valuations exist, and the only figures available from the Trade and Navigation Accounts are those for individual dutiable commodities expressed in physical units. To construct from these data an index of quantity entered of all dutiable commodities would be an elaborate task which it has not been considered necessary for our purposes to carry out. A weighted index of the quantities entered for consumption of eight of the most important imports, excluding corn, is shown ('import consumption

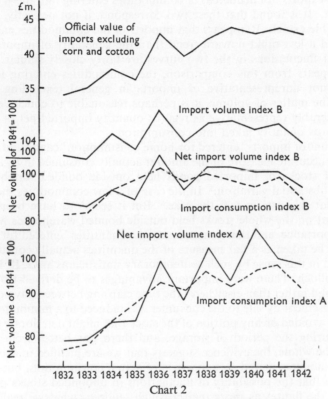

Chart 2

Indices of quantity of imports and of consumption of imports

index A') in Chart 2.[1] Between them the commodities represented in this index probably accounted for well over half the value of all non-corn imports in a normal year. For purposes of comparison with this index, 'net import volume index A' (see Chart 2) has been prepared on the same principles to show the volume of imports of the same eight commodities net of re-exports. The space between the two curves is a measure of the increase or decrease in the level of bonded stocks of the commodities in question in each year. The high weight necessarily accorded to cotton in these indices causes its fluctuations to dominate

[1] The eight commodities are cotton (6), wool (2), timber (3), sugar (4), tallow (2), tea (2), tobacco (1) and coffee (1), the numbers in brackets denoting the weight accorded in the index.

the results in certain years. To abstract from this, a further pair of indices ('import consumption index B' and 'net import volume index B') are also shown in Chart 2, based on the same material as the corresponding indices marked 'A' but excluding cotton; otherwise the commodities represented and the weights accorded them are the same in both pairs of indices.

It is desirable to test whether the commodities included in these indices are representative of imports as a whole. For this purpose Chart 2 also shows the Official value of imports exclusive of corn and cotton, together with the index of imports (re-exports not deducted) of commodities entering into the B indices for comparison. It is found that these two correspond, if not perfectly, at least to a considerable extent. It appears that imports of the commodities entering into index B had a less rapid upward trend than the generality of imports, but the year-to-year fluctuations in the two curves are fairly closely similar. If, therefore, as appears from this comparison, the commodities entering into our B index are not unrepresentative of imports in general (excluding corn and cotton) in the matter of volume, it is perhaps reasonable to conclude that they are also tolerably representative as regards quantity imported net of re-exports and as regards quantity taken into consumption.

The amount of imports 'entered for home consumption' cannot, of course, be taken as an accurate measure of the amount actually consumed in a given year if the level of stocks of imported goods held outside bonded warehouses was subject to substantial variation.[1] In the case of a few commodities there is clear evidence that this was in fact the case.[2] But it seems to have been generally assumed that on the whole stocks held outside bonded warehouses were not of the first importance, and that consequently the quantities 'entered for consumption' might be taken as a fair measure of the quantities actually consumed; they were quoted in this sense by such contemporary statisticians as G. R. Porter and J. R. McCulloch. There were important advantages to be derived from holding stocks in bond rather than elsewhere; the time elapsing between payment of duty and reimbursement by sale to the consumer was reduced to a minimum, payment of duty was avoided on any portion of the stock that might deteriorate or become unusable during the period of storage, and there was better security against theft. On the whole, the evidence suggests that we are justified in accepting the figures of amounts entered as a measure of actual consumption, but subject to the warning that the possibility of fluctuations in unbonded stocks prevents us from using the figures as more than a rough guide to what we really want to know.[3] For this reason, as well as because account is being taken of only a limited number of imports, it would be unwise, in particular, to conclude that

[1] This does not apply to cotton, since Ellison's consumption figures which have been used in the calculation of import consumption index A purport to take account of all stock holdings. See T. Ellison, *Cotton Trade of Great Britain* (1886), Table 1 (*ad fin.*).

[2] For example, flax and silk have been excluded from the indices shown in Chart 2, although their importance might appear to require them to be included, since it is known that stocks of them held by manufacturers were subject to considerable variation. See p. 17, n. 1, and sources cited there.

[3] For evidence relating to bonded warehouses and the use made of them, see G. R. Porter, *Progress of the Nation* (1851 edition), pp. 461–6; *Select Committee on Inland Warehousing*, 1840, v; Report of the Commissioners of Customs on the expediency of establishing bonding warehouses in large manufacturing and other towns, *Accounts and Papers*, 1859 (2nd session), XXVII.

the change in the levels of stocks of imports as a whole was necessarily always upwards or downwards when that is what appears from Chart 2. The indices there shown probably do indicate more or less correctly whether the rate of accumulation (or decumulation) of stocks was *faster* in one year than in another, but they are less reliable as a guide to whether there was in net in any particular year accumulation or decumulation.

It is useful to have general indices such as those shown in Charts 1 and 2 to form a framework of the discussion, and a good deal of use will be made of them

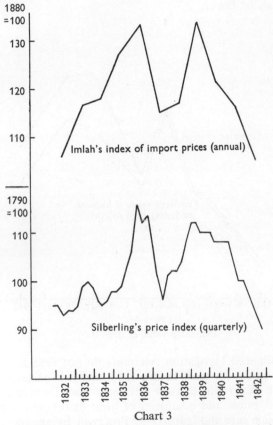

Chart 3

Imlah's import price index and Silberling's price index

in the following pages. But one of the most important features of the behaviour of imports in this period was the variety of behaviour manifested by individual commodities. For this reason it will often be necessary to go behind the general measures and examine particular cases.

Prices. In Chart 3 is shown Imlah's import price index, which is arrived at by dividing the estimated value of imports at current prices (see below) by the estimated value of imports at 1880 prices. The annual basis of this index reduces its value for the analysis of short-period fluctuations, since significant changes in

13

price often occurred over shorter periods than a year. There is therefore also shown in Chart 3 Silberling's general quarterly price index, about two-thirds of the commodities represented in which are, as has previously been mentioned, imports. There is in existence in contemporary prices-currents and elsewhere an enormous mass of material relating to individual commodity prices. The most convenient collation of this material is in Silberling's unpublished manuscript,[1] where monthly or quarterly figures are given of the prices of the thirty-five individual commodities from which his general index is constructed. For many of the leading imports, quarterly price figures are also to be found in Tooke and Newmarch's *History of Prices*.

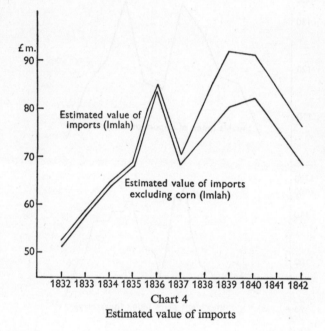

Chart 4

Estimated value of imports

Values. The Trade and Navigation Accounts do not include any figures for imports at current prices for years before 1853, and it is necessary to resort to estimates. The task of arriving at such estimates from the wealth of available material relating to prices and quantities of individual commodities has been carried out with much care and industry by Professor Imlah, and his figures are those which we shall use[2] (see Chart 4). Their accuracy is inevitably only approximate, but it is unlikely that they can be improved upon.[3] No similar calculations have been made, or indeed could be made with comparable accuracy, of the

[1] Norman J. Silberling, *Prices of 35 British Commodities* (1920), manuscript in the British Library of Political and Economic Science.
[2] A. H. Imlah, 'Real values in British foreign trade', *Journal of Economic History* (1948), pp. 133–52. Results that are broadly similar, though calculated on much cruder principles, had been obtained by W. Schlote, *Entwicklung und Strukturwandlungen der englischen Aussenhandels von 1700 bis zur Gegenwart* (1938).
[3] According to Professor Imlah, his results appear to be biased in the direction of overstating the value of imports in years in which rapid rises in prices took place (*loc. cit.* p. 145).

14

value of imports taken into consumption in each year; but we shall in the course of this chapter point out the general direction in which the value of imports consumed appears to have differed from the value of total imports at each stage of our period.

To assist the reader to form a picture of the structure of our import trade at this period, it may be useful before proceeding further to quote Professor Imlah's estimates of the value at current prices of twelve leading non-corn imports, after deduction of re-exports, in the fairly representative year 1838 (in £m.): cotton, 14·3; sugar, 7·6; timber, 6·1; silk, 4·0; wool, 3·8; flax, 3·7; tea, 3·1; tallow, 2·9; wines, 1·7; coffee, 1·2; hemp, 0·8; tobacco, 0·5; all other non-corn imports, 17·2; total non-corn imports, 67·1.[1]

3. FACTORS AFFECTING THE BEHAVIOUR OF IMPORTS

The pattern shown by the series depicted in Charts 1–4 is a complicated one. But if one neglects the fluctuations of shortest period, a certain regularity appears. The general impression is that the quantity of non-corn imports rose rapidly up till 1836, and that thereafter the rate of growth slackened or became negative. Slackening or reversal of growth stands out particularly in the series which exclude cotton (the B indices and the Official value of imports excluding corn and cotton given in Chart 2). This broad tendency is common both to the volume of imports and to the quantity of imports taken into consumption, but is more pronounced in the latter. The prices of imports also rise rapidly up to 1836, but, in contrast with volume, prices show a prominent second peak in 1839. The rise in agricultural prices contributed largely to this peak, but did not account for it entirely.

We may list five factors as generally relevant to the movement of prices, quantities and consumption of imports from one year to the next.

(1) The level of demand for imports from the consumer, whether the consumer be typically a firm or a household. This in turn depends on the state of trade and the level of real incomes. The general tendency to cessation or slackening of growth in the quantity indices after 1836 is fairly clearly to be explained in terms of this factor.

(2) The price elasticity of demand for imports.

(3) Variations in the supply schedule of imports, whether due to causes of a cyclical or of a non-cyclical character.

(4) The state of general business confidence, as affecting expectations of importers.

(5) Inventory and speculative fluctuations in individual commodity markets.

We shall now go through the period year by year in order to attempt to see the way in which these factors interacted to produce the observed results.[2]

---

[1] Professor Imlah's estimates of the values of individual commodity imports have not been published, and I am indebted to him for permission to quote those given in the text.

[2] The wide variety of behaviour found amongst individual commodity imports compels us in the following pages to engage in a discussion of some detail and complexity. Readers who wish to do so may omit the next three sections and turn straight to § 7 of this chapter (p. 24), where the chief results are summarised.

4. BEHAVIOUR OF IMPORTS, 1833–1836

From 1833 till 1836 the course of import quantities and prices was dominated by two forces: (1) a powerful upward trend in demand, rather more marked in the case of textile fibres and other industrial raw materials than in the case of consumer goods; and (2) inventory fluctuations. The extent of the latter is evident if comparison is made, for example, between the fluctuations shown in the import volume indices in Chart 2 with the steady rise of the corresponding consumption indices on the same chart.

The year 1832 was one of poor trade, and the level of prices, including the prices of imported commodities, was low. Accordingly, importers lacked incentive to make great increases in their commitments, and the volume of imports in 1833 was little higher than it had been in 1832. For a good number of commodities—compare net import volume index B—it was lower. But as 1833 advanced, a general improvement in the state of trade became apparent, and the conjunction of this with the relatively low level of imports created a tendency to rising prices which was soon markedly reinforced by speculative buying.[1] The fall in re-exports in 1833 (see Chart 1) may well have been due to the desire of merchants to sell their merchandise in the newly profitable home market. But the rise in prices affected demand,[2] and the amount of imports taken into consumption during 1833 was higher than during 1832 by only a moderate extent, though it did rise somewhat more rapidly than the volume of imports.

In 1834 the position was reversed. The recent rise in prices brought about a great increase in imports, and the speculative high prices of the previous year could no longer be maintained. The fall in prices is evident in Silberling's price index (Chart 3), and may also be seen reflected (with a slight lag) in a pronounced increase in bankruptcies in the last quarter of 1834.[3] But the fall in prices was beneficial to industry,[4] and consumption rose much more rapidly than in 1833. In fact, whether because of the fall in prices or because of the general improvement in business, consumption apparently rose even faster than imports. But the fall in prices in 1834 had evidently alarmed importers, and in 1835 there was a reduction in the volume of imports of a large number of commodities. In the meanwhile a variety of forces were bringing about a powerful upward shift in incomes and demand. As a result, net imports fell short of consumption by

---

[1] *Circular to Bankers*, 8 September 1833; T. Tooke, *History of Prices* (I and II, 1838; III, 1840; IV, 1848; V and VI, with W. Newmarch, 1857), II, p. 251; *Select Committee on Manufactures Commerce and Shipping*, 1833, VI, QQ. 11479–83 (W. R. Greg). Tooke (*loc. cit.*) speaks of speculation in colonial and other goods in the spring and summer of 1833; but the main rise in prices appears from the statistics actually to have come in the third and fourth quarters of the year. The *Circular to Bankers* cited here was a weekly publication edited by Henry Burgess, secretary of the Committee of Private Bankers, and is a source to which frequent reference will be made throughout the present work. On issues where the interests of private bankers were directly involved, and on a number of more general questions, Burgess shows a bias which has to be discounted; but the *Circular to Bankers* is of great value inasmuch as it provides a usually well-informed, though of course non-quantitative, commentary on fluctuations in the state of trade and credit from week to week. In this it serves in some limited degree the purpose for which *The Economist* has been so extensively drawn on by students of business cycles in Great Britain in the latter part of the nineteenth century.

[2] See Chapter IX for the application of this in the case of cotton.

[3] N. J. Silberling, 'British prices and business cycles, 1779–1850', *Review of Economic Statistics* (1923), p. 252.

[4] Cf. *Circular to Bankers*, 11 April 1834, 27 June 1834.

a greater margin in 1835 than in any other year in our period, and a large rise in prices became inevitable. Had it not been for this rise in prices, there can be little doubt that the increase in the tempo of the boom would have caused consumption of imports to rise more rapidly in 1835 than it had done in 1834, instead of slightly less rapidly, as actually occurred.

The reduction in stocks in 1835 was the background of the events of 1836. In the first half of 1836 the prices of imports continued to rise very steeply. This rise was to be attributed partly to the rapid growth in demand—the peak in business activity as a whole being generally reckoned to have come in spring 1836—but also in large part to the exceptional inroads on stocks that had been made in the previous year.[1] The rise in prices was accompanied by a great increase in the volume of imports, and an increase in the quantity of imports taken into consumption that was about as rapid, though not more rapid, than the increases registered in 1834 and 1835.

The increase in supplies brought about by the large imports of 1836 was bound to bring about some fall in prices, and this was what happened in the latter half of the year. But the very small extent of the decline that then took place indicated that the level of imports had not been excessive in relation to demand. It seems probable that stocks were not rebuilt to an adequate level till late in 1836.

The account that has so far been given of the behaviour of the quantity, consumption and prices of imports in 1833–6 is no more than a general summary. Considering the heterogeneous nature of our imports—colonial produce, textile fibres, dyestuffs and the rest—the price-quantity pattern was on the whole remarkably uniform; but of course many minor differences and a certain number of important ones are to be found between different commodities. The price rise in 1836 was least in the case of articles imported from Europe, the supply of which could be expanded at short notice more readily than, for example, the supply of colonial produce. Prices of goods imported from the United States, on the other hand, rose to an exceptional degree, largely, no doubt, because of the inflationary tendencies at work within the United States itself.[2] It has already been mentioned that the consumption of imported raw materials such as textile fibres rose more rapidly between 1833 and 1836 than the consumption of foodstuffs and other consumer goods; and the same distinction applied to prices. The exceptionally powerful upward trend in the demand for textile fibres may be the reason why imports of cotton did not share in the general fall (or slackening in rate of growth) in 1835. The rise in cotton imports in 1836 was not the result of a need for restocking but simply of the rise in demand and of the expansion in the productive potential of the American South.

Two other special cases may be mentioned. In the tea market, the East India Company, having recently lost its monopoly of the China trade, was engaged in selling off part of its stocks, and prices of tea in consequence fell throughout this

---

[1] There existed a strong consensus of opinion among contemporaries that speculation in 1836 was mainly confined to joint-stock company promotion and shares and did not, with a few exceptions, extend to the commodity markets or contribute to the rise in prices in the way that it had done on a number of occasions in earlier booms. See Tooke, II, pp. 255, 264; *Circular to Bankers*, May–June 1836, *passim*; *The Times*, 3 May 1836. The commodities which formed the most notable exceptions were silk and flax. (Tooke, II, p. 272; J. Sturrock, 'An account of the trade of the port of Dundee', *Statistical Journal* (1839), I, pp. 522–9.)

[2] See Chapter V.

period, even in 1836.[1] Sugar is an important case, which while preserving many of the typical features of the behaviour of imports generally, differs in a number of respects from the prevailing pattern, largely because of its high price-elasticity of demand. Consumption of this commodity rose a great deal in 1834 as its price fell and incomes increased, and again rose in 1835 despite a slight increase in price.[2] But a high level of importation had been maintained for several years previously, and the rise in price was therefore small, notwithstanding that the quantity imported was less than the quantity consumed both in 1834 and in 1835. Then towards the end of 1835 the price did at last rise substantially, and in 1836 a greater quantity of imports was secured. But in the meanwhile the rise in price choked off the demand, with the result that 1836 was both the first year since 1831 to show a rise in the quantity of sugar imported and the first year since 1832 to show a reduction in the quantity consumed. The fall in consumption of sugar in that year was in fact steep, notwithstanding the prosperous state of trade, and the supply when it did come in was found in consequence to be very excessive.

Having now surveyed the behaviour of prices and quantities of imports between 1833 and 1836, we are in a better position to understand the movement of import *values* (Chart 4). A general upward tendency in values was to be expected, since both prices and quantities were in general rising. But, as we have seen, quantities and prices to some extent tended to move in opposite directions as far as year-to-year fluctuations were concerned. Prices rose particularly rapidly in 1833 and 1835, largely because in those years quantities were relatively low; and the rise in prices was less rapid in 1834 because the quantities imported were especially high. The comparatively smooth growth in import values between 1833 and 1835 therefore masks a discrepancy between the experience of the individual years. The growth in values was not, it is true, perfectly smooth; the increase was slightly greater—*a fortiori*, greater proportionally—in 1833 than in the other years, presumably because in that year speculation increased the extent to which prices rose, and, on the other hand, in 1835 the fall in quantities involved a slackening in the rate of growth of values, notwithstanding the price rise. But the differences in the rate of growth of values between 1833, 1834 and 1835 were small in comparison with the difference between each of them and 1836, when, as we have seen, the rise in quantities was not inconsistent with a rise in prices, taking the year as a whole.

As has been explained, no satisfactory estimates are available of the annual values of imports taken into consumption; but in the light of what has so far been said and of the movements of stocks shown in Chart 2, it would appear that the value of imports taken into consumption must have been not so greatly different from the value of imports brought into the country in 1833 and 1834, but substantially above it in 1835 and substantially below it in 1836.

---

[1] The market in indigo was also subject to special disturbances arising out of the failure in 1832 of two of the largest Indian firms in the trade. (*Select Committee on Manufactures Commerce and Shipping*, 1833, VI, QQ. 2084–6 (G. G. de H. Larpent).)

[2] Porter (*Progress of the Nation*, pp. 542–3) remarks that 1835 was the only year between 1830 and 1849 when the price of sugar and the quantity of it consumed did not move in opposite directions. His own figures, however, show this to be an exaggeration, since 1842 and 1846, as well as 1835, constitute exceptions. But there is no doubt that the elasticity of demand was, as he maintained, very high.

5. BEHAVIOUR OF IMPORTS, 1837–1840

After 1837 the behaviour of imports becomes a good deal more complicated and harder to understand. Wide differences came to exist between the state of one commodity market and another, and even the most qualified generalisations become difficult to assert with confidence. This applies particularly to the years 1839–41.

By the beginning of 1837, stocks had risen sufficiently to make inevitable a fall in prices from the very high levels of 1836, and in the first half of 1837 the fall in prices that had started in the previous year became much more rapid. Part cause of this fall in prices was, of course, the general recession in business, especially in exports to the United States, and the credit stringency which accompanied the failure in June 1837 of certain finance houses engaged in trade between Britain and America.[1] But the commodity prices which fell most were, as Tooke remarked, 'those that had previously been raised by an exaggerated demand, and the fall in prices was not to so low a level as that from which they had risen'[2]—apart from cotton and silk, which were subject to peculiar circumstances.[3] The fall in prices was in large measure no more than the inevitable reaction from the high levels which had been attained in 1835–6 on account of the need to build up stocks at the same time as demand was abnormally high. The fall in demand in 1837 cannot have been too catastrophic, save in a few markets, since the consumption of many imports fell little or not at all.[4] None the less the situation was grave enough for the merchants, and the bankruptcy figures, with their usual close dependence on price movements, rose in the second quarter of 1837 to a level which was not surpassed till 1842.

Prices having started on their steep decline already at the *beginning* of 1837 (or in some cases earlier), the consequences were seen in a substantial fall in the volume imported in the *same* year The volume of imports in 1837 was considerably lower than it had been in 1836, though not so low as it had been in 1835. But the recession in trade in 1837 was shortly followed by a recovery, and the decline in the quantity imported proved in a good number of instances to have been excessive. Tooke described the result: 'Several articles of American and East India produce, having been unduly depressed in the first half of 1837, rallied towards the end of the year, and attained prices which, when the supplies for the season [1838] came forward, could not be maintained.'[5] The 'supplies for the season' were a good deal higher than they had been in 1837. Trade was felt to be recovering, and the price recovery alluded to in the last quarter of 1837 and the first quarter of 1838 showed that the low imports of 1837 had led to the absorption of surplus inventories and in some cases to the creation of deficiencies. As Tooke observed in the passage quoted, a number of prices declined somewhat in the second and third quarters of 1838, but by the end of the year the general tendency was again upwards. It appears, therefore, that the rise in imports in

---

[1] See pp. 58–9. [2] Tooke, II, p. 271.
[3] The former on account of the disruption of the trade on the American side, the latter on account of the speculation that had been practised in the boom.
[4] The fall in consumption shown by the indices in Chart 2 probably somewhat exaggerates the fall in the consumption of imports as a whole. A good many commodities not there represented registered rises in consumption in 1837 scarcely less marked than in 1836.
[5] Tooke, III, p. 55.

2-2

1838 was for the most part barely sufficient to restore depleted inventories and to provide for the needs of recovering trade. At the end of 1838 prices of most imports were at about the same level as they had been twelve months earlier.[1]

In 1839 the aggregate figures show a fall in the quantity of non-corn imports and a rise in prices; and in 1840 quantities rose and prices fell. But it would be a mistake to suppose that this represented merely a continuation of the two-year pattern of alternate high and low imports and falling and rising prices that had been in evidence in 1835-6-7-8. In the case of a certain number of commodities, it is true, the movement of quantities and prices in 1839-40 did represent a more or less similar continuation of the process initiated in the previous years; but the movements of the aggregate indices resulted from very diverse movements in individual commodity markets. In an attempt to find some sort of order in what is undoubtedly a confusing picture, we may separate commodities into three classes.

(1) In the case of a certain number of commodities—not very many—the quantity imported in 1838 turned out to have been excessive, and imports of these in 1839 fell, thus following the previous pattern of biennial alternation. These were mostly the articles which had felt especially severely the price recession in the second and third quarters of 1838, which had, however, in general, been relatively mild. In 1839 their prices naturally tended to rise. The most important commodity falling into this first group was sugar; others were coffee, indigo, tar and turpentine.

(2) A number of important articles which might at first sight appear to come into the first category in fact suffered a restriction in amount imported and a rise in price for special reasons on the supply side. To particularise: (a) an attempt was being made in the United States to drive up the price of cotton by artificially restricting supply, an attempt which was countered by concerted short-time working on the part of Lancashire cotton spinners. This episode is discussed more fully below (pp. 63-5 and 138-9). The price of tobacco was temporarily doubled for similar reasons. (b) In March 1839 the outbreak of the so-called Opium War marked the final breach in the never very harmonious relations between the Chinese authorities and the British trading community in the Far East. The consequent interruption to the supply of tea led to violent speculation in the London market.[2] (c) A less important case than either of the above, but one which attracted a good deal of attention, was that of sulphur (brimstone). British supplies were normally drawn from Sicily. In 1839 our total imports of the commodity were reduced by more than half as a result of the operations of a French syndicate which had been granted a monopoly in the trade by the King of Naples.[3]

[1] In Silberling's index the renewed cyclical movement in prices from the middle of 1837 to the end of 1838, described in the text, is obscured by the behaviour of corn and other agricultural prices. Agricultural prices are also responsible for the appearance in the index of a general upward tendency in prices over the year. (1838 was a year of exceptionally bad harvest; see p. 30.)

[2] Tooke, III, pp. 61-3. Cf. A. Redford, *Manchester Merchants and Foreign Trade, 1794-1858* (1934), pp. 118-20; M. Greenberg, *British Trade and the Opening of China, 1800-1842* (1951), Chapter VIII.

[3] The monopoly was abolished in 1840 after Palmerston had threatened naval reprisals. (J. R. McCulloch, *Dictionary of Commerce* (1844 edition), *s.v.* Palermo; Papers relative to the sulphur question, *Accounts and Papers*, 1840, XLIV, pp. 447-540 and 1842, XLV, pp. 225-37; *Hansard's Parliamentary Debates* (3rd series), LII, cols. 801-8.)

(3) The amount imported in 1839 of most commodities other than those already mentioned continued to increase. In a few cases (e.g. tallow) this increase was accompanied by a fall in prices, but for the most part prices were rising at the beginning of 1839, and fell little or not at all in the course of the year. The most likely explanation is that merchants had been made so cautious by the events of 1837 that the increase in imports in 1838 had been barely sufficient to restore inventories to a normal level. A further increase in imports was therefore requisite in 1839, and demand was still sufficiently high for this not to lead to any general downward tendency in prices.

In general, then, import prices were a good deal higher in 1839 than in 1838 in all but a small number of cases. The aggregate Official values (i.e. quantities) fell, but, as can be seen from Chart 2, the reverse result emerges if one abstracts from cotton. It is interesting to note that consumption index B which does not include cotton (as well as consumption index A, in which cotton is included) shows a decided fall, notwithstanding the stability in the corresponding net import index. This seems to dispose of the notion that an improvement in trade and hence in demand was the main reason for the conjunction in many commodity markets in 1839 of high prices and high quantities imported. Demand for certain imports such as wool, which benefited particularly from the high level of exports to the United States, did rise in 1839, but as far as the generality of commodities was concerned, it appears that the need for restocking was the main element in the situation, as it had probably been in 1836. But whereas 1836 had followed on a year of substantial disinvestment in import stocks, 1839 had been preceded by a year in which some rebuilding of stocks had taken place, and the rise in prices (always excluding corn) was therefore much less than it had been in 1836, except for commodities subject to peculiar conditions on the supply side.

In 1840 the cotton and sulphur monopolies had been broken, and imports were free to increase. In the case of cotton the increase was enormous, and the price fell heavily. But the supply of tea was even shorter in 1840 than in 1839, and, although the speculation in the commodity had passed its peak by February 1840, prices remained high throughout the year.[1] Sugar now came to be added to the list of commodities subject to disturbance on the supply side, in consequence of the failure of the year's supply from the West Indies.[2] Apart from cotton, tea and sugar, it appears that most non-corn imports were at about the same level in 1840 as they had been the year before. This was as was to be expected from the high but mostly fairly stable prices that had prevailed in the course of 1839. But whereas in 1839 the need for restocking had prevented prices from falling, in 1840 this was not so. Consumption was at about the same level in the two years (apart from cotton, tea and sugar), the consumption of some commodities, such as wool (affected by the fall in exports to the United States) declining, but consumption of timber and some others continuing to rise. Much the same was true of quantities imported. But prices in 1840 definitely tended downwards, though not very rapidly. A fall in prices was the inevitable consequence of the repetition in 1840 of the import quantities of 1839, since there was no great general increase in demand, and stocks by the end of 1839 had apparently been generally restored or nearly restored to an adequate level.

[1] Tooke, IV, p. 44.   [2] Ibid.

Such, then, was the prevalent pattern in 1840. But, as in 1839, there was a good deal of diversity between different commodity markets, and a certain number of commodities that in 1839 had entered into the first of the categories distinguished on p. 20 were imported in appreciably increased quantities in 1840, indigo being the most important example.

In summarising the forces governing the behaviour of non-corn imports in 1839–40, three principal factors may then be singled out:

(a) Several important commodities were subject to special reductions in supply which for our purposes may be classed as arbitrary. The effect of these was to raise prices, especially in 1839.

(b) Fluctuations in demand from the ultimate consumer were not for the most part of prime importance, though they were significant in some cases (e.g. wool). Demand was generally quite high, but not rising rapidly.

(c) Some restocking of almost all non-corn imports took place in 1838, but the amount of it varied. In a few cases it was excessive, and in a number of instances this led to the expected repercussions over the next two years. But as far as most commodities were concerned, importers were cautious, and the amounts imported in 1838 were insufficient to prevent prices from rising and inducing higher imports in 1839. Even then imports were not so high as to bring about substantial declines in prices. But a repetition of imports on a similar scale in 1840 proved more than sufficient to repair any remaining deficiencies in stocks, and prices fell.

It should be emphasised that this interpretation is largely conjectural. A full analysis would require much closer study of the circumstances affecting each of the most important commodity markets involved.

6. BEHAVIOUR OF IMPORTS, 1841–1842

In 1841 and still more in 1842, special shortages and inventory fluctuations became of lesser importance, and the principal force in the markets for imported commodities became the deepening depression.

Cotton remained an exception. Whereas in most commodity markets the two-year see-saw pattern that had marked the earlier part of the period became obscured after 1838, in cotton the amplitude of the see-saw movement was maintained and enhanced by the abnormally low imports of 1839. The enormous imports of 1840 led to lower prices, and hence to lower imports in 1841. This movement in turn was carried too far; during 1841 the downward course of cotton prices was perceptibly checked, and in 1842 the quantity of cotton imported actually showed a slight rise, despite the gravity of the depression then prevailing in Lancashire.

In 1841 the temporary deficiency in the sugar supply from the West Indies ceased, and with increased imports and falling prices a substantial increase in consumption was possible. In 1842 imports were slightly lower, but this did not prevent a further fall in prices; this time, however, consumption also fell. In 1841 the fall in prices had evidently more than offset the decline in incomes as far as sugar consumption was concerned, but in 1842 the influence of the slump was decisive.

The supply of tea was also slightly easier in 1841 than it had been in 1840, but it was not till 1842 that supplies became sufficient to bring prices down to a normal level. Consumption apparently rose somewhat in both years.[1]

Apart from the commodities mentioned, the general tendency was for a slight fall in quantity of imports in 1841, and a much more substantial fall in 1842.[2] Most prices had declined to a no more than moderate extent in 1840, and it was natural that the fall in imports should therefore also be no more than moderate in 1841. But in that year there were heavy falls in prices. The rise in consumption of imports shown in index B in Chart 2 is due to sugar, and consumption of most imported articles declined slightly; but, even so, the relatively small extent of the fall in the consumption of imports in 1841 is a little surprising in view of the prevailing depression in industry. The explanation is presumably that the fall in prices was partly the result of the maintenance of imports at a level which was only slightly lower than that of 1840, a level which even in that year had substantially exceeded consumption, and that the pressure of accumulating stocks, by driving down prices, helped to keep up consumption in face of declining incomes.

Imports were reduced drastically in 1842, but merchants had not foreseen the full extent to which demand would decline, and consumption fell faster than the quantity imported. Dealers were left with stocks at the end of the year higher than they had been at the beginning, and prices continued to tumble. The unintended accumulation of import inventories in 1842 was no doubt partly responsible for the continuing downward tendency in prices in 1843, when the recovery in general activity was unquestionable.

The behaviour of import *values* in the years 1837–42 presents no particular surprises. A big fall in 1837 and rise in 1838 were inevitable. In 1839 the value of most non-corn imports probably rose not less steeply than in 1838, but the rate of rise in the total was damped down by the special circumstances operating in the cotton market. On the other hand, in 1840 cotton pulled up a total which without it would have been about the same as in 1839. After 1840 the price fall dominated.

The value of imports taken into consumption must have exceeded that of imports in 1837, when stocks were being drawn upon. In all the later years it appears that stocks increased to some extent, so that expenditure on imports consumed must have fallen short of the total value of imports brought into the country. But the rate of stock accumulation varied greatly between the different years, being considerably less in the odd-numbered years than in the even-numbered ones. The excess of import value over value of imports consumed was apparently greatest in 1840.

---

[1] The figures for consumption of tea are a little suspect, since they tend to follow closely the fluctuations in quantity imported.

[2] Chart 2 shows a slight rise in 1841 in quantity of imports excluding corn and cotton, but this is replaced by a slight fall if sugar is excluded. Official value of imports excluding corn and cotton: 1840, £43·0m.; 1841, £43·5m. Official value of imports excluding corn, cotton and sugar: 1840, £37·7m.; 1841, £37·0m.

7. SUMMARY AND CONCLUSIONS

The relationship of imports to fluctuations in income and activity as a whole cannot be properly assessed until we have considered the influence of fluctuations in imports on foreigners' demand for our exports. We shall therefore defer discussion of it till a later chapter. At the present stage it will be sufficient to summarise briefly the causes of the movements that have been discussed in import prices and quantities, and consider some of the implications.

The general outline of the movement was determined by the state of demand: this accounted for the rising trend in prices and quantities up to 1836, the less rapid growth in the late 1830's, and the decline of 1841–2. Cyclical fluctuations in supply also played some part; the declining tendency in cotton prices after the year 1837 was due less to diminished demand than to the extra productive potential created during the boom years. But cotton was in this respect some-what exceptional, and the supply of articles produced outside the United States was both less expansive and less cycle-sensitive.[1]

But if cyclical movements in income and activity were the main factor, inventory movements and arbitrary fluctuations in supply also left a clear imprint on the pattern of quantities and prices of non-corn imports.

The extent of the price rise of 1835–6 and of the increase in import quantities in 1836 was largely the result of the low imports of 1835. The booming commodity markets of early 1836 would certainly have been impossible if trade in general had not been prosperous; but the need to restore depleted stocks was a very important adjunct without which prices would not have risen nearly as high as they did. And it was because they had risen so high under this influence that they had so far to fall in 1837. The recession of 1837 was bound to involve some reductions in the prices fetched by imported commodities, but this reduction would not have been felt so keenly if prices had not in 1836 been driven up for the reasons mentioned to abnormally high levels. What caused the bankruptcies and distress among the mercantile class in 1837 was not that prices were exceptionally low, but that merchants were obliged to sell for moderate prices goods which they had bought when they were exceptionally dear.

It appears that, taking the period 1833–7 as a whole, imports were rather less than adequate to provide for current consumption and for the need to increase stocks in proportion to the increase in consumption.[2] Imports were barely equal to consumption in 1833 and 1834, and were seriously short of it in 1835; the high imports of 1836 were, in most cases, no more than was required. The renewed decline in quantities imported in 1837 thus created arrears which had to be made up in the ensuing years.

These arrears in turn accounted for a large part of the upward tendency in prices in 1838–9. In 1839 the general level of prices was inflated by the special circumstances in the cotton trade and in a number of other commodity markets which have been described above (as well as by the effect of the bad harvest of 1838 on agricultural prices). Otherwise prices rose less in 1838–9 than they had

---

[1] For example, imports from the West Indies underwent not nearly so rapid an increase in volume over the period as imports of cotton, and the price of most articles of West India produce was no lower at the end of the period than it had been at the beginning.

[2] To quote a particular example: Ellison's figures show stocks of raw cotton as equivalent to 23 weeks' consumption at the end of 1832 and to 18 weeks' consumption at the end of 1837.

done in 1835–6. 1837 had had low imports, but it was a year of dull trade, and was not anomalous as 1835 had been with its boom in industry and decline in imports. The slow rebuilding of stocks in 1838–9 was therefore not accompanied by any spectacular price rises. For the same reason in 1840 when stocks had been restored to normal (or nearly so) prices did not fall very far. Consequently there was no really heavy fall in imports till 1842, and the average rate of inventory accumulation of imports from 1838 to 1842 was substantially higher than it had been from 1833 to 1837—a result to which the decline in demand owing to the slump also contributed in part.

In 1833 the shortage of certain commodities and the revival of business confidence led to an outburst of speculation which set off a 'cobweb' style fluctuation of two-year period in imports and import prices. This cyclical tendency was reinforced by the prosperity of 1836 and the recession of 1837. But after 1837 merchants became more cautious, and their pattern of expectations less responsive to short-period price fluctuations. In most commodity markets restocking was gradual and was not overdone. It was not till 1840, apparently, that stocks were fully restored, and when in that year prices fell, an insensitive pattern of exceptions was again manifested in a relatively small reduction in the quantities imported in the following year. There was more diversity between the behaviour of different commodities after 1837 than there had been before, and the two-year cycle was largely damped out. It was not entirely damped out; elements of it remained in the markets for certain articles of West India produce, and cotton was a still more important case in point. Just as the two-year cycle in imports generally had been amplified and sustained by the boom of 1836, so the cycle in cotton imports was sustained by the abnormal shortage of 1839. The repercussions of this were felt so strongly that anyone looking at the figures for import volume in Chart 1 might well suppose the two-year cycle to have continued in full force over the whole range of imports till the end of the period. Cotton in fact dominated the fluctuations in total import volume in the later years of the period, and if it is excluded the picture is completely altered.

It is not difficult to see how a tendency to a two-year cycle was liable to arise. Imports could not be immediately increased in response to a rise in prices, partly because of lags in transport and communications, and partly because of the agricultural nature of so many of the commodities concerned. Each merchant would be ignorant of the amount other merchants would be bringing forward by the time his own merchandise would be on the market. If all merchants took current prices as a guide to the prices that would prevail in the future, imports would tend to be excessive in years after prices had been high and deficient in years after prices had been low. This in turn would affect prices in the current year, and so the cycle would continue—a straightforward 'cobweb'. The movement of prices did not in fact observe an exactly annual pattern, and in such a year as 1837 when prices declined steeply in the first quarter, this was already reflected in the import total of the same year. But, presumably because in the case of so many imports the bulk of the supplies came in at one season of the year only, the cycle in *quantities* retained up till 1837 a two-year periodicity.

With the exception of a few articles such as sugar, the short-period price-elasticity of demand was not very high, and this increased the amplitude of the movements in prices. But a regular repetition of the same cyclical pattern was dependent upon merchants responding sensitively to the changes in prices that occurred. If traders were cautious, and when prices rose did not act on the assumption that they would stay at the same level indefinitely, a deficiency of imports in one year might not lead to a sufficient increase in supplies the following years to cause a fall in prices, or might even fail to raise imports to a sufficiently high level to prevent prices from continuing to rise. This is apparently what happened over a wide range of commodities in 1838–9.

Table 2. *Silberling's price index* (1790 = 100)

	First quarter	Second quarter	Third quarter	Fourth quarter
1832	95	95	93	94
1833	94	95	99	100
1834	99	96	95	96
1835	98	98	99	103
1836	106	116	112	113
1837	109	101	96	101
1838	102	102	104	108
1839	112	112	110	110
1840	110	108	108	108
1841	108	104	100	100
1842	97	95	92	90

Source: Norman J. Silberling, 'British prices and business cycles, 1779–1850', *Review of Economic Statistics* (1923), pp. 219–62. The index is an unweighted geometric mean of the prices of the following 35 commodities: Ashes (Canadian), beef (Irish), brimstone (Sicily), butter (Irish), coal (Sunderland), cochineal (West Indies), coffee (Jamaica), copper (British manufactured), cotton (Uplands), flax (St Petersburg and Riga), hides (Buenos Aires), indigo (East Indies), iron (wrought bars, Swedish), lead (British), leather (British), liquorice (Sicily), logwood (West Indies), madder root (Smyrna), mahogany (Honduras), olive oil (Gallipoli), whale oil (British South Sea fishery), pork (Irish), quicksilver (Spanish), rum (Jamaica), salammoniac (British), sumach (Sicily), silk (China), sugar (Jamaica), tallow (English), tar (Stockholm), tin (British), tobacco (Maryland), turpentine (American), wine (port), wheat.

26

Table 3. *Quantity, consumption, value and prices of imports*

Year	(1) Official value of imports (£m.)	(2) Official value of imports excluding corn (£m.)	(3) Official value of imports excluding corn and cotton (£m.)	(4) Official value of re-exports (£m.)	(5) Estimated value of net imports at 1880 prices (£m.)	(6) Net import volume index A (1841=100)	(7) Import consumption index A (same base as in (6))	(8) Net import volume index B (1841=100)	(9) Import consumption index B (same base as in (8))	(10) Import volume index B (same base as in (8))	(11) Index of import prices (1790=100)	(12) Estimated value of imports (£m.)	(13) Estimated value of imports excluding corn (£m.)
1832	44·6	43·7	34·2	11·0	42·6	77·8	75·3	87·6	82·8	97·4	106	52·5	51·3
1833	46·0	45·3	35·3	9·8	45·0	78·1	76·8	86·0	84·0	95·8	116	58·9	58·1
1834	49·4	48·8	37·9	11·6	47·9	83·3	83·5	92·8	92·4	106·2	118	64·7	64·1
1835	48·9	48·6	36·5	12·8	46·2	83·7	87·5	89·6	96·8	99·8	127	68·7	68·3
1836	57·0	56·3	42·9	12·4	56·8	99·3	94·0	107·8	102·6	116·6	133	84·9	84·1
1837	54·7	53·2	39·7	13·2	53·3	88·6	91·1	92·4	96·4	103·0	115	70·1	68·1
1838	61·3	58·9	42·2	12·7	60·7	103·0	97·0	102·6	98·6	111·4	117	80·1	75·8
1839	62·0	56·1	43·4	12·8	61·4	93·8	92·7	102·6	97·0	112·0	133	91·8	80·2
1840	67·4	62·5	43·0	13·8	67·4	107·6	97·0	100·8	94·6	108·2	121	92·1	82·1
1841	64·4	59·4	43·5	14·7	63·6	100·0	98·3	100·0	99·0	110·4	116	83·9	74·9
1842	65·2	60·0	42·8	13·6	65·1	98·7	91·6	94·2	89·0	103·4	105	76·4	67·9

Sources: (1), (2), (3), (4), annual *Finance Accounts* in *Accounts and Papers*; (5), (11), A. H. Imlah, 'Terms of trade of the United Kingdom, 1798–1913', *Journal of Economic History* (1950), pp. 170–94 (with revisions privately communicated); (6), (7), (8), (9), (10), for sources and method of construction see text, pp. 11–12; (12) A. H. Imlah, 'Real values in British foreign trade', *Journal of Economic History* (1948), pp. 133–52; (13), derived by deducting from (12) Imlah's estimates of value of corn imports, privately communicated.

27

CHAPTER IV

HARVESTS AND CORN IMPORTS

In the last chapter we confined our attention to imports of commodities other than corn, since the importance of the harvest factor and also of the peculiarities of the Corn Laws makes corn imports a very special case. Fluctuations in corn imports will be the principal theme of the present chapter, and we shall take the opportunity at the same time of discussing other respects in which harvest vagaries were liable to affect the level of effective demand.

1. Harvest Fluctuations and the Level of Effective Demand

It has generally been accepted that good harvests are good for trade and bad harvests bad for trade in the country affected (quite apart from the obvious effect of harvest fluctuations on the level of *real* income), and most students of economic fluctuations in Great Britain in the first half of the nineteenth century have agreed in assigning to harvest fluctuations a place of some importance. But there has been less agreement about the reasons responsible for the undisputed correlation between the state of the harvest and the state of trade.

Three main explanations have been put forward of why a bad harvest tended in this period to reduce the level of effective demand:

(1) A bad harvest increased corn imports, and this increase, being un-accompanied by a corresponding increase in exports, was deflationary both on account of the monetary effect and of the direct effect on incomes (to use the terminology of Chapter II). Foreign corn being usually taken out of bond and entered for consumption in August or September at the beginning of the harvest year, the gold drain and deflationary monetary effect were most often felt in the last quarter, when the bills in which payment for the corn had been made fell due (the well-known 'autumnal drain'); but the direct effect would be spread out throughout the period when the foreign corn was actually passing into consumption.

(2) Keynes, following Jevons, argued that in good harvest years stocks of corn would be accumulated (investment) and that in bad harvest years stocks would be drawn upon (disinvestment). In bad years, that is to say, a part of consumers' expenditure would go to the repayment of mercantile debt instead of creating incomes.[1] The consequent deflationary effect is analogous to the 'direct' effect of corn imports. Drawing on stocks would not, however, involve anything analogous to the monetary effect of increased imports, and a given reduction in stocks would on that account exercise a somewhat smaller deflationary effect than an equal increase in imports.

(3) The demand for corn was notoriously inelastic,[2] a point that requires to be borne in mind throughout this chapter. Hence in bad harvest years farmers'

---

[1] J. M. Keynes, *General Theory of Employment Interest and Money* (1936), pp. 329–32.

[2] Compare Gregory King's well-known estimates quoted and discussed in Tooke, I, pp. 10–20; v, pp. 66–72; D. Ricardo, *Protection to Agriculture*, in *Works and Correspondence of Ricardo*, edited by P. Sraffa, IV, pp. 219–22.

aggregate receipts must have tended to increase and a redistribution of income have taken place favourably to them at the expense of consumers. Bread being *par excellence* a wage-good, it is reasonable to suppose that consumers had a higher marginal propensity to consume than farmers. Even if farmers were not all particularly wealthy, a sudden increase in their incomes would probably not lead to a fully equivalent increase in their consumption, especially in such a period as the 1830's when the recent agricultural depression had left many farmers with debts to repay. Hence in bad harvest years aggregate expenditure on consumption would tend to be lower than in years when the price of corn was low.[1]

There is probably a certain amount of truth in all these three arguments, and the difficulty is only to decide their relative importance. Of the three, that relating to imports has the most secure empirical foundation, and it is for this reason that we are dealing with harvest fluctuations at the present stage of our inquiry. Fluctuations in stocks probably had some importance as well, and we shall have something to say about them in the following pages, though this is a matter on which firm results are difficult to reach. The peculiar machinery of the Corn Law sliding scale entailed some complicated connections between stock movements and imports, on which we shall have more to say presently.

The propensity to consume argument is of the three the least well attested, at least for our period. It must be remembered that by the 1830's the growing importance of imports had, despite the Corn Laws, reduced considerably the extent of the shifts in the distribution of income between farmers and consumers that resulted from harvest fluctuations. In a bad year prices no longer rose as high as they had done during the French wars, because supplies came in more freely from abroad; not merely was aggregate expenditure on corn thus not so high as it would have been in the absence of imports, but a substantial proportion of the expenditure that consumers did make went into the pocket of the foreigner. It remained true that bad harvests were on the whole more favourable to farmers than good ones; but as famine prices could no longer be maintained for any length of time, it seems not unlikely that farmers' receipts were highest not in really bad years but in moderately bad years, when prices were fairly high, but not so high as to make the Corn Law sliding scale (see p. 35) admit foreign corn at a nominal duty. The harvest of 1838/9, the worst of our period, was reckoned to be below the average of 1832–4 in quantity by fully one-third;[2] but prices only rose from the region of 45–50s. in the former period to about 70s. in 1838. We may perhaps conclude that changes in the propensity to consume consequent upon changes in distribution between farmers and others did contribute to the association between cheap bread and industrial prosperity, but that they were not the main cause of that association. However, in an earlier period when imports were of less significance, changes in the propensity to consume brought about in this way may well have been of the first importance.

[1] For a statement of this argument, see T. S. Ashton, *The Industrial Revolution* (1948), p. 145.
[2] Tooke, III, p. 12.

2. THE RECORD OF THE HARVESTS

We have no reliable figures on the produce of each year's harvest. The statistical material we have relates mainly to prices of corn and to quantities of corn entered for home consumption. The leading figures are presented in Table 4. In addition we have full commentaries on each year's harvest in qualitative terms in Tooke's *History of Prices* and elsewhere.

Table 4. *Corn prices and imports*

Year	(1) Wheat and wheat flour entered for home consumption (000's quarters)	(2) Average price of wheat per quarter (*s.*:*d.*)	(3) Estimated cost of all imported grain and corn entered for home consumption (£m.)
1829	1364	66:3	4·0
1830	1701	64:3	5·7
1831	1491	66:4	5·0
1832	325	58:8	1·0
1833	82	52:11	0·2
1834	64	46:2	0·2
1835	28	39:4	0·4
1836	24	48:6	0·3
1837	244	55:10	1·0
1838	1834	64:7	4·5
1839	2590	70:8	11·0
1840	2389	66:4	9·4
1841	2619	64:4	9·0
1842	2977	57:3	8·5

Sources: (1) and (2), G. R. Porter, *Progress of the Nation* (1851 edition), pp. 140, 148, derived from official returns. (3) Tooke, v, p. 181; these figures are estimates only, since there was no means of ascertaining the exact price fetched by foreign corn in years during which prices were subject to large fluctuations. Comparison with the weekly figures shown in *Accounts and Papers*, 1843, LIII, pp. 9–81, suggests, however, that Tooke's estimates are fairly accurate.

The outline of harvest fluctuations as chronicled by Tooke[1] is as follows. The harvests of 1828, 1829 and 1830 were all markedly deficient. That of 1831 was about average. There then ensued three exceptionally good years. 1835 was not quite so good but was still fully up to the average. The level of wheat prices was lower between 1834 and 1836 than it had been at any time since 1821–2. But the harvest of 1836 was no more than indifferent, and so was the harvest of 1837. 1838 had the worst harvest of any year since 1816, and the harvests of 1839, 1840 and 1841 were also all deficient to a greater or less degree. The harvest of 1842 was abundant.

What stands out from this record is the grouping of good and bad years—a phenomenon which, it may be observed, was almost equally noticeable in the years immediately before and immediately after the period with which we are concerned.[2] This grouping is still more prominent in the figures of corn im-

[1] *History of Prices*, II, pp. 194–209, 226–40; III, pp. 3–20; IV, pp. 3–16; summarised, VI, pp. 479–84.
[2] The harvests of 1819–22 were good; 1823–4 bad; 1825–7 average. 1842–4 were good; 1845–6 bad.

ports, which were high till 1831, low from then till 1837 and then high again in every year till 1842. It should be borne in mind that, with the exception of the years 1839 and 1840,[1] imported corn was mostly taken out of bond in August or September and passed into consumption during the ensuing harvest year. It appears therefore that 1833, commonly regarded as the year of cyclical revival, was the first full year for some time in which expenditure on imported corn was anything other than substantial. Corn imports remained low during the following years of improving trade and stayed low in the recession year 1837, but then increased in 1838 and stayed high during the whole of the succeeding five years, in which the state of trade was predominantly depressed.

3. THE GROUPING OF GOOD AND BAD HARVEST YEARS

It would be possible simply to point out the approximate (though not quite perfect) inverse correlation between the level of corn imports and the state of trade, conclude that harvest variations were at least partly responsible for fluctuations in the level of activity, and leave the matter at that. But one is reluctant to attribute so regular a pattern of corn imports as is revealed by the statistics entirely to the chance influence of weather conditions,[2] and although the possibility of natural causes creating in some way a general tendency for good or bad years to come in a sequence can certainly not be ruled out, one is tempted to ask whether some more strictly economic factors may not have been at work in producing the observed results.[3]

On *a priori* grounds one might look for a regular movement in the price of corn in so far as it might be expected to conform to the general pattern of business cycles. However, as far as our period is concerned this would lead to the opposite result from that which actually occurred, since bread was mostly dear in the years of bad trade. 1836 is about the only year in the period when the movement of wheat prices might with any plausibility be regarded as the consequence of shifts in the demand caused by income changes—unless one were willing to argue fancifully that the income-elasticity of demand for bread from all sections of the population taken together was negative, and that its price would therefore naturally have been high in the slump and low in the boom. The main contention of the sections on corn in Tooke's *History of Prices* is that short-run changes on the demand side were not responsible for the fluctuations that occurred in the price of corn; and in this Tooke seems to have been substantially right. The level of demand for bread was probably more a function of population than of anything else.

If general fluctuations in business will not help to explain the grouping of good and bad years, what other explanations may we seek? The most important factors to be considered in this connection are probably the movement of stocks

---

[1] Rather more than two-thirds of the imports of 1839 were entered in the harvest year 1838/9, and about a quarter of the imports of 1840 were entered in the harvest year 1839/40.

[2] For a general discussion of the alleged periodicity of harvest yields, see D. H. Robertson, *A Study of Industrial Fluctuation* (1915), pp. 144–55.

[3] The questions discussed in the remaining sections of this chapter are rather a side-issue from our main subject, and in parts are decidedly speculative; conclusions drawn about them are used relatively little in later chapters. The reader who wishes to omit the rest of this chapter may therefore do so without much loss to the continuity of the argument.

and the operation of the Corn Laws, with both of which we shall be dealing more fully in a moment. But there are also two other factors that may be thought of as mitigating in some limited degree the appearance of coincidence in grouping that has been commented on.

(1) Year-to-year fluctuations in agricultural prices cannot be viewed in abstraction from the long-run position of British agriculture. Historians of agriculture have commonly taken the year of Queen Victoria's accession as the turning point between the difficult period of readjustment after the Napoleonic wars and the beginning of what was subsequently to become, despite free trade, the golden age of British farming.[1] The choice of the exact date 1837 has probably been dictated by the pattern of harvest fluctuations; and the revision of the Poor Law in 1834, after the initial shock, has also been generally believed to have contributed to removing the feeling of malaise from rural districts. But long-run forces were at work as well. The enormous expansion of agricultural capacity undertaken in Great Britain and in Ireland during the wars meant that in the 1820's and early 1830's the rising trend of demand owing to the increase in population and in income per head could be met without any increase in price or even with falling prices in years of good harvests. But by 1840 the situation had begun to change. The failure of the harvest of 1838 and the absence of any especially good harvest in the ensuing years concealed from contemporaries the gradual development of a situation in which Britain could no longer feed herself except in years when the harvest was abnormally good. Soon even the best harvests were to prove inadequate. As the 1840's advanced, harvests improved, but the need for foreign corn continued almost unabated. There was only one year after 1838 when wheat imports amounted to less than a million quarters, and by the turn of the half-century nearly 25% of the nation's wheat supplies were being imported.

It is not unlikely, therefore, that long-run forces contributed in some degree to the high prices and high imports of the closing years of our period and were partly responsible for the prevailing feeling that harvests were then unusually deficient for several years in succession.

(2) Account should also be taken of the possible effect of past prices on acreage sown. Periods of high and low prices might be expected to alternate if farmers' production decisions were a lagged function of agricultural prices. It is difficult to be sure about the significance of this, since like so many other questions relating to corn and corn production in this period, the effect of price changes on production became an item in the Corn Law controversy, the danger of a reduction in acreage under cultivation being held out *in terrorem* by the protectionists as the likely consequence of too low prices owing to inadequate protection. The best opinion appears to have been, however, that short-run variations in agricultural prices had more effect on the relative production of different crops than on aggregate agricultural output. It seems that little land went altogether out of cultivation as the result of the low prices of 1833–5, but that there was a fairly pronounced switch away from wheat towards other crops.[2] In 1836–8 the prices of oats, barley and other agricultural products rose a good

[1] Lord Ernle, *English Farming Past and Present* (1927 edition), p. 346.
[2] Tooke, II, pp. 257–9; III, pp. 18–20, 42–3. Cf. also *Select Committee on the State of Agriculture,* 1837, v, QQ. 1876–7, 1909–17 (D. Hodgson).

deal less than that of wheat, and it appears that the rise in wheat prices in those years was partly due to a reduction in acreage under wheat caused by the earlier period of low prices. But in and after 1839 almost all agricultural prices were equally high. Not much is therefore to be deduced from this line of argument.[1]

We may now turn to the question of stocks. The level of the stock of corn carried over into any harvest year depended on the character of the harvest of the previous year, and to a lesser extent on the character of the harvest of earlier years as well. Since the level of stocks had an important influence on price, this meant that the price of corn in any year depended not merely on the most recent harvest but also on the character of earlier harvests. No reliable figures on stocks in existence within the country were available, and opinions often differed greatly as to whether the current level of stocks was higher or lower than it had been in previous years; but the general principle by which past harvests had an influence on current prices was well understood by contemporary observers. It was generally agreed, for example, that the decline in prices between 1832 and 1835 was not the result of a progressive improvement of harvests but of a *succession* of a series of harvests which were all above average, and that the carry-over of stocks from earlier years kept down prices in face of the indifferent harvests of 1836 and 1837.[2]

It is possible, however, that the influence of stocks on prices may have contributed in a more general way to the observed pattern of price movements. The argument may be put thus. The price of corn may be regarded, for the reasons just stated, as having been determined by a weighted average of recent harvest yields, with the greatest weight given to the most recent years. Now it is a well-known and easily verifiable property of moving averages that, even if the series from which they are derived shows entirely random fluctuations about the line of trend, the curve of the moving average will have a certain regularity. If the moving average for one year is above the line of trend, it is more likely that the moving average for the next year will be above the line of trend than that it will be below it. There will be no clear periodicity—no nine-year cycle—but in general there will be an appearance of good years going in groups and bad years likewise. It may perhaps be suggested that something of this sort accounted, at least in part, for the grouping of years of high and of low corn prices respectively that is found both in our period and in others. The tendency for movements in stocks to bring about groupings of years of high and low prices may have led contemporaries to overestimate the tendency of good and bad *harvests* to go together in groups, which is not the same thing. It is possible, for example, that the harvests of 1839–41 were not all quite so bad as was supposed, and that the high prices of those years were at least partly explicable by the shadow cast by the undeniably very bad harvest of 1838.

This suggestion presupposes, of course, that Tooke and others were capable of being sometimes mistaken in their estimates of the yield of the harvest. But there is a certain amount of reason to suppose that this was the case. There were no

---

[1] We shall throughout the remainder of this chapter confine our attention to wheat, since fluctuations in the prices of oats, barley and other crops had much less effect on farmers' incomes, and the annual imports of them rarely amounted to much more than £1 million.

[2] Tooke, v, p. 173.

satisfactory statistics to go on, and impressionistic estimates were bedevilled by the great diversity found between the yield of the harvest in different parts of the country.[1]

In the absence of statistical evidence relating to holdings of stocks, the hypothesis that the grouping of good and bad harvests was less marked than the grouping of years of high and low prices must remain no more than a hypothesis. It has, however, a certain plausibility, particularly as applied to years of low prices when imports did not enter into the situation. When imports did occur on a large scale, as they did in 1838–42, they introduced complications which can best be considered after we have discussed the peculiarities of the Corn Law sliding scale and their consequences.

[1] Tooke's estimates are the best known and have been mainly relied upon by historians, but they do not always perfectly agree with those of other authorities. It is interesting to compare Tooke's summaries of the quantity of the wheat harvest with those given by J. Scott, a Liverpool corn dealer, before the *Select Committee on Agricultural Distress* in 1836 (1836, VIII, Q. 5117). In the following list, Scott's statements (quoted verbatim) are given first, and Tooke's (extracted mainly from *History of Prices*, VI, pp. 474–81) second. 1809: Fair average. Deficient. 1810: Fair average. Deficient. 1811: Short. Very much below average. 1812: Very good. Very much under an average. 1813: Large. Very abundant. 1814: Deficient. Yield much inferior in quantity to last year, partly made good by an increased breadth sown. 1815: Good average. Abundant. 1816: Deficient. Very deficient. 1817: Middling average. About average. 1818: Deficient one-third. Better in yield than was expected in view of severe drought during the summer. 1819: Nearly fair. Full average. 1820: Fair, moderate. General and undoubted abundance. 1821: Large average. Large. 1822: Short. Average. 1823: Tedious (*sic*), fair. Decidedly deficient. 1824: Deficient. Deficient. 1825: Fair, moderate. Not large. 1826: Very moderate. About average. 1827: More moderate. Full average. 1828: Deficient. Greatly deficient. 1829: Nearly a fair average. Deficient. 1830: Very deficient. Less deficient than in 1828 or 1829. 1831: Fair, nearly full. Yield better. 1832: Large average. Abundant. 1833: Deficient. Good yield. 1834: Fair average. Abundant. 1835: Moderate average. Decidedly inferior to 1833 and 1834.

This comparison reveals a fair measure of agreement, particularly in the years when the harvest was especially good or bad (e.g. 1813, 1816, 1832); but there are also some striking discrepancies. Comparison may also be made with the estimates of Jacob for the years 1816–27 (W. Jacob, *Corn Trade and Corn Laws* (1828), p. 88), of Spackman for the years 1829–40 (W. F. Spackman, *Statistical Tables of the Agriculture Shipping Colonies Manufactures Commerce and Population of the United Kingdom of Great Britain and its Dependencies* (1842), p. 14), and of a large number of other authors for particular years (e.g. Porter, *Progress of the Nation*, pp. 538–9). All these reveal greater or less discrepancies from Tooke's estimates.

Another possible check may be sought in the returns of quantities of wheat sold. These were notoriously unreliable, particularly if taken as an indication of the volume of production (cf. *Select Committee on Agricultural Distress*, 1836, VIII, QQ. 23–4, evidence of W. Jacob, and QQ. 5167–72, evidence of J. Scott) but they may be quoted for what they are worth:

Quantities of wheat returned by corn inspectors as sold in
150 market towns in England and Wales, 1832–1841

Harvest year	1831/2	1832/3	1833/4	1834/5	1835/6	1836/7
Wheat sold (m.qr.)	3·2	3·7	3·4	3·9	4·1	4·3

Harvest year	1837/8	1838/9	1839/40	1840/1	1841/2
Wheat sold (m.qr.)	4·2	3·0	4·1	3·8	3·5

(*Source:* weekly figures given in *Accounts and Papers*, 1843, LIII, p. 65, corrected for change in coverage in 1842 on the basis of data, *ibid.* p. 1. The harvest year is taken to begin in the 36th week of the calendar year; cf. Tooke, IV, p. 414.) Taken at their face value, these figures confirm that 1838 and 1841 were bad years, but do not support the suggestion of any falling off in 1836 and 1837 or of any special deficiency in 1839.

4. THE EFFECTS OF THE CORN LAWS

The Corn Law of 1828, which was in operation for practically the whole of our period, was very far from being an ordinary tariff on imports. Under the Corn Law of 1815 (55 Geo. III, c. 26), even after it had been modified by the somewhat more liberal Act of 1822 (3 Geo. IV, c. 60), the import of foreign wheat was altogether prohibited until the price of wheat had risen above 80s. a quarter. This system was found to be altogether too rigid, and on several occasions the Act had to be suspended to prevent undue hardship. Growing awareness of its unsatisfactoriness led ultimately to its replacement by the Act of 1828 (9 Geo. IV, c. 60), which established what came to be known as 'the Duke of Wellington's Sliding Scale' and remained in force until it in turn was replaced by Peel's sliding scale in 1842 (5 & 6 Vict., c. 14). Under the Act of 1828, the rate of duty payable on foreign wheat when it was taken out of bond varied inversely with the 'averages', that is to say, the average price of wheat in the six weeks previous. If the averages were below about 67s., the rate of duty was so high as to be virtually prohibitive. As the averages rose the duty fell, not smoothly but jerkily, until when the averages were at 73s. or above the duty was reduced to the nominal level of 1s. The jerkiness of the scale was most pronounced at the higher price ranges; with the averages at 69s., 70s., 71s., 72s., and 73s., the duty was respectively 13s. 8d., 10s. 8d., 6s. 8d., 2s. 8d. and 1s. 0d.[1]

It is fairly clear that the general effect of the Corn Laws was to keep up the price of imported corn. The working of the sliding scale made the importation of corn into Britain an extremely risky and speculative business, and militated particularly severely against supplies sent from more remote sources, since a fall of a few shillings in the averages while the corn was in the course of shipment might prevent it from being sold save at a heavy loss.[2] In this way the supply of foreign corn was discouraged and prices kept up, even in years when the duty was low. It was sometimes disputed that this really had a great deal of importance, on the grounds that the available supplies were in any case bound to be very limited, duty or no duty. This view was based on the findings of William Jacob, Comptroller of Corn Returns, who in the late 1820's went to make a study of the regions of the Baltic from which our supplies of foreign wheat were then mainly derived.[3] He pointed out that the wheat grown in that area was for the most part deliberately cultivated for the English market on large estates as a cash crop of speculative character, since the local peasantry subsisted rather on rye bread and potatoes; and he accordingly argued that there was little surplus which might be tapped by a more liberal English import policy. His view was that the foreign supply would scarcely be capable of meeting a one-tenth deficiency of the British crop as a regular thing, though an *occasional* deficiency of that amount could be made up from stocks of foreign corn accumulated in years when British prices were low. But the subsequent course of events suggests that Jacob underestimated the extent to which supply could be expanded in

[1] For details of the Acts of 1815, 1822, 1828 and 1842, see D. G. Barnes, *History of the English Corn Laws* (1930), pp. 141, 174, 200; C. R. Fay, *The Corn Laws and Social England* (1932), pp. 62–8, 78–87.

[2] Tooke, III, p. 39; speech of Sir R. Peel of 9 February 1842, reprinted in Fay, *op. cit.* p. 174.

[3] For Jacob's views on this see his *Corn Trade and Corn Laws* (1828), pp. 125–31, and his evidence before the *Select Committee on Agriculture*, 1833, V, QQ. 50–3.

3-2

response to a steady demand—as was indeed argued against him at the time.[1] His view that a one-tenth deficiency could not regularly be met from foreign supplies was already falsified by 1838–42, for throughout that period over two million quarters of foreign corn were imported annually, which appreciably exceeded one-tenth of total consumption (this being variously estimated between 12 and 16 million quarters per annum).[2] After the Corn Laws had been repealed, the increase in imports was still more striking, and, as had been predicted, imports were then drawn from a much wider range of regions than formerly.[3] It is true that other causes besides the repeal of the Corn Laws may have contributed to this result, but it is difficult not to believe that the argument that the Corn Laws did have a discouraging effect on imports, even when prices were high, was substantially correct.

This conclusion means a bad mark for the Corn Laws from the point of view of their effect on real income and is important in the assessment of the economics of the Corn Laws generally; but it is not of very great relevance from the point of view of short-period fluctuations. Taken by itself the consideration advanced in the previous paragraph probably tended to reduce rather than increase the *value of expenditure* on imported corn in years of bad harvests, since the elasticity of demand can hardly have been so low that an increase in the supply of foreign wheat would have caused an equal or more than proportional fall in prices, in view of the small proportion of foreign supplies to the total amount of wheat consumed. But this is no more than a minor point, and is of much less importance, as far as the course of short-period fluctuations in expenditure on foreign corn is concerned, than certain other consequences of the Corn Laws which we must now examine.

The steep and irregular gradations of the Duke of Wellington's Sliding Scale made its working not so very different in many respects from that of the Act of 1815 which it replaced, under which importation was forbidden until the price reached 80s. Under the Act of 1828, once the averages had risen high enough for the duty to be brought down below the prohibitive level, a further rise of only a few shillings reduced the duty to a point where it became nominal; and if such a rise appeared at all likely, it obviously paid importers to delay taking their corn out of bond until it came about. The steepness of the scale meant that the bulk of the foreign wheat that was imported was entered at a very low duty, and the amount of revenue derived was consequently small. Out of a total of 13·6 million quarters entered while the Act of 1828 was in force, 5·8 million was admitted when the price was 73s. and 11·5 million when the price was 70s. or over.[4] It is this which explains the very marked contrast shown in Table 4 between the years of low imports on the one hand and the years of high imports on the other, and the comparative absence of years when imports were at an intermediate level. If the price of wheat was low, foreign supplies were virtually excluded; but if the price was above a certain level they were admitted at a very low duty. The Corn Laws in this way greatly accentuated the contrast between the amount of corn imported in high- and low-price years respectively.

[1] Cf. *Select Committee on Agriculture*, 1833, v, Q. 3220 (T. Oliver).
[2] Cf. *ibid.* Q. 53 (W. Jacob); James Wilson, *Fluctuations in Currency Commerce and Manufactures referable to the Corn Laws* (1840), pp. 12–13; Tooke, III, pp. 12–13, v, p. 107.
[3] Tooke, VI, pp. 450–3.
[4] *Accounts and Papers*, 1843, LIII, p. 74.

It is possible that the Corn Laws also accentuated this contrast in a different way, by artificially increasing the price paid for foreign corn in the years when it was imported. One of the main objectives aimed at when the sliding scale system was introduced had been to reduce inter-annual price fluctuations. Whether it succeeded in doing this to any extent is a debatable point; but the system certainly tended to increase rather than diminish the amplitude of price fluctuations of shorter period. Since the rate of duty depended on the average price over the previous six weeks, and was prohibitive until the averages approached 70s., prices had to stay very high for some time before any foreign corn was admitted. Then as soon as the averages reached the level of 73s.—or, alternatively, when importers despaired of their rising any higher, if they were still a little lower than that—virtually all the corn in bond would be entered and prices would fall. For a short spell of time, usually in August or early September, the level of prices was artificially raised, and the price prevailing at the time when the bulk of the foreign corn was entered invariably exceeded the average price for the year. The effect of this on the aggregate amount of expenditure on imported corn is difficult to assess, since it all depends on whether importers were able to realise their corn before prices had fallen very far. The general view seems to have been that the net effect was to increase somewhat the average price paid for foreign corn,[1] though to what extent is uncertain, and hence to increase the volume of expenditure on foreign corn in years when importation took place.

5. THE RELATION BETWEEN STOCKS AND IMPORTS

By preventing imports from showing any responsiveness to changes in price below the crucial level, the Corn Laws accentuated the tendency for several years of uniformly negligible imports to follow one another in succession. So long as the averages remained below 65s. or thereabouts, there was under the Act of 1828 virtually no question of wheat being imported on a significant scale, and if varying harvests caused prices to fluctuate below that level the effect on the amount of imports would be nil. If the year opened with a fairly high level of stocks, it would make no difference as far as the volume of imports was concerned whether the harvest was good or only moderate, though of course if it were really bad that would be different. It is clear that in such a year as 1837 imports of corn would have been considerably higher had the Corn Laws not imposed a severe duty. As it was, the fall in harvest yields in 1836 and 1837 as compared with previous years was met mainly by drawing on domestic stocks and by a diminution of the amount fed to animals and used for malting, distilling or other manufacture.[2] The reduction in stocks must have involved some deflationary consequences, but the deflationary pressure would evidently have been greater if the entire difference between the produce of the current harvest and the level of consumption established in the previous years had been made up by imports, as would presumably have happened under free trade.

---

[1] This appears to be the view taken by Alfred Marshall in his discussion of the working of the Corn Laws, *Industry and Trade* (1923 edition), pp. 751–4, though it is not quite clear whether what Marshall has in mind is the enhancement of the price due to the reasons mentioned in the text or the more general tendency in that direction discussed above, pp. 35–6. See also Tooke, III, pp. 30–9.

[2] Cf. Tooke, II, p. 257.

In years like 1837, then, in which prices were moderately high but not very high, the Corn Laws kept the volume of corn imports *below* their natural level. But for this very reason they were liable to *raise* the peak of imports in subsequent years to a higher level than would have been necessary under free trade. If imports had been regularly admitted, the most extreme stringencies would have been avoided, since the level of stocks would have been kept more nearly stable. Had wheat imports not been kept low by the duty in 1837, stocks would have been higher at the beginning of the harvest year 1838/9, prices would have risen less in face of the bad harvest of that year, and imports would not have needed to be so high.

When home supplies were so low as to make prices rise high enough to reduce the duty to a nominal level, the imports elicited were normally sufficient to send the price below 70s., at least for a while. Foreign supplies put a limit to the extent to which stocks might be reduced and prices driven up; the virtually free admission of foreign corn at the top end of the sliding scale prevented a cumulative rise of prices above the 73s. level. If it is true that the harvests of 1839, 1840 and 1841 were predominantly below normal, the absence of a cumulative rise in prices during those years may be explained by the safety valve of imports, and may be contrasted with the cumulative *fall* in prices that did take place as a result of the predominance of good harvests between 1832 and 1835.

It might perhaps have been expected that, when the price did at last rise sufficiently for foreign supplies to be entered without paying more than a low duty, the amount admitted would have been so great as not merely to afford a safety valve preventing prices from rising any further, but also to make up fully or more than make up both for the deficiency of the current harvest and for any previous depletion of stocks, and so drive down prices and prevent any shortage of stocks from being carried over to the next year. Had that been so, some modification would be called for in the hypothesis advanced on pp. 33–4, for prices would have shown a tendency to fall back rapidly as soon as they had reached the crucial level, and a succession of years of high imports would have been unlikely unless there really were a succession of unusually bad harvests. It is true that harvests on the Continent of Europe were subject to broadly the same climatic influences as the harvest in Britain and so tended to be deficient in the same years as the harvest here was deficient—a point often made by those who wished to belittle the benefits to be derived from free trade in corn—and that this acted to restrict the amount of foreign corn imported in dear years. But there was another argument not infrequently advanced[1] which tended to suggest the opposite conclusion. It was argued that when the price in England was too low for imports of corn to take place, stocks of foreign wheat tended to pile up in bond and in the countries of origin, so that, when at last the price did rise and the duty fall, several years' supply was imported into England in a lump. Hence, it was maintained, the amount of foreign corn imported in bad years exceeded both the amount required and the amount that would have been imported under free trade, and the result was to inflict upon home producers 'the misery of a low price, combined with a diminished portion of produce.'[2]

[1] See, for example, Jacob, *Corn Trade and Corn Laws*, pp. 126–7; *Select Committee on Agriculture*, 1833, v, Q. 784 (D. Hodgson).
[2] Jacob, *loc. cit.*

There are, then, really two questions to be answered here. Did imports tend to do more than fill the gap in home supplies in years when the duty fell to the lowest levels; and was a large proportion of the corn imported in such a year as 1838 derived from foreign stocks accumulated during earlier years?

The first of these questions is the more important of the two, but it is the more difficult to answer. The fundamental point to be explained is that after 1838 prices and imports did in fact remain consistently high until 1842, despite the extremely large imports that took place both in the harvest year 1838/9 and in the harvest year 1839/40. If in these latter years imports were sufficient both to restore stocks to a normal level and to supplement deficiency in the current harvest, the continuance of high prices and high imports in 1840/1 and 1841/2[1] can only be explained on the supposition that the harvests of those years were unusually poor and that there really was, therefore, a succession of bad harvests. But if, on the other hand, imports in 1838 and 1839 were scarcely if at all more than adequate to meet current requirements, the imports of the later years may have been necessitated at least in part by the need to rebuild stocks from the low level which they had reached in 1838. Unfortunately, we can only guess which of these interpretations of the facts is the correct one, since we know neither just how seriously deficient the harvests of these years were nor by how large a margin stocks had been run down below their normal level.[2] If the estimate of one-third deficiency of the crop of 1838 and of a normal annual consumption of not less than 12 million quarters were both correct, it is difficult to see how the imports of the harvest year 1838–9, which amounted to 3·3 million quarters, can have contributed very much to raising the level of aggregate stocks, and it would appear rather that the harvest of 1839 must have been approached with stocks even lower than they had been a year earlier. As far as this year is concerned, therefore, the hypothesis of 'excessive' imports does not seem plausible, and it is probable that continuance of a low level of stocks was largely responsible for the high imports of 1839/40. But just how large a proportion of the five million or so quarters of wheat imported in the next two years were needed for the replenishment of stocks and how large a proportion of them were needed to bridge the gap between consumption and current home production we can only guess. That all the imports of these years were needed for the replenishment of stocks is not a tenable hypothesis in view of the amounts involved, so it does appear that the harvests of 1839–41 must have been on the average insufficient to provide for current consumption. But when account is taken of the stock factor on the one

---

[1] The high corn imports of the harvest year 1842/3 represent in some respects a special case, on which see p. 41.

[2] The height of the normal level of stocks in our period is itself far from clear. On some occasions as much as 6 million quarters, equivalent to about six months' consumption, was said to have carried over from one harvest year to the next. This was computed to be about the level prevailing at the end of the Napoleonic war. But it was generally agreed that during the next ten years the normal stockholding was much reduced, and in 1833 it was reckoned to be equivalent to no more than one month's consumption. On the other hand, a considerable rise occurred during the next few years, and one spokesman whose experience in the corn trade went back for over thirty years stated in 1836 that stocks in the hands of farmers (though not of dealers) at that time were higher than he had ever previously known. See Tooke, v, p. 173; *Select Committee on Agriculture*, 1833, v, Report, p. v, QQ. 704–7 (D. Hodgson); *Select Committee on Agricultural Distress*, 1836, VIII, QQ. 6030–2 (J. Sandars), 8153 (G. Calthrop), 8541 (W. Umbers); *Select Committee on the State of Agriculture*, 1837, v, QQ. 1931–2 (D. Hodgson).

hand and the upward trend of demand on the other, it is at least arguable that there was not quite such a run of uniformly disastrous harvests as Tooke's narrative might suggest.

Reverting now to the second question posed on p. 39, that relating to the alleged accumulation of foreign wheat in years of low prices. The evidence suggests that the picture often painted of menacing accumulations of foreign corn piling up in years of low prices ready to be poured on to the English market at the first opportunity was somewhat exaggerated. Bonded stocks showed a slight tendency to diminish rather than to increase during the years between 1832 and 1837 when prices were low. Evidence is lacking with regard to the movement of stocks held in the Baltic and other producing areas, but there is no reason to suppose that the amount held there was really very large, even if it was tending to increase. It is to be borne in mind that the cost of holding stocks of wheat was not negligible, and importers could not afford to wait for an indefinite period. The annual cost of storing corn in bond was reckoned to be about 5s. 3d. a quarter, making no allowance for waste (which might amount to about 5%), and importers were sometimes driven to take their stocks out of the bonded warehouses and ship them away for sale elsewhere when it appeared that there was no prospect of the averages rising high enough to permit their being entered without a loss.[1]

It is true that wheat imports were, at 3·3 million quarters, higher in the harvest year 1838/9 than they were in any other year in our period, and this might be set down to the accumulation of stocks that had taken place in the Baltic in the preceding long spell of low imports. But it is more natural to attribute it rather to the great extent of the shortage in this country in that year. Less than half of the total imports of the harvest year 1838/9 were entered on the first occasion when the averages rose to 73s., which does not suggest that the bulk of the year's foreign supplies were drawn from the old stocks. The averages remained above 73s. for over three months on end, and foreign corn was entered at an increasing rate throughout that period. The fact that imports of wheat continued to run at an annual rate of over two million quarters until 1842 provides further evidence against the view that the imports of 1838 were so high that the bulk of them must have been drawn from stocks rather than from current production. A certain amount of them no doubt did come from old stocks, but the amount imported was not so much greater than the amount imported in subsequent years as to suggest that it represented the accumulation of several years' wheat production from northern Europe. It seems likely that Jacob and those who argued as he did overestimated the dependence of Continental wheat producers on the English market.

It is thus doubtful whether, at least in our period, the accumulation of foreign supplies during years of low prices was a factor of great importance. Indeed, it

---

[1] *Select Committee on Agricultural Distress*, 1836, VIII, QQ. 5270–6 (J. Scott). Since only a small proportion of the foreign corn entered in any year was thus drawn from bonded stocks imported in earlier years, we do not need to concern ourselves unduly with what would otherwise be a troublesome question, namely, whether stocks of corn in bond were normally owned by foreigners or by British merchants. If foreign corn was transferred to British ownership as soon as it was imported, the effect on the exchanges and on the balance of payments (though not the direct effect on incomes) would be felt then rather than at the time when it was entered for consumption. The most usual stage for transfer of ownership of foreign corn to take place from foreigners to British merchants is difficult to ascertain; the practice seems to have varied.

seems that there was some tendency in the reverse direction—namely, for the supply of foreign corn to be increased as a result of imports into England having been *high* for a spell of several years. When for a number of years in succession prices in England had risen high enough for importation to take place, foreign producers tended to increase their consignments to the English market in anticipation that the events of previous years would be repeated. This reaction on their part was subject to a certain lag, so that importation continued longer than was necessary or than was profitable to the importers. This happened most notably in 1842. At that time importers had hoped that prices would again rise as high as they had done in the four preceding years, and accordingly held substantial quantities in bond. But the harvest turned out to be exceptionally good, and most of the corn in bond had to be entered at a price and at a duty that carried a loss to the importer.[1] The same thing had occurred in 1831: 'as it almost inevitably happens on such occasions, the impulse to importation being given, the foreign supply continued to come in after the deficiency had ceased to be felt.'[2] The consequence on each occasion was that the deflationary effect of corn imports continued for longer than was necessary in the light of the harvest and stock situation, and the number of successive years of high imports was further prolonged. On the earlier occasion, moreover, the effect was not entirely exhausted for some time after the actual importation had taken place; some of the wheat entered in 1831 was still passing into consumption as late as the harvest year 1833/4.[3]

6. CONCLUSIONS

Any conclusions that may be reached on the complicated and often obscure issues that have been touched upon in this chapter must necessarily be tentative in a high degree. It is evident that harvest factors exerted substantial deflationary pressure in several years within our period, and that their working had a certain appearance of regularity, with good and bad years associated together in sequence. It is evident, too, that the observed behaviour of imports and of prices was influenced, to some extent at least, by factors other than the vagaries of the weather, more particularly by the movement of stocks and the operation of the Corn Laws. It is fairly clear that the effect of old stocks in keeping down prices and the effect of the Corn Laws in excluding imports till prices were above a certain level were together responsible in a large measure for the persistence of low imports for so long a period as 1832–7, and also contributed to the exceptionally high imports of 1838; it is also fairly clear that most of the imports entered in 1842 were the result of a lagged reaction to the preceding spell of high prices rather than of any serious inadequacy in the home supply. But it is more difficult to decide on the relative importance of the various factors—harvest deficiency, upward trend in demand, initially low level of stocks—which between them must have accounted for the high prices and high imports of the years 1839, 1840 and 1841.

[1] Tooke, IV, pp. 13–14. The losses suffered would have been even greater had it not been for the change in the Corn Laws effected by Peel's Act of 1842.
[2] Tooke, III, p. 37.
[3] *Select Committee on Agricultural Distress*, 1836, VIII, QQ. 108–15 (W. Jacob); 5285–91 (J. Scott).

In the absence of specific evidence to the contrary, it is natural to treat changes in the value of foreign corn entered for home consumption as a measure of the net inflationary or deflationary tendency arising out of the harvest factor from one year to the next. But the inflationary or deflationary consequences of investment or disinvestment in stocks of corn cannot be disregarded in assessing the effects of harvest fluctuations, even though their importance is difficult to judge. Some account must evidently be taken of such facts as that not all the foreign corn entered in 1831 passed into consumption immediately, that domestic stocks were drawn upon in 1836 and 1837, and that the high imports of the closing years of the period were accompanied by some increase—though not perhaps a very great one *in any single year* till 1842—in the aggregate holding of corn stocks within the country. Of course, if we follow Tooke in ascribing the amount of corn imported in each harvest year mainly to the deficiency in the yield of the home harvest in that same year—and it is by no means certain that we should be wrong to do so—then the inflationary or deflationary effects of changes in stock holdings can probably be passed over without a great deal of attention as of relatively small significance; but if, on the other hand, we believe that the need to rebuild stocks was an important contributory cause of the high prices and imports of 1839–42, corresponding importance must presumably be attached to the deflationary effects of disinvestment in home stocks between 1836 and 1838. This is an uncertainty that cannot readily be resolved.

CHAPTER V

THE AMERICAN MARKET AND ITS FLUCTUATIONS

THE broad commodity structure of Britain's export trade in our period can be inferred from the following figures of the value (in £ million) of the most important exports in 1838, taken as a fairly representative year: cotton piece-goods, 16·7; cotton yarn, 7·4; woollens, 5·8; linens, 3·6; iron and steel, 2·6; hardware, 1·5; all others, 12·2. The predominance of textiles, especially cotton, stands out very plainly. But whereas in our analysis of imports we found it necessary to draw frequent distinctions between the movements of prices and quantities of the several leading imported commodities, and in particular to treat corn imports under a separate heading, in the case of exports analysis by commodities is not a particularly fruitful approach. There was much diversity between the trend movements of the various items of export, but differences between commodities in the pattern of short-period fluctuations were mainly the result of differences between the markets for which the goods were respectively destined. Fluctuations in exports of woollens, for example, were largely governed by the state of the United States market, and those in exports of cotton yarn by the state of the market in northern Europe. The figures of value of British exports to individual countries, which are given in the Parliamentary Papers, therefore provide us with a more useful basis of classification.

Chart 6 (p. 71) shows the movements of export values in the three main categories which it is convenient to distinguish for this purpose, namely, exports to the United States, to 'northern Europe', here defined as consisting of France, Russia, Scandinavia, Prussia, Germany, Holland and Belgium,[1] and to other areas. The contrast between the behaviour of these three categories of exports is evident from the chart. We shall discuss the course of exports to the United States in this chapter, and that of the other two categories of exports in Chapter VI.

1. INTRODUCTION

Taking the average of the period 1833–42, the value of exports to the United States constituted 15% of the total value of British exports. This percentage may not seem very high. But the significance of the American market in determining the course of fluctuations in total exports was much greater than this figure would suggest, since the *proportional* fluctuations of exports to the United States were of much greater amplitude than in exports generally, as is evident from Chart 6. The proportion of export proceeds derived from sales in the United States was, as has been said, on the average 15%; but if we reckon instead the proportion of the average year-to-year *change* in exports to the United States to the average year-to-year *change* in total exports, the figure is 58%. And in the course of the period there was only one year—1834—when total exports and exports to the United States moved in opposite directions. The state of the

---

[1] The reasons for this definition are discussed in Chapter VI.

43

American market was therefore the most important single factor in bringing prosperity or depression to British export industries. For this reason it is appropriate to deal with it first in discussing fluctuations in exports.

Chart 5 and Table 5 show the value of British exports to the United States set against Cole's index of United States trade volume.[1] The close correspondence between the two is obvious, 1838 being the only year when they diverge. Evidently the course of British exports in these years cannot be understood

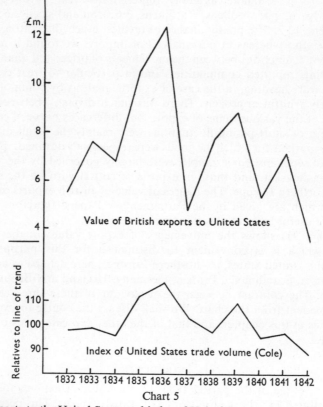

Chart 5

Exports to the United States and index of United States volume of trade

without reference to the varying fortunes of American business activity as a whole. It also appears from Chart 5 that the proportional amplitude of the fluctuations in British exports was substantially greater than that of United States trade. This, of course, partly reflects fluctuations in export prices, but high sensitivity of British exports to the state of business in the United States conforms to a pattern in Anglo-American trading relations that has prevailed up to the present day, and need occasion no surprise. Some of the circumstances that were responsible for it in the 1830's will emerge in the course of this chapter.

[1] W. B. Smith and A. H. Cole, *Fluctuations in American Business, 1790–1860* (1935), pp. 70–2.

In view of the importance to the British economy of fluctuations in the value of exports to the United States, and of the close relationship between these fluctuations and those of business activity in the United States, it is necessary to undertake a brief analysis of the nature and causes of these ups and downs in American economic activity, with special reference to those aspects which had a particular bearing on the value of American imports.

Table 5. *United States trade volume and value of*
British exports to the United States

Year	U.S. trade volume	British exports to U.S. (£m.)
1832	98	5·5
1833	99	7·6
1834	95	6·8
1835	112	10·6
1836	118	12·4
1837	103	4·7
1838	97	7·6
1839	109	8·8
1840	95	5·3
1841	98	7·1
1842	89	3·5

2. FLUCTUATIONS IN AMERICAN BUSINESS BEFORE 1835

The 1820's had been a period of steady and generally uneventful growth in the United States economy, unmarked by any such violent disturbances as characterised the ensuing decade.[1] There was a quickening of business around 1825 and some recession after that date, but this movement was not as pronounced as its counterpart in England, and there is reason to suppose that its origin lay in the country's external economic relations rather than in the logic of its own evolution.[2]

Towards the end of the decade growth became rather more rapid. Public land sales started to rise in 1829, and in 1830 some railway building began to be undertaken.[3] An upward turn is evident at about the same time in most of the principal statistical series, including commodity prices, which passed their trough by the autumn of 1830. But these hopeful signs were not accompanied by any particularly rapid rise in the volume of business. The upward trend was also interrupted by a slight recession in 1832.[4] From 1830 to 1833 the course of British exports to the United States—of which woollens, cotton textiles, linens, hardware and iron and steel goods were, in that order, the chief items—followed the pattern of cyclical fluctuations, with a decline in 1832 and rises in 1830–1 and

[1] Cf. T. S. Berry, *Western Prices before 1861* (1943), pp. 406 ff.
[2] Smith and Cole, p. 63. Almost all the most important statistics relating to the American economy of this period are presented in convenient and accessible form in this volume, and it has therefore not been considered necessary to reproduce them here. All statistics quoted in the present chapter are derived from this source unless contrary indication is provided.
[3] Figures of railway mileage constructed are in W. G. Sumner, *History of American Currency* (1875), p. 118.
[4] The recession is observable in the volume of trade index, in the commodity price index and in the movement of certain (not all) stock prices.

1833, and no obvious upward trend in value (as distinct from volume) over the whole. But the rise in exports in 1831 and 1833 and the fall in 1832 were a good deal larger than could plausibly be explained by the decidedly mild fluctuations in the volume of trade in the United States, and it seems likely that inventory movements were on this occasion acting as a destabiliser, picking up the fluctuations in trade as a whole and reflecting them in much exaggerated form.

In 1834 there took place a recession of some severity in American business. Its proximate cause was monetary stringency. Discount rates became 'high and variable.' This was commonly attributed to the curtailment of facilities by the Bank of the United States (B.U.S.) from October 1833, allegedly a step taken as a reply to the removal of the Federal deposits[1] with the object of proving the indispensability of the services normally rendered by the Bank to the public. More general fears of a crisis following the winding up of the B.U.S. no doubt also played a certain part;[2] and it should be noted that the United States had been running a substantial adverse balance of trade since 1831.

Some series—public land sales is an example—continued to rise in 1834 without showing any response to the recession. In general, however, its impact was quite sharp.[3] Throughout the year exchange on London was at a great discount, for not merely did the fall in incomes restrict demand for imports, but also, with discount rates ranging from 15 to 24%, capitalists had better use for whatever funds they had than to lock them up idle in the purchase of foreign exchange.[4] Had it not been for the generous short-term lending undertaken by British merchants, 'the credit of the Americans as customers would have been lost.'[5] Thanks to this finance, however, the United States was able to maintain a slight import surplus for the year as a whole.

3. ANDREW JACKSON AND THE BANKS

After 1834 hesitations were left behind and what has sometimes been known as the Jacksonian inflation commenced in earnest. The timing and nature of this boom were much influenced by the development of new banks and by a phenomenal increase in the more picturesque forms of bank finance. A tendency to wild-cat banking was endemic in the United States in this epoch, but the great outburst of the early 1830's owed its origin in large part to political factors, in particular the struggle between President Andrew Jackson and the Democratic party on the one hand, and the B.U.S. and its President, Nicholas Biddle, on the other.

The hostility of Jackson and his party to the Bank arose out of a variety of sources. The Bank had been founded in 1816 with its character clearly defined as that of banker to the Federal government.[6] Tax receipts, mainly from tariffs, were paid into the Bank through the Customs collectors in the form of notes on other banks. The subsequent presentation of these notes by the B.U.S. for payment at the bank of issue constituted a continual check on over-issue. In this way the influence of the B.U.S. throughout the 1820's placed a decided restraint

---

[1] See below.   [2] Sumner, p. 103.   [3] Cf. Berry, p. 427.
[4] R. W. Hidy, *The House of Baring in American Trade and Finance* (1949), p. 177.
[5] *Circular to Bankers*, 24 October 1834.
[6] For the early history of the B.U.S., see R. H. C. Catterall, *The Second Bank of the United States* (1903).

on monetary expansion. This was the result of the exercise of deliberate policy on the part of the B.U.S.[1] It was resented by other banks and also by the agrarian interests of the West and South, to whom easy credit was important as the means of facilitating territorial expansion. These interests carried much weight in the Democratic party. In addition to the strictly economic motive for agrarian hostility to the Bank, there was also a good deal of animosity felt against it in the West in its character as an aristocratic Eastern institution, and Jackson successfully exploited this animosity for political purposes.

The hostility towards the Bank amongst Jackson's supporters in the East was partly similar in nature to the feeling against it amongst the agrarians, but contained other elements as well. Small self-made business men and traders, who were anxious to raise themselves socially and economically, hated the aristocratic financial oligarchy which excluded them and seemed to stand in their way. Working men in the Eastern cities, recently grown in political consciousness and importance, disliked the Bank because they, like the agrarians, felt it to be unproductive and parasitic, and also because they tended to be supporters of a 'hard-money' policy and hence opposed to banks in principle as purveyors of inflationary paper money. There was here an evident inconsistency with the views of the agrarians, whose economic objections to the Bank were based on its *restraining* influence in the monetary sphere. Because of this divergence of interests amongst his supporters, Jackson in his campaign was careful not to give too much emphasis to the purely economic issues, and framed his attack rather in terms of more general and indeed demagogic hostility to the Bank as a symbol of undemocratic centralised authority and privilege.

The conflict between the Democratic party and the Bank had been brewing up since the late 1820's, and it was brought to a head when Biddle appealed for a renewal of the Bank's charter in 1831. The re-charter was vetoed by Jackson. The existing charter was due to expire in 1836, but before then, in September 1833, the Bank was by executive authority deprived of its position as depository of the Federal funds. Shortly afterwards this step was ratified by legislation. The deposits at the Bank were not actually removed, but were allowed to dwindle gradually as payments out were made.[2] Tax receipts were henceforward paid into selected banks in each state, the so-called 'pet banks'. The number of these banks, and the amount of the government's deposits at different dates, were as follows:

Government depository banks

Date	Number of banks	Government deposits ($m.)
1 Jan. 1835	29	10
1 Dec. 1835	33	25
1 Nov. 1836	89	49

Source: Dewey, p. 210.

---

[1] Speaking of the general monetary stability of the 1820's, W. G. Sumner wrote: 'there was scarcely anybody...who did not believe that the Bank of the United States was to be credited with having brought about this state of things' (*History of Banking in the United States* (1896), p. 198).

[2] D. R. Dewey, *Financial History of the United States* (1902), p. 206.

The mere freeing of these banks from the check on over-issue, which was brought about by the transfer of the Federal funds from the B.U.S., would have been a sufficiently important inflationary influence; but there were also certain special factors at work. The transfer of government deposits to the pet banks was of particular significance, and especially attractive to the pet banks, because the government's revenue consistently exceeded its expenditure. The 'compromise tariff' of 1832, unalterable for political reasons, was now bringing in a revenue in excess of the Federal government's needs. The surplus was at first used for the redemption of the national debt, and by January 1835 the whole debt had been repaid. The redistribution between the states of the steadily accruing surplus funds was carried out, after political wranglings, in 1837; pending the distribution the funds piled up in the pet banks and provided the basis for further inflationary loans. As the revenue from the sales of public lands mounted during the ensuing land boom, the surplus grew larger than ever.

Moreover, the encouragement provided by the policy of the administration to bank expansion operated also in rather more general ways. The Democratic party was by tradition the states' rights party, and it was hostile to the B.U.S. because, amongst other things, the B.U.S. was a strong centralised institution endowed with certain monopoly powers. The downfall of the B.U.S. was taken as a signal for the development of new local banks to take its place. 'Very many Democrats inferred it to be the wish of General Jackson's administration, that state banks should be created where they did not exist.'[1] And many banks were formed in the hope that they would be made depositaries of the Federal funds, even though the government had not given any indication that they would be favoured in this way, and did not in the event oblige them.[2] For these reasons the boom in the formation of new banks had already begun some time before September 1833, when the removal of the Federal deposits from the B.U.S. was ordered. As early as 1829 the impending battle of the administration with the Bank had been foreshadowed in the unfriendly references to the Bank in Jackson's first Message to Congress, and in some sharp exchanges between Biddle and the Secretary of the Treasury.[3] With the Bank's application for re-charter in January 1832 the war commenced in earnest, carrying with it a rapid development of new banks eager to fill the void the creation of which they foresaw. When the removal of the government's deposits was actually effected, the movement gained new momentum, and the operations of already established banks increased even more rapidly than the number of banks.[4]

The transfer of the deposits to the pet banks was of particular importance in its effects on purchases of the public lands. The public lands were on sale at this time at a minimum price of a dollar and a quarter an acre, payable to the local land receiver. As the general level of prosperity advanced and land purchase became

---

[1] T. Ford, *History of Illinois* (1854), p. 170.

[2] Sister M. Grace Madeleine, *Monetary and Banking Theories of Jacksonian Democracy* (1943), p. 69.

[3] Dewey, p. 200; F. C. James, *Growth of Chicago Banks* (1938), I, p. 77.

[4] For statistics on the growth of banks, cf. Dewey, p. 225 and Sumner, *History of American Currency*, p. 123. Unfortunately, the figures relating to the country as a whole are not reliable (Smith and Cole, pp. 74–5). Moderately satisfactory data are available for New York, Rhode Island, Massachusetts and Pennsylvania (Smith and Cole, *loc. cit.*), but the position of banks in these eastern states was different in fundamental respects from that of banks in the frontier states.

more and more the centre of speculation, buyers of the public lands came to finance their purchases increasingly out of bank loans. From the middle of 1835 onwards, the Treasury Department tried to tighten up the conditions on which bank notes might be used in payment at the land offices, but with little success. Now that the proceeds had no longer to be remitted through the B.U.S. branches to Philadelphia, a curious state of affairs was liable to arise. 'Borrowers found ready accommodation at local banks and with the loans thus secured made their purchases from the land receiver; the purchase money was in many cases thereupon redeposited by the government in the bank whence it came, where it once more served as a loan to another or even to the same land speculator.'[1] Judging by the relatively slight decline in receipts up to the end of 1836, the Specie Circular[2] itself did not altogether prevent this practice.

The result of all these developments was an unprecedented expansion of bank credit throughout the country, which fed on itself as any remnants of unwillingness on the part of the public to accept bank notes as money became overcome. The finance of real-estate speculation was what the banks were mainly concerned with, but they had a hand in all the forms of investment that were going forward.

4. TERRITORIAL EXPANSION AND INTERNAL IMPROVEMENTS

In all parts of the country, land development was the cornerstone of the boom. In some cases the land was purchased from the land offices by prospective cultivators, but in the final stages speculative purchases undertaken with a view to resale became predominant.[3] In the long run, when the boom and the ensuing slump had receded into past history, this land speculation could be seen in its perspective as merely the means by which the great shift of the American people westwards was carried forward. But at the time rational calculations of prospective cost and return from agricultural production were little to the fore.

Sales of the public lands first began to rise to spectacular heights in the last quarter of 1834; the peak was reached in the second quarter of 1836, but the level remained very high until the end of that year. This movement was accompanied by a rise in commodity prices and stock prices and by the other usual boom-time phenomena. But the boom definitely focused on land. The rise in the volume of domestic trade was by no means spectacular[4] and investment in manufacturing industry was not prominent.

Everywhere, urban real-estate speculation was rife.[5] In the South and Southwest, land development was associated with the other forms of investment involved in the expansion of cotton-growing capacity, for the rise in the price of cotton was here an important element in the situation. Cotton growing by slave labour was inevitably a highly capitalised business, and the increase in cultivation that took place was mostly financed by new banks—banks often sponsored by or connected more or less directly with the state authorities. These banks provided capital to planters at all stages of the productive process; they financed the

---

[1] Dewey, p. 225.   [2] See p. 55.
[3] This is demonstrated at length with reference to the prairie states by P. W. Gates, 'Land policy and tenancy in the prairie states', *Journal of Economic History* (May 1941), pp. 60–82. This article also discusses the influence of speculation on the subsequent pattern of land tenure.
[4] Smith and Cole, p. 73.   [5] Sumner, p. 119.

purchase of land and of slaves, and regularly gave advances on the year's crop as it was growing, or even before.

In the North and West, canal and railroad projects—'internal improvements' —proceeded apace. Backing by the states gave real or imagined security to foreign investors who were not in a position to inform themselves on the merits of each individual project, and rendered possible the execution of schemes for which private cost exceeded social cost.[1] The unexpected success of the Erie Canal, financed by the issue of New York State bonds in 1817–25 prepared the way for a host of other ventures of a similar nature, though not all so prudently conducted or so successful.[2] The repayment of the Federal debt not merely closed a conservative investment opportunity for Americans, but also provided for the European investor an unparalleled example of national financial soundness.

5. IMPORTS FROM BRITAIN DURING THE BOOM

As we have already seen in connection with the earlier years of the 1830's, the level of British exports was extremely sensitive to the level of activity in America; and this held also of American imports from other sources. The United States' total import surplus of goods in the year ending 1 September 1836 was $52 million. The greater part of these enormous imports were of consumption goods, including a large proportion of luxuries (e.g. silk goods to the value of $20 million), though iron for railway building already played some part. There were several special circumstances helping to explain the high income-elasticity of imports.[3] In the first place communications within the United States were still so slow that as the imported goods were transported into the interior the accumulation of stocks took place all over the country and was not at once perceived. Second and more important was the method of finance.[4] Most British exports to distant markets were undertaken at the risk of the British merchant or merchant-manufacturer, guided by his agents in the foreign country. This system had at one time prevailed also in the American market. The American agents of the English export houses had retained the bills of lading until they had received bills on Europe in payment from the American importer. After about 1827, the growth of commercial capital and enterprise in the United States led to the development of another system. American importers established agencies in England (also on the Continent and in the Far East) entrusted with the task of ordering goods for the American market either direct from a manufacturer or sometimes from another intermediary; payment was made in a four-month bill drawn on one of the seven Anglo-American houses engaged in this line of business. These bills could readily be discounted in London and the acceptance houses put into funds before the bills reached maturity. The Anglo-American

[1] Cf. G. S. Callender, 'Early transportation and banking enterprises of the states in relation to the growth of corporations', *Quarterly Journal of Economics* (1903), pp. 111–62.
[2] L. H. Jenks, *Migration of British Capital to 1875* (1926), p. 74.
[3] Smith and Cole's index of the volume of domestic trade rises sixteen points between 1834 and 1836; their index of the volume of foreign trade rises thirty-five points over the same period (*op. cit.* p. 73).
[4] The best contemporary description is in an article by J. R. McCulloch in the *Edinburgh Review* (July 1837), pp. 221–38. Cf. also N. S. Buck, *The Organisation of Anglo-American Trade, 1800–1850* (1925); Jenks, Chapter III; A. H. Cole, 'Evolution of the foreign exchange market of the United States', *Journal of Economic and Business History* (1928–9), pp. 384–421.

houses were not the risk-bearers unless remittances failed to be forthcoming in due time from across the Atlantic. Thus the enterprise was that of the American importer, and the capital that of the London money markets, made available to the Americans by the acceptances of the Anglo-American houses here. At first the American agents of these firms retained the bills of lading till payment had been received, but competition and over-confidence soon put an end to this check. The facilities this system had given to semi-speculative orders for imported goods became obvious as soon as the boom threatened to come to an end.

6. DOMESTIC AND INTERNATIONAL ANTECEDENTS OF THE AMERICAN BOOM

The rise of exports to the United States in 1835–6 played a significant part in determining the extent and character of the boom in Britain at the same time. As we are interested in the mechanism underlying fluctuations in Britain, it is important to decide whether the American boom should be regarded as being fundamentally independent in origin of events in Britain, so that its impact on Britain can be treated as that of an external and in a sense arbitrary shock; or whether, on the other hand, the American boom was itself largely the result of developments over here. In the latter case, it would follow that the main source of instability lay in Britain, and the picture of an inherently stable British economy being upset by disturbances from the other side of the Atlantic would already be shown to be false. Now it is obvious that there was *some* interaction both ways; prosperity in either country was bound to increase prosperity in the other. The question is in which direction the transmission of self-generated fluctuations in activity worked more strongly.

There were two main channels through which the state of trade in Britain affected the American economy; through the price of cotton, overwhelmingly the most important American export to Britain, and through the willingness of British capitalists to buy American securities.

With regard to cotton there are really two distinct questions to be asked. What part did cotton play in bringing about the boom in the United States? And in what sense, if any, could fluctuations in the cotton market be attributed to causes emanating from the eastern side of the Atlantic?

The central position occupied by cotton in the boom of the mid-1830's in the South was inevitable in view of its dominance in the Southern agricultural economy. Should we go further and say that cotton was the progenitor of the entire boom throughout the country or even its mainstay during the whole of its course?

Some light on this question may be sought from the two series which are available on a regional basis, commodity prices and public land sales. During the 1820's the tendency in the price of cotton was for the most part in a downwards direction. In 1831 this decline was arrested, and in 1833 prices advanced sharply. Prices in general were at this time already rising mildly, but the extent of the rise in cotton in 1833 was not paralleled in other commodities. After a setback at the end of 1833, the rise was renewed early in 1834 and reached its highest point in the late summer of 1835. In 1836 quotations remained high but did not in most cases attain to their previous peak. The recovery in cotton prices in early 1834 appears to have preceded slightly the turning-point in prices as a whole in that year, and the same is true of the general price level in New Orleans (and Charleston) relatively to the general price level in the North-east and in the West.[1] The lag was not great, but cotton was felt to be in the lead. In the interior the rate of increase in prices, especially of exportable commodities, was at first regulated by the rate of increase at the seaboard. But as the boom advanced pure speculation fed on bank credit became everywhere paramount, and the primacy of cotton disappeared.[2] Prices in the West in some cases ranged higher than prices in New Orleans, and agricultural commodities continued to advance throughout 1836, although cotton had already passed its peak.

The course of public land sales also suggests that in the early stages of the boom cotton was in the lead, but that it was not long before speculation acquired a momentum of its own. In 1833 public land sales in most states did not increase very much more rapidly than they had been doing since 1829. The exceptions were two cotton-growing states, Arkansas and Mississippi.[3] But in 1835 and 1836 the boom in land sales in the Southern states was not perceptibly more violent than elsewhere.

The answer to our first question—the part played by cotton in the boom as a whole—may therefore perhaps be summarised as follows: Following as it did on the moderate rates of territorial and other economic advance of the 1820's, the removal of restrictions on banking expansion and, indeed, the encouragement of banking expansion by Federal policy in the early 1830's produced a highly inflammable situation. Already as early as 1830 a steady rise in most series had begun, and it needed only a small further impulse to turn prosperity into boom. The rise in cotton prices was the spark which set the fire alight. The monetary stringency of 1834 created an interlude before the boom commenced with full force. Then in 1835 and 1836 all circumstances were at last favourable, and with cotton at first in the lead the speculative mania began in earnest. In the South, cotton naturally remained well in the forefront throughout, but in other districts land development and commodity speculation soon acquired a momentum of their own which carried all before it.

There remains to be answered the second question, relating to the causes of events in the cotton market and the part played by British demand in that sphere. The basic question is, why did the price of cotton turn up in 1833–6, making those years an interlude in the long downward course of prices?

There are three hypotheses to which more or less importance may be attached:

(1) The world demand for cotton may have been rising more rapidly in the 1830's than in the 1820's. This is what one would require to maintain if one wished to attribute the rise in cotton prices to developments on the British side. Britain took well over half of the total American cotton crop.[4]

[1] A. H. Cole, *Wholesale Commodity Prices in the United States, 1700–1861* (1938), charts 50 and 51 (opposite p. 106). For monthly prices of cotton in New Orleans, Charleston, Philadelphia, New York and Cincinnati, see *op. cit., Statistical Supplement.*

[2] Cf. *Cincinnati Daily Gazette*, 29 March 1836 (quoted Berry, *Western Prices*, p. 435): 'the causes which traders themselves have imagined and have persuaded themselves and others to believe in as foundation upon which to build increased prices are in verity but imagination.'

[3] It is interesting to note that almost the entire increase in cotton production between 1833 and 1842 came from the five newly developing states, Alabama, Mississippi, Louisiana, Arkansas and Florida (M. B. Hammond, *The Cotton Industry* (1897), p. 72).

[4] L. C. Gray, *History of Agriculture in the Southern United States to 1860* (1933), p. 692. The proportion of the crop sold in England was declining slightly during the period. Cf. also M. B. Hammond, pp. 246–7.

(2) There had been a tremendous land boom in the South and South-west in 1818, especially in Alabama. If the decline in prices during the 1820's is held to be the result of the gradual extension and intensification of the cotton culture in the territories then opened up, it could be argued that by about 1833 these possibilities were coming to be exhausted, and that a further increase in cultivation could only be obtained through striking out into more distant territories.

(3) Finally, it could be maintained that there was no special pressure of demand on supply in the 1830's in real terms—that the steady and unspectacular increase in acreage that had been going forward in the 1820's and early 1830's was adequate to cope with the rise in demand even after the potentialities opened up in 1818 had been fully exploited, and that the rise in prices after 1833 was the result of general inflationary tendencies within the United States, which in turn owed their origin to such causes as an excess of bank money.[1]

It is not easy to choose between these interpretations. It is interesting to note that, despite the disparity of price movements between the two periods, the rate of growth of cotton production was not notably different in 1831–6 from what it had been in the 1820's.[2] This would seem to imply that shifts on both the demand and the supply side played some part in bringing about the observed result.

As far as demand is concerned, there is little doubt that the rise in prices in 1833 owed something to speculation on the British side.[3] And demand in Britain was certainly sufficiently strong to bear the high prices of 1835–6. But it seems difficult to maintain that there was a general increase in the rate of growth of British demand for cotton in the 1830's as compared with the 1820's. There is no evidence of any such increase, nor is there any particular reason why one should have been expected. On the other hand, the evidence is clear that there was in the 1830's a major banking inflation in the United States, and also that by the early 1830's a long time had elapsed since any great land development boom. With two economies so closely and so multifariously linked to each other as Britain and America at this epoch, it is plainly futile to attempt a rigid division of the two into active and passive respectively in relation to any particular event or events. But when this has been said, it does still appear that the variations in cotton prices from 1818 to 1834 are to be explained for the most part in terms of events in the United States rather than in Britain.

The choice between hypotheses (2) and (3) above—or rather the decision as to the relative significance of the contribution made by each of the causes suggested —is a difficult one to make, but withal a matter of considerable importance for the right understanding of the nature of business fluctuations in the United States in this era. Was the land boom of 1836 in the South and South-west the result of a regular rhythm of territorial development, one period of expansion coming as soon as the previous one had been fully absorbed, or was it rather the result of largely political events in the monetary sphere?[4] Obviously no amount

---

[1] Other factors influencing production were the withdrawal of Indian claims to certain parts of the South-west and the liberalisation of Federal land-sale policy. For a detailed description of the cotton economy of the South in this period and of its geographical growth and shifting, see Gray, pp. 691–720 and 888–907.

[2] For statistics of production see Gray, p. 1026.

[3] See p. 16.

[4] The same problem could be posed with regard to the land boom in the West outside the cotton belt. But here it would be a good deal more difficult to make out a case for the paramountcy of real factors, since with an agriculture based largely on subsistence (and for external

of wild-cat banking would have inaugurated a land boom within a couple of years of 1818, and similarly a policy of rigid monetary deflation would evidently have checked the mania of 1836. And it is also clear that whatever set the boom in motion, its amplitude was greatly enhanced by the working of speculation. But there does remain a real problem in assigning weights to the real and to the monetary factors. This is not, however, a problem which the chronicler of British business cycles is called upon to resolve. Whether the cause of the fluctuations in question lay in some profound mechanism in land development or whether it arose more simply out of the political antipathies of Jackson and Biddle, on either interpretation the source of the disturbance lay in the United States, and Britain was a passive recipient of its consequences.

So much for the link between the economies of Britain and the United States created by cotton, and its part in the American boom. The importance of British finance, the other main link, is difficult to assess. Despite the great inflation of bank credit—including in some cases the use by railway and canal companies of their own notes with which to pay expenses[1]—the disposal of bonds to foreigners was extensively relied on in the United States during the boom. In 1835–6 the Bank of the United States was adding fuel to the flames by increasing its holding of bonds and reducing the proportion of more liquid items in its portfolio,[2] and the part played by foreign investors was rather similar. Foreign capital—mainly British capital, with a certain amount from France and the Low Countries—was especially prominent in the finance of internal improvements, and many banks whose operations depended primarily on the issue of their own notes required a certain amount of capital to set them going in the first instance. British capitalists were ready enough to assist. The rates of interest offered were high, and the security of backing by sovereign states seemed adequate. At the same time Britain had an obvious interest in securing an adequate supply of capital for the production of raw cotton, and British capitalists were not unaware of this.[3] Estimates of the total amount of British capital invested in the United States in the 1830's vary, but it was certainly very substantial.[4] The supply of this form of finance was of great assistance in the carrying out of many of the investment projects that were undertaken. Had the state of trade in Britain been such as to encourage a more cautious attitude on the part of investors, certain of these undertakings would probably have been impossible.

Yet the extent to which the Americans could rely on their own bank finance was very considerable. This applied to internal improvements as well as to land speculation pure and simple.[5] Cases are quoted where attempts were made unsuccessfully to finance a project by the sale of bonds, and the sponsors then

sales depending more on the domestic market than on exports) there could not be the same question as there was with cotton of the rate of territorial growth adapting itself to the relation between current supply potential and an (independently determined) level of demand for agricultural produce. As far as the West is concerned, at least, it is probably a mistake to regard the rise in commodity prices as the cause of the land boom. Both should rather be considered as parallel results of a common cause.

[1] James, *Chicago Banks*, p. 99.
[2] Madeleine, *Monetary and Banking Theories*, p. 81.
[3] A. Redford, *Manchester Merchants and Foreign Trade, 1794–1858* (1934), p. 221.
[4] Jenks, *Migration of British Capital*, p. 75; Chapter III of this book contains the best general account of British investments in the United States during the period.
[5] Cf. Bray Hammond, 'Long and short term credit in early American banking', *Quarterly Journal of Economics* (1934–5), p. 86.

found that, after all, what they needed could be obtained from banks.[1] The importance of foreign loans probably lay therefore not so much in the provision of finance as in enabling the United States to run a heavy import surplus without suffering a deterioration in the foreign exchanges.

This then is the sense in which British finance was a necessary condition of the American boom, or at least of British participation in it by way of increased exports. Had the United States developed an adverse balance of payments, the effect on the basis of the banking system might quite possibly have brought the boom to an end. But this is not the same as saying that British finance was the cause of the boom. And it is certainly implausible to maintain that a sudden *increase* in willingness on the part of British capitalists to buy American bonds was responsible for the upsurge in activity in the United States in 1835. The bonds were bought up as they came forward; but the initial propelling force lay in internal developments in the United States itself.

Our conclusion is, then, that although the American boom was encouraged and influenced in its character by events in Britain, in the most important respects, and especially in its timing, it was an independent development.

7. THE TURNING-POINT AND THE PANIC OF 1837

The nature of the turning-point in the United States was greatly affected, as the boom had been, by the intervention of the Federal government in monetary affairs. In June 1836 the prolonged political struggle[2] over the disposal of the Federal surplus revenue ended in the Deposit Act, a compromise by which the surplus was to be deposited for an indefinite period with the different states, each receiving a share in proportion to its representation in Congress; the name of distribution thus being avoided while the substance was retained. All funds in excess of five million dollars in the possession of the Treasury at the beginning of 1837 were to be distributed in this way in four instalments to be spread over the year with the first payable on 1 January. Then, almost immediately after the passage of this Act, the Treasury department on 11 July issued the order that came to be known as the Specie Circular, instructing land offices to accept only cash in payment for the public lands. The effect of this was to provide all banks in frontier states, whether they were banks of government deposit or not (though the Deposit Act gave to those that were, other and more urgent preoccupations), an incentive to increase their holdings of gold, as otherwise they would have to cease the profitable business of lending to land purchasers. To do so, they drew on the balances they kept in New York[3] or Philadelphia, or in the case of cotton-growing states, in the southern Atlantic cities; these balances came to be more considerable as the year's cotton harvest began to reach the outports and be sold from October onwards.[4]

---

[1] James, pp. 107–12.

[2] For the political background, see E. G. Bourne, *The Surplus Revenue of 1837* (1885). The details of the Deposit Act are set forth in Dewey, *Financial History of the United States*, pp. 228–9.

[3] For the extent of bankers' balance held in New York, cf. Margaret Myers, *The New York Money Market* (1931), I, pp. 103–25, 169.

[4] A. Trotter, *Finances of North American States* (1839), p. 34. Trotter's is a clear and useful account written from the English point of view.

The consequences of the Deposit Act were twofold. It aggravated the effects of the Specie Circular by causing a shortage of credit both in the East and in the West and South; and it drove exchange on the Atlantic cities in the interior to a tremendous premium. As soon as the contents of the Act became known, the 'pet' banks where the government balances were deposited had to take steps to ensure that by 1 January they should be in possession of sufficient cash to hand over, or else sufficient exchange on the district to which payment had to be made. The situation was therefore most embarrassing for the least liquid of the deposit banks, and these were the banks which had been lending most extensively for land purchase. The supposed receipts from land sales deposited with them gave them heavy liabilities to the Treasury; but what they had actually received in payment had been bank-notes, mostly their own notes, and these had been issued by way of loans secured usually by a hopelessly illiquid mortgage on the land to be bought. These banks therefore drastically cut down their lending for fear that the money lent might not be recoverable by the New Year, and at the same time attempted to increase their holdings of cash by drawing in their balances in New York; and their New York correspondents were accordingly subjected to another strain in addition to that already mentioned. The Federal revenue having been derived largely from land sales, and the proposed distribution of the surplus between the states being on the basis of population, the transaction was due to result in a net transfer of funds from the interior to the populous East;[1] so exchange on New York was at a premium by virtue both of the city's function as national financial centre and its position as net recipient of the transfer. As far as the latter was concerned, there should have been no need for actual movement of gold from East to West and back again, for it would have been sufficient for Western banks to hold on to their liquid balances in New York till the transfer had to be made.[2] On the other hand, gold would be required for the shares of the surplus that were to remain in the West; and furthermore, the banks must have been aware that cash would be required in January before they were informed exactly of the destination to which it was to be sent,[3] and they probably thought the safest policy was to accumulate what gold they could while there was yet time. While the specie was being transported from the East, it was out of active circulation; it continued idle while it was held by the deposit banks, who did not dare to lend it out; then while it was being transported from the deposit banks to the centres of distribution it was again not available for the benefit of the mercantile community. In the meanwhile, the transfer of funds from one bank to another and the consequent disruption of credit was increased by another provision of the Deposit Act, which required that the amount of government deposits held by any one bank should not exceed three-quarters of that bank's own capital; on account of the continual fluctuations in tax receipts this meant frequent transfers from one deposit bank to another. Even when the first instalment had been paid, the pressure was not relieved. Banks had to prepare for the second one; the funds that had been

---

[1] Myers, p. 172; Esther R. Taus, *Central Banking Functions of the United States Treasury, 1789–1941* (1943), p. 37.

[2] If this was done to any extent, it would help to explain the apparent inconsistency between the great premium in the West on exchange on New York and the not enormous accumulation of gold shown in the accounts of banks in the West (Trotter, p. 40).

[3] E.g. the New York deposit banks were not apprised of this till November (Myers, p. 171).

transferred to the states and deposited with their banks were not readily loanable for fear that they might at any time be required, and the distribution between the states bore no relation to their mercantile needs at that time of year.

The combined result of the Specie Circular and the Deposit Act was to precipitate the crisis by causing what was in effect an internal drain at a time when an external drain was imminent (see below) and domestic trade was already showing signs of sagging in some sectors. The mild decline in cotton prices in 1836 from the level they had attained at the end of 1835 was a warning—not heeded—that any further expansion of cotton cultivation was liable to be dangerous. Railway share prices, too, had passed their peak well before the end of 1835, and the mileage of railroads constructed fell heavily in 1836 compared to the previous year.

However, until near the end of 1836 the rising cost of credit was the only seriously alarming symptom. In 1835 credit had been abundant. Despite the booming condition of trade, discount rates were 'comparatively low'.[1] The cost of loans was rising throughout 1836, but the really high rates were not recorded till the demand for cash had ceased to be the reflection of active trade and had become due instead to a liquidity crisis. Discount rates began to rise more rapidly after June, and by the end of the year were around 30%. Land sales fell a good deal in the latter half of the year under the impact of the Specie Circular, but even in the last quarter they were still running at a higher level than had prevailed till the closing months of 1835. Commodity prices fell immediately upon the issue of the Specie Circular in July, but they then recovered again and had reached still higher levels by the end of the year.[2] There is certain reason to believe, too, that the volume of domestic trade continued to rise up till a late date and perhaps did not begin to fall until a little way into 1837.[3]

However, if domestic trade showed no spectacular decline before the end of the year, imports were much more seriously affected, for two reasons. The shortage of credit had for a while the same effect as it had had in 1834, namely, to make capitalists reluctant to lock up their cash in the purchase of bills on Europe.[4] Exchange on London fell to a discount and orders for imports fell off. Probably more important than this was the effect of unbalance within the United States between East and West. Because of the non-commercial demand for exchange on the East, dealers in the interior found it tremendously expensive to remit the sums which they owed to the coastal merchants and which they usually paid at this time of year on account of consignments of imported goods.[5] The import merchants therefore found difficulty in making their remittances to Europe, and hesitated to increase the volume of their outstanding debt by sending over fresh orders for imports. The result was growing depression in British export industries.

In the meanwhile financial developments in Britain were beginning to increase the difficulties of the Americans. In July the drain of gold led the Bank of

[1] Smith and Cole, *Fluctuations in American Business*, p. 83. By American standards this probably meant not less than 5%.
[2] The timing of the turning-point in prices varied substantially as between different centres. Cf. Cole, *Wholesale Commodity Prices in the United States, 1700–1861* (1938), p. 99.
[3] Smith and Cole, pp. 73, 84.
[4] *Circular to Bankers*, 21 April 1837; Hidy, pp. 218–19.
[5] *Edinburgh Review* (July 1837), pp. 221–38.

England to raise its discount rate to 4½%. It was said that at about the same time the extra discounting which the Bank had been undertaking with the East India Company's balances brought into its possession a large number of the acceptances of the Anglo-American finance houses, and called to the attention of the Bank's Court of Directors the amount of this paper in circulation.[1] In any event, it was in July that the Bank began to take a close interest in the affairs of these houses. On 20 August, Wiggin's, one of those that subsequently failed, were already feeling so unsure of their ground that they sent a request to their American agents to cut down the number of bills sent to them.[2] On 2 September the Bank Rate was raised to 5%, accompanied by an intimation that the Bank would refuse to discount any bills bearing the endorsement of a joint-stock bank of issue; and a few days later unintended publicity was given to a letter from Threadneedle Street to the Bank's Liverpool branch instructing it to cease to handle the acceptances of the Anglo-American houses.[3] At the same time it was reported that these houses had been refusing to accept some of the bills drawn on them and were returning them to America.[4] The result of these events, combined with the other circumstances tending to raise the London discount rate,[5] was to check greatly the flow of loanable funds from this country to America; it became more and more difficult for American firms to carry on by the repeated renewal of accommodation bills to be sold in London.

This form of finance had come to be increasingly relied on by American firms in the latter half of 1836, as the stringency in New York grew more acute; and the firms at the British end had been forced to continue their acceptances as long as possible for fear of precipitating a breakdown that would carry them with it. Consequently, in the early months of 1837 New York banks and merchants, still oppressed by the drain of specie to the West, found that the balance of payments with Europe was becoming more and more unfavourable as the bills they had drawn approached maturity and could not be renewed. The situation was aggravated by the condition of the cotton market. A drought had delayed the movement of cotton down to the ports,[6] so European exchange was slower than usual in coming in. This delay sustained cotton prices for a while,[7] but the collapse in credit in the Southern states combined with the ample stocks held in Europe soon led to a great fall. With the staple export yielding abnormally low returns and the supply of European credits drying up, the exchange on London, from being at a discount at the beginning of 1837, reached par in February; by the end of April it had 'no price but what is merely nominal'.[8] The first failure was of a bank in New Orleans, followed by its New York correspondent; caught between the internal and external drain, with a panic demand for gold now added, the New York banks suspended specie payments on 10 May, and were followed by banks throughout the country.

The first effect was to increase the panic. But with the removal of the obligation to pay specie, banks were able to give advances more freely to planters and traders, with the result that, after a further rise during the period of panic, discount rates fell right down to about 6% before the end of July, and stayed low

---

[1] *Edinburgh Review*, p. 232. Cf. pp. 171–2. [2] *Circular to Bankers*, 14 October 1836.
[3] Tooke, II, pp. 303–4. [4] *Circular to Bankers*, 2 September 1836.
[5] See pp. 92–3. [6] Trotter, pp. 103–4.
[7] *Circular to Bankers*, 28 October 1836. [8] *Circular to Bankers*, 26 May 1837.

for the remainder of the year. The B.U.S. began at this time to undertake the first of a series of operations in support of the cotton market, partly to provide itself with foreign exchange and partly to prevent the disruption of the normal credit mechanism in the South from leading to a complete collapse of prices.[1] But if suspension assisted domestic trade, for importers and others wishing to remit to Europe this abolition of the upper gold point had the effect of removing any limit to the costliness of foreign exchange. American importers' remittances to Europe dwindled. Hence arose growing difficulties for the Anglo-American acceptance houses in Liverpool, culminating in June in the suspension of the 'three W's', Wilson's, Wildes' and Wiggin's. Hence also the fall in the value of British exports to the United States from £12·4 million in 1836 to £4·7 million in 1837; in September, goods destined for the American market were being shipped back home again.[2] The situation might have been even worse had it not been for a new device to attract English capitalists into purchasing American securities. The states were no longer in a position to float loans, and the type of paper dealt in by the 'three W's' was discredited; but the credit of the B.U.S. still stood high, and when at the end of April[3] there arrived in London the first batch of B.U.S. postnotes, bearing a high rate of interest and payable in a year at Barings, they were eagerly bought up. Nicholas Biddle, the President of the B.U.S., had chosen to use these relatively long-dated securities, it was said,[4] because he was aware that the Bank of England had less power to restrain borrowing on the Stock Exchange than borrowing in the money market. It was estimated that in the course of the year £3 million were raised in this way.[5] By these means, in conjunction with the suspension of specie payments and the continuing premium on gold at home, it was possible for the United States in 1837 to maintain specie imports at an only slightly reduced level.

Despite the easing of credit conditions after the suspension, the year 1837 in the United States was one of violent recession in the financial sphere. Security prices and commodity prices fell catastrophically. The speculative real-estate boom came to an end, and public land sales fell back to their pre-1835 level. The volume of imports fell to a particular extent on account of the special reasons already mentioned. The volume of domestic trade fell a good deal less severely, but it too was affected. The prostration of banks was widespread, especially in the South.

The speculative nature of the boom determined largely the character of the crash. So long as funds are ample and confidence is not impaired, there exists no inherent force tending to bring to an end real-estate or commodity speculation based on expectation of ever rising prices. The analogy is rather to a stock-exchange boom than to a boom based, for instance, on industrial investment.[6] In the case of expansion of cotton-growing facilities, the satiation of the market

---

[1] Jenks, *Migrations of British Capital*, pp. 89–91. See pp. 61–3.

[2] *Circular to Bankers*, 11 September 1837.

[3] Exchange on Europe in New York having risen to a premium already before the suspension.

[4] *Circular to Bankers*, 28 April 1837.

[5] C. Juglar, *Des Crises Commerciales* (1889), p. 463.

[6] Railway building had, as already mentioned, begun to decline before the financial stringency set in; it was therefore just such an exception to the general pattern as was to be expected from its nature. It had not been 'a subject of unhealthy speculation' (W. G. Sumner, *History of American Currency*, p. 117) during the boom.

made a recession ultimately inevitable, but the end could be delayed so long as prices of cotton and of cotton-growing land were artificially maintained by the creation of new bank money. Similarly, state-financed internal improvements could presumably have gone on unabated if funds had not dried up. It was therefore inevitable that financial happenings should be mainly responsible for causing the unstable structure at last to topple over. It was not an objective fall in profit rates that was the cause of the crash, for calculation of objective profit rates had long ceased to be possible. What brought about the crash was the increasing difficulty of obtaining funds to support a speculative movement which up to that time had been feeding upon itself. This credit stringency was due partly to the change in the policy of the administration, represented by the Specie Circular and the Deposit Act, and partly to an adverse movement of the balance of payments resulting from high imports and diminishing willingness on the part of foreigners to fill the gap by lending. Suspension of cash payments, when it came, eased the credit shortage but destroyed what elements of confidence remained. After a speculative boom of this sort it was natural that prices should decline more than the volume of trade, and that the fall in individual commodity prices should be far from uniform. This was in fact what happened.[1] The fall in the prices of domestically consumed agricultural products was less than the fall in the prices of those staple commodities entering into international trade which had mainly attracted the attention of speculators during the boom. The consequent greater distress in the South compared to the West was to have important consequences in the next few years.

8. Resumption of Cash Payments

While cash payments were suspended the United States developed a favourable balance of payments for a number of reasons. The high cost of foreign exchange and the low level of incomes discouraged the purchase of marginal imports and the repayment of debts to foreigners so long as it could be postponed. Already as early as November 1837[2] the flow of American securities to purchasers in England had resumed—long-term securities, not the merchant bankers' acceptances of which the British public was still suspicious. With specie payments suspended, there was a free market in gold as well as in foreign exchange, so the usual mechanism by which a tendency to a favourable balance leads to gold imports was lacking; it might equally well have led to a reduction of the premium commanded by foreign exchange. But bankers in America were anxious to accumulate gold, and foreigners who expected resumption to be brought about in due course were anxious to profit by the favourable exchanges while they could. Furthermore, most bankers in Europe believed that the resumption of specie payments was a necessary prerequisite for the re-establishment of normal international trading relations, and sought to help to bring this result about. Assistance was provided by the celebrated loan of £1 million remitted in gold from the Bank of England to a New York banking house through the intermediacy of Barings. Barings, with whom the idea of this transaction probably originated, were particularly interested in helping to bring about

---

[1] Cf. Smith and Cole, p. 63.   [2] Hidy, *House of Baring*, p. 237.

60

resumption because they had remittances due to them from the United States which could not be made with foreign exchange in New York at its existing high premium. The sympathies of Wall Street banks in this matter were similar to those of Barings, since their interests were for the most part identified with those of the American importers who had debts owing to Europe and wanted to discharge them without inordinate expense. In the short run the efforts of these banks to accumulate specie tended to make the exchanges more adverse to the United States, but evidently it was believed that in the long run the re-establishment of the American currency system on a sound metallic base was the only way to ensure that exchange on Europe in New York should not chronically stand at a premium.

During the early months of 1838 banks throughout the United States, led by those in New York, were preparing themselves for the resumption of cash payments. The external position, as has been seen, was favourable for this purpose. So too was the domestic position. The demand for cash within the United States had been reduced by the collapse of the land sales boom and the general deflation of prices and incomes. Furthermore, the immobilisation of funds arising out of the working of the Deposit Act was no longer felt, since the third instalment had been made payable in bank notes irrespective of quality, and the fourth instalment was cancelled altogether.

In the months while the banks were rebuilding their reserves in preparation for resumption, discount rates naturally became a good deal tighter, especially in New York, where the banks were contracting their liabilities with particular vigour.[1] Stock and commodity prices declined, and exchange on London under the influence of dear money had actually fallen to a discount by the time cash payments were resumed. But the system soon readjusted itself, and it became apparent that even with specie payments enforceable the supply of credit was likely to be ample. Further assistance was provided by the repeal of the Specie Circular in May 1838 at the same time as the Wall Street banks resumed cash payments. Discount rates fell soon after resumption had been effected and stayed low until the middle of 1839.

9. POLICY OF THE BANK OF THE UNITED STATES IN 1837–1838

During 1837 the Bank of the United States—which since the lapse of its old charter was operating under a new one granted by the State of Pennsylvania—was pursuing a policy of its own. Biddle was not keen to see the resumption of cash payments. This was partly due to the general hostility to deflationary finance which animated his policy in his later years. But it may also be surmised that the Bank's large interest in the produce of the Southern states gave it the outlook of an exporter and caused it to regard with favour the premium commanded by foreign exchange under suspension. This was an important contrast between the attitude of the Philadelphia institution and the attitude of the Wall Street banks.[2]

---

[1] Sumner, p. 148.

[2] It has sometimes been stated (perhaps as a result of mis-reading a passage in Tooke, IV, p. 79) that the Bank of England's million's worth of gold was sent to the B.U.S. This is quite to misunderstand the situation. Resumption of cash payments was the last thing that Biddle wanted, and though in the event the B.U.S. did buy a certain amount of the gold sent, it was with great reluctance that it did so (Hidy, p. 245; Clapham, *Bank of England*, II, pp. 164–5).

Accordingly, the Bank made no efforts to curtail its operations and, indeed, was considerably more illiquid at the end of 1837 than at the beginning, as stocks and personal overdrafts came to replace bills in its portfolio.[1] The most commented-on aspect of its policy during 1837 was its extensive loans to Southern planters and banks to sustain cotton prices. These it defended on the grounds that the panic had destroyed the channels through which cotton was normally handled and that extraordinary assistance was therefore required to prevent a catastrophic fall in price. A similar defence could no doubt have been made—not quite so plausibly—for the other assets it acquired, largely railway stocks and such-like. But this argument that the Bank was merely filling a temporary gap in the financial facilities of the South was not altogether convincing, because, as its opponents pointed out, its cotton operations were often conducted in competition with the firms normally engaged in the trade.[2] Furthermore, in November 1837 the Bank set up an agency in London under Samuel Jaudon to organise the sale of American stocks to British investors, and at the same time a special subsidiary in Liverpool, Humphreys and Biddle, was established to act as consignee of cotton. The Bank was planning its operations on a long-term basis.

Exactly what the Bank's intentions were in these dealings is not perfectly clear. To say, as has often been said, that Biddle aimed to establish a corner in cotton for his own profit seems unjustifiable. No doubt he hoped to conduct the business in such a way as not to lead to a loss; but his firm at no stage controlled more than a moderate proportion, perhaps 30%, of the total supply. The extensive loans granted to planters and bankers in the South were not made conditional on the produce so financed being consigned to the Bank's subsidiaries.[3] The genuineness of the Bank's professed desire to support values in the South is not in doubt, nor are its generally inflationary predilections at this stage of its history; but another motive for the cotton transactions was probably to strengthen the Bank's position in the foreign exchange market. One of the sources of its previous supremacy in this field had been its position as banker to the Federal government. Federal tax payments in the Southern states were usually made in bills on Europe. Since the removal of the Federal deposits in 1833 the Bank had lost this source of foreign exchange, and it seems likely that one of the reasons for its entering the cotton market was to provide itself with an alternative source. Under suspension, and later during the boom of 1838–9, foreign exchange regularly commanded a premium, and so long as inflationary conditions persisted—as Biddle hoped they would—possession of bills on Europe conferred much profit and also much power over other banks.[4]

Banks in New York had been obliged by a state law to resume cash payments on 10 May 1838, exactly a year after the date on which they had suspended. By the time this date arrived, they were in a position to carry out their obligations. They were followed shortly by most other banks within the Union. The B.U.S.

[1] Cotton and tobacco did not officially figure in the list of the Bank's assets, since all its dealings in commodities were done through the intermediacy of its officers and directors, who were given accommodation for the purpose.

[2] Cf. *Circular to Bankers*, 24 August 1838.

[3] *Circular to Bankers*, 30 March 1838; Hidy, p. 543.

[4] In 1838 certain B.U.S. bonds held in Europe fell due to be repaid, and this was also quoted as an explanation of the Bank's desire to obtain bills on London (Buck, *The Organisation of Anglo-American Trade, 1800–1850* (1925), p. 95). It was probably not more than a minor element in the situation.

did not immediately follow. But as a result of its tardiness, prices came to range higher in Philadelphia than in New York; the balance of payments between the two became unfavourable to Philadelphia, and gold began to flow from there to New York.[1] The B.U.S. was forced to the realisation that the resumption of cash payments was of necessity indivisible and followed the example of the Wall Street banks on 10 August.

From then until the middle of 1839 the policy of the Bank does not appear to have undergone much alteration. Its interest in the cotton market continued unabated, and the comments of the British press, which had been not unfriendly in 1837, became decidedly more hostile.[2] A large part of the troubles of the South in 1837 had been traceable to the conjunction of an unusually abundant cotton crop with generally unfavourable business conditions, and it had been felt, even in Britain, that it was not altogether unreasonable in these circumstances to make some attempt to maintain values. But in 1838 the crop was much smaller and demand was recovering, so artificial attempts to enhance the price still further gave rise to a good deal of resentment.

How did the Bank finance its cotton operations? Its business was commonly represented as borrowing in Britain and lending in the United States, using British capital to bolster up the price of Britain's most important import and at the same time netting a handsome profit on the chronic excess of American over European interest rates.[3] This was certainly the case in 1837, when the sale of its post-notes in Europe enabled the Bank to make loans to planters in the South at a rate of 2% per month. But most of the bonds sold in London in 1838 were not obligations of the B.U.S. itself, but bonds of states and railway companies.[4] Jaudon's London agency was active in negotiating these bonds, sales of which provided the Bank with a further supply of *foreign exchange*; but the Bank did not in this way obtain any *capital* to work with, except in so far as (a) there was an interval between the sale of the bonds and the remittance of the proceeds to the issuers, or (more likely) (b) the bonds were part of the Bank's own portfolio, and sale of them represented a switch in the composition of its assets enabling it to hold cotton instead. A certain amount of capital for cotton transactions was obtained in this way and by smaller direct sales of B.U.S. obligations; but for the most part the Bank's operations in the commodity market seem to have been financed simply by a dangerous reduction of its liquidity.[5]

10. Contrast between the Boom of 1836 and the Recovery of 1838–1839

The recovery of activity in the United States in the summer of 1838 followed so immediately on the fall in discount rates that it is impossible not to suspect a direct causal relationship. Commodity prices and public land sales both rose very sharply in the third quarter of the year. The extent of the recovery was

[1] The authority for this statement is Sumner, pp. 144–5. The movement in relative prices alleged by Sumner is, it must be admitted, not very evident in the available statistics.

[2] Cf. *Circular to Bankers*, 11 May 1838.

[3] Cf. Sumner, p. 138.

[4] A shrewd discussion of the Bank's activities in the London market at this time was given in the City article in *The Times* of 17 September 1839. Cf. also Hidy, pp. 260–9.

[5] Under suspension the Bank had made a practice of paying out an old issue of its notes on which payment was not legally enforceable! An act was passed forbidding this early in 1838 (Sumner, p. 144; *Circular to Bankers*, 24 August 1838).

uneven, but by the end of 1838 prosperity had in general returned, and the peak reached in certain series approached or even surpassed the highest points attained in 1835–6. The boom of the 1830's had thus a double-headed appearance in the United States as well as in Britain, Older American writers were accustomed to make 'the panic of 1837' the focal point of their narrative, but recent historians have been disposed to give more attention to the recovery of 1838–9 and have been reluctant to single out any one date as marking *the* turning-point between the unquestionable boom of the middle 1830's and the unquestionable slump of the early 1840's.

The boom or semi-boom of 1838–9 differed in a number of interesting respects from that of 1835–6. Two differences may be singled out as of special significance.

(*a*) For the most part, the rises shown in the various indices were a good deal smaller in 1839 than in 1836. But there was a substantial difference between the pattern in different areas. The panic of 1837 had had particularly dire consequences in the South, and the agricultural West had suffered a good deal less. In 1838 the recovery came earlier in the West than in the South. The general level of prices was already rising steeply by the end of May, but the price of cotton in most centres did not show any important advance until the autumn. Not merely did the recovery in the West come earlier; it was also more powerful when it came. The general index of Cincinnati prices rose at the end of 1838 to a higher level than any it had reached in 1836, a result not paralleled in any of the other centres (New York, Philadelphia, New Orleans and Charleston) for which statistics have been prepared. Wisconsin was the only state to report a higher volume of public land sales in 1839 than in 1836. Several Southern states—Arkansas, Alabama, Mississippi—showed no recovery at all in public land sales in 1838–9, but instead a steady decline.

(*b*) Reference to public land sales raises the second interesting contrast between 1836 and 1839. In general, as has been said, prices did not rise so far in the latter year as in the former; the difference between the two peaks in prices was not, however, very great. The difference between the two years in the extent to which public land sales increased was much greater. There were exceptional cases, like that of Wisconsin quoted, and only in a few states was there no rise at all in 1839; but taking the United States as a whole, the 1839 boom in land sales was a very small affair compared to that of 1836.[1]

The events of 1838–9 are not perhaps too hard to understand in broad terms. The violence of the crash in 1837 had checked development at a moment when in many cases, especially in the West, it had not yet gone beyond a relatively early phase. Newly opened-up lands had as yet scarcely passed from the hands of the speculator into those of the tiller. Projects of internal improvements had had to be temporarily suspended on account of the credit stringency. Hence, when the immediate pressure passed off, as it did in 1838, it was inevitable that there should be quite a pronounced recovery. Land had been opened up, but there had not been such an increase in the amount actually under cultivation as to prevent a revival in the prices of agricultural produce. And where production *had* increased, a large part of the increase would be likely to be drawn off for

---

[1] Smith and Cole, *Fluctuations in American Business*, pp. 55–8, 63–4; Cole, *Wholesale Commodity Prices in the United States*, charts 50 and 51; *ibid. Statistical Supplement*, p. 271; Berry, *Western Prices*, pp. 450–6.

subsistence purposes. It was natural therefore that the revival should be marked by greater increases in commodity prices—with speculation again playing a part—than in sales of the public lands. The emphasis was on consolidating the advances roughly sketched out in the preceding boom.[1]

In the South and South-west conditions were less fortunate. The price of an exported cash crop like cotton was more closely tied to an externally determined level of demand than were the prices of corn and pork and whisky. It is probable, too, that by 1838–9 the land boom of the earlier years—which had started sooner in the South than in the West[2]—had led to a more considerable expansion of actual production of cotton than of foodstuffs. In 1838 this had been concealed by a short cotton crop, the result of drought,[3] but in 1839 it became manifest. Had it not been for Biddle's valorisation project, the cotton-growing area would probably have participated in the boom of 1839 to an even less extent than it did. In the event the recovery did bring with it some rise in cotton prices and also a certain amount of further territorial expansion, especially in Louisiana and Missouri. It must be remembered that at all times, so long as finance was available, there was some incentive to push into new lands, whatever the price of cotton and the other staples, since the best of the new land was bound to be superior in fertility to the worst of the old, especially where the latter had been exhausted by short-sighted husbandry.[4]

11. THE LAST DAYS OF THE BANK OF THE UNITED STATES

From the middle of 1839 the position underwent a sharp change. Already early in the year there were signs that the brief inflationary boom in the Western states was coming to an end. Prices and land sales began to fall. By the end of 1838 the high general level of incomes, unaccompanied as yet by any tightness in the credit market, was tending to make the foreign exchanges move adversely to the United States.[5] This adverse movement continued in 1839. Furthermore, at quite an early stage, during the summer of 1838, the British public had begun to be distrustful of the large volume of American stocks on the market. Bonds continued to be sent over in considerable quantities after that date, but merchant bankers found difficulty in disposing of them at a satisfactory price.[6] Furthermore, from March 1839 the price of cotton began to waver as the Bank's efforts to support the market were met with a concerted operation of short time on the part of Lancashire spinners.[7]

In face of this situation the B.U.S. embarked on the last and most extraordinary phase of its chequered career.[8] The Bank started an intensive campaign

[1] This is borne out by the increase in railway mileage constructed in 1838–41. The interpretation of Sumner's remark quoted earlier (p. 59 n. 6) is presumably that railway promoters did not attempt to push lines outwards until there was evidence that the region to be served was already properly settled and had attained some degree of stability.
[2] See p. 52.　　　　[3] Gray, *History of Agriculture*, p. 699.
[4] *Ibid.* p. 899.
[5] In October 1838 a certain amount of specie was shipped from the United States to England (*Circular to Bankers*, 19 October 1838).
[6] Hidy, pp. 261–2.　　　　[7] See pp. 138–9.
[8] Biddle resigned in March 1839 and the detailed conduct of the Bank's business passed into other hands. How much of the general policy continued to be inspired by him is impossible to say. The history of the Bank's actions in 1838–9 is fully analysed by Bray Hammond, 'The Chestnut Street Raid on Wall Street, 1839', *Quarterly Journal of Economics* (August 1947), pp. 605–18.

of borrowing in the New York money market on post-notes bearing from 18 to 24% per annum. At the same time, exchange on Europe being at a premium, it sold large quantities of drafts payable by its agent Jaudon in London. Both the post-notes and the drafts were naturally in great demand, and their sale provided the Bank with very large amounts of cash and claims on banks in New York. How was Jaudon expected to honour the drafts on the London agency? This was arranged partly by shipment to London of specie purchased in New York with the money realised by the sale of the drafts and post-notes—the Bank incurring a loss on each transaction to the general puzzlement of onlookers.[1] But specie shipments, in addition to being costly, were slow, and in the meanwhile Jaudon was often compelled to reduce his credit by borrowing in London at unpropitious moments.[2] Similarly, Humphreys and Biddle were forced frequently to make sales of cotton in order to put Jaudon in funds, when they would have preferred to hold on.[3] So if the object of the transactions was to supply the Bank with funds to support the cotton market, it was largely a failure; prices in general may have been sustained by the funds the Bank had at its command in the United States, but the position of their own cotton agency in Liverpool was much embarrassed in the process.

Probably finance for cotton speculation was one of the Bank's objects, and its lack of success can be put down in part to the stringency of the London money market and in part to the resort of spinners to short time working. But the Bank's behaviour had another purpose, revealed explicitly by one of its officers, J. Cowperthwaite, in the inquiry following its subsequent suspension. He said: 'Another crisis was anticipated, and it was feared that the banks generally would be obliged again to suspend. This was unhappily too soon to be realised, for the storm was then ready to burst; but instead of meeting its full force at once, it was deemed best to make it fall first upon the banks of New York.'[4] In other words, those responsible for the Bank's policy thought that the fall in prices, which had set in early in the year, together with the adverse state of the exchanges, would shortly lead to another suspension, and to anticipate that event they acquired enormous claims on New York banks by the sale of drafts on Europe and post-notes, with a view to forcing these banks to suspend immediately by presenting to them their notes for payment at awkward moments. The Bank's apologists have maintained that the motive here was simply in accord with the well-known views held by Biddle in his later years in opposition to the deflation necessitated by a metallic currency base. On the other side, naturally, there were not lacking critics who argued that the Bank was trying to conceal the leaf of its own unsoundness in the forest of a general suspension. It is not our business here to arbitrate between these two interpretations. In any event, the attempt failed. In

[1] Bray Hammond, p. 608.
[2] It was decidedly unfortunate for Biddle that corn imports into England in 1839 should have led to tightness in Lombard Street and so made it more difficult for Jaudon to raise money on bonds or Bank of the United States post-notes; but American securities had already been difficult to dispose of before money started to become dear. Cf. *Circular to Bankers*, 13 September 1839.
[3] This and other aspects of the Bank's closing years are discussed at length in *Report of the Committee appointed at the meeting of stockholders of the Bank of the United States held January 4th, 1841*.
[4] Letter of 23 March 1841 from J. Cowperthwaite to N. Biddle, *United States Commercial and Statistical Register*, edited by S. Hazard, vol. IV (1841), p. 259.

October confidence in the Bank was impaired to such an extent that it was unable to sell in the New York money market a sufficient amount of new post-notes to repay those that were coming to maturity, and on the 9th of the month the Bank was obliged itself to suspend payments. Its agents in Europe had not been able to remit back any money to Philadelphia, for they were barely able by the sale of cotton and American securities to raise enough cash to meet the drafts drawn on them by the head office.[1] Indeed, they themselves were scarcely less embarrassed than the head office.[2] Once the desperate attempt to break the New York banks had failed, and public confidence in the Bank of the United States had weakened, its position was hopeless, for the inquiry after its suspension revealed that most of its assets were completely illiquid.[3] Cotton was by no means the only source of the trouble; the Bank's portfolio was found to be made up largely of dubious stocks of railway companies and the like which the Bank had acquired over the previous few years—in a number of cases by way of repayment of debts incurred by its own officers—and which it had perhaps hoped to dispose of in due course to investors in Europe.

The effects of the Bank's policies from the middle of 1839 on are clearly perceptible in the statistics. Interest rates rose steeply as the post-notes drained away other banks' reserves. Most interesting, however, is the large import surplus of goods, accompanied by an export surplus of specie, that is recorded for 1839. The Bank's willingness to supply foreign exchange at a loss was undoubtedly largely responsible for this. The Bank's policy enabled the flow of British goods into the United States to continue longer than would have been possible had foreign exchange not been made available to American importers at artificially low prices. In this respect B.U.S. policy was actually of assistance to the maintenance of activity in Britain in 1839, and this must be set against the discouragement to activity here which was caused by the cotton valorisation scheme.

With the suspension of the Bank in August 1839, the recession in the United States which had been threatening since early in the year could no longer be deferred. Interest rates rose for a short while to crisis heights, then slumped. Commodity prices crashed immediately. At first foreign exchange rose to a premium as the abnormal supplies made available by the B.U.S. dried up; but presently the fall in incomes proved effective in reducing the demand and a large discount appeared. The volume of trade in 1840 was even lower than in 1837. For some reason that is not altogether clear there was a decided recovery in 1841; it was regarded as 'comparatively a year of prosperity'.[4] Banks were still very shaken, but it was reported that in some cases new men were taking over functions that banks would normally have performed.[5] But the recovery proved

---

[1] *Circular to Bankers*, 27 September 1839.

[2] Their embarrassment was not, however (as has sometimes been supposed), the immediate cause of the Bank's suspension. The news that one of the Bank's agents, Hottinguers, had refused to honour some of its drafts did not reach the other side of the Atlantic until after 9 October, the date on which the Bank suspended payments. This is shown by Bray Hammond, p. 615.

[3] There were also allegations of malpractices by Bank officers, but, from the tangle of personalities in the controversy that ensued, it is not possible at this date to draw any conclusion.

[4] Sumner, p. 153. It is interesting to note that, as in 1838–9, the recovery in 1841 was more pronounced in the prices of the agricultural produce of the West than in the prices of Southern staples. Smith and Cole, p. 64.   [5] *Circular to Bankers*, 17 September 1840.

to have no substantial foundations, and in 1842 the country plunged again into depression, with prices falling to unprecedentedly low levels. An increase in tariff rates made matters worse for the British exporter, but had no immediate effect in restoring prosperity. 'The year 1843 was one of the gloomiest in industrial history.'[1]

Many factors contributed to the gravity of the slump. Most important undoubtedly was the violence and speculative nature of the boom that had preceded it. Public land sales had reached in 1836 a level which was never again to be equalled. The renewed suspension of the B.U.S. in 1839, following as it did on the widespread bank failures of 1837, caused a profound public mistrust of banks and bank credit generally. The failure on the part of nine of the states to pay the interest due on their debts destroyed American credit in Europe and made it out of the question for any more loans to be obtained in that way.[2] And the state of the cotton market in Britain after 1840 could scarcely have been less hopeful.

The course of British exports to the United States in the years 1838–42 conformed closely with what was to be expected from the fluctuations that have been described in the state of American business.[3] The only apparent anomaly was in 1838. Through most of 1838 business was on the upgrade in the United States, but for the year as a whole the volume of trade appears to have been somewhat less than in 1837, when business was declining but from an initially high level. The value of British exports to the United States, on the other hand, was much higher in 1838 than in 1837. The reason for this was evidently that our exports in 1837 had been reduced to an exceptional degree as a result of circumstances already mentioned. During 1836 stocks had been accumulating, and during 1837 exchange on Europe was extremely difficult and costly to obtain, both because of the low levels of American banks' reserves and because of the disruption of the facilities formerly provided by the Anglo-American finance houses. It is noteworthy that British sales in the American market were lower in 1837 than in 1840, when trade generally in America was worse but when there were not the same special circumstances operating to discourage imports. It was not surprising, therefore, that our exports rose in 1838. In 1839 they rose again, and in 1840 they crashed. The recovery in exports in 1841 was perhaps rather larger than the recovery in trade might appear to justify, and here it is possible that, as on previous occasions, inventory movements acted as a destabilising factor. The renewed decline in 1842 was correspondingly severe.

12. CONCLUSION

In this chapter the interrelations of British and American cycles have been viewed from the American end. The impact of the fluctuations in America on the British economy will be further discussed in Chapter XII after we have con-

---

[1] Sumner, *loc. cit.*

[2] The state repudiations and their consequences are brilliantly described by Jenks, *Migration of British Capital*, pp. 99–108. Analogous to the cessation of European lending to the United States in the slump was the drying up within the United States of the flow of capital from East to West. Cf. Berry, *Western Prices*, pp. 465–7.

[3] See Chart 5 at the beginning of this chapter.

sidered the other sources of instability affecting British industry. As has already been remarked, it is in the nature of things futile to try to draw any hard-and-fast line assigning to either country causal primacy in the cycle as a whole or in its individual phases. But enough has been said in the present chapter to indicate the powerful nature of the forces making for instability from within the United States in this period.[1]

[1] A. H. Cole (Smith and Cole, p. 73), commenting on the greater amplitude of the fluctuations of United States external trade volume compared to United States internal trade volume, remarks: 'possibly with a clarity not conveyed by non-statistical accounts of this troubled era, the table [of the fluctuations in the volume of trade] suggests the important role played by foreign influences in the "crisis of 1837"'. In a sense this is true. Yet it is to be observed that in almost all years in this period when the volume of United States foreign trade increased (decreased) there was an adverse (favourable) movement in the United States balance of trade (*ibid.* p. 79). This implies that the greatest variability was in imports rather than exports, which in turn suggests that the fluctuations in the volume of external trade were the result rather than the cause of fluctuations in the United States business as a whole. One reason for the variability in the volume of United States commodity imports was no doubt the variability of United States capital imports. Yet the amount of capital imports was mainly governed—subject to the need of European banks to safeguard their reserves—by the conditions of trade and credit within the United States.

CHAPTER VI

EXPORTS TO OTHER MARKETS

1. Exports to Northern Europe

Exports to markets other than the United States were, it will be recalled, divided at the beginning of the last chapter into exports to northern Europe and exports to other areas, northern Europe being defined for this purpose as France, Russia, Scandinavia, Prussia, Germany, Holland and Belgium. The value of exports to these areas is shown in Table 6 and Chart 6. We shall deal first with exports to northern Europe. The characteristic feature of exports to this area, as appears from Chart 6, is the smallness of their year-to-year fluctuations, which cannot properly be described as cyclical.[1] In some years the upward tendency of exports was less pronounced than in others, and occasionally there was even a slight fall, but variations in the level of exports to these countries contributed much less to short-period fluctuations in the value of total British exports than they did to the upward trend of the total.

Table 6. *Declared value of total exports and exports to northern Europe, United States and other markets (£m.)*

Year	Total	To northern Europe*	To United States	To other markets
1832	36·1	10·6	5·5	20·1
1833	39·3	10·2	7·6	21·6
1834	41·3	10·6	6·8	23·8
1835	47·0	11·8	10·6	24·7
1836	53·4	11·6	12·4	29·4
1837	42·1	13·2	4·7	24·2
1838	50·1	14·4	7·6	28·1
1839	53·2	14·6	8·8	29·7
1840	51·4	14·7	5·3	31·5
1841	51·6	16·1	7·1	28·4
1842	47·4	17·2	3·5	26·7

* For countries included under this head see text.

Source: G. R. Porter, *Progress of the Nation* (1851 edition), pp. 359–67 (derived from official returns).

Endogenous fluctuations in economic activity on the continent of Europe assumed importance on one occasion only in our period; there was a minor boom, particularly in Belgium, which reached its peak in the course of 1838 and was reversed by the end of the same year. The impact of this movement on Britain

---

[1] It is because exports to France share this short-period stability and do not resemble in their behaviour exports to other Mediterranean countries that they are included in the present category. A notable feature of exports to France in this period was the extreme rapidity of their upward trend. Between 1827 and 1830, their annual value was consistently less than £½m., while in the early 1840's it averaged about £2½m. France's imports from all sources approximately doubled over the same period. Cf. Sir John Clapham, *Economic History of Modern Britain* (1930 edition), I, p. 479; idem, *Economic Development of France and Germany, 1815–1914* (1936), p. 114; G. R. Porter, *Progress of the Nation* (1851 edition), p. 400.

was more marked in the financial than in the commercial sphere, so full consideration of it is deferred to Chapter VII. It was reflected to some extent in the behaviour of British exports to France and the Low Countries in 1838, when they rose well above trend. The impact on our exports of the recession from this boom was very mild, for although in 1839 complaints of slack continental demand for cotton twist were commonly made,[1] the figures reveal only a very slight reduction in sales in the area, which remained well above their pre-1838 level.

The other occasion when cyclical forces appear to have exercised a perceptible effect on the level of exports to northern Europe, though in quite a different

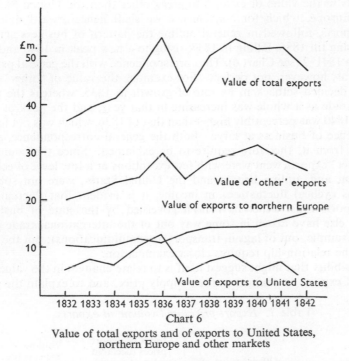

Chart 6

Value of total exports and of exports to United States,
northern Europe and other markets

way, was in the slump years 1841 and 1842. At that time it was widely argued that the relatively moderate extent of the fall in total export values was due to the amount of dumping in overseas markets that was being forced on producers by the depression of trade at home.[2] The rapid rise in the value of exports to northern Europe in 1841 and 1842 suggests that it was in this area that reductions in prices were most effective in bringing about increased sales. It is possible that the same cause contributed to the rise in exports to northern Europe in the recession year 1837.

[1] *Circular to Bankers*, 24 May 1839, 7 June 1839.
[2] 'A considerable exportation of goods has taken place, but their extremely low prices from the depression of the home market accounts for this.' Lord Brougham in the House of Lords, 11 July 1842 (*Hansard's Parliamentary Debates* (3rd series), LXIV, col. 1244). Cf. also *Report of the Assistant Poor Law Commissioners sent to inquire into the state of the population of Stockport*, 1842, XXXV, p. 252.

It appears, then, that there is nothing very much in the behaviour of exports to northern Europe over the period which stands in need of explanation. However, it *is* necessary to explain why exports to this part of the world should have been immune from the influences that dominated the course of exports to other countries. This, accordingly, is a matter to which we shall return when the nature of these latter influences has been examined.

2. ALTERNATIVE HYPOTHESES REGARDING THE BEHAVIOUR OF EXPORTS TO 'OTHER' MARKETS

Movements in the value of exports to areas other than the United States and northern Europe, which for convenience we shall henceforward describe as 'other' exports, followed in general outline the pattern of business activity in Britain, rising till 1836, falling in 1837, rising to a new peak in 1840 and falling off again in 1841–2 (see Chart 6). The correspondence with the general pattern of business was, however, not perfect. For example, the value of 'other' exports suffered a decided setback in its rate of growth in 1835, whereas the pace of revival in trade as a whole was increasing in that year, and the peak of 'other' exports in 1840 was perceptibly higher than that of 1836, which was not felt to be the experience of business at large. Both the general correspondence, and the departures from it, therefore require to be explained. Since the countries to which 'other' exports went were with few exceptions at a low level of economic development and, unlike Britain and the United States, were not subject to endogenous cyclical fluctuations in income, it is evident that fluctuations in 'other' exports must either have been governed by the state of business in Britain, or else have arisen in some way out of the international trade process itself (for example, out of lags in transport or communications); but the precise nature of the relationship requires closer examination.

One possibility that might suggest itself is to relate changes in the value of this category of exports to changes in their supply price, and to explain the general

Table 7. *Export prices and volume of exports*

Year	Official value of exports (£m.)	Index of export prices (declared value of exports as percentage of Official value of exports)	Volume of 'other' exports (declared value of 'other' exports ÷ index of export prices)
1832	65·0	56·2	35·8
1833	70·0	56·7	38·1
1834	73·8	56·4	42·2
1835	78·4	60·5	40·7
1836	85·2	62·6	47·0
1837	72·5	58·1	41·6
1838	92·5	54·2	51·8
1839	97·4	54·6	54·4
1840	102·8	50·0	63·0
1841	102·2	50·5	56·2
1842	100·3	47·3	56·6

Source: Porter, p. 356, and Table 6 above.

conformity of movements in 'other' export values to the British business cycle by supposing that the demand for British goods from the countries concerned had typically a low elasticity. On this view it is unnecessary to suppose that any cyclical *shifts* took place in the demand for 'other' exports. Table 7 and Chart 7 present the evidence required for the consideration of this hypothesis. In them are shown, in addition to the declared value of 'other' exports, the index of

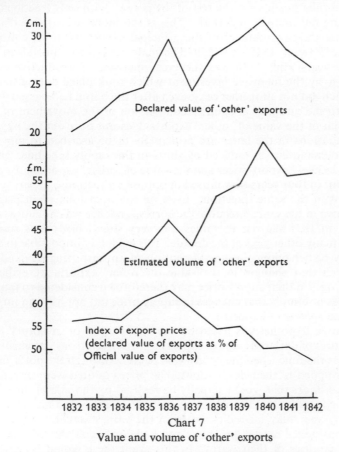

Chart 7

Value and volume of 'other' exports

export prices (obtained by dividing the declared value of exports by the Official value of exports), and the volume of 'other' exports (obtained by deflating their declared value by the export price index).[1]

The explanation of the movements in export *prices* shown in Chart 7 is to be sought in the history of the leading British export industries over the period, and

[1] The export price index is an index of the prices of all exports, not only of 'other' exports; but there is no reason to suppose that the course of 'other' export prices was so different from the general course of export prices as to affect the outlines of the movements shown. The main difference between the composition of exports to the United States and northern Europe and the composition of 'other' exports was the greater preponderance in the latter of cotton piece goods. For this reason an index of the prices of 'other' exports would probably rise rather more steeply than does the index shown in the years 1835 and 1839. This does not affect any of the conclusions reached in the text.

73

therefore belongs properly to Chapters IX and X rather than to the present chapter. But it is worth while to point out, in parentheses, at the present stage the striking contrast which emerges if one compares this index with an ostensibly general price index such as Silberling's, which is in fact made up mainly from the prices of primary products. The Silberling index (Chart 3) has two peaks of roughly equal altitude in 1836 and 1839. The export price index has a peak in 1836 and then falls steadily for the rest of the period, with only fractional interruptions to the fall in 1839 and 1841.[1] This is the more remarkable if it is remembered that the raw material of the principal export industry, cotton, was rising in price between 1837 and 1839. The main reason for this fall in export prices in the years after 1836 was the great increase in productive capacity brought about by the intensive investment which took place during the boom years and which did not altogether cease even after the boom had passed its peak.

To revert to the question in hand: a comparison of the movement of export prices with that of the value of 'other' exports does not bear out the hypothesis that the fluctuations in the latter are principally to be ascribed to movements along stable demand curves induced by shifts in the supply schedule. In six of the ten years 1833–42 export prices and the value of 'other' exports moved in the same direction; in four years they moved in opposite directions—a bare majority for movement in the same direction. Even on the occasions when prices and values did move in the same direction, the correspondence was not always close; for example, in 1835 the rise in values was very slight, but prices rose more steeply than in any other year of the decade. It is evidently impossible to explain such diversity of behaviour on the assumption of an unshifting demand curve. The hypothesis that changes in the value of 'other' exports were the result mainly of changes in their supply price may therefore be considered to fail. (This, of course, does not imply that changes in supply price did not have an important bearing on the *volume* of exports.)

An alternative hypothesis is based on the supposition of inventory fluctuations. The figures of declared value of exports were derived from statements made by exporters at the time when the goods were passing through the ports and were about to be shipped to their destinations. The prices quoted were therefore not necessarily the prices that would actually be realised by the sale of the goods to the ultimate consumer in the foreign market. It is possible that the declared values for any year may have differed from the values actually realised if exporters had misjudged market prospects and had consigned abroad excessive or insufficient quantities of their wares. In this event there would be unforeseen changes in the prices fetched, or fluctuations in the level of stocks of British goods held abroad, or both. This might give rise to 'cobweb' cycles in exports analogous to those which we found to have occurred in certain years in imports.

The hypothesis that fluctuations of this sort were of chief importance in the explanation of the movements in export values in the earlier part of the nineteenth century has been advanced by Professor W. W. Rostow:

Acting, in fact, on similar or identical intelligence, British merchants tended, roughly, to behave in the same manner. When inventories fell off, and prices rose abroad, word was received from overseas agents and fully circulated; and more goods were shipped

[1] This fall in prices has as its counterpart the rapid growth in the Official value (volume) of total exports till 1840. See Table 7.

from Britain. Such actions, individually taken, tended to reverse the conditions in foreign markets which justified the increased shipments, in the first instance; and the reversal could not be reported instantaneously, nor the production decisions which stemmed from it instantaneously reversed within Britain. And so the curve of British exports did not rise smoothly, in continuous accord with market conditions abroad. It moved upward, with occasional setbacks, fluctuating about the imaginary line which, at any moment of time, would have represented the equilibrium volume of exports. There was, undoubtedly, a tendency for British foreign trade to fluctuate cyclically, in what we might call an inventory cycle.[1]

Does this hypothesis help to explain the movement of 'other' exports between 1833 and 1842?

If we have regard merely to the *value* of 'other' exports, the view that their course during our period was the result of an endogenous inventory cycle of the sort described appears somewhat lacking in plausibility. The chart does not show short-period fluctuations of regular duration, and it seems rather unreasonable to suppose that an independent inventory cycle should by coincidence have corresponded in timing so closely to the behaviour of trade in other sectors of the economy. If instead of regarding values, we consider the *volume* of 'other' exports, rather more case does emerge for postulating the existence of a short cycle of two years' duration, since volume rises and falls in alternate years from 1834 to 1842, with the one exception of 1839, when instead of a fall there is a slackening of rate of growth. But a moment's reflection will show that these fluctuations, so far from supporting the hypothesis of an inventory cycle as conceived, actually go far to refute it. The foundation of the theory is that exporters increase their consignments (to an excessive extent) when market reports are favourable and lead them to expect that good prices will be fetched. On this assumption, years of high export prices should be years of high export volume—for it must be remembered that the declared values from which our estimate of export prices is derived are based on prices *expected* by exporters at the time they were sending off the goods. But an inspection of Chart 7 reveals that in the majority of years prices and volume moved in the *opposite* direction. For this reason, as well as because of the *a priori* unlikelihood of an endogenous inventory cycle leading to fluctuations in export values so similar to those in business at large, it must be concluded that inventory cycles cannot be regarded as constituting the main explanation of the fluctuations in 'other' exports that took place during our period. It is possible, however, that they did play a subordinate part, and we shall revert to this again later in the chapter.

3. The Relationship between 'Other' Exports and Imports

The two hypotheses so far advanced to explain the movement of 'other' exports have both proved unsatisfactory. A more promising line of approach to the problem is suggested by the comparison of the behaviour of 'other' exports with that of imports. The value of 'other' exports and the value of imports exclusive of corn are plotted together on a logarithmic scale in Chart 8. The

[1] W. W. Rostow, *British Economy of the Nineteenth Century* (1948), pp. 39–40 (quoted by courtesy of the Oxford University Press).

correspondence between the two series is remarkable. Not merely are their fluctuations similar, but the trend rate of growth of each over the period is almost identical. Even such discrepancies as are to be found between them are mostly in respects for which a ready explanation is available; thus the high figure of imports relatively to exports in 1836 is probably largely the result of the tendency for Imlah's estimates of import values to be excessive in years of steeply rising prices,[1] and the relatively high values of exports in 1840–2 may be attributed to the dumping which manufacturers were impelled to engage in in those years on account of the depression of the home market.[2]

That Britain's purchases of imports should have exerted an important influence on the overseas demand for British exports is in a general way not particularly surprising. But the exact nature of the relationship requires to be more closely considered.

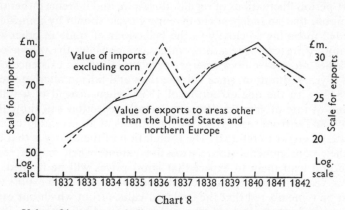

Chart 8

Value of imports, excluding corn, and value of 'other' exports

Changes in the value of British imports were likely to affect the demand for British exports in two ways: first, by their effect on the level of income in the countries from which the imports were derived, and, secondly, by their effect on the availability of sterling.

The latter of these two effects was probably the more important. As far as the former is concerned, it is true that the leading British export markets outside the United States and northern Europe were countries lacking in industrialisation and hence not subject to regular fluctuations in income except in so far as these were transmitted to them through their foreign trade, and that for this reason changes in their exports to Britain, the world's largest importer, were probably the main source of regular or cyclical fluctuations in their income level. On the other hand, exports accounted for no more than a small proportion of the national income of most of these regions—the West Indies being the chief exception—and arbitrary causes such as harvest variations probably played a much larger part than changes in the value of exports in bringing about year-to-year fluctuations in their real income levels. Consequently, although the effect of

---

[1] See p. 14, n. 3.   [2] See p. 71.

changes in British imports on incomes in the supplying countries was not necessarily unimportant, it can scarcely be considered to provide an adequate explanation of the relationship between exports and imports revealed by Chart 8.

The economically backward character of the countries in question is, in conjunction with the geographical remoteness of most of them, the crucial point to be emphasised in connection with the other and more important factor, the effect of variations in British imports on the availability of sterling. In trading relations between Britain and other financially advanced countries, it was not necessary for an exact year-to-year balance to be struck between imports and exports (even abstracting from long-term capital movements), because, if there were substantial excess demand for either country's currency, shipments of gold could take place to cover the difference. Short-term capital movements could also help to bridge the gap, whether motivated by movements of the exchanges within the specie points, or, as more often, by the international discount rates differentials which resulted from specie movements. But trading relations with the more backward countries that comprised the main markets for 'other' exports were on a different footing. Even if their currency system was on some sort of metallic basis, which was not always the case, the absence of an organised and large-scale market in bullion—as well as their geographical distance—made the shipment to them of treasure an expensive and unattractive method of remittance save in exceptional circumstances, and it was likewise difficult without inordinate expense to mobilise any substantial quantity of treasure for transmission from there to Britain. Much the same contrast between advanced and backward countries applied with regard to accommodating capital movements. The absence of an organised market in bills of exchange in backward countries eliminated the possibility of regular arbitrage by short-term capital movement such as was practised between London and the leading financial centres of the continent. If in any year there were an increase in exports to a backward country unaccompanied by any offsetting increase in its exports to the United Kingdom, the gap could only be bridged out of the resources of the export merchant himself, or by any borrowing he might be able to do by the issue of accommodation bills or similar means. For a deficit to be covered in this way was not, of course, impossible, and no doubt the use of such means sometimes enabled a balance to be struck over rather a longer period than a year. But there were limits beyond which this could not be pushed, and merchants would be anxious to avoid the risk and cost which would inevitably be entailed if their business had to be financed in this way.

The reason for the contrast between the behaviour of exports to the United States and northern Europe on the one hand and the behaviour of 'other' exports on the other should now be clear. In the case of the latter, but not of the former, the availability of means of remitting the proceeds appears to have imposed the most powerful restraint on the ability of overseas markets to absorb our exports.[1] As the value of imports fluctuated under the influence of the various forces described in Chapter III, exports followed suit. As a rule the difficulty was to obtain means of remitting back the proceeds derived from our

[1] With the consequence that the price elasticity of demand for 'other' exports can normally have departed by only a small extent from unity.

exports rather than to find exports with which to pay for imports[1]—a natural consequence of the rapid growth of productivity in British export industries. It is clearly right to regard exports rather than imports as the dependent variable in the relation between the two, partly for the reason just mentioned, and partly because changes in the value of imports are readily explicable with reference to fluctuations in Great Britain, whereas no analogous forces operated on the demand for 'other' exports—a further contrast with exports to the United States—so that, if exports were treated as the independent variable, the explanation of their movement would be left in the air.

4. SOME DIFFICULTIES

So much for the general principle explaining the relationship between 'other' exports and imports. There are a number of points that call now for further comment.

In the first place, the value of British imports would not be a fair measure of the availability of sterling to the countries in question if long-term capital movements were substantial. However, it so happens that long-term lending—or at least fluctuations in long-term lending—to countries other than the United States was not of major importance during our period, with one exception which does not affect the general principle.[2]

In the second place, comment is called for on the exclusion of corn imports from the total of import values to which the movements of 'other' exports have been related. If corn is included along with other imports, the correspondence between the two series becomes much less good. The justification for deducting corn is that in this period imports of corn were drawn almost entirely from northern Europe, and fluctuations in expenditure on imported corn did not therefore result in changes in the availability of exchange on London for the finance of 'other' exports. As has been argued above, the supply of sterling with which to effect remittance was not of primary importance in determining the course of short-period fluctuations in British exports to northern Europe, and it was, indeed, notorious that in years when corn imports were abnormally

[1] For the applicability of this to the boom year 1836, cf. *Circular to Bankers*, 1 July 1836: 'Foreign markets are not...overstocked; the difficulty is in getting returns of produce from countries willing to purchase our manufactures'. Cf. also more generally, Clapham, *Economic History*, I, pp. 488–9.
[2] The exception arises from the speculation in Spanish and Portuguese securities that took place in 1834 and 1835 (see pp. 87–8). This was accompanied by an increase in British exports to the Iberian peninsula from £1·9 million in 1833 to £2·5 million in 1834 and £2·7 million in 1835. From certain points of view it is arguable that Spain and Portugal should be grouped with north European countries rather than 'other' countries, since Lisbon, in particular, possessed well-developed financial facilities, and sizeable movements of treasure between there and London were not uncommon. On the whole, however, it has been deemed preferable to include the Iberian peninsula with 'other' countries, partly in order to keep the north European group on a roughly geographical basis, and partly because, despite the movements of treasure just mentioned, the statistics suggest that the supply of exchange on London exercised an important influence on the fluctuations of British exports to these parts. The main effect of the exclusion of exports to Spain, Portugal and Gibraltar from the category 'other' exports would be to reduce slightly the rate of growth of the latter in 1834. The general correspondence between the fluctuations of 'other' exports and of non-corn imports would not be affected, being rendered slightly more close in some years and slightly less close in others.

high they had to be paid for in gold and did not stimulate British exports to any appreciable degree.[1]

There would in principle be something to be said for deducting non-corn imports from northern Europe from the total of imports in the same way as we have deducted corn imports; but the statistics in the form in which they are available do not enable us to distinguish readily between the values of imports from different sources. This need not be considered too serious a source of error, since with the exception of corn, fluctuations in the value of imports from northern Europe appear to have been roughly similar to those in imports generally.

In the third place, comment is required on the propriety of including imports from the United States in the total of imports in the present context, for the same reasons as those mentioned in the last two paragraphs. It cannot be claimed that the exclusion of imports from the United States would have no effect on the fluctuations of the total, since imports and prices of cotton, the chief article involved, were on a number of occasions a law unto themselves. But even apart from the statistical difficulties of estimating the value of imports from the United States, it is doubtful whether to deduct them from the total would really be the right thing to do. The justification for including them lies in the importance of multilateral settlement of payments between Britain, the United States and certain other areas, particularly the Far East. Britain's balance of payments with India and China (taken together) was consistently favourable, and that of the United States with India and China was consistently unfavourable. Bills on London enabled the Americans to pay for their purchases in the Far East, and provided a convenient means of remitting British Far Eastern earnings back to Britain. The extent of the United States' favourable balance of payments with Britain was thus a factor in determining the extent to which British exports to India and China could be expanded. It is probable that a similar triangle was in operation in our trade with certain other areas, such as the West Indies and South America, but it was in the Far Eastern trade that its importance was greatest.[2]

For this reason fluctuations in the value of British imports from the United States were not without influence on 'other' exports. On the other hand, it must be conceded that the supply of bills on London available to finance triangular trade in the way described can be only very approximately measured by the value of British imports from the United States, since the other items in the balance of payments between Britain and the United States—capital movements and British exports—were liable to very substantial fluctuations as well. But in the absence of any statistical information on capital movements between Britain

[1] This was, of course, essentially a short-period phenomenon. One of the most widely canvassed arguments in the anti-Corn Law agitation was that it was the *irregularity* of corn imports under the Corn Laws that led to the drain of gold in bad harvest years, and that free trade, by establishing a more regular (as well as a larger) import trade in corn would stimulate the growth of British exports to corn-producing countries.

[2] For a discussion on the multilateral system of balancing in this period with special reference to the China trade, see M. Greenberg, *British Trade and the Opening of China, 1800–1842* (1951), Chapters I and VI. The position was somewhat more complicated than is stated in the text, since India's favourable balance with China (owing to opium exports) was used to offset Britain's unfavourable balance with China. A good contemporary statement of the system of payments between Britain and India in this period is to be found in the evidence of J. C. Melvill before the *Select Committee on East India Produce*, 1840, VIII, especially QQ. 10–118.

and the United States, the approximation reached by taking the import figures alone is perhaps not too hopelessly bad, since, as may be seen from Chapter V, there was a strong tendency for British purchases of United States securities and United States purchases of British goods to rise and fall together and so in some measure to cancel out.

5. THE NATURE OF THE RELATIONSHIP POSTULATED

Accommodating movements of short-term capital or treasure between Britain and the main markets for 'other' exports were as a rule expensive and inconvenient to arrange, but they were not impossible. For this reason, as well as because of the various points mentioned in the last section, it would be foolish to expect more than a rough correspondence between the movements of 'other' exports and those of non-corn imports. The excellence of the fit revealed in Chart 8 must in part be set down to coincidence. All that is here suggested is that the availability of means of remitting was in this period the most important single factor governing the movement of British exports to the countries in question.

It is interesting to compare the experience of our period in this respect with that of earlier and of later years. In the 1840's and 1850's the relationship between the value of 'other' exports and the value of non-corn imports revealed by the statistics remains fairly close, though not so close as in the 1830's. From 1843 to 1857 inclusive, the two magnitudes rose and fell together in every year, with only one exception (1847). The proportional amplitudes of the fluctuations of the two remain very similar after 1843, though the similarity is not quite so close as it had been between 1833 and 1842. It seems, therefore, that no fundamental change took place in the forces determining the level of British exports to 'other' markets in the period immediately after that with which we are concerned. The big change came with the growth to substantial proportions of capital exports from the United Kingdom to these areas in and after the late 1850's. 1858 is the first year in which the relationship we have been discussing is shown by the statistics to have broken down altogether. 1858 was a year of trade recession in which import values fell pronouncedly, and the rise in the total of 'other' exports in that year was entirely due to the increase in exports to India which accompanied the intensive railway-building projects set on foot there after the Mutiny.

The evidence is therefore not inconsistent with the view that the value of British imports remained of major importance in determining the level of exports to the less economically advanced of our export markets for some time after the period with which we are concerned. But in the 1820's the picture revealed by the statistics is quite different. The relationship between the fluctuation of shortest period, at least, in the two series in that decade is by no means close, and the behaviour of the export curve is difficult to explain without recourse to the hypothesis that there were, as well as large exports of capital, substantial fluctuations in export inventories. The fall in 'other' exports in 1831 apparently requires to be explained in this way, and may have contributed to raising the level of exports in 1832 above the level that would otherwise have prevailed.

It would be wrong to suppose that inventory movements in exports were necessarily altogether absent between 1833 and 1842. As we have argued, there is not much evidence that they were responsible for the overall movement of 'other' exports during these years, but it is quite possible that there were inventory fluctuations *in individual markets* which in the aggregate largely cancelled out. The course of exports to the four leading areas which may be distinguished outside the United States and northern Europe are shown in Table 8 and Chart 9. The outlines of the four curves shown is far from identical. Whether the differences between them are to be explained as the result of inventory movements in the individual markets or as a result of differences between the availability of sterling to each of the respective areas must remain an open question until more detailed research has been carried out into the structure and organization of British trade with each of the regions concerned.

Table 8. *Declared value of exports to principal 'other' markets (£m.)*

Year	Total 'other' exports	Exports to			
		West Indies	Latin America	Asia	Southern Europe
1832	20·1	3·6	4·3	4·2	5·0
1833	21·6	3·6	4·8	4·7	5·4
1834	23·8	4·0	5·2	4·6	7·4
1835	24·7	4·3	4·9	5·5	6·7
1836	29·4	5·0	6·0	6·8	7·4
1837	24·2	4·5	4·3	5·6	6·2
1838	28·1	4·7	4·7	7·0	7·8
1839	29·7	5·3	6·0	7·6	6·2
1840	31·5	4·7	6·2	9·3	6·8
1841	28·4	3·6	5·1	8·2	6·8
1842	26·7	3·4	5·0	7·5	6·7

Source: Porter, pp. 362–5.

Precisely why inventory fluctuations should have come to exercise less influence on the total of 'other' exports after the beginning of our period than they had done previously is difficult to say. General improvement in merchanting arrangements and a reduction in the speculative element in the export trade perhaps played a part. But it is not too difficult to suggest reasons to explain another prominent contrast, the greater persistence and regularity in our period of cycles in import inventories as compared with cycles in export inventories. In the first place, British imports were mainly composed of primary products, British exports of manufactures. Primary products, on account of their homogeneity, provided a more convenient object of speculation than manufactures, and the fixed period of production of many of them helped to secure synchronisation between fluctuations in different commodity markets. In the second place, the amplitude of fluctuations in inventories was more likely to be sustained by external 'shocks' in the case of imports than of exports. Such shocks might arise either at the British end or at the foreign end. Shocks at the foreign end were likely to affect exports and imports to about the same degree. But whereas in the case of imports shocks at the British end would tend to arise from changes in income and *demand*, in the case of exports shocks at the British end would arise from changes on the *supply* side; and supply schedules, being mainly dependent on the amount of capacity in existence and the state of technique, were less liable than were income levels to substantial changes from one year to the next.

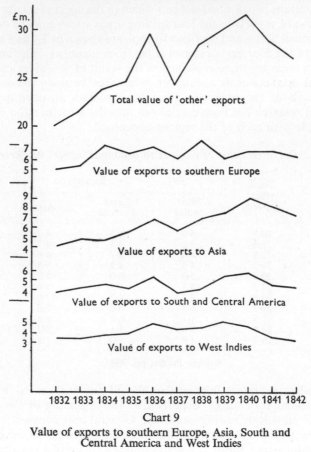

Chart 9
Value of exports to southern Europe, Asia, South and
Central America and West Indies

6. IMPLICATIONS FOR THE CYCLICAL PROCESS

The apparent dependence of 'other' exports on imports involves consequences of some importance for the mechanism of the cycle in income and activity as a whole.

The tendency for certain categories of imports and exports to march together was a stabiliser from the point of view of the balance of trade, by definition, and also, *ceteris paribus*, from the point of view of the balance of payments. Since fluctuations in the foreign balance create corresponding fluctuations in effective demand, it might appear that this tendency also helped to promote stability in incomes. But this is true only from one point of view. It is true that, in so far as the value of 'other' exports was governed by the value of imports, they did not constitute an independent source of fluctuations in income in Britain. This is the

82

fundamental respect in which their role differed from that of exports to the United States. In this sense 'other' exports were not such a source of instability as might appear from superficial observation of their fluctuations. But although the behaviour of 'other' exports was thus not an independent source of instability, it tended to increase the amplitude of any fluctuations in income which had origins elsewhere. In the theory of international trade the fact that a certain proportion of the extra incomes earned in the boom is spent on imports appears as a factor tending to damp down the increase in incomes in the boom, since the expenditure in question constitutes a leakage from the circular flow. Similarly, when incomes are declining, if part of the decline in expenditure falls on imports, this lessens the impact of the depression on the home market. But if it is true that in our period changes in the value of imports led to equal proportional changes in certain important categories of exports, then the stabilising influence of changes in expenditure on imports must have been correspondingly weakened. In so far as the balance of payments was stabilised, that is to say, it was prevented from fluctuating contra-cyclically.

These conclusions are subject to a qualification on account of movements in import inventories. As explained in Chapter III, accumulation of import inventories appears to have proceeded rather more rapidly after 1837 than before. Since accumulation of import inventories added to foreigners' demand for our exports without, as such, involving any diversion of British consumers' demand away from home-produced goods, this tendency for the rate of change in import inventories to vary inversely with the level of activity served in some measure to help to stabilise income levels. But although investment in import inventories tended in a general way to move contra-cyclically, year-to-year fluctuations were not always in this direction, and hence were not always stabilising in character. In 1836 and 1837 particularly, the investment and disinvestment respectively in import inventories meant that the value of imports fluctuated much more widely than the value of consumers' expenditure on imports, and the effect of this on exports was to accentuate the boom in 1836 and to accentuate the recession in 1837.

CHAPTER VII

THE BALANCE OF TRADE AND THE BALANCE OF PAYMENTS

OUR task in the present chapter is to give a general survey of the movements in Britain's balance of payments and their effect on economic fluctuations in the period, in the light of the analysis of particular aspects of the balance of payments that has been given in the foregoing chapters.

In accordance with the distinction drawn in Chapter II between the 'direct' and the 'monetary' effect of changes in the foreign trade balance on the level of effective demand, the matter requires to be looked at from two points of view. The 'direct' effect is a function of certain items only in the balance of payments, being unaffected, for example, by capital movements (except, of course, in so far as these lead to movements in other items). The balance between the various items which are relevant for the 'direct' effect will be termed the income balance.[1] This is distinguished from the overall balance of payments, which is the quantity that is relevant for the analysis of international gold movements and the 'monetary' effect.

1. THE OVERALL BALANCE OF PAYMENTS: INTRODUCTION

We shall consider the overall balance of payments first. In the present chapter we shall be concerned with the *causes* of fluctuations in the foreign exchanges and the gold movements they gave rise to. The effect of the gold movements on the volume of credit within the country will be considered in Chapter XI, where it will be shown that the relationship between the balance of payments and fluctuations in the rate of discount was very close. Just how great was the effect of discount rate movements on the level of economic activity is a more debatable point, and for this reason it is possible that a good deal of what will be said in the following pages is really of more interest for the theory of the balance of payments than for the theory of the trade cycle. This also is a matter which will be further discussed in Chapters XI and XII.

In tracing the course of fluctuations in the balance of payments and their effects on the Bank of England's reserve, it will be necessary to take into account not merely the behaviour of imports and exports but also the behaviour of invisible items in the balance, both on current account and on capital account, in so far as it is possible to make estimates of these. The inadequacy of the statistics makes it very difficult to decide which of the items in the balance of payments were primarily responsible for the various movements of bullion into or away from the Bank of England; but it is important to attempt some analysis, since it

---

[1] This is not the same as the balance of payments on current account because of the distinction between the volume of imports entered for consumption, which is relevant for the 'direct' effect, and the volume of imports brought into the country, which is what is included in the balance of payments on current account as commonly understood.

must make a considerable difference to our view of the interrelation between the cyclical process and the balance of payments whether the observed movements of the latter were caused chiefly by fluctuations in the balance of trade or by fluctuations in the balance of lending.

The figures of the Bank of England's bullion holding are necessarily the starting point of any study of Britain's balance of payments in this period. The quarterly average of the amount of bullion[1] held by the Bank is shown in Chart 13 (p. 170).

Fluctuations in the Bank's reserve were liable to result either from changes in the amount of coin required for internal circulation or from import or export of bullion. The statistics do not distinguish between internal and external bullion movements, but Bank officials reckoned that they were able as a rule to judge for which purpose gold was being sought in times of drain and whether it was drawn from internal or external sources in times of reflux.[2] Their views on the nature of the movements occurring at most phases of our period[3] are set forth in pamphlets and in testimony before Parliamentary committees, so that the distinction between internal and external movements does not present any great difficulty for the historian. It is sometimes less easy to ascertain the precise destination or source of the bullion on occasions when the drain or reflux was known to be external, though contemporary commentators usually had a certain amount to say about this too. The bulk of the short-period movements of gold and silver that affected the London money market were to or from the Continent of Europe, with the United States next in order of importance. Other countries, as has already been argued, in general lacked sufficiently large or highly organised markets in the precious metals to enable treasure to provide a regular means of bridging short-period disequilibria in the balance of payments, save on a small scale.

The plan of the next four sections of this chapter is as follows. We shall consider in § 2 the evidence relating to the balance of trade and the balance of payments on current account, and in § 3 that relating to long-term and short-term capital movements. Consideration of short-term capital movements will require us to make a short digression and describe briefly the course of economic fluctuations in France and Belgium during certain phases of the period. We shall then go on to try to explain the origins of the various bullion movements recorded (§4) and to draw some more general conclusions (§5).

2. THE BALANCE OF TRADE

Estimates of the United Kingdom's balance of trade for the years 1790–1850 have been obtained by Professor Imlah by setting alongside the declared value of exports his own estimates of the value of imports and of re-exports which we used in Chapter III above. His results for the years embraced in our period are

---

[1] Bullion in this context includes indifferently gold and silver, bars and coin.

[2] Cf. *Select Committee on Banks of Issue*, 1840, IV (henceforward referred to as *S.C. of 1840*), QQ. 1838–40 (G. W. Norman).

[3] Evidence relating to the years 1841–2 is rather jejune. There was no Parliamentary inquiry into the currency between 1841 and 1848, and by the latter date interest had shifted to more recent events. Contemporaries were, moreover, always more interested in explaining drains than in explaining refluxes.

reproduced in the first column of Table 9. Unfortunately these data are much affected by being based on what is in effect a c.i.f. valuation of imports and an f.o.b. valuation of exports. This is of particular importance in view of the much greater bulk relative to value of British imports at this period compared with British exports, the former being composed principally of primary products and the latter of textiles and other manufactures (exports of coal being as yet unimportant). If appropriate allowance could be made for shipping and other transport costs, it might well eliminate not merely the persistent excess of imports over exports that appears in the figures, but also some of the violence of the fluctuations of the balance. In the figures as they stand an equal *proportional* rise (or fall) in exports and imports is bound to involve a deterioration (or improvement) in the balance on account of the chronic excess of imports, and it is not at all certain that this result is really significant.

Table 9. *Estimated balance of trade and ratio of imports to exports*

Year	Estimated adverse balance of trade in £m. (Imlah)	Percentage ratio of estimated value of imports (minus re-exports) to declared value of exports
1832	8·1	125
1833	12·3	132
1834	15·1	137
1835	12·1	127
1836	22·3	142
1837	19·0	145
1838	20·8	142
1839	29·4	153
1840	29·8	158
1841	22·4	143
1842	20·6	143

Source: A. H. Imlah, 'Real values in British foreign trade',
Journal of Economic History (1948), pp. 133–52.

For this reason it is possible that the *ratio* of imports to exports (Table 9, second column) may provide a better guide—though still a very rough one—to the course of fluctuations in the commodity trade balance. With the important exceptions of 1837 and 1838, the direction of year-to-year change in this series is the same as that found in Imlah's reckoning of the balance of trade, but there are substantial differences between the two series in the order of magnitude of the changes shown.

The results shown in Table 9 will be further commented on later in the chapter. It will be observed that the movements in the ratio between imports and exports suggest a marked improvement in the balance in 1835, a period of gold influx, and a marked deterioration in 1839, when gold was flowing out; but, on the other hand, there are several years, such as 1837, when the behaviour of the ratio is notably at variance with what might have been expected in the light of recorded bullion movements.

A striking feature common to both the series shown in Table 9 is the apparently adverse trend movement in the balance of trade over the period as a whole. It is probable that up till 1840 this was in some degree offset by the movement in invisible items in the balance of payments on current account. In the first place, the upward trend in the volume of foreign trade was not arrested till after 1840, and the freight rates earned by British ships did not move in a manner precisely similar to that of commodity prices but instead rose more or less steadily from the early 1830's to a peak in 1839 or 1840.[1] Hence between 1836 and 1840, when many commodity prices were falling but freights were still rising, the growth of shipping earnings probably caused the balance of payments on current account to move rather less unfavourably than would be suggested by Table 9. In the second place, at least until 1839 Britain was engaging in substantial, albeit somewhat uneven, net long-term capital export, and interest earnings on foreign investments must therefore have been rising. After 1840 further long-term lending abroad was checked, and in 1841–2 interest earnings were reduced by default on the part of American borrowers.

With so many items to which quantitative magnitudes cannot be attached, it is evidently impossible to form more than a hazy impression of the course of movements in the balance of payments on current account. As far as quantitative estimates are concerned, the situation is even worse with respect to the balance on capital account; but a good deal of qualitative evidence is to be found concerning the main features of our lending, both long-term and short-term, and to this we now turn.

3. Capital Movements and Economic Fluctuations on the Continent of Europe

The revival of activity on the Stock Exchange after the long period of quiescence that had followed the crash of 1825 was ushered in by a phase of speculation in Portuguese and Spanish bonds. The course of events was thus described by J. Horsley Palmer, a Director and formerly Governor of the Bank of England:

The speculative action. . . originated in the loans to Don Pedro upon his first attempt to recover the throne of Portugal. The money advanced effected the overthrow of Don Miguel, and upon that overthrow followed the speculative mania in the foreign stock-market. More loans were contracted in aid of Donna Maria, and provided the contractors could only secure their agency and commission, the public were left to take care of themselves. The rage for speculation being further excited by the popular idea of overthrowing absolutism and establishing liberal Governments throughout the Peninsula, Spain came in for her share of the plunder obtained through English credulity. These loans were going forward from July, 1833, until towards the end of 1834, when the profit realised upon the daily extending engagements in the foreign stock-market engendered a further spirit of speculation in almost every kind of previously neglected South American, Spanish, and Portuguese bonds, causing an enormous advance in all, and in some nearly 100 per cent. In short, until the spring of 1835 hardly a packet arrived from the Continent which did not come loaded with every sort of foreign securities for realisation upon our foreign stock-exchange.[2]

[1] See p. 119.
[2] J. H. Palmer, *Causes and Consequences of the Pressure upon the Money Market* (1837), pp. 27–8. Cf. also Palmer's evidence, *S.C. of 1840*, QQ. 1183–90. For the history of the Portuguese episode, see E. L. Woodward, *The Age of Reform, 1815–1870* (1930), pp. 220–2.

The episode was essentially a speculative one—fostered perhaps by the rising price of the funds[1]—and the lending undertaken had little to do with the economic development of the countries concerned. Many of the bonds negotiated had their origin in the stock-market boom of 1825.[2] When the crash came in May 1835—allegedly as a result of a bear raid on the part of Rothschilds[3]—it was sudden and violent. Over half the members of the Stock Exchange suffered losses, but the general public for the most part emerged unscathed.[4]

Lending from Britain to the United States had consequences of a much more far-reaching nature. Its course has already been described in Chapter V, and here a brief outline of events as they affected the balance of payments will suffice.

It was not until 1836 that widespread publicity was given to the extent of dealing in American securities in London, but large and growing capital export to the United States had by then already been taking place for several years. The increase in the pace of capital export in 1836 was manifested partly in the purchase of bonds, but the growth in short-term lending on the basis of merchant bankers' acceptances was probably of still greater importance. Both forms of lending came practically to a standstill in 1837, and that year, as also 1838 to some extent, was marked by American repayment of short-term indebtedness incurred in 1836. But already in 1838, with the Bank of England's £1 million loan leading the way, the purchase of United States securities in London had begun to revive, including, apparently, the purchase of certain stocks previously held by capitalists on the Continent.[5] The short-term American securities marketed in Europe in 1838–9 were principally liabilities of the B.U.S., not, as in 1836, merchant bankers' acceptances. With the suspension of the B.U.S. in 1839, the flow of capital ceased, and in 1840 and the following years, British capitalists were concerned in endeavouring to induce the Americans to honour their existing debt and interest obligations, and did not contemplate throwing good money after bad.

The category of foreign lending which remains to be considered is short-term capital movements between Britain and Continental Europe. It will be convenient to preface discussion of these with a brief account of the course of economic fluctuations generally in France and Belgium during the period. These appear to have been the only Continental countries to manifest any pronounced tendency to independent fluctuations in economic activity at this time.

In both France and Belgium the mid-1830's were years of great development of the banking system and of a boom on joint-stock company promotion.[6] But,

[1] Cf. S. Ricardo, *Observations on the Recent Pamphlet of J. H. Palmer, Esq.* (1837), pp. 8–9, 16. On the prices of the funds see pp. 188–90.
[2] They thereafter became 'for half a century the football of the stock exchanges' (L. H. Jenks, *Migration of British Capital to 1875* (1926), p. 58).
[3] R. W. Hidy, *The House of Baring in American Trade and Finance* (1949), p. 198.
[4] *Circular to Bankers*, 5 December 1835.
[5] *S.C. of 1840*, Q. 1362 (J. H. Palmer).
[6] The principal sources on which the following pages are based are: *Annuaires Statistiques*; J. H. Clapham, *Economic Development of France and Germany* (1936), pp. 126–9; B. S. Chlepner, *Belgian Banking and Banking Theory* (1943), Chapter i; *idem*, 'La Première Crise Bancaire en Belgique', *Bulletin de la Banque Nationale de Belgique* (January 1939); G. Ramon, *Histoire de la Banque de France* (1929), pp. 177–82, 201; E. Levasseur, *Histoire des Classes Ouvrières et de l'Industrie en France* (1881), II, pp. 158–95; A. Courtois, *Histoire des Banques en France* (1881), pp. 148–64; C. Juglar, *Des Crises Commerciales* (1889), pp. 411–14; A. L. Dunham, 'How the first French railways were planned', *Journal of Economic History* (1941), pp. 12–25.

especially in Belgium, the newly formed banks, of which the Banque de Belgique, founded in 1835, was the most important, found the monetary habits of the public a serious obstacle to the establishment either of a wide note circulation or of extensive deposits, and the total liabilities of the Banque de Belgique, for example, never rose as high as twice its paid-up capital. For this reason the loans to industry and the purchase of shares which the banks were anxious to make could be pushed far only at the cost of endangering the banks' liquidity. A further source of embarrassment to Belgian banks was the conservatism of the Belgian moneyed classes, who were reluctant to buy the industrial securities which the banks had hoped to be able to dispose of on the open market. The consequent illiquidity of the banks meant that they were in a weak position to meet the crash when it came.

In Belgium, activity continued to grow up till 1838, especially in the mining and metallurgical industries, the Anglo-American troubles of 1836–7 having no visible effect on trade. During most of 1838 activity continued high, but the turning-point was felt to have been passed before the year was very far advanced. The recession was said to be partly due to the procrastination of the French Parliament in deciding on its further railway-building plans. In December, with the recession already under way, a raid on the Banque de Belgique by its most important rival in the sphere of individual banking, the Société Générale pour Favoriser l'Industrie Nationale, forced the Banque to suspend payments. Panic followed. Firms who were in the habit of relying on accommodation from the Banque could not pay their current expenses, and there was a run on the Société Générale itself. Aid from the government to the Banque prevented complete collapse, but rates of interest remained high. Henceforward all the Belgian banks became reluctant to encumber themselves with illiquid assets, and confined themselves to short-term lending. Activity for several years continued low.

The evidence relating to France gives a more complicated picture, with more windows on the outside world but rather less endogenous fluctuations than in Belgium, France being more advanced financially than industrially. The year 1836 had been preceded by a period of rapid credit expansion by the Bank of France and also by newly chartered issuing banks in competition with it, and there was a pronounced tendency to inflation of prices as activity grew. In 1836, as in Britain at the same time, the foreign exchanges became unfavourable. There was a sharp reduction in the amount of gold presented to the mint for coinage, and specie was shipped to the United States. Throughout most parts of France (though some departments remained unaffected) discount rates rose, and the Bank of France found itself faced with an internal drain as well as an external one. Prices fell, and 1837 opened with distress borrowing from the central bank at a high level. But although prices did not regain their former level, recovery seems to have come quite quickly. In fact, outside the trades reliant on the American market, the recession of 1837 in France appears to have been confined principally to the financial sphere. Employment in the iron industry continued to rise. But the check encountered before the end of 1838 was of a more substantial nature. The discount rate again rose, partly under the influence of renewed United States borrowing. This time the foreign exchanges did not give trouble, but confidence had already become very shaky before it was given the *coup de grâce* at the end of 1838 by the failure of the Banque de

Belgique. There followed a run on Lafitte's Bank in Paris, and what Tooke described as 'a much more severe pressure on...trade and manufactures than has been experienced here'.[1] This crisis reached its height in January 1839. Distress borrowing from the Bank of France again rose for a while to a high level.[2] But by the summer of 1839 the Bank of France was in a comfortable position again. In its issue of 31 May 1839 the *Circular to Bankers* was already expressing regret that conventional etiquette forbade the transference of some of the Bank of France's surplus gold to the Bank of England—a sentiment which later events demonstrated had crossed the minds of the members of the Bank of England's Committee of Treasury. Apart from some revival of railway building, activity and prices remained low after 1839, and discount rates and the volume of transactions on the Bourse continued to decline steadily till 1844–5.

It can be seen that fluctuations in industrial activity and in the money markets of France and Belgium in these years manifested a fair degree of independence of the contemporaneous ups and downs in Britain and the United States. The effect of continental fluctuations on Britain's exports was comparatively slight, for Belgium was not an important British market, and relatively violent fluctuations in French industry and finance had probably only a small effect on France's total national income. But in the London money market the influence of events on the Continent was felt more. Liberal banking policy in France, and still more in Belgium, kept discount rates on the Continent low in 1837 and encouraged the movement of short-term capital to London. But when the crash came in Belgium at the end of 1838, money was fairly plentiful in London, and the opportunity to earn crisis rates of interest led to a substantial though not long-lasting outflow of short-term capital from Britain.[3] The movement began to abate before the end of February 1839. In 1841 there was a repetition of a similar pattern of events. The continuing depression of trade led to a series of liquidity crises or near-crises in financial centres on the Continent, including a number of centres that till that time had escaped relatively unscathed. Failures of important firms were reported from Paris, Vienna, Frankfurt, Antwerp and elsewhere, and there was a movement of short-term funds from London to earn the high interest rates temporarily available.[4]

The capital movements described in the previous paragraph were motivated principally by interest-rate differentials. Those that took place in 1839 were of a different and rather more abnormal character, and require to be described at greater length.

The full story of the Bank of England's actions in 1839 did not emerge till some time after the event. In April 1839 the Bank's bullion was down to £4½ million, and the exchanges showed no signs of improvement. The Committee of Treasury—the committee responsible for most of the day-to-day conduct of the Bank's affairs—therefore decided to enter into a confidential arrangement with Rothschilds to negotiate the sale of bills to the value of a million sterling on

---

[1] Tooke, III, p. 75.

[2] Belgium was unfortunate by comparison in having no lender of last resort except the Treasury, whose performance of that function was very spasmodic and unsatisfactory.

[3] Tooke, III, pp. 74–75; *Circular to Bankers*, 25 January 1839, 22 February 1839; *Select Committee on Banks of Issue*, 1840, IV, Q. 1931 (G. W. Norman); Sir John Clapham, *The Bank of England* (1944), II, pp. 166–7.

[4] *Circular to Bankers*, 30 July 1841, 15 October 1841.

Paris and Hamburg. This arrangement enabled the Bank to carry through the month of May without any further serious encroachments on its reserve. In June, however, rumours of the agreement with Rothschilds began to reach Directors of the Bank who were not members of the Committee of Treasury and so had not previously been aware of what was going on. On the matter being raised at a meeting of the Court of Directors, a resolution was passed to the effect that direct action upon the exchanges was improper and should cease. The agreement with Rothschilds was accordingly terminated, and there naturally ensued a sudden further deterioration of the exchanges. It was not long before reports of what had happened became current on the Royal Exchange, and the belief spread to financial circles on the Continent that the Bank, having tried and then abandoned a policy of direct borrowing abroad, would shortly be obliged to suspend payments altogether. Continental finance houses therefore hastened to send all English bills in their portfolios to London for immediate discount.[1]

The drain on the Bank was therefore intensified, and it soon became apparent that vigorous action would be necessary to prevent suspension. The decision reached was to resort to a similar expedient to that which had been adopted earlier in the year, and had then been rejected in consequence of the resolution of the Court. This time the agents were Barings, and the success of the venture depended on the co-operation of the Bank of France. Bills were drawn on various French banking houses in favour of Barings, to whom the Bank of England transferred English securities as a guarantee. These bills were then sold in the normal way to satisfy the demand for foreign exchange, the Bank of France having undertaken to discount bills up to the value of 48 million francs should any difficulty be experienced in discounting them in the open market. By November 1839 the drain of gold from London had ceased, and by the beginning of 1840 Barings were able to liquidate all their engagements in Paris without detriment to the exchanges, and to restore the pledged securities to the Bank of England.[2] At the time, the policy adopted by the Bank was commonly considered unprecedented, and, by some, discreditable; but direct action by the Bank on the foreign exchanges was rather less of an innovation than was supposed, since it had been resorted to in 1832 and again in 1836, when about £500,000 was apparently raised in Paris by the Bank to help meet the drain to the United States.[3]

4. THE COURSE AND CAUSES OF INTERNATIONAL BULLION MOVEMENTS

We are now in a position to attempt to piece together an account of the factors responsible for the bullion movements which occurred during the several phases of the period.

The exchanges had been very favourable during 1832 and the first half of 1833,

[1] *Select Committee on Commercial Distress*, 1847–8, VIII, Part III, QQ. 838–9 (J. H. Palmer). That fears for the convertibility of the pound accounted for a large part of the drain of 1839 was also stated by Palmer, Norman and Loyd before the Committee on Banks of Issue in 1840: 1840, IV, QQ. 1362, 1481–2, 1932, 2851. Cf. also *Bankers' Magazine* (1847), p. 210.
[2] For details of these transactions, see Clapham, II, pp. 168–70 and references there; also *Bankers' Magazine, loc. cit.*
[3] *S.C. of 1840*, QQ. 1440–52 (J. H. Palmer).

and by the autumn of 1833 were returning to more normal levels.[1] By the end of 1833 a decided turn against us was felt, and the Bank of England's reserve began to fall (see Chart 13, p. 170). This state of affairs continued until the spring of 1835. The exchanges then turned sharply in our favour and the drain of gold ceased. A few months later a reflux of gold began and persisted till the spring of 1836.

Between 1833 and 1835 capital and current items in the balance of payments were working in much the same direction, and it is not possible to decide the relative importance of each in causing the adverse tendency of the balance of payments in 1833 and 1834 and the improvement in 1835. No doubt both played a part. In 1833 and 1834 the growth of imports was outstripping that of exports, but in 1835 the fall in the volume of imports of many commodities,[2] together with the expansion of exports to the United States, caused this tendency to be temporarily reversed. On capital account, the course of the Spanish security speculation (see above) also conformed well to the behaviour of gold movements, growing in intensity till May 1835 and then collapsing; Horsley Palmer endeavoured to explain the movement of the exchanges entirely with reference to this cause.[3]

There is some uncertainty about the destination of the gold that was exported from England in 1833–5. Palmer evidently supposed that it had gone to the Continent, but it is difficult to believe that there was not also a drain to the United States, at least in 1834. 1834 was a year of recession in the United States in which imports from Britain were reduced and even so had to be bought largely on credit.[4] Exchange on London in New York fell to greater discount in 1834 than it did in 1836, a year when gold movement from England to the United States undoubtedly took place. In 1835 the tremendous recovery of exports to the American market was sufficient to restore the rate of exchange between London and New York more nearly to normal, but not to cause the gold to flow back again to London. The reflux of that year was European in origin.

From the spring of 1836 till September of the same year the exchanges were unfavourable and there was a drain of gold from the Bank of England. The Bank's reserve continued to fall till early in 1837, but the exchanges had ceased to be unfavourable by September 1836 and the drain that took place after that was internal in character.[5]

For 1836, as for the previous years, the distinction between the effects of capital movements and of current account movements is not easy to make. The need to rebuild stocks of imported goods depleted in 1835 made the balance of trade more unfavourable, apparently, than in any of the earlier years of our period— though by no means as unfavourable as it became a few years later—and there is

---

[1] Statistics of rates of exchange in London on leading Continental centres may be found in appendices to the reports of the Select Committees on money and banking that sat in 1832, 1840, 1841 and 1848 (1831–2, vii, 1840, iv, 1841 (1st session) v, 1847–8, viii, Part ii). For the dollar-pound exchange rate, see W. B. Smith and A. H. Cole, *Fluctuations in American Business, 1790–1860* (1935), p. 77.

[2] See p. 16.

[3] Palmer, *Causes and Consequences*, pp. 28–9; *S.C. of 1840*, QQ. 1183–90. Cf. Tooke, ii, pp. 281–4.

[4] See p. 46.

[5] *S.C. of 1840*, Q. 1264 (J. H. Palmer); Tooke, ii, p. 304.

no doubt that this applied still more to our relations with Continental Europe than to our relations with the United States. But the drain of gold that took place was exclusively to the United States, and the Paris and Hamburg exchanges were only moderately unfavourable throughout the year. In public discussion of the causes of the drain, all the emphasis was placed on the increase in lending to the United States. An increasing proportion of exports to the American market were being financed by acceptances of the Anglo-American finance houses discounted in the London market,[1] and at the same time the purchase of United States bonds was proceeding apace and Americans were being granted large credits by British firms to finance imports from the Far East. In addition, the United States administration was pursuing a deliberate policy of increasing the amount of gold in circulation, and to that end had recently reduced the gold content of the eagle (= $10).[2] Gold shipment from London to New York was reported to be clearly profitable for the first time in *The Times* of 20 May, but a slight drain had by then already been in progress for some weeks.

In speaking of the drain of 1836, Horsley Palmer observed: 'if all these circumstances be adverted to...the surprise will be not that some, but that so small a portion of bullion should have been abstracted from the Bank of England'.[3] The amount lost by the external drain was in fact about £2½ million, rather less than had been lost in 1834, though, since the reserve had been higher at the start of 1834, the drain then had caused less anxiety. The extent of the drain in 1836 was indeed surprisingly small, and it was also rather surprising that there was no loss of gold to countries other than the United States. The explanation was probably that the rise in interest rates, together possibly with a certain amount of direct borrowing on the part of the Bank of England, caused a movement of short-term capital from the Continent to London, of a rather greater magnitude than was immediately appreciated at the time.

The action undertaken by the Bank of England effectively restrained the growth of capital export to the United States,[4] and by September 1836 the external drain was checked. When exactly gold began to flow back from abroad is not clear, but it was probably already doing so early in 1837, and this continued throughout 1837. The internal drain of gold from the Bank that marked the earlier months of 1837 ceased later in the year, and the Bank's reserve then increased rapidly.

In 1837, as in 1835, the forces tending to bring about a reflux of bullion from abroad were not precisely the reverse of those that had caused the preceding drain. The drain of 1836 had been to the United States; but in 1837 United States net imports of specie were higher than in 1836, and there is no suggestion that any of the gold recovered by the Bank of England came from that source. Instead the reflux was from Europe. The great fall in the value of British imports in 1837 applied to goods imported from northern Europe no less than from other sources, and at the same time there was a marked expansion of our exports to northern Europe. There was also, as has been seen, some further transfer of

[1] It was estimated that by the middle of 1837 there was still £8 million of mercantile indebtedness outstanding from the United States to England (*Edinburgh Review* (July 1837), pp. 236–7).
[2] Palmer, pp. 29–33. Cf. D. R. Dewey, *Financial History of the United States* (1902), pp. 210–12.
[3] Palmer, p. 32.   [4] See pp. 57–8.

short-term capital to London, since discount rates still tended to be higher in London than on the Continent. As far as our balance with Europe was concerned, however, it seems that the main source of improvement was in the balance of trade. The main source of improvement in our overall balance, on the other hand, appears to have lain in the reduction of lending, since although Imlah's figures show a certain improvement in the balance of trade, this is, for reasons earlier explained, of questionable significance. The ratio of aggregate imports to aggregate exports was actually higher in 1837 than it had been in 1836. The main reason for this was the precipitous fall in exports to the United States, which was rendered not inconsistent with a more or less neutral balance of payments between Britain and the United States by the virtual cessation of British purchases of American long-term and short-term securities.

In 1838 the Bank's reserve position was felt to be sufficiently strong to justify the celebrated transmission of £1 million to the United States. At the time when the gold was sent to America the influx from the Continent was still continuing, and no adverse tendency in the exchanges was felt till near the end of the year. The slight reduction in the Bank's bullion during 1838 was attributed to an increase in domestic demand for coin consequent upon the recovery of business from the recession of 1837.[1] At the end of 1838, however, the exchanges turned, and from then until November 1839 they moved against us very steeply. Gold flowed out, and the Bank's reserve fell to a lower level than at any other time in the period. The causes of this drain are, for once, relatively easy to discern. Chief among them was the sudden and enormous rise in expenditure on imported corn. The corn being imported as soon as the harvest of 1838 was known to be deficient, bills drawn in payment for it were becoming due towards the end of the year. For a while the flow of short-term capital to support shaken banks in France and Belgium was also a source of anxiety to the Bank; but the drain of bullion continued unabated after this had ceased. Finally, in June, came the weakening of foreigners' confidence in the soundness of the Bank which has already been described. The balance of payments with the United States in 1839 was not one of the sources of the drain, and, indeed, there was a certain import of specie from the United States during the year, notwithstanding the further increase in British purchases of foreign securities. The peculiar circumstances giving rise to this result were outlined in Chapter V.

The drain was halted by the loan negotiated through the good offices of Barings and the Bank of France. But this could not have provided a permanent solution had the balance of payments not shown any improvement on other scores. In fact in 1840 the drain of 1839 was not repeated, but the Bank's reserve did not register any substantial recovery. Corn imports remained high, and the ratio of imports to exports was actually slightly higher than in 1839. It is therefore rather surprising that the Bank managed to avoid further loss of bullion. The suspension of the Bank of the United States had put a stop to purchase of American securities, and evidently this and the reversal of the flow of 'hot money' to Europe that had occurred in 1839 were sufficient to counteract any adverse tendency there may have been from the balance of trade.

In 1841 the movement of the Bank's reserve was similar to what it had been in 1840, tending slightly upwards but not increasing to more than a moderate

[1] *S.C. of 1840*, QQ. 1334–7 (J. H. Palmer).

extent. In 1842 the tide turned decisively, and by the end of the year the reserve was at a higher level than it had been since 1833.

In 1841 and 1842 corn imports remained fairly high; contrary to what has sometimes been asserted, the recovery in the Bank's reserve in 1842 was not to any great extent the result of an improvement in the harvest. (The further increase in the reserve in 1843 was a different story; then the reduction in corn imports did play a large part.) But the prices of most imports were falling steeply, and although exports to most parts of the world were languishing, exports to northern Europe were doing very well. The overall ratio of imports to exports was not, indeed, much lower than it had been in the years before 1839. But the cessation of capital export meant that our balance of payments with the United States was approximately in equilibrium, notwithstanding the low level of commodity exports to the American market.

The statistics do not suggest that the balance of trade was much more favourable in 1842 than in 1841, so the failure of the gold reflux to assume large dimensions until 1842 must be attributed to the movements of short-term capital to the Continent of Europe in 1841 that were alluded to on p. 90 above.

5. STABILITY AND INSTABILITY IN THE BALANCE OF PAYMENTS

We may now turn to consider some of the conclusions suggested by the foregoing chronicle of events.

The first point which attracts attention is the contrast between the behaviour of the balance *vis-à-vis* Europe and that of the balance *vis-à-vis* the United States. In the theory of international trade, it is commonly supposed that a country will tend to have an active balance of payments during periods of depression and a passive balance of payments during periods of prosperity, the argument being that low incomes and prices discourage imports and encourage exports, while high incomes and prices have the reverse effect. As far as our relations with France and the other leading countries on the Continent were concerned, this conception of the interaction between the level of activity and the balance of trade seems to have a considerable measure of truth, although its application stands out less obviously in the prosperous years than in the depressed ones. The most evident instances are to be found in the reflux of gold in 1837 and 1842, both these being years of contracting trade marked by low import values and high values of exports to northern Europe. On the other hand, even in our relations with Europe this tendency was not infrequently outweighed in its influence on the balance of payments by forces tending in a different direction. Complications arose from corn imports and from capital movements. The cyclically arbitrary factor of corn imports had a great effect on the balance of payments between 1839 and 1842; in its absence there would probably have been little or no drain in 1839 and a tendency to a much more favourable balance of payments in the subsequent years.

Capital movements between Britain and the Continent also bore no unique relation to the state of trade, though unlike corn imports they were much influenced by it. The tendency of short-term capital movements was normally to equalise by arbitrage discount rates between London and Continental centres.

There was thus a flow of funds to London in 1836 and 1837, when first the drain to the United States and then the internal discredit caused money to be in shorter supply in London than on the Continent. Similarly, there was an outflow in 1838 and 1841, when there was greater credit stringency abroad. The tendency to equalise discount rates did not mean that this type of capital movement was uniquely associated with either the state of trade or with the behaviour of other items in the balance of payments, since credit stringency might result either from a boom or from a crisis, and either from an internal or from an external drain. This, moreover, was not the only type of capital movement between Britain and the Continent; there was, in addition, the movement of long-term capital in the Spanish security speculation of 1833–5, which was probably fostered by the recovery of trade at home but which collapsed well before trade had reached its peak, and also the peculiar short-term capital movements of 1839—the disequilibrating flow of 'hot money' and the credit arranged with the Bank of France to offset it.

In general, therefore, the balance of trade with Europe tended to move in what may be called the orthodox, anti-cyclical, manner, but this tendency did not always communicate itself to the balance of payments because of the irregularities of corn imports and capital movements. The balance of trade with the United States, in contrast, did not tend to move anti-cyclically but rather the reverse. The United States was subject to fluctuations in income and activity which corresponded roughly in time with those in Britain and were not less violent, and at the same time her marginal propensity to import was very high. Hence cyclical fluctuations in the value of British exports to the United States apparently tended to be greater in proportion than cyclical fluctuations in the value of British imports from the United States, so that the balance of trade tended to move favourably to Britain in the boom and unfavourably in the slump. However, in years of boom American securities found a good market in Britain, while in the slump they represented an unattractive proposition. The behaviour of capital movements therefore tended to offset in some degree that of the trade balance, and this to an important extent helped to stabilise the balance of payments between the two countries. With the two forces pulling in opposite directions, there was no regular relationship between the phase of the cycle and the state of the balance. In 1834 it was an American recession that turned the exchanges against us; in 1836 it was an American boom; while in the early 1840's the fall in British lending to the United States and the movement in Britain's disfavour of the balance of trade appear to have been of approximately equal magnitude.

On two occasions (1834 and 1836) the bullion lost by the Bank of England appears to have found its way, at least in part, to the United States, and in 1838 a further transfer of bullion of a rather different character took place in the same direction. Only once, on the other hand, in 1839, was there a record of a reverse movement of gold back from the United States, and that was not of any great extent. In each of the years when there was a substantial reflux of bullion (1835, 1837 and 1842), the source from which it came was the Continent. Since the Bank's reserve was at about the same level at the end of the period as it had been at the beginning, it follows that the movements of bullion which took place served to effect a net transfer of gold from the Continent of Europe through

London to the United States, as well as serving as a stop-gap to fill temporary disequilibria in the British balance of payments.

From what has been said, it is evident that the orthodox conception of the relation between the trade cycle and the balance of payments, according to which the boom leads to an outflow and the slump to an inflow of gold through their effects on imports and exports, does have a certain applicability to our period (especially if the consequences of corn imports are neglected), but that it is, on the other hand, far from being the whole truth. Not merely was the anti-cyclical movement of the balance of payments much blurred by the working of various complicating factors, but even in so far as the overall movement was anticyclical, this was as much the result of capital movements as of movements in the balance of trade. For example, in the recession of 1837 the improvement in the balance of payments on capital account with the United States was apparently not accompanied by any general improvement in the balance of trade, though there was an improvement in the balance of trade with Europe. Similarly, in the early 1840's it was largely the cessation of lending to the United States that enabled the high level of corn imports to be sustained without damage to the overall balance of payments. The orthodox view described above may thus be said to be a more or less accurate description of the behaviour in our period of Britain's balance of trade (excluding corn) with European countries, but it is not applicable to the balance of trade with other areas, and it fails to give sufficient attention to the importance of capital movements.

Over the period as a whole the Bank of England's reserve remained roughly constant, and though some difficult passages were experienced, fluctuations in the reserve for the most part were kept within bounds. It is natural, before leaving discussion of the overall balance of payments, to inquire briefly what was the mechanism by which this result was attained.

Some parts of the answer have already been suggested. The gold standard mechanism was not called upon to maintain equilibrium in the balance of payments between Britain and the more economically backward of her customers and suppliers, since these countries could scarcely be said to be effectively on the gold standard. In relations with the United States, moreover, the tendency for capital movements to cancel out movements in the balance of trade tended to keep disequilibria in the aggregate balance of payments within bounds. The magnitude of the problem was thus subject to important limitations at the start. However, equilibrium in the balance with the United States was far from perfect, and there remained the problem of the balance with Europe.

The nature of the mechanism of international adjustment was one of the principal points at issue in the contemporary controversy between the Banking School and the Currency School.[1] The Banking School emphasised what they called 'the terminability of drains', that is to say, the tendency of forces giving rise to balance of payments deficits to come to an end of their own accord before any great period of time had elapsed. Corn imports necessitated by a bad harvest were a favourite example. A natural implication of this view was that a major contribution to preventing balance of payments disequilibria from causing disruption in the economy would be brought about if the Bank of

---

[1] For further brief discussion of this controversy, with references to the literature, see pp. 166–8.

England could contrive to increase the normal level of its reserve, since as things stood the reserve was usually equivalent to less than the value of two months' imports, and even relatively small disequilibria in the balance of payments were therefore liable to be a source of embarrassment. As against this point of view, the Currency School were the precursors of gold-standard orthodoxy. They argued that the effect of gold movements on prices and hence on imports and exports was the natural way for equilibrium in the balance of payments to be preserved, and they emphasised the importance of not allowing banking policy to stand in the way of this adjustment. Currency School authors were usually vague on the exact mechanism by which gold flows were supposed to affect prices. Later gold-standard theory placed all the emphasis on the rate of interest —what we have called the monetary effect of balance-of-payments disequilibria—whereas the modern theory of international trade gives more prominence to the direct or foreign-trade multiplier effect. The two aspects of the matter can be considered together, since in either case the argument is that an adverse balance of payments, by lowering prices and/or incomes, brings about, or at least helps to bring about, its own corrective.

As applied to the events of the 1830's, the Banking School doctrine of 'the terminability of drains' has a good deal to be said for it. The forces making for drains and refluxes were mostly either cyclical, with a short period of oscillation, or else arbitrary, and hence again of short duration. Thus the speculation in Spanish securities was in its very nature bound to be short-lived. The fall in United States imports in 1834 was the result of a very temporary recession. The financial stringencies on the Continent which led to the export of short-term capital in 1838–9 and 1841 soon passed off. Even the purchase of United States securities in 1836 would probably by itself have reached a natural terminus, though the steps taken by the Bank of England undoubtedly hastened the end. The same thing was largely true of periods of reflux; for example, the low level of imports which contributed to the favourable balance of 1835 was achieved at the cost of disstocking which could not continue. In contrast to these cases, the flight of 'hot money' in 1839 was not terminable in character, but rather tended to feed upon itself; precisely for this reason the Bank of England was obliged to resort to unusual measures in order to counteract it.

It is difficult to gauge the importance of adjustment effected either by the orthodox gold-standard mechanism or by the foreign-trade multiplier. As is the case with later periods in the nineteenth century,[1] the temporary adjustment brought about by the effect of discount-rate movements on the flow of international capital is much easier to discern than any adjustment effected through the price level. The sensitivity of capital movements to changes in the discount rate in itself largely justified the efforts of the Bank to maintain an association between the state of exchanges and the ease of credit.[2] The most obvious example was in 1836, when the restrictive policy of the Bank of England helped to check the export of capital to the United States and to attract short-term funds from Europe. In 1839 also the volume of American securities sold in London would

[1] Cf. R. S. Sayers, 'The development of central banking after Bagehot', *Economic History Review* (1951), pp. 109–16.
[2] See pp. 168–75 for a demonstration that, despite charges to the contrary, the Bank did endeavour to maintain this association.

almost certainly have been a good deal higher if conditions in the money market had not been tight.

As far as adjustment through incomes and prices is concerned, it may be observed that the foreign-trade multiplier effect can have helped to stabilise the balance of payments only on occasions like 1839 when the source of the disequilibrium lay in items which influenced incomes directly. It would not operate when the adverse tendency had other origins, as in 1836. The significance generally of adjustment through incomes and prices, whether by the foreign-trade multiplier or through the operation of the discount rate, cannot really be assessed without anticipating the conclusions of Chapter XII, since, although fluctuations in incomes and prices undoubtedly had much effect—and on some occasions, at least, a stabilizing effect—on the balance of payments, it is another matter to say that these fluctuations were themselves principally the result of anterior movements in the balance of payments. In fact, as will be seen in Chapter XII, this can scarcely be said normally to have been the case.

But in any event it seems fairly clear that in the three years of most conspicuous decline in the Bank's reserve, 1834, 1836 and 1839, the *immediate* cause leading the drain to be arrested did not lie in a general deflation. In 1835 the boom was gaining momentum rather than being checked at the time when the exchanges turned in our favour. In 1836 the external drain was corrected before any marked recession in incomes or prices had been felt. In 1839 the drain was stopped only by the loan from France. It is possible, however, that when some adverse element in the balance persisted for several years, as happened with the corn imports of 1838–42, the consequent depressing effect had time to bring about a reduction in the demand for imports and an increase in the supply of exports. Corn imports undoubtedly contributed to the gravity of the slump in the early 1840's, and this in turn was partly responsible for the improvement in the balance of payments at the end of the period. But it is hard to resist the conclusion that in general adjustment through incomes and prices played a much smaller part in the correction of balance-of-payments disequilibria than did the various other factors that have been mentioned.

6. THE THEORY OF THE INCOME BALANCE

We have now endeavoured to deal, as far as it is possible to do so, with the course and causes of changes in the overall balance of payments and the bullion movements with which they were associated. It remains to discuss the behaviour of those items in the balance of payments which contributed to the direct or foreign-trade multiplier effect.

As was argued in Chapter II, the magnitude which is relevant for this purpose is the difference between the value of exports, which constitute an inflationary factor, and the value of expenditure by consumers upon imports, which are a deflationary factor. This difference will be referred to as the income balance. Changes in this magnitude from year to year indicate the nature of the direct effect exercised by foreign trade on incomes. Thus, if the income balance is said to rise, this means that the net direct effect of foreign trade in the year in question was such as to cause either a rise in incomes, or else, if deflationary forces were at work independently of foreign trade, a smaller fall in incomes than would otherwise have occurred.[1]

It is not necessary at the present stage to discuss the *causes* of the movements which took place in the overall income balance, since the various constituent elements in the income balance have already been analysed at length in Chapters III–VI. What is required now is to assess the net effect of the workings of these various factors, and to comment on the implications of the results shown.

The statistical difficulties of arriving at an estimate of year-to-year changes in the income balance preclude anything more than a rough approximation. There are also certain difficulties of interpretation which are economic rather than statistical in character, and these require brief discussion at this point.

The difficulties arise principally from the distinction between 'induced' and 'autonomous' changes in imports, and to a less extent from a similar distinction with regard to exports. A change in expenditure on imports may be the result of a change in the level of the national income, in which case it is termed 'induced', or it may be due to an 'autonomous' shift in consumers' expenditure from imports to home-produced goods or vice versa. Examples of autonomous increases in imports would be when a bad harvest leads to importation of foreign corn or when there is for some reason a reduction in the supply of some imported commodity in inelastic demand. Likewise a rise in exports might be due to an increase in foreign demand and so be autonomous from the British point of view, or else it might be the result of a cyclically induced change in supply price coupled with a foreign demand elasticity significantly different from unity. The statistically observed movements in the income balance reflect a combination of autonomous and induced elements which cannot be separated. What is the significance of this? Not, assuredly, that we should endeavour to eliminate induced elements before arriving at an estimate of the inflationary or deflationary tendency of the income balance; an increase in imports represents an equal drain from the circular flow of incomes regardless of whether it is autonomous or induced.[2] But the distinction does affect the interpretation to be placed on any observed movement in the income balance, in two important respects.

In the first place, the distinction affects the activity or passivity of the role to be ascribed to the income balance in relation to changes in the level of income. Induced movements in the income balance, unlike autonomous ones, cannot by definition initiate a change in the level of income in either an upwards or a downwards direction. All that they can do is to alter the magnitude—not the direction—of a movement in income that has been initiated in some other way.

[1] If we had evidence to enable us to calculate the marginal propensity to consume—which we have not—and if the conditions necessary for this type of analysis to be legitimate could be assumed to be satisfied—which is very uncertain—the size of the net effect on income would be measured by the product of the income balance and the multiplier, the latter being given by the formula $1/(1-c)$, where c is the marginal propensity to consume. This multiplier is, of course, different from the investment multiplier, the formula for which in an open system is $1/(1-c+m)$, where m is the marginal propensity to import. On this point, and also more generally on the matters discussed in the present section, see D. H. Robertson, 'Mr Clark and the foreign trade multiplier', *Economic Journal* (1939), pp. 354–6, and G. Haberler, *Prosperity and Depression* (1943 edition), pp. 461–73.

[2] In terms of the multiplier analysis, the multiplier applicable to the actual income balance is $1/(1-c)$, irrespective of the relative importance of induced and autonomous items in the balance. On the other hand, the multiplier that would be appropriate to the autonomous items in the balance, if they could be isolated and taken by themselves, would be the same as the investment multiplier, viz. $1/(1-c+m)$.

In the second place, although the effect *on the level of income* of a given change in the income balance does not depend on the relative importance of induced and autonomous items, the same is not true of the effect of the income balance on the level of expenditure on home-produced consumer goods. A fall in imports which is induced by a fall in the national income will reduce the extent to which expenditure on home goods falls, but it cannot altogether prevent it from falling. On the other hand, an autonomous fall in imports (assuming no change takes place in the propensity to consume) represents a switch in the pattern of consumer spending away from imports towards home goods which is a positively favourable factor and which might in certain circumstances result in a rise in expenditure on home goods, even if there took place simultaneously an autonomous fall in exports larger than the fall in imports, and hence an adverse movement occurred in the overall income balance and in income. If this seems paradoxical, consider the limiting case where there are autonomous falls of equal extent in both imports and exports. Aggregate income will then remain unaltered, and the decline in incomes earned in the export industries will be exactly offset by the increase in incomes earned in industries catering for the home market. It is plain that if the autonomous fall in exports had somewhat exceeded that in imports, so that income had fallen, expenditure on home goods might still have risen to some extent. Some examples of these difficulties will be encountered as we proceed.

7. THE WORKING OF THE INCOME BALANCE

In order to calculate with accuracy the net direct effect of the foreign-trade balance on incomes we should require not merely to know the volume of imports actually consumed in each year and their prices, but also to make the corrections called for by the c.i.f. valuation of imports and the f.o.b. valuation of exports and by the presence of other unrecorded invisible items in the balance. This we can do only by a great deal of guesswork. The results which emerge when we make what appear to be the most plausible assumptions are shown in Table 10. The figures given in the second column (and hence also in the final column) contain a large margin of error, but it is hoped that the principal conclusions suggested by the figures are not misleading.[1]

The main impressions to be derived from inspection of Table 10 are that the cessation of corn imports at the beginning of the period helped to initiate the up-

---

[1] The procedure by which the figures in Table 10 have been arrived at is as follows. The figures for corn imports are derived from Table 4, adjusted for certain movements in stocks on which there is reliable information, in particular the tendency for the supply of imported wheat for a whole harvest year to be entered for consumption in the preceding autumn. The figures for exports are derived directly from the declared values. The real difficulty is to calculate expenditure on non-corn imports and to allow for the invisible items in the balance. The figures given in Table 10 are based on the assumption that the commodities included in the 'A' indices given in Chapter III (see above, pp. 11–12, 27) are representative of the generality of non-corn imports with respect to the ratio between net volume imported and volume taken into consumption. The method used has been to multiply Imlah's estimated cost of net non-corn imports by the ratio of import consumption index A to net import volume index A, and reduce the result by one-third so as to provide a rough allowance for shipping and other invisible earnings. [Very closely similar results are yielded by recalculation of these figures on the basis of the more elaborate estimates of invisible earnings given in Professor A. H. Imlah's article, 'British balance of payments and export of capital, 1816–1913', *Economic History Review* (1952), pp. 208–39, which appeared after the present work had been completed.]

swing; that between 1834 and 1836 the rise in imports and the rise in exports to a large extent cancelled each other out; that the decline in expenditure on imports in 1837 was insufficient to offset the deflationary consequences of the fall in exports; that the foreign balance contributed to an important extent to the recovery of 1838—especially when account is taken of the fact that the rise in corn imports did not become substantial till the closing months of the year; that in the absence of favourable factors outside the sphere of foreign trade the year 1839 must have witnessed a serious recession; and that in the concluding years of the period foreign trade acted as a stabiliser in face of the general downward trend of income. These impressions require expansion and elucidation in a number of respects.

Table 10. *Estimated year-to-year changes in the income balance* (*in £ million*)

Year	Increase (+) or decrease (−) in			Net favourable (+) or unfavourable (−) change in income balance
	Expenditure on imported corn	Expenditure on other imports minus invisible earnings	Exports	
1833	−5	+5	+3	+3
1834	−1	+4	+2	−1
1835	0	+4	+6	+2
1836	0	+6	+6	0
1837	0	−7	−11	−4
1838	+3	+1	+8	+4
1839	+6	+4	+3	−7
1840	−1	−3	−2	+2
1841	0	−1	0	+1
1842	−1	−6	−4	+3

On the face of it, the smallness of the movements in the income balance in most years (especially when corn imports are excluded) and their tendency as often as not to offset rather than aggravate the prevailing movements of income and activity as a whole must occasion some surprise, in view of the importance commonly attached to the foreign balance in explaining the course of British business cycles. But it is perhaps rather less surprising when one considers the mechanics of the process.

Some of the points raised earlier in this chapter apropos of the overall balance of payments are also relevant in discussion of the income balance. The income balance, like the balance of trade, appears as a rule to have moved cyclically as far as trade with the United States was concerned and contra-cyclically as far as trade with Europe was concerned; the two thus tend to cancel each other out, at least in part. It was argued above that the balance of payments with more backward countries was not subject to important fluctuations; but the same does not necessarily hold with regard to the income balance, since, even apart from capital movements, fluctuations in the holdings of import inventories in Britain meant that consumers' expenditure on imports was liable to differ significantly from the aggregate value of imports brought into the country in a given year. In years when stocks of imports were increasing, exports from the countries from which they were drawn and hence also British exports to those countries tended to rise more (or fall less) than consumers' expenditure on the imports in question, with net inflationary effect. Inventory fluctuations had on some occasions important consequences of this sort. However, they did not usually operate with any force in the same direction for more than a year or two at a time, and they therefore affected the main cyclical movement less than they affected fluctuations of shorter duration.

Taking the period by stages, we find that after the important improvement in 1833 owing to the fall in expenditure on imported corn, the upswing till 1836 was characterised by the approximate cancelling out of favourable and unfavourable elements in the income balance such as we should expect on the grounds stated above.[1] When allowance is made for the tendency of Imlah's estimates of import values, on which Table 10 depends, to be excessive in years of steeply rising prices, it appears probable that there was actually some favourable movement in the income balance in 1836, although the figures given show no change in either direction in that year. The behaviour of the income balance in 1835 and 1836 would seem on this reckoning to have been much the same. The slight favourable movement in 1835 and 1836 contrasts with the slight unfavourable movement in 1834 and with the tendency of non-corn items in the balance to yield an unfavourable result in 1833. But the similarity between the behaviour of the income balance in 1835 and its behaviour in 1836 was due to dissimilar causes. In 1835 exports to America rose very rapidly, and the improvement in the income balance would have been still greater had there not been a decided check to the rate of growth of exports to other non-European markets on account of the relatively low volume of imports and the heavy drawing on import inventories that accompanied it. In 1836, on the other hand, the rate of growth of exports to the United States was much less than in 1835, but the extremely high value of imports which resulted from a combination of high prices, high consumption and stock accumulation caused exports to other markets to rise spectacularly.

In 1837 the trends of 1835-6 were violently reversed, and the net effect of the simultaneous steep fall in exports and in imports was evidently seriously deflationary. 1837 is a year with respect to which the distinction discussed earlier in this chapter between autonomous and induced movements in the income balance assumes some importance. The net movement in the income balance was decidedly unfavourable, and there can be little doubt that the working of the foreign-trade multiplier brought about a substantial fall in incomes. But if it could be shown that the very large fall in expenditure on imports was to an important extent autonomous in character, it would follow that the effect of the income balance on *the level of expenditure on home-produced goods* was not necessarily very severe. In theory, as was argued above (p. 101), the effect might even have been positively favourable, in which case the deflationary consequences of the fall in the income balance would have been confined entirely to

[1] The balance is shown in Table 10 to move favourably in 1833 and unfavourably in 1834; but it may be observed that measurement by calendar years is here probably slightly misleading, since import prices fell pronouncedly in the middle of 1834 before they began to rise again towards the end of the year. The period when the income balance was moving most unfavourably was probably at the end of 1833 and the beginning of 1834, when import prices were at their highest and the most rapid fall in corn imports was already over. The minor recession in the United States also contributed to the deterioration of the income balance in 1834.

the export trades. The question really turns on whether the fall in import prices in 1837 was chiefly induced or autonomous. That it was in part autonomous has been argued in Chapter III, where it was suggested that some fall in prices was inevitable after the high levels that had been attained as the result of the need to build up stocks in 1836. It is unlikely, however, that a sufficient part of the fall in import prices in 1837 was autonomous to prevent the income balance from exerting a depressive effect, possibly a severe one, on the level of demand for home goods; but none the less the autonomous element in the fall in import prices probably does go some way to account for the surprising firmness of certain indices of home consumption in 1837.[1]

Until the growth of corn imports in the closing months of the year, the movement of the income balance in 1838 was very favourable, and the recovery of this year is the clearest case in the period when a change in the income balance (independent of corn) had a substantial share in the responsibility for causing trade as a whole to move in the direction it did. There was a revival of exports to the United States, and for once this was not offset by an adverse movement in the income balance *vis-à-vis* the Continent of Europe, in parts of which a boom of moderate proportions, as we saw earlier in this chapter, in this year reached its peak.[2] At the same time, import stocks were again being built up, and exports to other countries therefore rose to a somewhat greater extent than did our consumers' expenditure on imports derived from them. 1838, then, like 1837, was one of the occasions such as was naturally liable to come about from time to time when the various elements in the income balance failed to cancel out. But such a combination of favourable factors could not be of long duration, and already by the autumn of 1838 corn imports were turning the tide.

Corn imports dominated the income balance in 1839. In their absence he interaction of the various complicated factors at work in the balance of trade—recession in Belgium and France, moderate expansion of exports to the United States, rises in many important import prices, with in some cases decreases and in others increases in import inventories—would have produced a certain deterioration in the income balance; but this deterioration would not have been very great, and in the event corn imports were responsible for much the greater part of the serious adverse movement that took place.

The movement of the income balance in 1840–2 was favourable and acted as a stabilizer in face of the general downward tendency of income. The improvement in the income balance in 1840 was largely due to the disappearance of certain of the abnormal (non-cyclical) circumstances that had adversely affected the balance, particularly on the import side, in 1839, and was not mainly caused, as far as we can tell, by an income-induced fall in the demand for imports. Likewise in 1841 the recovery in exports to the United States, again not a characteristic feature of the recession phase as such, was largely responsible for such improvement as occurred in the aggregate income balance. Only in 1842, when there was apparently substantial involuntary accumulation of import inventories, was there a considerable improvement of the income balance attributable to the contraction process itself.

[1] Cf. pp. 209–11.
[2] Above, pp. 88–90. The rise in exports to northern Europe in 1837 was probably also due in part to this.

The general conclusions to be drawn from the foregoing discussion of the behaviour of the income balance will appear in better perspective in Chapter XII, where the various domestic and foreign influences bearing upon the level of income and employment will be viewed in conjunction. The results so far reached appear to suggest that the direct effect of the foreign trade balance on incomes, while going a long way to explain the recession of 1837 and the recovery in 1838, and to a somewhat less extent the recovery of 1833, does not serve in itself to explain the main cyclical swing. However, this conclusion is derived from an inspection of figures in which induced and autonomous changes are combined and are difficult to disentangle. Since the broad cyclical movement of the value of non-corn imports was undoubtedly largely induced by changes in income, it is perfectly possible and indeed likely that *autonomous* movements in the balance of trade did operate in a cyclical rather than a neutral or anti-cyclical fashion. But since the aggregate income balance as often as not moved anti-cyclically, it remains true that fluctuations in the sphere of foreign trade were not in themselves *sufficient* to account for observed fluctuations in business as a whole, even though certain parts of our foreign trade balance—most obviously that arising out of trade with the United States—may have behaved in such a way as to support whatever other forces were tending to produce cyclical movements in the economy.

CHAPTER VIII

CONSTRUCTION: RAILWAYS, BUILDING
AND SHIPBUILDING

1. INTRODUCTION

IN the previous chapters, we have discussed the circumstances underlying the impact on incomes in Britain of fluctuations in different components of the nation's balance of payments. We now pass on to a discussion of the behaviour of domestic investment. In this field our knowledge is inevitably much more fragmentary and unsatisfactory than it is in the sphere of foreign trade. As far as foreign trade is concerned, the Trade and Navigation Accounts, for all their shortcomings, do provide a fairly adequate statistical skeleton. For home investment, and indeed for domestic production generally, there is nothing comparable at our disposal.

A large proportion of the total of domestic investment consisted of investment in industrial capital—for example, in plant and equipment in the cotton industry. It is not possible to analyse the course of this type of investment without discussing the general cyclical experience throughout the period of the industries in which the investment took place. Investment of this description will therefore be dealt with in Chapters IX and X below. In the present chapter we shall be concerned with the leading forms of constructional investment, namely, the building of railways, houses and ships. Some of the theoretical implications of the topics discussed in this chapter will be further commented on in Chapter XII.

2. RAILWAYS

At the beginning of 1833 there were less than 200 miles of railway in operation in Great Britain. By the end of 1842 the railway mileage opened was nearly 2000.[1] This was the net result of the railway boom of the 1830's. It was on a smaller scale than the 'mania' of the next decade, which added some 4500 miles of track to the national network.[2] But the lines projected in the 1830's were more than just a foretaste of things to come. The mileage then undertaken became the foundation of the British railway system. By the end of the 1830's, railway building ranked among the most important of the nation's investment industries. Between 1833 and 1843 a sum in the region of £50 million was spent on the construction of railways and the purchase of rolling stock, and this figure does not include the substantial sums required for the expropriation of landowners. To give a rough indication of the order of magnitude involved, it may be pointed out that during the peak years of railway building activity, 1838–40, the rate of expenditure almost certainly exceeded the value of exports to the United States.

Before work on constructing a railway could begin, it was necessary to pass through Parliament an Act granting the right of eminent domain and similar

---

[1] H. G. Lewin, *Early British Railways, 1801–1844* (1925), p. 186.
[2] D. Lardner, *Railway Economy* (1850), pp. 54–5; Tooke, v, pp. 349–52.

privileges to the company. The cost of securing such an Act was considerable, and an Act would not normally be sought or obtained until the plans for the line in question had passed beyond mere aspiration and had reached a fairly advanced stage. Figures relating to these Acts therefore give a fair index of investment *planned* in each year. These figures are shown in Table 11.

Table 11. *Number of companies, mileage and capital sanctioned by railway acts*

Year	(1) No. of companies sanctioned	(2) Mileage sanctioned	(3) Capital authorised (£m.)
1833	4	218	5·5
1834	5	131	2·3
1835	8	201	4·8
1836	29	955	22·9
1837	15	543	13·5
1838	2	49	2·1
1839	2	54	6·5
1840	—	—	2·5
1841	1	14	3·4
1842	5	55	5·3
1843	3	90	3·9

Sources: (1) and (2) Lewin, p. 186; (3) James Wilson, *Capital Currency and Banking* (1847), p. iv.

It will be our purpose in the following pages to analyse the reasons which led investment plans to move in this way, and to consider the course of the actual investment to which the plans gave rise.

In order to understand why the first railway boom came when it did, it is necessary to go back to the beginnings that were made in the 1820's.[1]

The authorisation of the Stockton and Darlington Railway in 1821 marked the beginning of the railway age. During the following five years, especially in the boom of 1824–5, a good many schemes were mooted, with traction by horses or stationary engines usually in contemplation. Apart from the Liverpool and Manchester, and a few unimportant lines, these projects bore no immediate fruit. Many were mere bubbles and were pricked when the crash came in December 1825. But there was an appreciable number of lines for which careful surveys and estimates of prospective costs and receipts were carried out in the early and middle 1820's by responsible persons. The reason why most of them fell through was simply that the prospective profits were held to be insufficient to justify the investment. Others were frustrated by opposition from canal interests and landed proprietors.[2] In the years from 1826 to 1829, nothing happened to render these obstacles any less formidable. The example of the Stockton and

---

[1] For many years scholars have felt the lack of an adequate history of railway building that would make full use of the vast bulk of evidence in existence; but the lack has yet to be made good. Much the best contemporary treatment is J. Francis, *History of the English Railway* (1851). Valuable brief modern accounts are W. T. Jackman, *The Development of Transportation in Modern England* (1916), pp. 510–72 and Sir John Clapham, *Economic History of Modern Britain* (1930 edition), I, Chapter IX. Lewin, *op. cit.*, is useful for reference.

[2] Francis, I, pp. 135–51.

Darlington (opened in September 1825) had not been so startling as to give rise to great developments in imitation. The use of locomotives on a line open to the public was a novelty; but the line was a short one, and catering as it did mainly for coal traffic, it was not in principle such a great departure from the private colliery lines that had long been familiar.[1] The experience gained on it in the use of locomotives was by no means decisive in their favour.[2] In the late 1820's, moreover, the depressed state of general business activity made the financial climate less favourable than it had been in 1824–5, so until the Liverpool and Manchester showed the way, there was little likelihood of projects being revived which had not been considered to offer attractive profit prospects even in the boom.

The prominent position traditionally accorded to the Liverpool and Manchester Railway in the development of the British railway system is no more than it deserves. The first attempt in 1825 to secure an Act authorising this line failed to get Parliamentary assent. The route was then replanned so as to reduce the amount of opposition from landed interests, and in 1826, after the necessary alterations had been made, Parliamentary sanction was secured. Work was begun immediately, but owing to the difficulties of construction the line was not completed until 1830.[3] Regular traffic started in December of that year. Already, in 1829, the performance of Stephenson's 'Rocket' at the Rainhill locomotive trials organised by the Liverpool and Manchester had revived interest in railways, and the price of the company's shares at once rose by 10%.[4] The successful construction and operation of the pioneer line were what set the stage for subsequent developments and largely determined their timing.

The ways in which the experience of the Liverpool and Manchester encouraged further developments were manifold. In the first place, formidable difficulties in the construction of the track were shown to be not insuperable for a good engineer, and the locomotive was found to be capable of a standard of performance not previously considered within the realm of possibility.

Secondly, the line had been open only a short time when it became apparent that the traffic was well above expectation, and the passenger traffic spectacularly so. Hitherto calculation of the prospects of any line had usually been based on the assumption that the traffic would, at best, amount to no more than that previously conveyed along the route by canal or road or whatever was the existing method. It was not appreciated to what extent cheaper and speedier transport would *create* the traffic, even in the short run.[5] The lesson of the Liverpool and Manchester in this respect was soon learnt. Indeed, it was learnt too well, and the difficulty of calculating exactly how much traffic would be created by a line and the consequent opportunities for exaggerations on the part of promoters were among the main causes of the speculative nature of the railway manias of the 1830's and 1840's alike.

Thirdly, the exaggerated fears of damage to property adjoining a line were

[1] Jackman, pp. 481–3.   [2] Clapham, pp. 381–2.
[3] These difficulties, particularly the carrying of the line over Chatmoss, and George Stephenson's success in surmounting them, have been many times described. Cf. Samuel Smiles, *Lives of the Engineers* (1862), III, pp. 219–39. For the early history of the line generally, cf. C. R. Fay, *Huskisson and his Age* (1951), pp. 15–30.
[4] Francis, I, p. 130.   [5] Francis, I, p. 137.

soon set at rest. The value of the land crossed by the Liverpool and Manchester increased rather than the reverse.[1] Lord Sefton and Lord Derby contested the bill to authorise the Liverpool and Manchester; when their estates were again threatened a few years later by the London and Birmingham, neither offered any opposition.[2] In view of the power which lay with the landed interests to prevent the passage of railway Acts—a power which they had not hesitated to exercise in the 1820's—the importance of this consideration was substantial.

Fourthly, as soon as some lines had been built or were firmly in prospect, the construction of others to feed or connect them became much more promising—an elementary case of external economies. An obvious example was the Grand Junction Railway, authorised in 1833 to connect the Liverpool and Manchester with the projected London and Birmingham.[3]

Such then was the background for the new interest shown in railways at the beginning of the 1830's. Despite the depressed condition of trade in 1829 and much of 1830,[4] the Rainhill trials and the subsequent opening of the Liverpool and Manchester caused projects that had been shelved in the 1820's to be immediately reopened. Many lines that had been unable to secure authorisation in the previous decade now came before Parliament again in the more favourable atmosphere created by the example of the Lancashire line, and were successful. A few examples may be quoted to illustrate the way in which events developed.

Much the most important from every point of view of the lines projected in the early 1830's was the London and Birmingham, the nation's first trunk line. Schemes to connect London and Birmingham by rail had been mooted in the 1820's, and a bill to authorise such a line was brought before Parliament in 1826, but thrown out. Then in 1830 'the progress of the Liverpool and Manchester line revived the spirit of the projectors'.[5] At first two rival companies were formed, one planning a route via Oxford and Banbury and the other a route via Coventry. The folly of such competition was soon perceived, and the two companies amalgamated, deciding on the Coventry route, on advice obtained from George Stephenson. By 1832 affairs had sufficiently progressed for an Act to be petitioned for, but this first attempt failed and the bill was thrown out by the House of Lords. The bribes offered to the interested landowners had not been high enough, and this matter had to be adjusted before the company could finally procure its Act in 1833.[6]

The history of most of the other companies undertaken in this early phase of the railway boom was similar. Plans to build a railway from London to Bristol were under consideration in 1832, but the obstacles in the way prevented the Great Western from securing its Act until 1835.[7] The London and Southampton was carefully planned to pass through land devoid of agricultural value or

---

[1] Jackman, p. 527. [2] Francis, I, p. 173.

[3] The complementary nature of different lines was, it is true, not universally understood at the time. The adoption of the 7 ft. gauge on the Great Western (in the face of opposition) was an indication of this. Brunel's supporters argued that 'the Great Western railway is complete in itself between the two sides of the island' (E. T. MacDermot, *History of the Great Western Railway* (1927), p. 78).

[4] Cf. W. Smart, *Economic Annals of the Nineteenth Century, 1821–1830* (1917), Chapters XLIII, XLVII.

[5] *Osborne's London and Birmingham Railway Guide* (1840), p. 46.

[6] Francis, I, pp. 182–9.

[7] Jackman, pp. 554–64.

amenity, but the company was unfortunate in its first choice of an engineer, and although the line was originally projected in 1831, it was not authorised till 1834.[1] The Grand Junction Railway from Birmingham to Liverpool was another line that had been proposed—under a different name—in the 1820's, but had not then prospered. Acts had been unsuccessfully sought in 1824 and 1826.[2] In 1832, when the project was revived, one complementary line, the Liverpool and Manchester, was already in operation and the other, the London and Birmingham, seemed certain to obtain sanction at an early date. The Grand Junction's Act was therefore secured with little difficulty in 1833.

The first phase of the railway enthusiasm of the 1830's ended about the middle of 1835 and is to be fairly sharply distinguished from the second phase, the 'mania' proper. The lines projected in this first phase may be considered the direct result of the technical and other advances brought before the public eye by the Liverpool and Manchester. There is little reason to suppose that the improvement in trade conditions in 1831 and again after 1833 played anything more than a subsidiary part in motivating these undertakings. It would be erroneous to connect the increase in authorisations in 1833 (the amount of railway capital authorised in 1832 having been negligible) with the improvement in trade in that year, since the Acts passed in 1833 were mostly for lines that had been in preparation for several years and had been held up for technical reasons.[3] Had the difficulties in the construction of the Liverpool and Manchester been less than they were by a sufficient extent to permit of its completion, say, in 1828 instead of 1830, there is every reason to suppose that the first phase of the railway boom would have been correspondingly antedated.

The lines projected in the first phase of the railway boom in the early 1830's were not in any sense speculative bubbles. They were decided on because in the light of the experience so far gained in the construction and operation of railways it was thought that the return would justify the cost. A prominent part in their finance was played by the group of hard-headed Lancashire business men known in railway circles as the 'Liverpool party'. The interest of these men in railways was as investments, not as speculations. They owned a majority holding in the London and Birmingham, and put up a substantial portion of the capital for lines as remote from Lancashire as the Eastern Counties and the London and Southampton.[4] Many of the early lines were also powerfully backed by local business men whose primary interests lay in the indirect advantages that would accrue to trade in the districts served when the lines had been completed.[5]

In the latter part of 1835 there began the second phase, the 'mania' properly so called.[6] Up till that time some very important lines had been projected, but their number was not large. From September 1835 prospectuses for new lines

---

[1] G. F. D. Marshall, *A History of the Southern Railway* (1936), pp. 69–76.
[2] *Osborne's London and Birmingham Railway Guide*, p. 46; Francis, I, p. 208.
[3] The preoccupation of the Houses of Parliament with the Reform Bill in 1832 may also have contributed to the delay.
[4] Tooke, II, p. 275; Lewin, p. 71; Marshall, p. 78.
[5] Cf. Clapham, pp. 386–7, who makes much of this point.
[6] The division between the two phases was not, of course, absolute. A number of companies authorised in 1836 or even later had been planned four or five years earlier but had been delayed by one or other of the many obstacles that might arise. Cf. C. S. Stretton, *The History of the Midland Railway* (1901), pp. 36–7 (on the Midland Counties Railway) and Francis, I, pp. 242–261 (on the Eastern Counties Railway).

began to multiply. The peak was reached in May 1836, but the flow continued until nearly the end of that year.[1] The authorising Acts lagged behind the prospectuses by about a year—for the climate of opinion no longer favoured the factious opposition that had delayed some of the earlier lines by three years or more. The result may be seen in Table 11. The railway capital authorised by Parliament in 1836 was nearly double that authorised in the whole period 1833–5. In 1837 the figure was smaller, but still very large.

In this second phase the professional company promoter and the gullible small shareholder replaced the local chamber of commerce and the Quaker capitalist as the leading actors in the drama.[2] There had not been any tangible evidence of increased profit prospects to justify such a sudden expansion as took place after 1835. Neither the London and Birmingham nor any other of the important lines that had been authorised between 1830 and 1835 was yet in operation, and if the traffic on the Liverpool and Manchester had exceeded expectations, so had the cost.[3] There is no doubt that in this second phase, in contrast to the first, confidence engendered by the prosperous state of trade and the relatively easy conditions in the money market mainly accounted for the extent and timing of the boom.

Share speculation was rife, alike in the stocks of established and of new companies. 'Ladies and clergymen'[4] were tempted by the facility with which shares in newly projected companies could commonly be bought for a deposit amounting to only a small proportion of their nominal value. It was inevitable that, after a few pioneering companies had led the way, decisions to undertake long-term investment in an untried project like railways, financed, moreover, by public subscription, should be exceptionally sensitive to speculative influences and more or less irrational changes in business confidence. Many of the promoters were rogues who were interested only in quick profits for themselves at the expense of shareholders, and never intended that any actual construction should be undertaken. Many others, even if they did intend that the lines they canvassed should be built and expected them to yield some return, regarded the question of the profitability of the projected company as subsidiary to their own personal takings. Much of the railway development decided on in 1835–6, though perhaps not the greater part of it, emerged—in Keynes's phrase—as a by-product of the activities of a casino.[5] In any case, for better or for worse, the number of the lines then projected that reached the stage of procuring Parliamentary sanction was sufficient to lead to the expenditure of many million pounds on construction in the next few years.

The consequences of the railway mania can be quickly described. It was inevitable that few new lines should come forward once the peak of boom-time confidence had passed and had turned first into recession and then, in the early summer of 1837, into something near panic. The attention of railway promoters and directors was fully occupied during the next few years in surmounting the difficulties involved in the actual construction of the lines they had undertaken.

---

[1] Particulars on the prospectuses and their dates of issue are in *Select Committee on Joint Stock Companies*, 1844, VII, pp. 358–63.
[2] Clapham, p. 388; Francis, I, pp. 288–300.   [3] Jackman, pp. 529–30.
[4] Francis, II, pp. 1–2.
[5] J. M. Keynes, *General Theory of Employment Interest and Money* (1936), p. 159. The need to secure Parliamentary authorisation did offer some safeguard against utterly foolish schemes.

The cost was almost invariably found to be in excess of what had been predicted, and extra cash had to be raised in circumstances that were often unpropitious. Repeated calls left many shareholders in arrears with their subscriptions. Cases were recorded where shares were offered with a premium for whoever would accept them, and many companies were obliged to seek Parliamentary sanction for an increase in their capital.[1] In these circumstances, with most lines still incomplete, the promises of high dividends so lightly given in 1836 naturally proved difficult to honour.

The railway mania of 1836 was a promotion boom, not a construction boom. Actual expenditure on the building of railways came to a peak several years later. It is not easy to reach precise conclusions on the amount of such expenditure in each year. Some of the relevant evidence is reviewed in an appendix at the end of this chapter. The conclusions which appear to emerge are broadly as follows. Up till 1835 investment expenditure brought about by railways was small, and it is doubtful if it amounted to as much as £1 million in any one year. In 1835 and 1836 there was an increase attributable, not to the lines that were currently being promoted, but to the undertakings that belonged to the first phase of the boom and that had now at last begun to reach the stage of substantial expenditure on physical construction. But even so aggregate expenditure was probably still a good deal below £5 million in 1836. That was perhaps about the level reached in 1837 as a result of a further increase of activity, again mainly on the older lines.

In 1838 work on the lines projected during the 'mania' itself at last reached substantial dimensions. The three years 1838, 1839 and 1840 mark the peak. In 1839 expenditure appears to have amounted to some £9 million, and 1838 and 1840 were scarcely less active. In 1840 over 500 miles of line were opened, a far greater amount than in any previous year. By 1841 the bulk of the work planned in 1835–6 had been carried into execution, and expenditure fell steeply. It fell again in 1842. But in each of these years there was still much to be done in building tributary lines and extensions, and in the purchase of rolling stock and other equipment required for the actual operation of the lines.[2] Consequently the rate of expenditure in 1841–2, though much lower than that of the three preceding years, was still probably not much less than the rate of expenditure in 1836–7.

The timing of the first phase of the railway boom was, as has been seen, relatively little affected by fluctuations in the state of trade, being determined mainly by the example of the Liverpool and Manchester Railway. The timing of the second phase, the mania, on the other hand, was very much affected by the state of trade, and particularly by the state of confidence. The timing of the actual construction of the lines was determined by the state of trade, in so far as their inception had been so determined. But it does not seem that the state of trade had much to do with the rate at which the work went forward once it had been started.

Nor does it seem probable that the relative absence of new railway projects

---

[1] Francis, I, pp. 299–300; Clapham, p. 389. It may be seen from Table 11 that the amount of capital authorised in the later years was much higher relatively than that of the new mileage sanctioned—a result of costs exceeding expectation.

[2] Cf. *Companion to the British Almanack*, 1841, p. 60.

between 1838 and 1843 was mainly the result of general business stagnation. Even if the state of business had been better than it was after 1837, it would still have been a matter of common prudence for promoters to wait before starting anything fresh until they could see what the railway map of the country would look like when the lines so far projected had been completed. The depression of 1841–2 undoubtedly made things difficult for many companies;[1] but it is interesting to note that it was in these exceptionally gloomy years that George Hudson was successfully pushing forward plans for what was in many ways the most ambitious project of all, the northern section of the line that was to connect London and Edinburgh.[2] By 1841 there was already in existence a continuous line from London to York, and the prospect of a through route to the north could therefore be considered within the bounds of possibility. The time was approaching when the railway investment undertaken in the 1830's would be completed and absorbed, and the stage set for a further burst of expansion.

3. BUILDING

The index of brick production is one of the best known of statistical indicators of economic fluctuations in the first half of the nineteenth century.[3] It is of particular interest for the years after 1829, since it is one of the few indices of production that is available on a regional basis. The excise duty payable on bricks was collected at some fifty local centres, and the returns give the annual receipts at each of these points. For the years after 1836 receipts are also given by county,[4] but unfortunately the figures for the earlier years cannot be reduced to this basis. It is not possible to make any accurate calculation of the contribution made by building to the national income, but it was, of course, a very great industry. The total numbers engaged in the building trades in 1841 exceeded the number of cotton operatives. The fluctuations in output and employment would not, however, be as large as this would suggest viewed solely in conjunction with the brick index, since many of those listed in the census as employed about houses were presumably occupied with maintenance work rather than with new construction. But there is no doubt that fluctuations in building made a very important contribution to fluctuations in total investment.

The movement of total brick production in England and Wales is shown in Chart 10a.[5] Between 1832 and 1843 the curve describes a large M, with twin peaks in 1836 and 1840. The fluctuations shown are of very substantial amplitude, production in the trough year 1832 being little more than half of production in 1840, the higher of the two peaks.

The brick index is undoubtedly the best measure available of fluctuations in

---

[1] Cf. Lewin, pp. 99, 115–16.

[2] Cf. R. S. Lambert, *The Railway King, 1800–1871* (1934), pp. 70–90.

[3] *Accounts and Papers*, 1839, XLVI, pp. 14–15, and 1846, XXV, p. 209; H. A. Shannon, 'Bricks—a trade index', *Economica* (1934), pp. 300–18.

[4] *Accounts and Papers*, 1837–8, XLV, p. 5, and 1846, XXV, pp. 212–15.

[5] For the figures themselves, see Tables 20 and 21 at the end of this chapter. Figures of brick production in Scotland are not included, since the predominant use of stone renders the appropriateness of brick production as an index of building activity in that part of Great Britain extremely dubious.

building activity.[1] But the building activity which it reflects includes the building of factories, warehouses and offices as well as of houses; and it is also much influenced by the extensive brickwork required in the construction of railways. It is not possible to segregate that part of brick production that was due to house-building, as it would be desirable to do. But a certain amount of interest can be learnt from the index none the less.

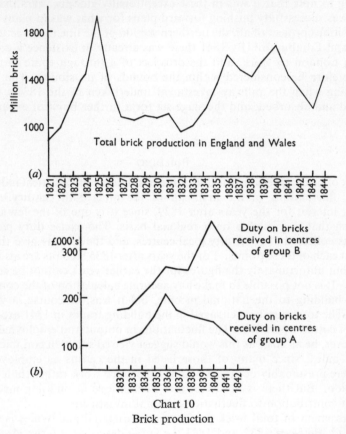

Chart 10
Brick production

[1] Timber imports have also sometimes been used as a measure. The figures are as follows:

Year	Official value of timber imports (in £000's)	Year	Official value of timber imports (in £000's)
1832	653	1838	843
1833	627	1839	932
1834	690	1840	983
1835	803	1841	915
1836	771	1842	581
1837	783		

Source: Accounts and Papers, annual *Finance Accounts.*
These figures correspond moderately well with the brick index, but not perfectly. It is to be remembered that the volume of timber imports was much affected by fluctuations in ship-building.

As pointed out by H. A. Shannon in the article which first drew the attention of economic historians to the brick index, the movements of brick production in different parts of the country in the 1830's and early 1840's were markedly diverse. In particular, although aggregate brick production shows two peaks of roughly equal altitude in 1836 and 1840, this is true of very few individual local series.[1] This is brought into greater prominence in Chart 10*b*. Here we divide the regional series into two groups according as their highest point between 1832 and 1843 was reached before 1839 on the one hand (group A) or in or after 1839 on the other hand (group B).[2] The result that emerges is rather curious, and provides a good example of the dangers of uncritical use of economic aggregates. In both groups there was a strong rise up to 1836 and a falling off in 1837–8, though both the rise and the fall were more rapid in group A—which incidentally is the smaller of the two groups. But in 1839–40, while group B was rising to a peak that made that of 1836 look a trifling affair, group A showed no rise whatsoever, but merely continued the mild decline that had begun in the previous two years. Finally, in 1841–2, the rate of decline in group A increased and output in group B at last turned down.

The rise in brick production up to 1836 was most marked in the textile districts, especially in Lancashire. Duty paid on bricks in Manchester and Lancaster in 1836 was three times as high as in 1832. Much of this was accounted for by the building of factories and other business premises,[3] but house-building was not neglected. As early as 1833 the number of houses that were under construction in Manchester and its environs was arousing comment,[4] and in 1835 and 1836 there was a great speculative boom in cottage-building in the cotton districts.[5] But the regional centres in group A (the group showing a peak in 1836) were by no means all located in textile districts; and, as has been remarked, a good many of the centres in group B also rose strongly in the years ending 1836. Shannon therefore appears to be guilty of some overstatement when he sums up: 'except for the...group of textile towns, bricks and building pass through the 1830's relatively unmarked.'[6] The group of textile towns alluded to in fact accounts for barely a third of the total rise in brick production between 1834 and 1836. It seems that the upswing of business in these years had a fairly widespread effect on building. Building activity had been almost everywhere at a low level from 1827 to 1834, and there was therefore no great recent accumulation of new

---

[1] The only important centres which show two peaks of comparable height are Uxbridge and Northwich. Most of the others either have one clearly defined peak or else move erratically or non-cyclically.

[2] The centres included in group A are: Bedford, Cambridge, Coventry, Exeter, Halifax, Hereford, Lancaster, Leeds, Lichfield, Liverpool, Manchester, Northampton, Reading, Salisbury, Salop, Sheffield, Stafford. Those in group B are: Barnstaple, Bath, Bristol, Canterbury, Chester, Cornwall, Cumberland, Derby, Dorset, Durham, Essex, Gloucester, Grantham, Hants, Hertford, Hull, Isle of Wight, Lincoln, Lynn, Newcastle, Northwich, Norwich, Oxford, Plymouth, Rochester, Stourbridge, Suffolk, Surrey, Sussex, Uxbridge, Wales, Wellington, Whitby, Worcester, York, London. An additional point of collection was established at Wigan in 1839. Half of its total in 1839–42 has been assigned to each group. It does not materially affect the result.

[3] See pp. 134–5.

[4] *Select Committee on Manufactures Commerce and Shipping*, 1833, VI, QQ. 764, 790 (Joshua Bates).

[5] *Report of the Assistant Poor Law Commissioners sent to inquire into the state of the Population of Stockport*, 1842, XXXV (henceforward cited as *Report on Stockport*), p. 221.

[6] *Loc. cit.* p. 309.

houses to depress rents and prices. It was doubtless the rise in incomes that was the immediate cause of the rise in brick production and building after 1833—an increase in the demand for house-room, that is to say, rather than any actual fall in the supply. But the relatively low rate of addition to the supply at the beginning of the period was an important permissive factor.

There was not, it is true, in every part of the country anything that could fairly be described as a building boom. Only in the textile districts were the results spectacular. Incomes there were particularly affected by the boom of 1835–6 and the increase in activity tended to cause an inflow of labour from the rural districts to the towns. After 1836 this flow slackened; by 1841–2 it had actually reversed, and unemployed operatives were returning to the villages from which they had been attracted a few years previously.[1]

Shannon's attribution to railway building of the renewed rise in brick production in 1839 and 1840 seems undoubtedly correct.[2] The regions where brick production rises most pronouncedly in those years—the home counties, the north-east and parts of the west country—were those where railway building was active. It appears that brick production lagged slightly behind railway-building activity, if what has been said above about the timing of railway building is correct, for it continued to fall in 1838 and stayed at a high level in 1841. Another lag is shown by the continued fall of brick production in 1843 when trade was for the most part looking up. The tendency of the building trade to lag behind other sectors of the economy in its cyclical movement has, of course, frequently been observed.

What the figures do not tell us, and what it would be interesting to know, is whether the rise in 1839–40 was entirely due (directly or indirectly) to railways or whether in those districts—including the metropolis—in which the boom of 1836 had been relatively little felt, *house*-building continued to rise, or at least did not fall, until the depression set in in 1841–2. It seems not unlikely that this was the case, for the rise up to 1836 had been in many places fairly mild and did not lead to any very violent reaction in 1837–8; but we cannot say more.

Our conclusions about the timing of fluctuations in house-building are therefore rather jejune. But it is evident that with the exception of the textile districts in 1835–6, there was no feverish building boom. House-building played its part in the cyclical process, but was not one of its most striking manifestations. This becomes more evident if a general comparison is made between the 1820's and the 1830's. In the ten years 1821–30 the total number of bricks on which duty was paid in England and Wales was 12·3 thousand million. In 1831–40 the number was 13·4 thousand million. If allowance is made for the appearance in the latter decade of a great new demand for bricks arising out of railway building, it is evident that the rate at which houses were being put up can have increased little if at all between the two periods. If the 'appropriate' rate of house production during any period—that is to say, the rate which will leave housing standards constant—is considered to be determined by the increase during the period in the size of the population, house-building did not perhaps put up a worse performance in the 1830's than in the 1820's;[3] but it did not, on the

---

[1] Tooke, IV, pp. 56–7; *Report on Stockport*, p. 203.
[2] Shannon, p. 307.
[3] Population of England and Wales (millions): 1821, 12·0; 1831, 13·9; 1841, 15·9.

other hand, register any progress, and its proportional contribution to the national income must have fallen.

As is apparent from Chart 10*a*, there was no year in the period 1833–42 when brick production reached or even approached the level established in 1825. In that year house-building made a much larger contribution to the boom than it did in 1836. The contrast is especially noteworthy in the case of London. Production of bricks in London in the peak year 1840 was considerably less than half of production in 1825—a remarkable drop.[1] Presumably the tremendous amount of building executed in London around 1825 created a legacy which prevented any great activity in the following decade, just as the extensive cottage-building in Lancashire and elsewhere in 1835–6 depressed the building trades in the early 1840's. This co-existence of longer swings in the rate of building activity with the shorter swings induced by the business cycle has been a feature of the building industry in the United States as well as in Great Britain over a very long period. In our period the longer swings appear to have been mainly regional, in contrast with the large national swings that were especially characteristic of the last quarter of the nineteenth century in Britain.[2]

Table 12. *Uninhabited houses in* 1831 *and* 1841

Date	Percentage of uninhabited to inhabited houses			
	England and Wales	Middlesex	Lancashire	Yorks., W. Riding
1831	4·9	8·0	4·9	6·4
1841	5·9	4·7	8·2	8·3

Sources: Census of 1831, 1833, xxxvii, p. 832; Census of 1841, 1843, xxii, p. 440.

The hypothesis that the state of the building trade in London in the 1830's was less prosperous in comparison with the textile districts receives confirmation from the census figures (Table 12). It seems reasonable to guess that the movement in the ratio of unoccupied to occupied houses in the different districts is some measure of the relative intensity of house-building activity in the preceding decades. It is true that the high proportion of empties in the north in 1841 was probably partly accounted for by the great severity of the depression there at that time. 1831 had been relatively a year of prosperity, and the depressed state of trade in 1841 was clearly the reason for the increase between the two years in the proportion of empty houses in the country as a whole. The income-elasticity of demand for accommodation in the districts worst hit by the slump was well attested.[3] But that this is not the whole of the explanation for

[1] Regional figures are not given in the bluebooks for before 1829, but those relating to London are available in the manuscript Excise documents and are quoted (in part) by Shannon, p. 309.
[2] For long cycles in building in Britain, cf. W. H. Beveridge, *Unemployment* (1931), pp. 335–9; for an introduction to the extensive literature on the phenomenon in the United States, Alvin H. Hansen, *Business Cycles and National Income* (1951), pp. 39–52.
[3] Cf. *Hansard's Parliamentary Debates* (3rd series), LXIV, cols. 1188, 1248.

the difference in the proportion of empties in Middlesex and the north is suggested by the fact that the number of inhabited houses per hundred of population fell in Middlesex between 1831 and 1841, but rose in the country as a whole and in Lancashire and the West Riding of Yorkshire.[1]

4. SHIPBUILDING

Fluctuations in the shipbuilding industry provide some interesting comparisons and contrasts with the fluctuations in brick production that have just been discussed.

In our period shipbuilding was already a substantial industry, but it had not by any means come to occupy the prominent position in the national economy to which it had attained by the end of the nineteenth century. It is possible to get a fairly good idea of the order of magnitude of its contribution to the national income. The tonnage built in the United Kingdom from 1833 to 1842 varied from rather below 90,000 in the worst years to rather over 210,000 in the best. The cost per ton differed a good deal from one class of ship to another. A West Indiaman of the first class might cost up to £25 per ton; on the other hand, an inferior vessel without elaborate outfitting might be obtained for as little as £12 per ton. Costs were generally higher in London shipyards than elsewhere. If we take £20 per ton as the average cost at the beginning of the period we shall probably be erring if anything slightly on the side of excess.[2] On that reckoning the value of ships built in 1833 fell somewhat short of £2 million. Assuming no change in costs, the value of output in the peak year 1840 would be around £4 million. In fact, there was probably a certain rise in costs between the two dates, and allowance for this might bring the figure for 1840 to £4½ million.

Rough as these calculations are, they are adequate to show that the shipbuilding industry cannot have contributed more than a minor part to fluctuations in the national income. It is doubtful if there were in this period any two consecutive years between which the value of the industry's output altered by as much as £1 million. Its fluctuations have, however, a certain interest on their own account and may therefore be briefly discussed.

The tonnage built in each year is shown in Table 13. There was some rise in 1834 and more in 1835, but this was followed by a sharp drop in the generally prosperous year 1836. In 1837 the rise recommenced and continued rapidly until the peak was reached in 1840, at a level over double that prevailing at the beginning of the period. In 1841–2 output declined but still remained relatively high.

If attention is directed to the excess of tonnage built over that falling out of use in each year, the magnitude of the boom in 1839–41 is brought out still more startlingly. Between 1827 (the first year when reliable figures are available) and 1839, the average annual increase in tonnage belonging to the United Kingdom

---

[1] Census of 1841, *loc. cit.* p. 6. The Census figures on number of houses are well known to be unreliable on account of the ambiguity of the term 'house'; but the result quoted is consistent with the other evidence.

[2] For evidence on shipbuilding costs, see *Select Committee on Manufactures Commerce and Shipping*, 1833, VI, QQ. 3614–20 (R. A. Gray), 5734–5 (W. Woolcombe), 7793 (T. Young); *Select Committee on Import Duties*, 1840, V, Q. 3030 (J. Mitchell); *Select Committee on British Shipping*, 1844, VIII, QQ. 120–2, 149, 176 (G. F. Young).

was approximately 18,000 tons. Between 1839 and 1841 it was no less than 213,000 tons.[1]

A considerably greater tonnage was built in each of the years 1838–41 than at any other time between Waterloo and the Great Exhibition. There had been some rise in output in the boom of 1824–5, but it had not reached any great heights. The position of the shipping interest in the 1820's resembled in many ways that of agriculture; the war had created an expansion of capacity which was excessive in relation to peace time needs. As a result of this—with Wallace's much-complained-of alterations of the Navigation Laws in 1822 and Huskisson's reciprocity treaties perhaps playing some small part as well[2]—shipping and ship-building were in a generally depressed state in the 1820's, and freights had a strong downwards tendency.[3]

Table 13. *Tonnage of vessels built and registered in the United Kingdom and possessions in Europe (thousands)*

1832	93	1838	161
1833	92	1839	187
1834	103	1840	217
1835	122	1841	168
1836	90	1842	133
1837	136	1843	85

Source: G. R. Porter, *Progress of the Nation* (1851 edition), p. 395.

By 1834, shipping, like agriculture, was beginning to emerge from its troubles. The steady rise in the volume of trade was at last arresting the fall in freights, and in 1835 there was a short outburst of speculative building of ships by joint stock companies. 'Amongst other objects of the speculative mania of 1835 was the formation of shipping companies, in which capital to an enormous extent was involved, the result of which has been an almost universal failure.'[4] Presumably the unsound quality of this investment, rather than any glutting of the market, is to be held responsible for the surprising setback in 1836, since in 1837 the recovery was vigorous. From so querulous a class as the shipowners,[5] such admissions as that 'from 1837 to 1840 things were considerably better'[6] or that during these years freights were 'remunerative'[7] may be taken to indicate a very satisfactory level of prosperity.

The shipbuilding boom of 1838–41 is to be regarded as a natural sequel to the slow rate of increase in tonnage that had characterised the 1820's and the early 1830's. That it should have reached a peak as late as 1839–40 can only be attributed to the internal dynamics of the industry. In 1835–6 the volume of foreign trade had not yet become sufficiently high in relation to the available

[1] G. R. Porter, *Progress of the Nation* (1851 edition), p. 394. The excess of this figure over the average level of production in the United Kingdom during the same period is explained by the admission to the United Kingdom register of tonnage built in Canada and other colonies (*Select Committee on British Shipping*, 1844, VIII, Q. 93 (G. F. Young)).
[2] Cf. Clapham, *Economic History*, I, pp. 330–4.
[3] *Select Committee on British Shipping*, 1844, VIII, Q. 1930 (R. Anderson).
[4] M. Dunn, *A View of the Coal Trade* (1844), p. 204.
[5] Cf. Porter, p. 390.
[6] *Select Committee on British Shipping*, 1844, VIII, Q. 1468 (G. Smales).
[7] *Ibid.* Q. 1368 (G. Smales).

tonnage for a major boom to result; by 1839–40 it had.[1] In the latter years there were also one or two special factors pushing up the demand for shipping, in particular the war with China[2] and the large corn imports.[3]

In such favourable circumstances, it was not surprising that, despite the high rates of interest prevailing, shipbuilding in 1839–40 should have been pushed further than could be justified on a sober estimate of the future. There was a great revival of speculative building by joint-stock companies, many of them run by men inexperienced in the trade.[4] There was also a very large increase in the inferior class of vessels built in the North American colonies for sale in London, and in production on the Continent of Europe.[5]

After 1841 a strong reaction was inevitable in shipping and shipbuilding alike. Already in 1840 freights were slightly lower than in 1839,[6] and most of the tonnage completed in 1841 had probably been commissioned in the previous year. The increase in tonnage came on the market at a time when the world-wide depression had temporarily arrested the upward trend in the volume of trade. The ending of the China war caused East India freights to be especially depressed. A fall in emigration in 1843 was also felt.[7] Even the recovery in trade later in the 1840's did not bring shipbuilding nearly up to the level established in 1838–41. As with the case of London house-building discussed previously, the magnitude of one boom largely determined the extent to which production could rise in the next.

APPENDIX

Statistics of the railway boom

Despite the enormous amount of statistical material on railways that is available in Parliamentary Papers and elsewhere, it is unfortunately not possible to construct a year-to-year index of expenditure on railway building for our period that could claim accuracy even in a very broad way. In this appendix, an attempt is made to analyse the facts as they appear from what is admittedly only a small selection from the vast quantity of chaotic and not infrequently contradictory evidence in existence.

The capital which railway companies were authorised to raise in each year by Act of Parliament (see Table 11) has sometimes been taken as an index of their current expenditure on construction.[8] This procedure is altogether illegitimate.

---

[1] It may also be that shipowners waited until freights had been ranging high for some time before deciding to place orders for extra tonnage; in view of the violent short-period fluctuations in freights that were customary this would have been a natural policy.

[2] *Select Committee on British Shipping*, 1844, VIII, QQ. 40–3, 194–5 (G. F. Young).

[3] *Ibid*. QQ. 753–4 (G. F. Young). Most of the extra corn imported was carried in foreign ships, however (*ibid*. QQ. 835 (H. C. Chapman), 2276 (J. Smith), 2952–56 (J. Straker)).

[4] *Ibid*. QQ. 1675–6, 1695–1711 (H. Tanner).

[5] Some of the witnesses before the Committee of 1844 attempted to fasten all the blame—or nearly all the blame—for the current depression in the industry on the increase in production of ships from the North American colonies in 1839–40. Their argument was not convincing, since the increase in the production of such ships was less than the increase in the output of United Kingdom shipyards in the same years (*ibid*. QQ. 93, 750–2 (G. F. Young)).

[6] *Ibid*. Q. 2513 (T. Thompson).

[7] *Ibid*. QQ. 221 (G. F. Young), 454 (J. Somes).

[8] Cf. Sir William Beveridge, 'The trade cycle in Britain before 1850', *Oxford Economic Papers* (1940), pp. 75 and 104, and criticism of Beveridge by C. N. Ward-Perkins, 'The commercial crisis of 1847', *Oxford Economic Papers* (1950), p. 91.

In the first place not all the money authorised was ever actually raised. In the second place the money that was raised was called up and spent gradually and not immediately upon the passage of the authorising Act. The usual practice was to require from shareholders initially only a small deposit on the nominal value of their shares, the remainder being called up as required to finance the progress of the work. In the case of the shares issued around 1836, five years or more often elapsed before full payment had been made. Subscriptions on shares created after 1838 were usually more rapidly called up, since by that time companies did not as a rule issue new securities unless they currently needed the cash.[1]

If it were available, the amount of capital actually called up in each year would be a better index of expenditure on construction in that year. The total amount of capital raised is shown in Table 14.

Table 14. *Capital raised by railway companies prior to* 31 *December* 1843 (£m.)

Total capital raised	66
Capital raised on shares	44
Capital raised by loans	22
Total capital authorised	86

Source: Lords' Committee on Commercial Distress, 1847–8, VIII, Part III, p. 524.

It is not possible to ascertain the amounts raised annually, but a certain amount of evidence exists for individual companies, and this has been combined into an index (Table 15).

Table 15. *Calls on railway share capital*

Year	Calls on share capital made by 12 leading companies (1838 = 100)
1833	10
1834	16
1835	25
1836	64
1837	72
1838	100
1839	124
1840	116
1841	52
1842	38
1843	12

Source: Calculated from figures in H. Scrivenor, *The Railways of the United Kingdom* (1849). The twelve companies are: London and Birmingham, Grand Junction, Great Western, Manchester and Birmingham, North Midland, Midland Counties, London and South Western, London and Brighton, Manchester and Leeds, Birmingham and Derby, Eastern Counties. These comprise most of the more important lines under construction during the period.

The impression gained from the figures in this table is very different from that given by the amounts of capital annually authorised, shown in Table 11. The peak is in the years 1838–40, and 1836 does not figure as more than a stage on

[1] See H. Scrivenor, *The Railways of the United Kingdom* (1849), *passim*.

the way up. In conjunction with Table 14, the figures in Table 15 suggest that expenditure was at a rate of over £10 million per annum in 1838, 1839 and 1840; that up to 1835 inclusive annual expenditure was less than £3 million; and that although the rate of expenditure in 1836 was more than double that in 1835, it was scarcely above the rate of expenditure in the depression year 1841.

The figures so far given are interesting, but they are not conclusive. In the first place, a more than negligible period may sometimes have elapsed between the calling up of funds and their expenditure. In some cases companies may have been influenced by easy conditions in the money market to call up funds in advance of their actual needs, for fear that trouble might be experienced in collecting them later on.[1] In the second place the figures in Table 15 take no account of funds raised by loans, which, as shown in Table 14, were substantial.[2]

We may therefore turn for further light to another set of figures, those relating to mileage completed in each year (Table 16).

Table 16. *Mileage of railway lines completed and opened*

Year	Mileage of lines currently completed	Estimated cost in £m. of lines currently completed	Mileage currently opened
1833	—	—	42
1834	35	0·4	90
1835	6	—	40
1836	—	—	65
1837	27	0·2	137
1838	357	11·5	202
1839	78	2·7	227
1840	219	8·4	528
1841	423	17·5	277
1842	355	10·5	164
1843	66	3·1	105

Sources: First and second columns, *Select Committee on Railways*, 1844, xi, pp. 600–1. Third column, H. G. Lewin, *Early British Railways, 1801–1844* (1925), p. 186. The source of Lewin's figures is said to be 'various Parliamentary Papers'.

The difference between the first and the third columns in Table 16, assuming both to be accurate (which is far from certain), arises because the latter includes sections of lines which were opened before the line had been finished in its entirety, and the former also excludes certain lines for which date of completion was not ascertainable.

Like the figures given in the previous tables, those shown in Table 16 are useful but inconclusive. In using them to help to form an estimate of the annual expenditure on railway building, the following points are to be observed: (1) The figures for mileage of lines currently completed are tolerably well authenticated,

---

[1] It was well known that many companies found difficulty after 1839 in raising the money needed when the work got going. Cf. G. H. Evans, *English Corporation Finance* (1936), p. 84.

[2] The common practice in railway Acts was to authorise the company to borrow on mortgage or otherwise up to one-third of the maximum permitted amount of its share capital. But as the permitted amount of share capital was commonly not fully called up, the proportion of loans in the total capital actually raised was higher than this would at first sight imply.

but in the years for which the highest figures are returned, the total is made up to a large extent by a few very important lines that had been under construction for a considerable period of time. These figures can therefore give only a rather general indication of the amount of work done in any year. They also exclude several hundred miles of line for which date of completion was not known. (2) The figures in the third column therefore correspond more closely to what we need. Unfortunately, there exists some uncertainty about their accuracy. Their compiler does not give the sources from which they are derived, and the present author has not been able to find in the Parliamentary Papers adequate material from which to check them. However, such checks as have been found tally fairly well,[1] and so in the absence of any alternative we may accept them as a correct indication of the broad drift. (3) There remains the doubt about the period of time that normally elapsed between the start of work upon a given section of line and its completion, which varied a good deal from one case to the next. Evidence has been presented to suggest that in the railway boom of the mid-1840's the average period of construction was about two years.[2] In the 1830's the period of construction was probably rather longer, since engineers were less experienced in the difficulties of the work; but how much difference this made we cannot tell.

If we accept a roughly two-year period of construction and take as an indication of the amount of work on hand in any year the mileage opened in that year plus the mileage opened in the two succeeding years, we get as a measure of annual expenditure the results shown in Table 17 (reducing to an index with $1838 = 100$).

Table 17. *Index of expenditure on railway building based on mileage opened*

1833	18	1839	107
1834	20	1840	102
1835	25	1841	57
1836	42	1842	48
1837	59	1843	62
1838	100		

The general tendency of this index, it will be observed, quite closely resembles that shown in Table 15, the main difference being that the present index does not rise so rapidly in 1836 and 1837 and stays more nearly level from 1838 to 1840. The leading conclusions already suggested would therefore appear to be confirmed. On the other hand, there is a substantial discrepancy between the two series for 1843, and this is evident to a lesser extent also for 1842.

A few further words may therefore be said on the opening and closing years of the period, seeing that it is these which have been left in the greatest doubt by the evidence so far presented.

How quickly did work start on the railways projected in the early 1830's and in the 'mania' period? The index of Table 15 suggests a higher rate of activity in

---

[1] For example, D. Lardner, *Railway Economy* (1850), p. 54, gives mileage opened in 1843 as 95; *Companion to the British Almanack*, 1841, p. 84, gives 483 miles opened in 1840 up to October, and *Companion to the British Almanack*, 1842, p. 56, gives 247 miles 'brought into use for the conveyance of passengers' during 1841.

[2] E. Victor Morgan, *Theory and Practice of Central Banking, 1797–1913* (1943), p. 153.

1836 and 1837 than does the index of Table 17. Table 18 gives some further evidence.

It appears that as far as these railways were concerned, the commencement of expenditure after the passage of the authorising Act was leisurely. Although a fair amount of work was in hand on the older lines by 1836 and more by 1837, it would seem doubtful whether, if this performance was typical, the lines which were authorized in 1836–7 can have been responsible for a great deal of expenditure before 1838. A good deal of the relatively large amount of share capital called up in 1836–7 is no doubt to be explained by legal and Parliamentary expenses and by the cost of expropriating landowners. The cost of the land commonly accounted for over 10% of the total cost of a railway.[1] In the years before 1836, both calls on share capital and mileage completed probably rather exaggerate the annual expenditure on construction, the former for the reason just mentioned and the latter because with a few important exceptions the lines or sections of lines completed were unambitious affairs designed for the conveyance of coal and other bulky materials over short distances and not planned on an expensive scale.[2]

Table 18. *Annual expenditure on construction by four railway companies*

	Date of authorising Act	Date of completion of line	Expenditure on construction, rolling stock etc. in £000's						
			1834	1835	1836	1837	1838	1839	1840
Great Western	1835	1841	—	93	350	966	1196	1157	1522
London and South-Western	1834	1842	25	150	385	385	609	402	325
London and Brighton	1837	1841	—	—	—	—	384	548	758
London and North-Western (southern division)	—*	—*	277	727	1230	1696	1036	579	193

* Company formed by amalgamation. The two most important constituent companies, the London and Birmingham and the Grand Junction, were both authorised in 1833 and opened the main portions of their lines in 1838.

Source: Accounts and Papers, 1847, LXIII, p. 77.

As far as concerns the years 1841–3, the index based on mileage completed probably gives a better measure of expenditure on construction than does the index of calls on share capital. By this date lines built by the companies represented by the latter index were for the most part already completed or nearing completion, and such construction as was going forward, especially in 1843, was due to newer undertakings. The share index therefore understates the rate of expenditure in these years. As evidence of this may be quoted some figures given

[1] See figures for individual companies in *Select Committee on Railway Acts Enactments*, 1846, XIV, Appendix 2. The cost of land together with the legal and other expenses of securing a company's authorising Act appear normally to have amounted to about a seventh of the total capital cost of the line.

[2] Cf. Lewin, *Early British Railways*, pp. 21–33.

in a Parliamentary Paper of 1847 purporting to show the amount of expenditure on construction by all railway companies (a) prior to 1841, (b) in the years 1841, 1842 and 1843 taken together.[1] These figures for all companies add up to approximately £32 million for the years prior to 1841 and £13 million for 1841–3. The figure for the latter period is therefore even higher relatively to the previous period than would appear from the index based on mileage completed. The explanation is probably that work still went forward after a line had been opened on improving facilities, acquiring additional rolling stock, etc.[2]

It is interesting to note that the figure of £45 million for total expenditure on construction up to the end of 1843, which results from the statistics just quoted, tallies well with the figures given above in the second column of Table 16. The latter add up to £54·3 million. If to £45 million we add an allowance of one-sixth of £45 million for Parliamentary and legal expenses and for purchase of land (see p. 124, n. 1) we get a total of £52·4 million. The discrepancy between the two figures, £54·3 million and £52·4 million, is accounted for to some extent by the exclusion from the latter of expenditure on lines completed before 1838 (see n. 1, below). Adding to the figure of £45 million an allowance for the expenses of companies that never got to the stage of completing their projected lines—and for running expenses, not to say dividends, paid out of capital[3]—we shall not be far wrong if we estimate the total amount of income-creating expenditure on railway building (i.e. excluding compensation for land but including at least a part of legal and such-like expenses) throughout the period at about £50 million.

What has been said already sufficiently demonstrates how impossible it is to determine accurately expenditure in each individual year. But if pressed to give an estimate of how the expenditure of this £50 million was distributed between the different years of the period, the author would, on the basis of all the evidence and considerations given, favour some such rough assignment as shown in Table 19.

Table 19. *Estimate of income-creating expenditure on railway building (£m.)*

1833	—	1837	5	1841	5
1834	1	1838	8	1842	3
1835	2	1839	9	1843	5
1836	4	1840	8		

[1] *Accounts and Papers*, 1847, LXIII, pp. 63–76. The figures are given as 'amount of money expended in the actual cost of construction and of working stock...of all railways in Great Britain and Ireland in each triennial period previous to the first day of January respectively in the years 1841, 1844 and 1847'. But a comparison of the figures given for the pre-1841 period with those given in *ibid.* p. 77 and quoted above in Table 18 shows that as far as these lines are concerned expenditure in *all* years before 1841 has been included and not merely expenditure in the triennial period 1838–40. The same presumably applies to the other lines as well. The word 'triennial', as far as it relates to the first of the periods distinguished, must therefore be a slip. However the figures given do not include any items for the cost of construction of the Liverpool and Manchester, of the Stockton and Darlington, and of a few other unimportant lines which had been completed at an early date, and which incurred *no* constructional cost in 1838 or later years.

[2] According to the figures in the source quoted in the preceding footnote, expenditure on purchase of working stock bore a much higher proportion to expenditure on construction between 1841 and 1843 than it did prior to 1841.

[3] Cf. R. S. Lambert, *The Railway King, 1800–1871* (1934), p. 60; W. W. Tomlinson, *The North-Eastern Railway* (1914), p. 433.

Table 20. *Total brick production in England and Wales (million bricks)*

1821	899	1827	1103	1833	1011	1839	1569
1822	1019	1828	1078	1834	1152	1840	1678
1823	1244	1829	1109	1835	1349	1841	1424
1824	1463	1830	1091	1836	1606	1842	1272
1825	1948	1831	1125	1837	1478	1843	1159
1826	1350	1832	972	1838	1427	1844	1421

Source: H. A. Shannon, 'Bricks—a trade index', *Economica* (1934), p. 318.

Table 21. *Duty received on bricks in two groups of local centres (£000's)*

	Group A	Group B
1832	110	177
1833	114	184
1834	130	209
1835	164	233
1836	208	264
1837	175	259
1838	164	256
1839	156	304
1840	151	359
1841	123	314
1842	107	283

For sources and methods of calculations see pp. 113, 115.

CHAPTER IX

THE COTTON INDUSTRY

WHETHER measured by the amount of employment it gave or by the value of its output, the cotton industry was easily the most important branch of manufacturing in Britain in the second quarter of the nineteenth century. For this reason and because of the relative abundance of the evidence concerning it, it is proposed now to trace the development of this industry throughout the period 1833–42 in some detail. In Chapter X the experience of some of the other leading British industries over the period will be dealt with more briefly.

1. VOLUME AND VALUE OF OUTPUT

Because of its exclusive reliance on an imported raw material, it is possible to obtain a tolerably accurate index of the volume of production in the cotton industry. Chart 11 shows the quantity of raw cotton consumed in the United

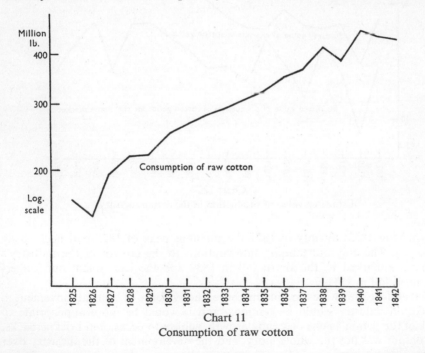

Chart 11
Consumption of raw cotton

Kingdom between 1825 and 1842. This may be taken as a fair measure of the volume of output in the industry. The behaviour of this series is remarkably in conflict with the simple-minded concept of the trade cycle according to which all important economic magnitudes, including *par excellence* the volume of production, rise until the 'turning-point' and then fall. The date of the turning-point

127

in the 1830's is universally agreed to have come in 1836—and contemporary comments on the *profitability* of the cotton industry would certainly give support to such a view. But from a mere inspection of the curve shown in Chart 11, no one could discern a major peak in 1836—far less a minor peak in 1839.[1] After the slump year 1826, output rose in every year up to 1838. Furthermore, with the exception of the year 1829, when the increase was very small, the rate of growth did not vary greatly from one year to another. Output increased rather more rapidly in 1836 and rather less rapidly in 1837 than in other years, but the difference is by no means striking. There was no increase in the rate of

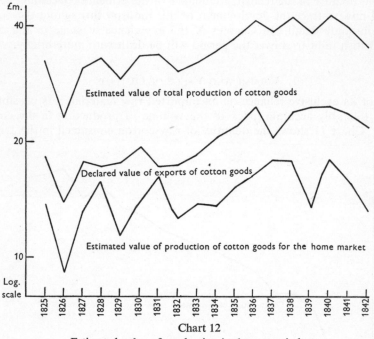

Chart 12

Estimated value of production in the cotton industry

growth after 1833; already in 1827 the previous peak of 1825 had been easily surpassed. The only outstanding interruptions to the growth of the industry's output are marked by the sharp fall in 1839 and the less violent but longer-continued fall in 1841–2.

If, therefore, this were the only measure, the evidence of cyclical movement in the cotton industry would be tenuous, and it would be more appropriate to think of the period as one of steady growth, subject to occasional brief setbacks. But output was not the whole story, and the development of the industry over these years was more complicated than would appear from the output figures alone.

This is already apparent if we have regard to the value of output instead of to its volume. A conjectural estimate of the value of output in the cotton industry

[1] See pp. 1–2.

in each year of the period, and of its distribution between home and export trades, is shown in Chart 12.[1] The results correspond rather more closely with what we should have expected than did the series of output volume shown in Chart 11, though there are still some peculiar features. We find a trough in 1832, followed by a rise up to 1836. A fall in 1837 is followed by another and very slightly higher peak in 1838, and another fall in 1839 is succeeded by a third peak which is again slightly higher than the previous one. The decline in 1841 is not of quite so great extent as the decline in 1839, but it is followed by a further steep fall in 1842—the only occasion during the whole period 1825–42 when the value of output declined for two years in succession.

In analysing the history lying behind these figures, it is convenient to divide the period into four phases. A concluding section will be devoted to a discussion of the impact on the labour force employed in the industry of the fluctuations taking place during the several phases.

2. 1826–1833: GROWING OUTPUT AND FALLING PROFITS

According to our calculations, the aggregate value of the industry's output between 1825 and 1834 showed a mild upward trend of rather less than 1% per annum, while fluctuating a good deal from one year to the next both in total and in distribution between home and export markets. The upward tendency was in the main confined to exports of yarn, which were mostly sold in northern Europe. It did not extend to exports of piece-goods, which were sold mostly in those distant territories classified as 'other' markets in Chapter VI.[2] There, as in the home trade, the growth in the volume of sales was made possible only by a fall in prices of about equal proportional magnitude.

The fall in prices was the outstanding feature of the industry's history during this phase. It was the result not of decline in raw-material prices but of a reduction in manufacturers' costs and profit margins. Between 1826 and 1832 the price of raw cotton altered relatively little. Yarn and cloth prices, on the other hand, tended steadily downwards till 1830. Towards the end of 1830 prices of finished goods stabilised, and profit prospects temporarily improved 'to such a degree as...to allow accumulation of capital on the whole to take place'.[3] But this brighter phase was of short duration, and by the autumn of 1831 the trade was again in the doldrums. Costs had fallen and were falling, but not sufficiently to avoid a decline in profits. It was observed that the numerous failures taking place around this time were not the result of 'overtrading' as in 1825–6 but simply the result of a steady decline in profit margins. Throughout 1832 only the most efficient firms were able to show any profit—that is to say, 'profit' in the sense customary in the trade, reckoned after deduction of interest on own capital as well as on borrowed capital at a rate of 4 or 5%.

Apart from the brief interlude in 1830–1—years marked by a temporary improvement in the economy as a whole—profits were generally agreed to be

---

[1] The basis of these estimates is explained in the Appendix at the end of the chapter, along with a table of the relevant statistical series.

[2] Except in the years 1835–6 the United States was not one of the chief buyers of British cotton manufactures.

[3] *Circular to Bankers*, 7 January 1831.

low and on balance falling between 1827 and 1833. In 1833 the situation for a while became even worse. The state of raw-cotton stocks in the country at the beginning of that year had been such that some rise in prices had been expected, but the rise that actually took place went much further than was justified on any reasonable reckoning of the state of the market for finished goods, and was largely the result of speculation. The consequence was a still further reduction in margins for spinners and manufacturers, since the price of yarn and cloth did not rise as much as the price of the raw material. Not till the beginning of 1834 did the price of cotton fall a little and allow the trade to return to a more profitable footing.[1]

In view of the general agreement that profits were so low during this first (pre-1834) phase, it is natural to ask how it came about that the volume of output rose steadily and already in 1827 far surpassed that of the boom year 1825.

In seeking an answer to this question, there is one point that needs to be placed in the forefront of the discussion. Contemporary writers never ceased to emphasise it, and it was much heard again when depression returned in the early 1840's. In the representative cotton mill of the period, overhead costs were so high in relation to prime costs that, however low the price of the product, it was in general bad policy to reduce output below the level of full-capacity working. One can conceive of the situation schematically as one where there is a reverse L-shaped short-run average prime cost curve and a horizontal or nearly horizontal demand curve, the latter in normal times intersecting the former on its vertical stretch. The difference realised between total receipts and total prime costs will be required to cover overheads and provide a profit. In such a situation, if the demand curve facing the firm falls, nothing will be gained by reducing output unless the demand curve falls right down to the level of the horizontal stretch of the cost curve or below. If overheads constitute a large proportion of total costs and were initially being fully covered, the extent of the fall in the demand curve will plainly have to be very substantial before there is any contraction in output. In the meanwhile the firm will have nothing better to do than carry on as before until its financial resources are exhausted.[2]

This appears to have been the position facing many cotton manufacturers in the late 1820's and early 1830's. Under-utilisation of capacity was not common. Short-time working is occasionally mentioned, but as often as not it was a concerted move agreed to by a number of producers in the hope that it might lead to an improvement in the market—for instance, in order to force down the artificially inflated price of the fibre in 1833. It was not the normal reaction on the part of a single firm working under competitive conditions.[3]

What has just been said helps to explain part of the paradox of the years

[1] For evidence on prices and profits in the cotton industry till 1834, see *Circular to Bankers*, especially the issues of 1 July 1831, 13 July 1832, 1 February 1833, 26 July 1833 and 8 September 1833; *Select Committee on Manufactures Commerce and Shipping*, 1833, VI (henceforward referred to as *S.C. of 1833*), evidence of K. Finlay, H. Houldsworth, W. Graham, G. Smith, W. Greg and J. Milne, *passim* (the tables given there, pp. 568–70, illustrate statistically the fall in margins as it affected one particular firm).

[2] Among the most explicit of the many passages dealing with this point are *Circular to Bankers*, 22 February 1833 and *S.C. of 1833*, QQ. 1232–9 (Finlay), Q. 11553 (Greg), QQ. 11045–6 (Milne).

[3] On short-time working, cf. *S.C. of 1833*, QQ. 10646–7 (Sefton) and QQ. 11474–80 (Greg); T. Ellison, 'The great crises in the history of the cotton trade', *The Exchange* (1863), p. 46.

1825–33, namely, why firms did not *reduce* output when they found profits falling. But it does not explain the *increase* in output that actually took place. Indeed, all the emphasis placed on the inadvisability of working at less than full capacity makes the increase in output in a way yet more difficult to understand, since if there was little idle capacity in the early years like 1827, the subsequent increase in output can only have been made possible by an *expansion* of capacity. A further question has therefore to be asked. Why did not merely output but also capacity continue to expand when profits were low and falling?

It is true that as a joint result of the causes just set out and of the steady march of technical progress, *some* net expansion of capacity was to be expected for obvious reasons. In the late 1820's and early 1830's the textile machinery coming on to the market was steadily improving in quality and declining in cost,[1] and even those firms which for one reason or another found it impossible to take advantage of technical advances involving a complete reconstruction of their mills were yet able to profit by innovations requiring no more than adaptation of existing machinery. Innovations of this sort were fairly numerous.[2] At all times except the very worst, there will in a progressive industry always be a certain number of firms which, being above the average in efficiency, find it worth while to expand in circumstances which afford little or no profit to the representative firm. In the period under discussion this expansion undertaken by the more efficient firms in the cotton industry was not matched by an equal contraction of output on the part of the substandard firms because of the inelasticity of short-period supply already discussed.

Technical progress is thus part of the answer to the question which was asked —why capacity expanded notwithstanding a more or less static (albeit fairly elastic) demand and an indifferent level of profits. However, it is not the whole answer. Another important element in the situation was the presence of what may be termed semi-reserve capacity. It has been asserted above that there was little unused capacity in the cotton industry during these years. This is true, in the sense that output could not be increased without installing more machinery and equipment. But in the boom years ending in 1825 a fair number of firms built factories of a size and with a power supply in excess of their immediate needs. These factories were then gradually filled with machinery as the years advanced.[3] For some time, therefore, floor space and power were not being fully utilised, although there was no excess capacity in the sense of idle spindles or looms. It was consequently possible to expand production, not, indeed, altogether without further capital investment, but with an amount of investment that was relatively small. As time progressed and floor space and power supply became gradually more fully used, expansion of this type became more difficult and greater capital expenditure had to be undertaken in order to make possible a given increase in output. But the delay in filling mills with machinery in some cases extended till as late as 1833.

In some respects analogous to the filling of factories with machinery was the installation of power-weaving equipment by firms that had previously been engaged solely as spinners. This was possibly the most important form of

---

[1] *S.C. of 1833*, Q. 11012 (Milne), QQ. 11564–5 (Greg).
[2] *S.C. of 1833*, Q. 702 (Finlay).
[3] *S.C. of 1833*, QQ. 9166, 9229–31 (Smith); QQ. 11495–6 (Greg).

investment undertaken in the industry between 1825 and 1834.[1] Spinning had a longer history as a factory industry than weaving, and power-looms were at this time still relatively a novelty in practice, though their invention belonged, of course, to a much earlier date. Consequently, although a considerable number of power-looms were set in operation in 1824–5, it was to the spinning department of the industry that speculative capital was principally attracted in those years, and it was that department of the industry which felt most severely the pressure of increased capacity on prices and profits in the ensuing years. It was generally agreed that spinning was more depressed than weaving throughout the phase of the period which we are considering.

There was a further reason for this, related to that just mentioned. Just as in the boom the expansion of capacity was proportionately greater in spinning than in weaving because weaving was still far from being entirely a factory industry, so in weaving the burden of slack trade could to a large extent be passed on by employers to the already chronically depressed hand-loom weavers, who were by this time suffering from the mechanisation in their own section of the trade as much as they had benefited a quarter of a century earlier from the mechanisation of spinning.[2] The concern of power-loom manufacturers with overhead costs made them anxious to keep their factories in full operation as far as possible. In good times most of them also gave work out to hand-loom weavers. But the employers were not called upon to bear the overhead costs of supporting hand-loom weavers and their families, so it was they who first felt the consequences when trade became slack. 'The factories', a contemporary observer noted, 'are for what is expected to be the steady and permanent demand, and the hand-loom weavers are a body to meet the fluctuations of the market.'[3]

For these reasons power-loom weaving was generally found to be more profitable than spinning; but it was not sufficiently so to attract newcomers to the industry. For a variety of more or less technical reasons, pure weaving firms were relatively uncommon at this stage of the industry's history,[4] and anyone seeking to enter the business from outside would have had to set up a mixed undertaking, doing both spinning and power-weaving. The low-profit rate in the spinning section made this an unattractive proposition. But the case was different for those who had already sunk capital in spinning, and it was they who were chiefly responsible for the extensive investment in power-looms that was carried on in the years preceding 1833.[5]

This particular form of investment may be considered to have been essentially a manifestation of technical progress. But, as was suggested above, the instal-

---

[1] *S.C. of 1833*, QQ. 1191 (Finlay), 9161–8 (Smith), 11369–75 (Greg). The statement by Baines (E. Baines, *History of the Cotton Manufacture in Great Britain* (1835), p. 236) that few power-looms were built between 1825 and 1832 is not supported by the evidence of the witnesses before the Committee of 1833, cited above, which Baines himself refers to. These witnesses speak of such investment as having been carried out 'in late years' or 'in the last few years', without conveying the impression that it was entirely a very recent development.

[2] Cf. Sir John Clapham, *Economic History of Modern Britain* (1930 edition), I, pp. 551–8; S. J. Chapman, *The Lancashire Cotton Industry* (1904), pp. 36–49.

[3] *Report of Hand-loom Weavers Commissioners*, 1841 (1st session), x, p. 306.

[4] Chapman, pp. 161–2.

[5] Power-looms were also being built to some extent by former hand-loom weaving manufacturers whose own line of business was depressed and who were anxious that the knowledge of the trade which they had acquired should not be entirely wasted. (*S.C. of 1833*, QQ. 5259–60 (Houldsworth), 9277–9309 (Smith).)

lation of power-looms in these years of low profits may also be regarded as analogous to the filling of existing mills with more machinery. In both cases what happened was that in the previous boom one part of the firm's establishment—factory space or power supply in the one instance, spinning capacity in the other—had been expanded relatively to the rest, and there was therefore an incentive to expand the remaining parts in proportion in the following years.

On the face of it, expansion in either of the two ways so far discussed—technical improvements (shifting of cost curve) and fuller utilisation of fixed factors of production (movement along downward-sloping cost curve)—would have been advantageous whether the rate of profit were high or low, so long as it was not so low as to induce complete stoppage. Obviously the rate at which surplus factory space was drawn into use and the rate at which power-looms were added to spindles were to a large degree a function simply of the passage of time. But contemporary writers state frequently, and with such emphasis as to leave no room for doubt, that the expansion which took place up till 1833 was largely motivated by the *low* level of profits. Mill-owners, it is said, were spurred into expanding their operations by the depression of the trade and the consequent need to spread their overheads over a larger volume of output.[1] An enlargement of the scale of operations was, it appears, a laborious and possibly risky business, demanding time and thought and effort from the entrepreneur. When trade was good, he might very likely prefer to leave well alone, even though there were a number of ways in which he might increase his profits yet further if he cared to give his mind to the matter.

Thus, although the decline in prices and margins meant that few new firms entered the industry, it apparently served to stimulate increases in output on the part of existing firms. Since it was the increase in output which was principally responsible for the decline in prices, there was here evidently the possibility of a cumulative downward movement of prices setting in. But there was necessarily a limit beyond which this process could not go, a limit imposed by the gradual absorption of semi-reserve capacity (or in the last resort by the fall of profits to a point compelling firms to close down). As through time this reserve came to be more nearly used up, the extent to which output could be expanded without any great new capital outlay was reduced, and the previously dominant tendency for output to rise irrespective of falling prices (or even because of them) was correspondingly weakened. The stage was set for the next phase of the cycle.

The conclusions so far reached may now be briefly summarised. Taking the period 1825–33 as a whole, the money value of the cotton industry's output was rising only very slowly. The rapid expansion in the volume of output was accompanied by a great fall in prices and manufacturers' margins, though the elasticity of demand was sufficient to prevent this fall from reaching catastrophic dimensions, and the general drift of demand was probably upwards rather than downwards. Very few new firms entered the industry and few completely new mills were built,[2] but capacity was substantially enlarged as entrepreneurs were impelled by the pressure of competition to seek ways of spreading their over-

[1] Cf. *S.C. of 1833*, QQ. 563 (Lewis Loyd), 5218–24, 5292–8 (Houldsworth), 9166 (Smith) 11495–6, 11533–4 (Greg); *Circular to Bankers*, 22 February 1833 (also 5 November 1841); *Select Committee on Bank of England Charter*, 1831–2, VI, Q. 4398 (J. B. Smith).
[2] *S.C. of 1833*, QQ. 5259–60 (Houldsworth), 9159 (Smith); Baines, p. 395.

heads over a larger volume of output. A variety of minor technical improvements were sought out and applied; spinners extended their businesses to include power-loom weaving; new machinery was installed in order to make fuller use of floor space and power brought into existence in the earlier boom period. At the end of the phase, in 1833, there was relatively little idle capacity in the industry. Despite the fall in prices most mills continued in full work, and although there were large falls in margins per unit of output, the fall in profit rates per unit of capital was a good deal less severe on account of the adoption of the various cost-reducing expedients that have been described. Fundamentally, it was the reductions in cost brought about by these means that enabled surplus capacity or semi-reserve capacity to be absorbed, and so made possible the creation of substantial quantities of new capital in the ensuing period.

3. 1834–1836: PROSPERITY AND HIGH INVESTMENT

The outstanding feature of the second phase, running from 1834 to 1836, was the rise in demand and in the value of output. The rise in exports of cotton goods followed much the same pattern as that described in earlier chapters for exports generally. In 1833–4 the rise was accounted for mainly by sales to 'other' markets, but in 1835 practically the whole of the increase in piece-goods exports went to the United States. Then in 1836 the value of cotton exports to the United States fell somewhat, and the 'other' markets again took the lead. The rise in the value of sales in the home market over the period was, according to our calculations, less than the rise in exports, but it too played its part in 1835–6.

The period of more or less unqualified prosperity for the cotton industry was considered to have begun early in 1834.[1] In 1834 the price of raw cotton remained nearly stable till October,[2] and yarn and cloth prices moved in such a way as to ensure satisfactory profit margins. In 1835 a shortage of raw cotton was again felt, but demand was sufficiently buoyant to stand the consequent rise in prices. Till near the end of the year trade was prosperous, but profit margins were apparently not abnormally high, and the high rate of return enjoyed by a number of firms was largely the result of capital gains derived from holding raw cotton in stock or in process on a rising market. In 1836, however, there was a decided rise in cloth and yarn prices without any corresponding advance in the cost of the fibre. Indeed, taking the year as a whole, raw cotton was slightly cheaper in 1836 than it had been in 1835, notwithstanding the large increase in the quantity imported.[3] Profit rates for spinners and manufacturers therefore rose most at the very end of the boom.

The amount of investment stimulated by the rise of profits in the cotton industry in 1834–6 was very great. The distribution of this investment between the individual years cannot be ascertained, but it is possible to get a good idea of its magnitude over the years 1835–7 taken as a whole, these three years including the most active period, 1835–6, and the recession year 1837 in which there was probably a good deal of work still in hand. The relevant figures may now be briefly reviewed.

[1] *Circular to Bankers*, 13 February 1835, 3 July 1835.
[2] *Circular to Bankers*, 24 October 1834. For annual figures of prices of raw cotton, yarn and cloth, see T. Ellison, *Cotton Trade of Great Britain* (1886), Tables 1 and 2 (*ad fin.*).
[3] See p. 57.

According to a survey made by the Factory Inspectors early in 1835, the total horse-power of steam engines in cotton mills in Lancashire at that date was 20,302. The figure given in a second survey made three years later was 29,566.[1] The latter was probably somewhat of an underestimate, since it took no account of engines in mills currently unoccupied—a category which had been included in the 1835 estimate.[2] If the figures for the two years could be set on a comparable basis in this respect, the increase in horse-power between the two dates could scarcely be less than 50%.

These figures are fairly well confirmed by another contemporary calculation made on a rather different basis. The horse-power of steam engines *erected* between 'January or July 1835' (the survey in this year having been spread over six months) and July 1838 in all factories in 'Lancashire and its immediate vicinity' was estimated at 13,226, of which nearly 12,000 were to be found in cotton mills.[3] If allowance is made for the slight differences in coverage, this result is much the same as that obtained by the Factory Inspectors.

Estimates for the total amount of capital invested in the cotton manufacture naturally rested on much shakier foundations than estimates of horse-power. For what they are worth, however, it is interesting to note that the estimates that were made of the increase in capital between 1835 and 1837 were somewhat lower than those just quoted for horse-power. 25% seems to have been the usual reckoning.[4] If this figure is roughly correct, the smaller rate of growth of all capital invested in the industry compared to that quoted for horse-power of steam engines (50%) may perhaps be held to indicate that, as in 1824–5, installation of power supply was temporarily outstripping installation of equipment to use it.

In face of the general agreement that the rate of investment in the cotton industry increased so rapidly after 1834, it is natural to ask why there was not at the same time a corresponding increase in the rate of growth of the quantity of cotton goods produced.

The rise in the price of raw material provides part of the answer. Already in February 1835 shortage of cotton was mentioned as imposing a decided check on output.[5] In 1836, when increased supplies of the fibre came forward, the rate of growth of output did accelerate to some degree.

It is unlikely, however, that this is the entire explanation. It is unfortunately not possible to analyse the evolution of the industry between 1834 and 1836 so confidently as for the earlier years, since there is no source material for the later phase of comparable value to that provided by the evidence of witnesses from the cotton trade before the Select Committee on Manufactures Commerce and Shipping in 1833. But it seems probable that the increase in the money value of investment after 1834 did not entail an equivalent increase in the rate of growth of capacity. By 1834 the semi-reserve capacity inherited from 1825 must

---

[1] *Accounts and Papers*, 1836, XLV, pp. 55–79 and 1839, XLII, pp. 16–17 (returns from Factory Inspectors). Cf. also *Statistical Journal* (1838), I, pp. 315–18, 444.

[2] In number, unoccupied mills in 1838 constituted about 6% of the total. It is possible, however, that their size was typically less than average; see p. 142, n. 2.

[3] *Forty-eighth report of Select Committee on Poor Law Amendment Act*, 1837–8, XVIII, Part III, p. 506.

[4] *Circular to Bankers*, 4 August 1837. *London Shipping and Mercantile Gazette*, 2 January 1840 (quoted Jenks, *Migration of British Capital to 1875*, p. 362) gives 30%.

[5] *Circular to Bankers*, 13 February 1835.

have been largely exhausted, and each addition to productive potential must have become correspondingly more expensive. Moreover, if it is true that the various forms of expansion undertaken in the period before 1833 were in large part the result of competitive pressure and fear of loss, it is reasonable to infer that established manufacturers may have relaxed their efforts when they found profits improving.

The change which took place around 1834 was not, it may be suggested, so much an increase in the rate of growth of capacity as a change in the nature of that growth. Instead of cautious expansion and technical improvement carried out by existing firms, the strengthening of demand and the rise in profits led to an influx of new capital to all sections of the industry, involving the construction of complete new mills instead of the adaptation of old ones. Much of this investment required time before it could bear fruit in increased output. It has already been suggested that investment in looms and spindles did not keep pace with investment in sources of power. Such technical delays—possibly accentuated in some cases by the recession in 1837—were among the reasons why production did not rise more rapidly during the boom years. And if it is conceded that the innovations and expansions to which entrepreneurs had been driven by their difficulties before 1833 were afterwards executed with a good deal less energy, it is unnecessary to seek further explanations for the more or less unaltered rate of growth of output of cotton goods during the years when investment expenditure in the industry was increasing in so spectacular a manner.

The position of the cotton industry in 1834–6 differed from its position in the years before 1834 on both the demand side and the supply side. In the earlier period any increases in demand that might from time to time take place tended not to have any great effect on profits because they were outweighed by the steady growth of production on the part of firms which were seeking to make fuller use of fixed factors of production. Consequently investment in money terms was not great. After 1833 not merely was demand more buoyant (for reasons external to the industry), but a given increase in demand stimulated a greater amount of income-creating investment. The behaviour of demand in general is a matter which we cannot discuss fully till Chapter XII, but here evidently was an important factor in the mechanism of the cyclical upswing.

The joint-stock banks that were newly being promoted in this period were more active in Lancashire than in any other part of the country, and the finance they provided for the construction of new cotton mills attracted much attention and comment at the time. Just how important was the part they played in this respect is not very easy to gauge. Finance for investment usually tends to be available in some form or other if profits are sufficiently high. But entry to the cotton industry was not altogether easy for the outsider at this period—to set up in spinning, capital of £5000 or so was necessary[1]—and there seems no reason to deny that the development of joint-stock banks did enable a greater amount of investment—possibly a substantially greater amount—to be carried out than would otherwise have been possible.[2] This was perhaps particularly important in 1835 when, as mentioned above (p. 134), profit rates were apparently not much higher than in 1834 and there was none the less a great increase in investment.

[1] *S.C. of 1833*, QQ. 5304–5 (Houldsworth).
[2] The growth of joint stock banks and their importance are discussed more fully in Chapter XI.

4. 1837–1840: CONFLICTING TRENDS

The period 1837–40 is the least homogeneous and the most difficult to understand of the four phases that we have distinguished. With the striking exception of 1839, the volume of output continued to rise more rapidly than ever, and employment—at least for factory hands—was steady.[1] But the value of output fluctuated violently with little upward trend, and the trade was never felt to be as prosperous as it had been in 1835–6. The period 1837–40 was, indeed, summarised as having been one of 'great loss of capital' in the industry, in consequence of the competition from the large number of recently erected mills.[2]

The year 1837 has gone down to history as one of great depression in the cotton trade, as in manufacturing industry generally. Piece-goods exports fell steeply both in value and in volume, for reasons that have been explained in earlier chapters with reference to exports as a whole.[3] Raw-cotton imports declined, and there was a headlong fall in prices, due partly to the prostration of the American South and partly to the high stocks accumulated in this country in 1836. Yet it is evident from Chart 11 that whatever depressive tendencies may have been at work did not extend to the volume of output, since the amount of raw cotton consumed continued to rise at a scarcely slackened rate.

The collapse of prices undoubtedly hit merchants hard, and the fall in exports meant hardship for manufacturers and workers whose products were specific to the export trades—for example, hand-loom weavers engaged on the production of fancy goods for the American market. But most entrepreneurs seem to have been able to switch over to the home market, and the value (not merely the volume) of sales there appears to have risen to a remarkable extent (see Chart 12). On account of manufacturers' reluctance to work their factories at less than full capacity, they were evidently driven by the fall in export demand to sell in the home market a much greater proportion of their output than they had been willing or able to do in the boom times of 1836—with advantage to home consumers and operatives alike.

The impression that most manufacturers in the cotton industry managed to survive 1837 without too much loss is confirmed by an illuminating incident that took place in April of that year. A deputation from Liverpool prepared a petition for presentation to the government and to the Bank of England to request that special assistance be given to Lancashire to relieve its difficulties, and an invitation was sent to the Manchester Chamber of Commerce to join in sponsoring this petition.[4] In reply, the Manchester Chamber of Commerce acknowledged that the plight of merchants in Liverpool fully justified a request

[1] *Circular to Bankers*, 9 April 1841; *Statistical Journal*, III (1840), p. 370; *Report of the Assistant Poor Law Commissioners sent to inquire into the state of the population of Stockport*, 1842, xxxv (referred to as *Report on Stockport*), pp. 201–2.
[2] *Circular to Bankers*, 5 June 1840; and many other passages in similar vein.
[3] Yarn exports to the northern European market continued to rise in 1837.
[4] A. Redford, *Manchester Merchants and Foreign Trade, 1794–1858* (1934), p. 80; *Circular to Bankers*, 21 April 1837 and 28 April 1837. Amongst other requests, the deputation suggested that the Liverpool branch of the Bank of England should consent to discount bills on Liverpool brokers, contrary to its normal practice, in order to prevent further declines in the price of raw cotton. This request the Bank rejected, on the reasonable grounds that if artificial obstacles were placed in the way of the fall in prices, output in the industry would be adversely affected. It was apparently informally hinted, however, that the Bank's Liverpool branch would in future be rather more lenient in granting discounts on the sort of paper in question.

for special assistance of the sort desired, but argued that manufacturers in Manchester could not really claim that their position was so bad as to call for extraordinary aid. For this reason the Chamber declined to be a party to the petition, contenting itself with giving the Liverpool deputation good wishes for the success of their mission.

Manufacturers responded with alacrity to the improved prospects opened up by the recovery of exports in 1838. The volume of output rose even more rapidly than it had done in 1836. Sales in the home market were slightly lower than in 1837, but were still well above the 1836 level, by value as well as by volume. But prices of finished goods continued to sag, and by the end of the year stocks of manufactured goods were reported to be increasing to a disturbing degree.[1] The continuing increase in capacity was evidently exerting a steady pressure on profits and prices.

Output fell in 1839 to an extent unparalleled in any year since 1826. The circumstances underlying this fall were peculiar. At the beginning of the year, prospects for the industry appeared rather poor, though not seriously alarming. The high stocks carried over from 1838 depressed the market, and the disastrous harvest threatened a deterioration in the home trade. Yarn exports to the Continent, moreover, were held up by the financial crises in France and Belgium in December 1838.[2] Then to add to these troubles came the attempted valorisation of cotton on the part of the B.U.S.[3] As early as February short time was being worked as a result of agreement between Lancashire spinners in an endeavour to defeat this scheme. It was the persistent working of short time during the next few months that was responsible for the striking fall in the volume of output over the year as a whole.[4]

It would be a mistake to suppose that this short-time working was resorted to because the valorisation of raw cotton had driven up prime costs to such an extent that manufacturers were incurring losses on marginal units of output. There is no reason to suppose that anything of that sort took place. Manufacturers' margins were undoubtedly poor, but it is unlikely that they were any worse than they had been, for example, in 1832 and 1837. In those years, in contrast with 1839, the growth of output did not suffer any interruption. In 1839 the rise in raw-cotton prices that caused so much fuss was really of very moderate dimensions. Prices even at their highest point were much lower than they had been on many occasions between 1833 and 1836. Nor was demand hopelessly bad; the value of exports actually rose a little, and home demand was stated to be 'tolerably satisfactory, notwithstanding the high price of bread'.[5] As has already been seen, profit margins had normally to fall very low indeed before the representative competitive firm found it worth while to curtail output, and there is no evidence that this stage was reached in 1839.

In fact, the working of short time in 1839 was not the result of decisions taken independently by individual firms. It was a concerted step taken in order to checkmate Nicholas Biddle—in short, a monopsonistic restriction of output.

---

[1] *Circular to Bankers*, 5 July 1839 and 3 April 1840; T. Ellison, 'The great crises in the history of the cotton trade', *The Exchange* (1863), p. 48.
[2] See pp. 88–90.   [3] See pp. 62–5.
[4] Tooke, III, p. 74; *Circular to Bankers*, 8 February 1839, 3 May 1839, 7 June 1839, 26 July 1839.
[5] *Circular to Bankers*, 3 January 1840.

In normal times the advantages to be gained by concerted output restriction on the part of spinners were not sufficient to overcome the various obstacles in the way; the demand for finished goods and the supply of raw material to the industry were both too elastic. In normal times it was unlikely that concerted short-time working would reduce the price of cotton enough to make it worth while. In 1839, on the other hand, the rise in price was due to exceptional circumstances, and if Biddle's speculation could be broken, there was every chance of a substantial fall. Much the same sort of thing had happened on a smaller scale in 1833, when British rather than American cotton speculators were the enemy aimed at.[1]

We may sum up by saying that what was unusual about 1839 was not so much the *magnitude* of the difficulties facing cotton spinners as the peculiar nature of these difficulties. Because of the valorisation scheme, spinners for once felt it worth while to combine to reduce output instead of each endeavouring to press more and more of his wares on the market, as was usual when profits were low. Whether they judged correctly in so deciding is somewhat doubtful. Prices of cotton did fall, but the sacrifice of output (falling entirely on the home market, apparently) that had to be made in the meanwhile was severe. Hence 1839 was summed up as having been 'a singularly disastrous year for manufacturer, spinner and merchant'.[2]

In 1840 came a natural reaction. Exports continued at about the same level, but the home market, having been starved in the year before, now took an enormously increased amount of cotton goods. Profits were not especially good, but the increase in the volume of output was tremendous. Accusations of over-trading came to be heard again from time to time.[3]

Having now traced the course of year-to-year fluctuations in the cotton industry between 1837 and 1840, it remains to survey the industry's position and development during these four years regarded as a whole.

In 1837–40, as in each of the two earlier phases we have distinguished, the capacity of the industry continued to grow. This is apparent alike from the increase in output (for there was no idle capacity in 1836) and from direct evidence quoted below. Since the *value* of the industry's output showed virtually no upward trend, the growth in capacity created, as it was bound to do, a heavy pressure on prices and profits. The situation was in many ways analogous to that which had prevailed in the years before 1834.

Some expansion of capacity after 1836 was to be expected, for reasons which are obvious. As after 1825, many mills projected in the boom period were no doubt still incomplete or not yet filled with machinery, and older firms were compelled to seek ways of meeting the new competition. Much of the expansion that took place—probably the greater part of it—was evidently to be explained in such ways. The analogy to the pre-1834 period is, however, incomplete in one important respect. It will be recalled that in the earlier phase the expansion that took place was undertaken almost entirely by existing firms, and the construc-

---

[1] On each occasion moral as well as practical considerations probably played a part. The rise in prices being 'artificial', it was legitimate to combine to thwart it. In normal times combination to drive down prices would be improper as well as likely to fail.

[2] *Circular to Bankers*, 3 January 1840.

[3] Cf. W. F. Spackman, *Statistical Tables...of the United Kingdom of Great Britain and its Dependencies* (1842), p. 77.

tion of complete new mills was very rare. In 1837–40 this appears not to have been the case. The expansion of capacity apparently involved extensive new building, both in the spinning and in the weaving sections of the industry.

Some of the evidence for this may be briefly quoted. Where horse-power increased substantially, it may be taken that more than mere adaptation of old mills was being undertaken. Total horse-power (steam and water) in the Lancashire cotton industry was a little over 23,000 early in 1835 and about 34,000 three years later.[1] At the end of 1841 it was about 38,500.[2] In other words, in the three years beginning spring 1835 an annual average of about 3500 h.p. were erected, and from then until the end of 1841 an annual average of about 1250 h.p. There was thus a substantial falling-off in the latter period, but the level of investment was still not negligible. It represented an addition of about 4% per annum to the capital stock of the industry.

This investment was not carried out regularly in each of the years in question. Leonard Horner, the Factory Inspector for Lancashire, collected the following figures for horse-power erected in the years specified in 'new mills or additions to mills' producing cotton textiles: 1839, 641; 1840, 1513; 1841, 1172.[3] Taken in conjunction with the earlier figures, this implies that about 1200 h.p. were installed in the latter part of 1838; the amount installed in the whole of that year was probably therefore not less than 2000 h.p.[4] The positive correlation between these figures and the year-to-year fluctuations in the prosperity of the industry is very evident,[5] and is itself an indication that the investment recorded was not entirely of the type prevalent before 1834 and characteristically induced by the fear of loss.

We must not exaggerate the amount of completely new investment initiated in 1837–40. The rate of increase in horse-power in those years was much lower than it had been in the boom, whereas the rate of growth of output (abstracting from the peculiar events of 1839) was higher than ever. There need therefore be no doubt that most of the increase in output was made possible by expansion on the basis of existing factory space and power on the part of firms established during or before the boom, in the manner already witnessed in the period between 1826 and 1834. Moreover, that some new factories should have continued to be erected when 'great loss of capital' was being complained of is not in itself necessarily a paradox, for the newer and more efficient mills were no doubt able

---

[1] The sources of these figures are as quoted above, p. 135, n. 1.

[2] The figure 38,500 is obtained from tables on pp. 357–9 of *Reports of the Inspectors of Factories*, 1842, XXII, adjusted (from detailed figures, *ibid.* pp. 370–412) so as to exclude mills situated outside Lancashire.

[3] *Reports of the Inspectors of Factories*, 1842, XXII, p. 414. The figures there given show that the investment extended to spinning and weaving alike.

[4] For this relatively high rate of investment in 1838 there is other corroboration. Dr J. P. Kay (*Forty-eighth report of Select Committee on Poor Law Amendment Act*, 1837–8, XVIII, Part III, p. 506) calculated that the horse-power of machines *in course of erection* in July 1838 exceeded 4000. His estimate included all manufacturing industry, not merely cotton, and covered certain parts of Cheshire in addition to Lancashire. Correction for this would probably reduce the figure to about 3000. This is broadly consistent with the estimate quoted of 2000 h.p. for the amount *completed* in 1838. On the considerable amount of new building carried out in the cotton industry in 1838, cf. also *Circular to Bankers*, 16 February 1838.

[5] The high rate of interest in 1839 may also, in addition to the depression of trade in that year, have played a part in causing the figure for it to be low. 1841 was not a good year for the industry, but trade continued tolerable until about May, and the investment carried out during the year had probably been started before that date.

to show a profit when others could not. The capital whose loss was lamented was the capital of the established firms. A low rate of profit per unit of turn-over did not necessarily preclude an adequate rate of profit per unit of capital for low-cost producers.

But there does remain in this continuing expansion of new undertakings in the late 1830's something of a contrast with the aftermath of 1825. The financial facilities afforded by the joint-stock banks no doubt continued to make entry to the industry easier than it had formerly been, though they were no longer able to pursue such generous lending policies as in 1835–6; but probably the principal cause for the contrast mentioned is simply that, taking the three years 1838–40 as a whole, the fall in profits was not so severe as it had been in the aftermath of 1825, on account of the effects of railway building and a number of other factors in maintaining the national income for most of the three years in question at a tolerably high level.

5. 1841–1842: DEPRESSION

With demand at the level prevailing in 1840, profits in the cotton trade were barely adequate. In 1841–2 demand fell steeply, and dull trade gave way to disastrous depression. The years 1841–2 constitute the only instance of consumption of raw cotton falling for two years in succession in the whole period between the end of the Napoleonic Wars and the cotton famine of the 1860's.

Serious falling-off in demand was first noted early in the spring of 1841.[1] From then on demand continued to deteriorate. The export trade was not good, but sales in the home market were considerably worse, and many manufacturers resorted to dumping abroad in order to keep up the volume of their trade.[2] The total value of the industry's output did not, according to our calculations, fall as low as it had done in 1837, but the vast increase in capital invested in the industry since that year meant that the rate of profit was now far worse. By the autumn of 1841 little completely new investment was being done, but many firms were installing labour-saving devices and other innovations to keep down costs, and this increased still further the difficulties of firms which for one reason or another were not in a position to adapt themselves.[3]

By 1841–2 the state of the industry was so bad that in contrast to the earlier years of low profits some reduction in output could no longer be avoided, even though there was none of the concerted restriction of production practised in 1839. The extent to which production fell was in fact greater than appears from Chart 11, for the depression caused spinners to concentrate to a greater extent than usual on the coarsest counts, and the output of finished goods was therefore lower relatively than the amount of raw material used.[4] However, even if account is taken of this, it is probably still true to say that, although the volume of output was declining in 1841 and 1842, it was still higher in each of these years than it had been at any time before 1840.

[1] *Select Committee on Distress (Paisley)*, 1843, VII, Q. 293 (R. Wilson); *Circular to Bankers*, 2 April 1841.
[2] *Hansard's Parliamentary Debates* (3rd series), LXIV, col. 1211 (speech by Cobden); *Report on Stockport*, p. 252; T. Ellison, 'The great crises in the history of the cotton trade', *The Exchange* (1863), p. 49. Cf. above, p. 71.
[3] *Reports of the Inspectors of Factories*, 1842, XXII, pp. 342, 362; *Circular to Bankers*, 29 July 1842.　　　　　[4] *Hansard's Parliamentary Debates, loc. cit.*

What happened in 1841–2 was the natural sequel to what had happened in 1837–40. Because of the burden of overheads, the generality of firms endeavoured to avoid curtailing output and even increased it in so far as they were able. This was emphasised by commentators in the early 1840's no less than it had been ten years earlier.[1] The volume of output therefore remained high in comparison with earlier years. But by this time a new feature had appeared: things were so bad that firms began to go bankrupt in large numbers. Profits having been poor for a number of years, many entrepreneurs faced the further deterioration in trade in 1841–2 with their reserves already almost exhausted. The banks were in no position to help, for mortality amongst them was scarcely less high than amongst manufacturers. In the inter-war years of the twentieth century, bank finance enabled many firms in the cotton industry to carry on a losing trade for years, since the banks could balance the losses they made in Lancashire by profits earned in less depressed regions. In the 1840's this was not possible, for the Lancashire joint-stock banks were heavily dependent on the prosperity of local industry.

Table 22. *Estimated weekly loss of wages in cotton mills in Stockport in 1841*

	£
By stoppage of mills	3116
By reduction in wage rates	945
By time lost* about	1000
By reduced number of hands	422
Total	£5483

* This includes the effects both of short time working and of strikes against proposed reductions in wages.

Source: Report on Stockport, p. 237.

It was the bankruptcies and consequent complete closures of firms that were mainly responsible for the unemployment and fall of production in 1841–2. Those firms that could keep going often produced more than ever. As evidence of this may be quoted the interesting figures (Table 22) given by the Assistant Poor Law Commissioners. They show the relative importance of the different contributory causes of reduction in the weekly wage bill in cotton mills in Stockport in 1841, compared to a hypothetical prosperity level. Table 23 covers a wider field in less detail. Well over half the unemployment recorded appears as the result of complete closure of mills. The under-employment resulting from short-time working was probably not very great; according to particulars provided to the Factory Inspectors by mill managers, 'short time' most frequently meant 'hours of daylight'.[2]

[1] *Report on Stockport*, p. 200; *Circular to Bankers*, 5 November 1841, 24 November 1841; *Reports of the Inspectors of Factories*, 1842, xxii, pp. 343, 415–18; H. Ashworth, 'Statistics of the present depression of trade in Bolton', *Statistical Journal*, v (1842), pp. 74–81. Horner and Ashworth, in the last two places cited, gave figures to demonstrate statistically the predominance of fixed costs in manufacturers' total outgoings.

[2] Horner's figures from which Table 23 is compiled provide a good deal of material beyond what is here discussed. For example, it appears from Table 23 that mills not at work were on the average smaller than those working full time, and that mills working short time were the largest of all. This relationship holds for all three of the main types of firms (spinners, weavers and mixed) considered separately, so it was not due to differing severity of the depression in

The firms which closed down were those which had been unable to reduce their costs and had now no longer sufficient reserves to carry on at a loss. For example, Stockport was particularly hard hit because it was an old centre of the industry and many of the mills there were 'not fit for the reception of the most improved machinery'.[1] Unemployment amongst factory hands being largely the result of complete stoppages, it was natural that it should be delayed for a long time after profits had passed their peak, and that when it did come its impact should be correspondingly sudden and severe. The figures quoted show, it is true, that an appreciable number of firms were by the end of 1841 working at less than full capacity. But had it not been for the complete stoppage of many mills, output in aggregate would almost certainly have continued to rise in 1841–2, albeit at a slackened rate.

Table 23. *Cotton mills in Lancashire in the last quarter of* 1841

	No. of mills	Total h.p. of machinery	H.p. of machinery idle	Employment (000's)	
				When in full work	At end of 1841
Mills working full time	844	29,531	2,617	147	137
Mills working short time	129	5,668	656	29	27
Mills not at work	131	3,303	3,303	17	—

Source: Reports of the Inspectors of Factories, 1842, XXII, pp. 357–9, 370–412.

6. SUMMARY AND CONCLUSIONS

Some of the conclusions reached so far in this chapter may now be briefly summarised.

The steady growth in the volume of output that characterised the entire period from 1826 onwards, with the exception of 1839 and 1841–2, is explained by the joint working of two factors:

(*a*) The pressure of overheads normally made full utilisation of capacity relatively more profitable than any lower level of output, even if demand was not very good. In 1839 the reduction in output was the result of monopsonistic agreement between spinners to drive down the price of cotton, undertaken at a time when profits were poor but not disastrously so. In 1841–2 the state of the trade became so bad that marginal producers were compelled to close down completely.

(*b*) The rate of growth of capacity was fairly even, since, although the amount of new building and hence the amount of investment in money terms was much

---

different sections of the industry, or anything of that nature. That the smallest firms should have been most prone to close down is intelligible, but it is not obvious why short time should have been especially prevalent in large firms. Was the demand for their products perhaps less elastic than for the products of other firms? This is one of the many interesting points raised by Horner's figures which we cannot here pursue. Cf. the use made of them for quite a different purpose by John Jewkes, 'The localisation of the cotton industry', *Economic Journal* (*Economic History*) (1930), pp. 93–5, where a well-deserved tribute is paid to Horner and his associates for the skill and energy displayed in the preparation of this and other reports.

[1] *Report on Stockport*, p. 239.

higher in 1834–6 than in other years, yet at times when profits were not adequate to attract much fresh capital to the industry (i) entrepreneurs were driven to seek ways of lowering their costs and spreading their overheads over a larger volume of output, and (ii) there was usually a fair amount of work to be done in completing and making fuller use of investment projects started in the preceding boom.

The high rate of profit and consequently of investment in 1834–6 was the result, first of an unusually rapid rise in money demand both at home and abroad, and secondly of the increasing cost of adding to capacity as the factories built in the mid-1820's were gradually filled with machinery, and established firms slackened their efforts to find cheaper and better methods. The latter factors raised the supply price of increased output from existing firms and so encouraged the establishment of new firms, and the former factor enabled a higher price to be charged without losing custom. After 1837 demand stagnated and increases in output again came to be effected without very much new capital expenditure being required. In consequence the years 1837–40 marked a period of recession as far as profits were concerned. In 1841–2, demand declined, and recession turned into depression.[1]

The distribution of sales between the home market and exports fluctuated considerably from year to year and did not follow any regular pattern. Producers evidently found it tolerably easy to make a switch if either branch were especially depressed. For example, in 1837 the steep fall in exports led to an increase in the value of sales at home, and in 1841–2 the depression in the home market led to dumping abroad.

7. The Impact on Labour

Before concluding the chapter, something must be said about the impact on labour of the fluctuations in the cotton industry that have just been surveyed.

Employment of factory workers apparently moved more or less in line with that of the volume of output, growing steadily until 1840 and then declining. The fall in output in 1839 resulted in under-employment—short-time working—rather than the laying-off of hands. In 1841–2, however, the stoppage of mills threw many operatives completely out of work. Up till then the same considerations as prevented manufacturers from curtailing output impelled them to provide employment to their workpeople, and it was generally agreed that entrepreneurs suffered much greater proportional loss in money earnings between 1837 and 1840 than the operatives did. The generally steady employment enjoyed by factory workers during these years did not extend to the hand-loom weavers, the supply of whom was chronically excessive in relation to the demand. Hand-loom weavers could be sure of employment only when trade was exceptionally busy.

The amount of unemployment amongst cotton operatives did not move in a simple obverse relation to that of employment, on account of the rapid increase in the labour force attached to the industry. This increase resulted from immigra-

---

[1] It is interesting to note that this pattern is apparently totally different from that which obtained after 1825. Then the really bad year (1826) came immediately after the boom, and was followed by a long period of slack but not disastrously depressed trade.

tion to the cotton towns of workers from rural districts of England and from Ireland, and to a less degree from the natural increase in the population already employed in the industry.[1] It was therefore possible for there to be widespread unemployment in the industry in 1841–2 notwithstanding that the actual number employed was well in excess of what it had been in the boom years 1835–6. When the slump came, those who ten years earlier had been under-employed in agriculture found themselves unemployed in manufacturing districts. Short-period fluctuations in the rate of townwards migration cannot be traced on account of the lack of statistics for inter-censal years, but it appears that, as was to be expected, townwards migration was highest in 1835–6 and slackened off or reversed after 1840. In 1843–4, when trade in general was recovering, there remained a labour surplus of unusual magnitude in the country-side in consequence of the failure of the towns to absorb the customary number of immigrants during the preceding years of depression.[2]

As has been said, employment of factory operatives in the cotton industry fluctuated roughly in step with the volume of output. But over the period as a whole output grew more rapidly than employment, in consequence of technical improvements. The Factory Inspectors' returns show an increase of 33% in the number of operatives in cotton factories in Lancashire between 1835 and 1841. In the same period the volume of output rose 38%. The difference between these two figures is admittedly small, but the increase in productivity was greater than this would suggest, since in 1841 a good deal of short time was being worked, and, moreover, weaving that had formerly been given out to hand-loom weavers (not included in the numbers quoted) had been increasingly transferred to the power-looms in factories. The increase in horse-power between 1835 and 1841 was no less than 52%, considerably greater proportionally than the increase in output.

In the slump years, the increase in productivity was accompanied by a substantial amount of technological unemployment. The item 'reduced number of hands' in Table 22 (p. 142) relates mainly to operatives displaced by improvements in machinery. It does not bulk very large in the table, but then, as we saw (p. 143), Stockport was a town where improved methods were being relatively less practised than in newer centres of the industry. Horner wrote in 1841 that 'especially in the last four or five years' efforts have been made to cut costs 'by rendering existing machinery more productive; by superseding manual labour by mechanical contrivances; and where manual labour is still necessary, by getting it performed by children and young persons instead of adults'. This was of particular importance in the department of spinning the yarn on mules, where labour was most skilled and most expensive. Longer mules and 'double-decker' mules were installed in order to increase output per man. The introduction of the self-acting mule went ahead especially rapidly.[3]

Much of the unemployment that occurred in the slump may be considered technological in a rather more general sense.[4] Technological unemployment need not necessarily involve that operatives are discharged because in the

[1] Cf. A. Redford, *Labour Migration in England, 1800–1850* (1926), *passim.*
[2] Tooke, IV, pp. 56–7; *Annual Register*, 1838, p. 200.
[3] *Reports of the Inspectors of Factories*, 1842, XXII, p. 362.
[4] Cf. J. A. Schumpeter, *Business Cycles* (1939), II, pp. 515–16.

factory where they were employed the work formerly done by them is now being performed by a machine. Essentially the same result is brought about when the competition of new efficient firms with low labour (and other) costs per unit of output forces high-cost firms to work short time or to close down. This sequence of events was one of the most characteristic features of 1841–2.

Much of the technological unemployment of the early 1840's was the result of the slump in this way. Yet something similar had been going on for a longer period as a result of more fundamental forces. The advance of technique and the elimination of jobs like that of the spinner by mechanisation led not merely to a reduction in the number of operatives per unit of output, but also, as Horner pointed out in the passage quoted above, to the substitution of the labour of women and children for that of men. According to the Factory Inspectors' returns, employment of adults (aged 18 and over) in all mills in the Lancashire district rose between 1835 and 1838 from 76,000 to 85,000—12%; employment of children (under 13) and young persons (13–17) together rose from 47,000 to 64,000—36%. Unfortunately, precisely comparable figures are not available in the returns for 1841, but Horner computed that at that date those aged 20 or under comprised 60% of the industry's labour force, and this suggests that the trend evident in the earlier years did not cease. In 1841 barely 20% of operatives in cotton factories were aged over 30.[1]

This predominance of juveniles, and its tendency to become still more marked through time, is the more remarkable when it is observed that the general age-group distribution of the population was moving in the opposite direction. The proportion of the population aged over 20 was increasing substantially in the 1830's and 1840's as a result of the abnormally high birth-rate in the second decade of the century.[2] In 1841 the proportion of those aged over 20 was considerably higher for the population as a whole than it was amongst operatives in cotton factories,[3] a remarkable result, especially when it is borne in mind that the Factory Act of 1833 forbade the employment of children under 9. In view of this tendency for the proportion of juveniles in the industry's labour force to increase, it is hard to resist the conclusion that adult males must often have found it difficult to get employment in the cotton districts. In the one department where unskilled adult male labour was needed—in the blowing room—competition from Irishmen kept wages low.[4]

This conclusion is not inconsistent with the continued influx of labour from the countryside to the cotton districts, for it would be erroneous to suppose that such immigration necessarily implied full employment for those already in the

---

[1] *Accounts and Papers*, 1836, XLV, pp. 55, 70–9; 1839, XLII, pp. 16–17, 68–9; *Reports of the Inspectors of Factories, loc. cit.* p. 365. The figures quoted for 1841 are at first sight inconsistent with those given in the Census of that year (1844, XXVII, p. 16), according to which cotton workers aged over 20 were more than twice as numerous as those below that age. (Similarly Horner gives the proportion of female operatives as 54%, whereas the Census shows male operatives in a majority.) The seeming inconsistency is explained by the fact that the Census figures include hand-loom weavers (commonly considered to number about a quarter of a million in all), most of whom were adult males, while the Factory Inspectors' returns relate exclusively to factory operatives.

[2] Cf. T. H. Marshall, 'The population of England and Wales from the Industrial Revolution to the World War', *Economic History Review* (1934–5), p. 69.

[3] Census of 1841, 1843, XXII, p. 17.

[4] *First Annual Report of the Poor Law Commissioners for England and Wales*, 1835, XXXV, pp. 295–6.

locality. The inducement to agricultural labourers to migrate to the cotton towns often lay less in the opportunity to increase their own earnings than in the improvement in the earning power of their children. Dr Kay, Assistant Poor Law Commissioner, discussing in 1835 the prospects for the migration of workpeople to Lancashire from the south of England, wrote: 'widows with large families of children or handicraftsmen, such as shoemakers, tailors, blacksmiths, etc., etc., with large families will be the most successful immigrants.' 'The English adult labourer', he added, 'would be preferred to the Irish, but the child would also be exceedingly more valuable to the manufacturer than the man.'[1]

It is evident that the concept of 'full employment' is too vague to be very useful in analysing the condition of labour in the cotton industry in this period. In the first place, immigration from rural districts provided a reserve supply of labour that was capable of expanding or contracting according to the demand. In the second place, the supply of children might be inadequate but that of adults superabundant.[2] Furthermore, the number of children seeking employment was liable to vary from year to year in accordance with the fluctuations in the earnings in real terms of the chief bread-winner of the family, who might, for example, be a hand-loom weaver.[3] Amongst the hand-loom weavers themselves, under-employment was the normal state of affairs.[4]

Children and young persons constituted a larger proportion of the labour force in cotton mills than in any other industry of comparable importance.[5] The tendency for this proportion to rise still further in the 1830's may help to explain why wages of cotton operatives had a downward trend over the period (see Table 24).

This downward trend is not apparent in most of the statistics which have been collected of money wage-rates in other occupations.[6] These on the whole tend to rise over the period, although not very rapidly. Children's wages were low because of their lack of bargaining power and restricted opportunities for employment outside the cotton industry. Hence, since the distinction between

[1] *Ibid.* p. 300.
[2] Whether even in busy times there was any *general* shortage of children's labour is rather doubtful, though local and temporary shortages were always liable to occur. The matter is discussed in *Reports of the Inspectors of Factories*, 1837, xxxi, p. 60. Horner (writing in October 1836) was disposed to regard shortage of labour as an exceptional occurrence, and argued that objections to further statutory limitation of hours of work on such grounds were much exaggerated. 'When the Factory Act first came into operation...I heard it confidently predicted that the certain result...would be that half the mills in the country would be stopped for want of hands, and that thousands of children would be thrown out of employment and reduced to a state of starvation: two consequences of an opposite nature which it never appeared to me very possible to reconcile.' (*Ibid.*)
[3] 'In the country we have extreme difficulty in getting young children, *especially in times when bread is cheap*' (italics added). *Select Committee on the Factory Acts*, 1840, x, Q. 9185 (J. Nussey).
[4] A further difficulty in applying the concept 'full employment' or 'unemployment' to this period is that the line between the wage earner and the small master was not always a hard-and-fast one. This was perhaps less important in cotton textiles than in industries where the representative unit of production was smaller. In the cutlery trades, for example, a notable feature of the depression of the early 1840's was the great increase in the number of small masters, men unable to find employment as wage earners. (G. I. H. Lloyd, *The Cutlery Trades* (1913), p. 194.)
[5] *Select Committee on the Factory Acts*, 1840, x, QQ. 3475–6 (J. Stuart). The proportion of children to total labour force was even higher in silk mills; cf. G. R. Porter, *Progress of the Nation* (1851 edition), p. 232.
[6] See Table 33, p. 221.

skilled and unskilled labour in cotton corresponded to a considerable degree with the distinction between adult labour and child labour, the displacement of skilled workers by mechanisation carried with it a correspondingly larger reduction in the average rate of wages than would have been the case had the unskilled labour been that of adults, and thereby tended to reduce the average rate of wages and with it the extent to which the workers in the industry benefited from technical progress.

Table 24. *Wages of operatives in cotton factories (pence per week)*

1832	114	1838	116
1833	114	1839	112
1834	115	1840	112
1835	116	1841	113
1836	117	1842	113
1837	117	1843	110

Source: G. H. Wood, *Wages in the Cotton Trade* (1910), p. 127.

APPENDIX

Statistics of value of production in the cotton industry

The purpose of this appendix is to explain the methods which have been used to derive the estimates shown in Chart 12 of the value of the cotton industry's annual output and so (by subtracting the declared value of exports) the value of its output of goods for the home market.[1] It should be emphasised that these estimates are extremely inexact. It is hoped that their accuracy is sufficient to justify the conclusions drawn from them in the text; for other purposes they might well prove inadequate.

The basic data on which the calculations are founded are the quantity of raw cotton consumed (in lb.) which is taken as an index of total volume of production; the money value (declared value) of exports of yarn and of piece-goods respectively; and the volume of exports of yarn and of piece-goods respectively, measured either in natural units (lb. of yarn and yards of cloth) or in Official values.[2] All these figures are available on a fairly reliable basis. Unfortunately, they are not sufficient by themselves to give us what we want, and they therefore require to be supplemented by some calculations and assumptions of more dubious validity.

Several contemporary authorities made attempts to calculate the total value of the cotton industry's output in 1833,[3] and we therefore take this year as the base year. In 1833 the declared value of yarn exports was £4·7 million and that of piece-goods exports £13·8 million. Baines estimated the total value of the industry's output in that year at £31·3 million, setting the value of sales in the home market—the unknown item—at £12·9 million. Bannatyne's estimate in the *Encyclopaedia Britannica* was £34 million for the total, making £15·5 million for

---

[1] See also Table 25.
[2] For the Official valuation system see pp. 9–10 above.
[3] J. R. McCulloch, *Dictionary of Commerce* (1844 edition), *s.v.* Cotton; *Encyclopaedia Britannica* (1842 edition), *s.v.* Cotton; E. Baines, *History of the Cotton Manufacture* (1835), pp. 399–413; G. R. Porter, *Progress of the Nation* (1851 edition), pp. 212–13.

the home trade. The same figure as Bannatyne's was arrived at by McCulloch and given in the earlier editions of his *Dictionary of Commerce*; but at a later date he came to believe that a rather lower estimate would be preferable.[1]

The means by which all these authorities arrived at their conclusions were, it must be said, decidedly crude, and on the evidence they adduce any figure between £30 million and £34 million would be almost equally plausible. We have therefore assumed as a reasonable compromise, and one which leads to simplicity in calculation, that the value of the home trade in 1833 was equal to the value of piece-goods exported, viz. £13·8 million.[2] This puts the total value of the industry's output for the year at £32·3 million. If we had assumed a slightly different figure, it would not have made any great difference to the course of *fluctuations* displayed in the result. The figures we reach therefore probably indicate year-to-year fluctuations more accurately than they indicate absolute values.

Having arrived at the figure mentioned for the base year, it remains to make calculations for the value of output in the other years. The procedure that has been adopted to this end for each year is as follows:

The weight of the raw cotton used in the manufacture of piece-goods is first estimated by deducting from total weight of raw cotton consumed in the industry the weight of yarn exported, plus an allowance of 10% of the latter for the weight lost in spinning.[3] The estimated weight of raw cotton used in the manufacture of piece-goods is then reduced to a relative with 1833 = 100, and is divided by the Official value of exports of cotton piece-goods, also expressed as a relative with 1833 = 100. The result provides an index of the proportion of quantity of piece-goods exported to quantity of piece-goods produced in the year in question, expressed as a relative of the corresponding proportion in 1833. Now we have found that there is reason to believe that in 1833 the total *value* of piece-goods production was approximately double that of piece-goods export. Unless there was great variation in quality between home and export trades from one year to another (see next paragraph), the figure we have just calculated (the proportion of *quantity* of piece-goods exported to *quantity* of piece-goods produced in any year, expressed as relative of same proportion in 1833) should therefore also enable us to calculate the relation in any year between piece-goods production and piece-goods exports *by value*. Thus, for example, in 1836 the ratio of the quantity of piece-goods output to piece-goods exported was 0·95 of that ratio in 1833. Therefore since in 1833 the value of piece-goods production is assumed to have been equal to twice that of piece-goods export, we may estimate that in 1836 the value of piece-goods production was 1·90 times the value of piece-goods export. Since we know the declared value of piece-goods exported in each year, the rest is plain sailing. Total output of the industry is obtained by adding the value of yarn exports to the value of piece-goods production, and the

---

[1] *Dictionary of Commerce* (1880 edition), *s.v.* Cotton.

[2] Various *obiter dicta* are to be found in the literature on the relative importance of the home and export trades in cotton. Baines (*op. cit.* p. 398) considered the home trade to be nearly equal to the foreign trade in value. Two witnesses before the Select Committee on Manufactures Commerce and Shipping in 1833 (Greg, QQ. 11403–4 and Thomson, Q. 3541) gave one-third as the proportion of home trade to total trade, one of them considering this to be a high estimate.

[3] Cf. Baines, p. 376.

value of home sales is obtained by deducting the value of exports from the total value of production.

Certain assumptions upon which the validity of the above method depends may be briefly discussed. The question of variations in quality has already been mentioned. There were sometimes appreciable variations in quality of piece-goods exported from one year to another.[1] As these depended to a considerable extent on the destinations to which the goods were to be sent, it is probable that corresponding variations did not take place in the home trade, at least not to the same extent. Hence the ratio of value of exports to value of home sales is not necessarily the same as the ratio of the lb. weight of the two. This difficulty has, however, already been allowed for in an approximate manner by taking Official values instead of natural units (yards) as an index of quantity of piece-goods exported. In years when the quality of exports is low, the Official values (which take some account of quality) tend to understatement when taken as an index of the *weight* of raw cotton entering into piece-goods exported, and hence lead to too high an estimate of the *quantity* of piece-goods produced for the home market. On the other hand, in these years the value of home relative to export trade will tend to be higher than the relative quantity, because the deterioration of quality found in exports is assumed not to have taken place—or to have taken place to a less extent—in the home trade. The two sources of error thus tend to cancel out. Had we believed that year-to-year variations in quality were normally of equal extent in the home trade and in exports it would have been appropriate to measure quantity of piece-goods exports in yards instead of in Official values. It may be observed, however, that this would have made very little difference to the final result.

Both declared and Official value of exports are strictly speaking indices of *sales*, or rather of consignments to foreign markets. The procedure we have adopted assumes implicitly that they are an adequate index of *production*, since we set them against the quantity of raw cotton taken into consumption. We are thus in effect disregarding the consequences of any fluctuations that may have taken place in stocks of manufactured goods held in this country. However, it seems to have been generally supposed that such fluctuations were small—by no means of the same order of magnitude as fluctuations in stocks of raw cotton. The only instance when fluctuations in stocks of finished goods are commented on is in 1838/9.[2] Allowance for this could hardly alter the general movement found in our figures for these years.

---

[1] This is evident in the variations in the ratio of unprinted to printed goods exported. Cf. Porter, p. 180.

[2] See p. 138.

Table 25. *Value of production in the cotton industry*

Year	(1) Consumption of raw cotton (m. lb.)	(2) Yarn exports (m. lb.)	(3) Estimated raw cotton used for piece-goods production (m. lb.)	(4) Official value of exports of cotton piece-goods (£m.)	(5) (Quantity of raw cotton used for piece-goods production as relative, 1833=100) ÷ (Official value of exports of cotton piece-goods as relative, 1833=100)	(5) Declared value of exports of cotton piece-goods (£m.)	(7) Estimated value of total production of cotton piece-goods (£m.)	(8) Declared value of yarn exports (£m.)	(9) Estimated total value of production of all cotton goods (£m.)	(10) Declared value of cotton exports (£m.)	(11) Estimated value of cotton production for home market (£m.)
1825	167	33	131	26·6	0·95	15·2	28·9	3·2	32·1	18·4	13·7
1826	150	42	104	21·4	0·93	10·6	19·7	3·5	23·2	14·1	9·1
1827	197	45	148	29·2	0·97	14·1	27·4	3·6	31·0	17·8	13·2
1828	218	51	162	29·0	1·08	13·6	29·4	3·6	33·0	17·2	15·8
1829	219	61	152	31·8	0·92	13·6	25·0	4·0	29·0	17·6	11·4
1830	248	65	177	35·4	0·95	15·3	29·3	4·1	33·4	19·4	14·0
1831	263	64	193	33·7	1·11	13·3	29·5	4·0	33·5	17·3	16·2
1832	277	76	193	37·1	1·00	12·7	25·4	4·7	30·1	17·4	12·7
1833	287	71	209	40·1	1·00	13·8	27·6	4·7	32·3	18·5	13·8
1834	303	76	219	44·3	0·95	15·3	29·0	5·2	34·2	20·5	13·7
1835	318	83	227	44·8	0·97	16·4	31·8	5·7	37·5	22·1	15·4
1836	347	88	250	50·6	0·95	18·5	35·1	6·1	41·2	24·6	16·6
1837	366	103	253	41·9	1·15	13·6	31·6	7·0	38·6	20·6	18·0
1838	417	115	291	54·6	1·03	16·8	34·6	7·4	42·0	24·1	17·9
1839	382	106	266	58·5	0·83	17·7	31·2	6·9	38·1	24·6	13·5
1840	459	118	329	62·6	1·04	17·6	35·6	7·1	42·7	24·7	18·0
1841	438	123	303	58·8	0·99	16·2	32·1	7·3	39·4	23·5	15·9
1842	435	137	284	56·4	0·97	13·9	27·0	7·8	34·8	21·7	13·1

Sources: Columns (1), (2), (6), (8) and (10) from T. Ellison, *Cotton Trade of Great Britain* (1886), Tables 1 and 2 (*ad fin.*). Column (4), from annual *Finance Accounts* in *Accounts and Papers*. For method of calculation of other columns, see text.

151

CHAPTER X

CYCLICAL MOVEMENTS IN OTHER INDUSTRIES

1. INTRODUCTION

WE have been able to trace the history of the cotton industry in some detail because the figures of raw-cotton consumption provide us with an index of the volume of production. The absence of any production index for the great majority of other industries prevents us from forming so clear a picture of the pattern of fluctuations in them. Scattered comments on the fortunes of individual industries in individual years are plentiful in contemporary writers; but even if time and space permitted a full recital of these, their value would be limited, since the writers were most commonly concerned with the *profitability* of business, and what they said is liable to be misleading if taken as an indication of the volume of production or even of its value. Had figures for the volume of cotton consumption not survived and exclusive reliance been placed instead on contemporary comments of a qualitative nature, a very faulty picture of the fluctuations undergone by the industry would almost certainly have been obtained. Again, ample statistics are available on both the volume and the value of exports of particular commodities. But we have seen that in the case of cotton the home and export trades by no means always marched in step; and in other industries it would be still more dangerous to take exports as a criterion of total production, for there were few industries in which exports were as high a proportion of total output as they were in cotton.

In the present chapter, therefore, no attempt will be made to analyse the cyclical experience of each of the nation's major industries. All that will be done is to call attention to certain features of interest in a number of industries on which evidence is fairly readily to be found. For many very important industries—boots and shoes, for example—it would be difficult to find any substantial body of evidence without a search in local newspaper files or the records of individual firms. The student of business cycles can do no more than wait for such industries to attract specialised attention from historians.

2. WOOLLEN AND WORSTED INDUSTRIES

Contemporary comments on the experience of the woollen and worsted industries in 1833–42 suggest that the timing of fluctuations there followed the same broad outline as in cotton, with 1833–6 prosperous and the subsequent period dull or depressed.[1] Such, at any rate, was the way profits fluctuated; exactly how the volume of production moved is difficult to ascertain.

The volume of foreign wool taken into consumption is shown in the first column of Table 26. The steep rise up to 1836 is followed by a recession in 1837,

[1] Cf. H. Heaton, 'An early Victorian business forecaster in the woollen industry', *Economic Journal* (*Economic History*) (1933), pp. 553–74. This contains an account of the periodical surveys of the state of the trade which appeared during these years in the *Leeds Mercury*.

a recovery in 1838 and then a gradual and irregular tendency to decline. In the depressed years at the end of the period consumption of imported wool was below that of 1836 (contrasting in this respect with the consumption of cotton), but it was higher than it had been in 1833–5.

Table 26. *Imports and exports of wool and woollens*

Year	Wool entered for home consumption (m. lb.)	Volume of woollen and worsted exports (1880=100)	Value of woollen and worsted exports (£m.)
1832	28	13	5·2
1833	39	15	6·3
1834	41	13	5·7
1835	43	15	6·8
1836	61	15	7·6
1837	43	9	4·7
1838	56	13	5·8
1839	53	13	6·3
1840	50	11	5·3
1841	53	13	5·7
1842	45	13	5·2

Sources: Wool entered for home consumption, and value of woollen and worsted exports, *Accounts and Papers*; volume of exports, A. H. Imlah, 'Terms of trade of the United Kingdom, 1798–1913', *Journal of Economic History* (November 1950), pp. 186–7.

Unfortunately, consumption of imported wool cannot be taken as an index of the volume of output in the industry, since home-grown wool comprised on the average about two-thirds of the supply,[1] and we have no means of gauging the amount of it used in each year. It is probable, moreover, that the proportion of imported wool used showed a tendency to diminish during this period, (*a*) because the worsted industry, which used English wool almost exclusively, was growing more rapidly than the woollen industry, and (*b*) because within the woollen industry less attention was coming to be paid to the finer cloths for which foreign wool was essential.[2] It is therefore probable that the figures of foreign wool consumed understate the rate of growth of output over the whole period.

The same is probably true of the export figures (second and third columns of Table 26). These also show production in the concluding years as higher than at the beginning of the period but not so high as during the boom. However, since the United States was the industry's main export market, and since the falling off in the concluding years relatively to 1835–6 was very great in wool, as in all exports to the United States, it is probable that the figures of exports, if interpreted as an indication of total output in the industry, give an unduly favourable picture of the mid-1830's relatively to the later years. Sales of woollen and worsted goods in the home market were considered at all times to exceed exports by a substantial margin.

The woollen industry was still largely based on out-work in the 1830's, and the power-loom had there made little progress. In worsted, on the other hand, the factory system was well established, and the unit of production was large;

[1] J. James, *History of the Worsted Manufacture in England* (1857), p. 489.
[2] Heaton, pp. 562, 572–4.

153

here power-loom weaving was exerting a heavy pressure on hand-loom weavers' earnings, as in cotton.[1] During this period the rate of growth of the worsted industry was considerably more rapid than the rate of growth of the woollen industry, partly because of the greater susceptibility of the former to mechanisation, and partly because of the important innovation, first generally introduced about 1837, of using a cotton instead of a woollen warp in worsted manufacture.[2] Between 1835 and 1838 the number of woollen mills in the West Riding of Yorkshire increased by 30%, and the number of worsted mills by 65%. Similarly, employment in woollen mills in the West Riding increased from about 24,000 in 1835 to about 26,000 in 1838 (the increase being almost entirely in persons under 18); employment in worsted mills was only about 17,000 in 1835, but in 1838 had risen to a level about equal to that in woollen mills.[3] It appears, moreover, that in addition to growing more rapidly during the boom, the worsted industry suffered relatively the less severely of the two in the slump in the early 1840's.[4]

Wool and worsted, like cotton, had had a long dull period after 1826; but the recovery in Yorkshire decidedly antedated that in Lancashire. By 1832 the state of trade in Leeds was already good and in 1833 it was better; the level of prosperity was such as to induce extensive new investment in the industry.[5] Similar revival in cotton, it will be recalled, had to wait till 1834. Perhaps there had been a smaller expansion of capacity in the woollen industry in the years between 1825 and 1832. The five years 1832–6 were all marked by high prosperity in the West Riding, and great numbers of new mills were built. In autumn 1836 there was a very sudden reverse, in consequence of the collapse of the American demand, and for the next year trade was bad. There was a recovery in 1838, but towards the end of that year and in 1839 the home demand was weakened by the bad harvests, and this apparently more than offset the rise in exports. In 1840 the home demand improved and the trade as a whole was felt to be rather better off than in 1839. In 1841 there was a temporary revival of exports to the United States, but in that year and in 1842 business was none the less considered to be bad and getting worse.[6]

In the trough of the slump wool and worsted were even harder hit than cotton. Unemployment in Leeds in 1842 was worse than in Manchester.[7] Halifax—after Bradford the most important centre of the worsted industry—showed a greater proportional decline in brick production between 1836 and 1842 than anywhere else in England, although until 1839 the level maintained was quite high.[8] The

---

[1] The best brief comparison of the structure and development of the woollen and worsted industries in this period is E. Baines, 'On the woollen manufacture of England; with special reference to the Leeds clothing district', *Statistical Journal* (1859), xxii, pp. 1–34.

[2] James, pp. 470–6.

[3] *Accounts and Papers*, 1836, xlv, pp. 136–7; 1839, xlii, pp. 18–19, 292–3 (Returns from Factory Inspectors).

[4] Cf. James, p. 450.

[5] Heaton, p. 562; *Select Committee on Manufactures Commerce and Shipping*, 1833, vi (*S.C. of 1833*), QQ. 540 (L. Loyd); 754, 763, 790 (J. Bates); 1104, 1287–9 (H. Hughes); 1878, 1903 (J. Brooke).

[6] Heaton, *loc. cit.*; James, pp. 440–50, 477–94.

[7] *Hansard's Parliamentary Debates* (3rd series), lxiv, cols. 1244–5 (Lord Brougham).

[8] Duty paid on bricks in Halifax (thousand £):

1836	1837	1838	1839	1840	1841	1842
7·2	6·5	6·3	4·8	2·1	1·3	1·1

burden of the extra capacity created during the boom was very widely complained of.[1] Woollen and worsted manufacturers did not have the same facilities for dumping their wares abroad as were enjoyed by cotton manufacturers. Moreover, it was to be expected that in the slump output and employment should be more seriously affected in wool (though not on this account in worsted) than in cotton, since over a large part of the woollen industry out-work was still the rule. Where that was the case, entrepreneurs' overhead costs were small relatively to their prime costs, and they lacked the incentive to keep output high despite low profits which was so prominent a feature of the slump years in Lancashire.

3. THE COAL INDUSTRY

The great north-east coal-field, which supplied coal by sea to London and the east coast, was still at this period the most important in the country. As information on other coal-fields—in Lancashire, in the midlands, in south Wales and in Scotland—is relatively sparse, we shall in this section confine our attention to the north-east.[2]

The outstanding feature of the history of the coal industry in the north-east in this period was the development of new mines in districts too far from the coast or from navigable waterways to have been commercially workable before the advent of the railways. By 1841 a whole series of short railway lines had been built running from west to east to connect inland coal-fields with the coast,[3] and the competition created by the new pits served by these lines was directly responsible for the break-up of the Limitation of the Vend, the cartel of Tyne and Wear coal-owners which up to that time had controlled the shipment of coal from Newcastle to London.

Already in the early 1830's there was a marked increase in shipments of coal from the Tees, made possible by the Stockton and Darlington Railway (opened 1825) and the Clarence Railway (opened 1833). However, the upward movement of demand was for a while sufficient to enable this extra capacity to be absorbed without a fall in prices, and the price of coal in London tended upwards from 1833 to 1838. The year 1833 had been one of 'fighting trade', in which the Limitation had been temporarily in abeyance on account of dissensions between coal-owners, and the return of regulation after 1834 also contributed to the recovery of prices from the low level obtaining in 1833.[4]

The railways that served the Tees coal-fields had been completed some time before 1836, and it appears that expansion of capacity in that area proceeded a good deal less rapidly after 1836 than before. But the opposite was true of collieries farther north in County Durham, and taking the north-east coal-field as a whole, there is good reason to believe that capacity expanded to a much

---

[1] *Circular to Bankers*, 3 January 1840, 22 January 1841. Cf. also a petition from the master spinners of the West Riding for a further legal limitation on the hours of work of young persons—ostensibly on 'moral and educational' grounds—but with the hope that, incidentally, it would alter a 'state of things which affords constant opportunity to persons who are disposed to take advantage of it to glut the market' (*Accounts and Papers*, 1843, LII, p. 191). The petition was drawn up in May 1842.

[2] This section is based mainly on P. M. Sweezy, *Monopoly and Competition in the English Coal Trade, 1550–1850* (1938).

[3] Compare the map facing p. 5 of H. G. Lewin, *The British Railway System* (1914).

[4] Sweezy, pp. 101–8, 155, 158.

greater extent between 1836 and 1843 than it had done between 1829 and 1836.[1] This appears to have been the result of two main factors:

(a) The timing of the railway-building boom in Durham was broadly similar to that in the country as a whole; that is to say, many of the lines built did not come into operation till 1839 or later.[2]

(b) The long gestation period elapsing between the decision to sink a new pit and its coming into full production meant that the new mines opened up under the influence of rising prices in the mid-1830's, especially in the years around 1836 (when the flotation of joint-stock companies in the coal industry was attracting attention), did not begin to produce any great impact on the market till about 1838, and in the meanwhile capacity continued to increase.

When the new pits did come into operation, the machinery of the Limitation proved ineffective in preventing a fall in prices, and owners who had hitherto abided by the regulations of the Limitation and restricted their output to the prescribed level therefore became discontented with the whole scheme and disposed to break away. The working of the Limitation had encouraged the creation of excess capacity throughout the area, since the quota accorded to an owner under the scheme bore a relation to the estimated capacity of his mine or mines; so, as the Limitation gradually weakened, old mines as well as new ones were able to bring increased supplies on to the market.[3]

For these reasons the most rapid expansion of output came at a relatively late date,[4] and up to 1838 prices continued to rise. The recession of 1837 produced no visible effect on the coal industry in the north-east, probably because its main market, London, was relatively little hit by the slump (the principal impact of which was on the export trades); in 1837 new pits continued to be sunk at a great rate.[5] But owners were becoming restive, since the admission of new pits to the Limitation involved reductions in the quotas accorded to old pits. It proved possible to persuade most of the newcomers to the industry to join the scheme, but 'the trouble was fundamentally the new collieries, not whether they joined the Limitation or not'.[6] It was not possible to prevent the increase in the number of collieries, and restricting the output of the new pits once they came into operation was not a sufficient substitute.

Prices turned down in 1838, but output continued to rise (with a break in 1839) till 1841, when a peak was reached.[7] Up till that time the fall in prices did not prevent many new pits from being opened, but then for a while the flow ceased. The system of railway lines from inland to the coast was for the moment complete; in 1842 no new lines were opened in the Vend area, and in 1843 only one.[8] In response to the fall in prices, moreover, the trade in 1842 succeeded in agreeing on a stricter enforcement of the rules of the Limitation, and some semblance of stability in output was attained for the next couple of years.[9]

[1] Sweezy, pp. 110–11. [2] Lewin, p. 65. [3] Sweezy, pp. 113–27.
[4] The same appears to have been the case in south Wales, where, as in the north-east, the development of new coal mining enterprises in this period seems to have been influenced as to its timing more by railway building than by the general state of trade. The special virtues of south Wales coal for steam purposes were in the 1830's attracting attention for the first time. (R. L. Galloway, *Annals of Coal Mining and the Coal Trade* (second series, 1904), pp. 18–19.)
[5] Sweezy, pp. 122–3. [6] *Ibid.* p. 124. [7] *Ibid.* chart, p. 160. [8] Lewin, p. 65.
[9] The equilibrium was fundamentally unstable, and the Limitation finally collapsed in the confusion left behind by the great miners' strike of 1844 (Sweezy, pp. 126–9). On the strike, cf. F. Engels, *The Condition of the Working Class in England in 1844* (English edition, 1892), pp. 253–8.

4. THE IRON INDUSTRY

In broad outline, the picture presented by the iron industry in this period is one of rapid growth of demand but, except for a brief period around 1836, a still more rapid growth of supply.

On the supply side the outstanding event was the growth of the industry in Scotland, where the number of blast-furnaces more than doubled in the course of a decade. The technical innovation mainly responsible for this development was the application of the hot-blast invented by Neilson in 1828. In the course of the next ten years the hot-blast came into general use in Scotland. The special significance of the hot-blast for the Scottish industry lay in its particular suitability for the smelting of blackband ironstone, of which large reserves existed in central Scotland. The qualities of this ore had not been generally appreciated before the advent of the hot-blast. In addition, the economy of fuel rendered possible by the hot-blast was apparently especially great in Scotland on account of the technical qualities of the coal used in Scottish iron-works. In England the hot-blast had not yet come into general use by 1840, partly because the fuel economies to be gained were not so great, but partly also because of the conservatism of ironmasters in the older centres of the industry.[1]

On the demand side railway building was already dominant. Demand for iron from this source continued to increase strongly till about 1840. There was also a large and rapidly expanding domestic demand for iron for a variety of purposes —bridge-building and other constructional uses being now added to the established trade in kitchen utensils, locks, carpenters' tools and the like.[2] Exports of iron did not normally constitute more than about a quarter of the industry's output, if the figures of output in Table 27 are to be trusted.

Table 27. *Estimated production of iron (million tons)*

1828	0·7	1840	1·5
1835	1·0	1841	1·5
1836	1·2	1842	1·2

Source: G. R. Porter, *Progress of the Nation* (1851 edition), p. 575. The figures in Scrivenor, p. 290, are broadly similar though not identical.

Up till about 1834 or 1835, the iron industry was a good deal less prosperous than most other sectors of the economy. Low prices and over-production were the great complaints, and the industry was exceptional in having an appreciable amount of unemployment.[3] In 1830 and 1831 practically no new blast furnaces were erected in Staffordshire.[4] In 1832 there was a revival in production, but not in prices. In 1833 pig-iron prices rose, and this led to a situation similar to that prevailing in the cotton industry at about the same time. Ironmasters concerned with later stages of production were faced with higher raw-material costs at a

---

[1] H. Scrivenor, *History of the Iron Trade* (1854 edition), pp. 290–1; Clapham, *Economic History of Modern Britain*, I, pp. 425–7; H. Hamilton, *The Industrial Revolution in Scotland* (1932), pp. 179–92.

[2] Clapham, p. 149; *S.C. of 1833*, QQ. 9625–31 (W. Mathews).

[3] *S.C. of 1833*, QQ. 9517–18 (S. Walker); *Circular to Bankers*, 16 April 1830, 20 August 1830, 19 September 1831, 13 July 1832, 27 June 1834.

[4] *Ibid.* 21 October 1831.

time when their selling prices were still being squeezed by competition.[1] Iron ore and pig-iron prices continued to range high for several years. By 1835–6 the industry was enjoying general prosperity. The price of bar iron was higher in 1836 than at any other date in our period. Many new blast-furnaces were in the course of construction, and, as is apparent from Table 28, this expansion of capacity was not confined to Scotland.

Table 28. *Estimated number of blast-furnaces and output of iron in United Kingdom, in Scotland and in Staffordshire*

	In United Kingdom		In Scotland		In Staffs	
	1828	1839	1830	1839	1830	1839
No. of furnaces in blast	277	396	—*	54	75	120
Total no. of furnaces	367	538	27	60	123	226
Output of iron (000's tons)	703	—*	37	197	223	346

* Not known.

Sources: Number of furnaces in blast in Staffs. in 1830, *Circular to Bankers*, 21 October 1831; total iron output in 1828, Porter, p. 575; all other figures, *Royal Commission on Coal Supply*, 1871, xviii, pp. 878–80.

In 1839 the demand for railway iron was at its peak and output was higher than ever before, but the trade was considered to be in a depressed condition. Attempts were made to carry out a concerted restriction of output, but they were not successful. Renewed attempts in 1840 met with rather more support, but were unable to prevent a further increase in production on account of the still continuing growth of capacity in Scotland.[2]

What had happened is fairly clear, and in many respects resembles the contemporary history of the coal industry. It can be seen from Table 28 that, in the course of the ten years or so before 1839, although the increase in the total number of furnaces was very great and extended throughout the country, the number of furnaces out of blast increased in a substantially greater proportion than the number of active furnaces, particularly in Staffordshire, the old centre of the industry. It is true that there was at all times a considerable number of furnaces out of blast because they were too old or outmoded to be of service, but this remarkable *increase* in the proportion of furnaces out of blast—notwithstanding that demand in 1839 was, on account of railway building, still very high—can only have been due to competition driving out the high-cost producers. In 1835–6 capacity had evidently been expanded to an excessive degree, the period of gestation obscuring from ironmasters the inevitability of a fall in prices as soon as the new furnaces should come into operation. On top of this, when prices had passed their peak, low-cost producers—the Scots ironmasters— did not cease to expand. There was thus taking place in the late 1830's an increase in capacity from two sources. High-cost producers were forced to put their furnaces out of blast even though demand was still rising. In contrast to cotton manufacturers (and also to coal-owners), ironmasters appear to have been fairly

[1] *S.C. of 1833*, QQ. 4268–78 (J. Dixon). For price statistics, see Porter, p. 577.
[2] Scrivenor, pp. 257–8, 290.

ready to put their furnaces out temporarily when prices were low, instead of striving to compensate for low-profit margins by a large turn-over.[1] The high proportion of fuel and other prime costs in total outgoings was no doubt the main reason.

After 1840 the demand for railway iron fell off and the domestic market in ironmongers' goods also deteriorated.[2] Exports were increased sharply in 1841–2 in an attempt to find alternative outlets to replace the waning home demand, but this did not restore prosperity to the industry. Iron prices fell steeply and did not recover again till 1845, with the arrival of the second railway boom. Output also fell and for several years stayed at about the level attained in 1836.

To summarise: demand and output grew rapidly till 1840, with probably a short recession between 1836 and the beginning of the railway building boom of 1838–40. Up till about 1835 the growth in capacity, especially in Scotland, was sufficient to prevent there being any great increase in the profits of the trade as a whole, though the earlier stages of production yielded good profits. Then in 1835–6 for a while profits rose and there was an outburst of investment not confined to Scotland. From 1837 to 1840 output continued to rise and capacity to be extended in the low-cost districts, and also in other districts in so far as decisions taken during the boom years were only now bearing fruit; but profits were declining, and high-cost furnaces being put out of blast. Finally, after 1841, the railway demand fell away and output had to be reduced. As a result of the increase in capacity, however, the volume of production remained at a relatively high level by previous standards.

The resemblances between the behaviour of iron and coal industries in the period are very pronounced, despite the peculiarities in the latter owing to the Limitation of the Vend. In both industries technical innovations (railways in coal, and the hot-blast in iron) opened up new sources of supply which continued to expand after the general boom phase of 1835–6 had passed. In neither industry does demand appear to have fallen off to any serious extent before 1841. But when the slump did finally arrive, output fell to a greater extent in iron than in coal, because putting out a blast-furnace was a less costly operation than closing a coal-mine.

5. THE JOINT-STOCK COMPANY BOOM

Mention has already been made several times of the joint-stock companies that were formed in a number of industries between 1834 and 1836, and it will be convenient at this point to say a few words about the joint-stock company boom in general and its effect on industry.

Prosperity was general throughout the economy in 1835 and 1836, but joint-stock company flotation was the only sphere in which this prosperity culminated in a 'mania'. Speculative dealing in commodities was not general, and although

---

[1] Cf. D. H. Robertson, *A Study of Industrial Fluctuation* (1915), pp. 32–3.

[2] *Circular to Bankers*, 18 November 1842; *Select Committee on Import Duties*, 1840, v, QQ. 1583–6 (J. Walker). In the cutlery trades the state of business was felt to be deteriorating steadily from 1836 to 1842, and the year 1842 went down to history as one of greater depression in the industry than any other year in the nineteenth century. Output, however, continued to rise after 1836 till at least 1840. (G. I. H. Lloyd, *The Cutlery Trades* (1913), pp. 341–2.)

United States stocks and bonds were bought in large amounts, and *The Times* thought it necessary to warn its readers against investment in foreign banks,[1] foreign stocks did not command the centre of the stage in the way they had done in 1825. There was a rise in the prices of home railway shares concomitant with the growth of the mania for railway promotion, but otherwise share-prices rose comparatively little.[2]

The first signs of a joint-stock company mania were observed during 1834.[3] There was then a lull till the end of 1836, when the excitement revived. The peak was reached in spring 1836.[4]

The underlying causes of the mania were to be found in the steady improvement of trade that had been taking place since 1833, together with the further stimulus received in 1835 from the growth of exports to America. The crash of the Spanish security speculation in May 1835, moreover, closed the avenue which had been followed by speculatively inclined investors in the previous year.[5] It appears that in timing, at least, the joint-stock mania was a good deal affected by movements in discount rates. Table 29 shows monthly movements of the market rate of discount, of Gayer's share-price index, and of the number of joint-stock company prospectuses issued, as given in the Report of the Select Committee on Joint Stock Companies in 1844. The latter series appears not to be comprehensive,[6] but there is no reason to doubt that the general pattern it reveals is correct.

The market rate of discount showed a rising trend in the first part of 1835, reaching 4% by the middle of the year. It fell to $3\frac{1}{2}$% in August and then stayed at $3\frac{3}{4}$% till February 1836. In March and April 1836 it fell, and it remained low in May. In June began the sharp rise which was to continue into 1837. The other two series in Table 29 show a slight tendency to decline after the beginning of 1835, but recover at the end of the summer. The peak in the joint-stock mania was reached in April–May 1836, the two months when the rate of discount was at its lowest.

The movements in the discount rate, which were mainly caused by fluctuations in the balance of payments—themselves not unconnected with the collapse of the Spanish security speculation referred to above—were too small to have exerted any great influence other than a psychological one; but the joint-stock company mania, like all speculative bubbles, was itself largely a psychological phenomenon, and it seems probable that the rather unusual occurrence of a downward trend in interest rates at a time of rapid increase in business activity did predispose joint-stock company promoters and the subscribing public to take an irrationally optimistic view of business prospects.[7]

During the whole of the period of the mania, railway promotion was the dominant item, and after it the promotion of banks and other financial institu-

---

[1] *The Times*, 11 May 1836.

[2] See figures of share prices in A. D. Gayer, A. Jacobson and I. Finkelstein, 'British share prices, 1811–50', *Review of Economic Statistics* (1940), pp. 78–93.

[3] *Select Committee on Joint Stock Companies*, 1844, VII, QQ. 2358–9 (J. Parkes). Cf. B. C. Hunt, *Development of the Business Corporation in England, 1800–1867* (1936), pp. 60–1.

[4] Cf. Tooke, II, pp. 274–9.   [5] See pp. 87–8.

[6] The nominal capital of the companies included in the list adds up to £135 million, which falls well short of the figures given by Poulett Thomson, quoted below, p. 162.

[7] On the causes of the movements in discount rates in 1835–6, see pp. 92–3; on their effects see also pp. 197–8, 207–8.

Table 29. *Market rate of discount, share prices and number of joint stock company prospectuses issued monthly, 1835–36*

Year	Market rate of discount %	Share prices (June 1840 = 100)	Number of joint stock company prospectuses issued
1835 Jan.	3¾	104·0	2
Feb.	3¼	104·1	8
Mar.	3½	105·1	6
Apr.	3¾	107·6	1
May	3¾	101·8	1
June	4	98·9	—
July	4	101·8	2
Aug.	3½	101·9	3
Sept.	3¾	102·1	8
Oct.	3¾	106·2	4
Nov.	3¾	108·8	8
Dec.	3¾	110·0	3
1836 Jan.	3¾	117·9	11
Feb.	3¾	123·5	13
Mar.	3½	125·2	11
Apr.	3¼	125·9	29
May	3¼	133·7	22
June	4	129·9	22
July	4	124·5	18
Aug.	4½	128·1	2
Sept.	5	126·7	8
Oct.	5	122·0	5
Nov.	5½	112·9	2
Dec.	5½	115·7	3

Sources: Market rate of discount, *Select Committee on the Bank Acts*, 1857 (2nd session), x, Part I, pp. 463–4. Share prices, Gayer, Jacobson and Finkelstein, *loc. cit.* Company prospectuses, *Select Committee on Joint Stock Companies*, 1844, VII, pp. 358–63 (companies for which month of issue of prospectus is not given are omitted from the table).

tions. Next most important came mining enterprises.[1] Railways, banks and mines were lines of business where the joint-stock principle was familiar, if not universally approved, so it was natural that promoters and investors should show greater interest in them than in manufacturing industry. Joint-stock companies were formed for the mining of coal and of iron-ore, but the greatest amount of speculative attention was paid to Cornish tin and copper mines. These were notoriously unsuccessful. 'For the greater part they are not only complete failures, but are memorable proofs of the folly and cupidity of British capitalists on the one hand, and of the knavery of their projectors on the other.'[2] A similar verdict was passed on new joint-stock ventures in shipbuilding.[3]

The many miscellaneous projects set on foot in 1836 were ably described in the following well-known passage from a speech by J. Poulett Thomson, President of the Board of Trade, in the House of Commons on 6 May 1836.[4]

[1] Of the companies whose prospectuses were listed by the Select Committee on Joint Stock Companies (*loc. cit.*), the distribution of nominal capital was as follows: railways, £70m.; banks, etc., £32m.; mines, £7m.; others, £26m. The mining companies were numerous but small.

[2] W. F. Spackman, *Statistical Tables...of the United Kingdom of Great Britain and its Dependencies* (1842), p. 153.   [3] See p. 119.   [4] Quoted by Tooke, II, pp. 276–8.

It is impossible not to be struck with the spirit of speculation which now exists in the country; but I believe that there is a great difference in the state of things and what took place in 1825. The spirit of speculation was then turned to foreign adventures of the most extraordinary description; but now speculation is turned to home objects...I felt it my duty, some time ago, to direct a register to be kept, taking the names merely from the London and a few country newspapers of the different joint-stock companies and of the nominal capital it was proposed to embark in them. The nominal capital to be raised by subscription amounts to nearly £200,000,000, and the number of companies is between 300 and 400. I am just now reminded of the speculation for making beet-sugar but that is a sound speculation compared with some in my list. The first is the British Agricultural Loan Company, with a capital of £2,000,000....Another company is proposed for supplying pure spring water, capital £300,000. Then there are the Patent Steam-paddle Company, with a capital of £30,000; the Safety Cabriolet Company, capital £100,000; the British and American Intercourse Company, capital £2,000,000; the London Whale Fishery Company....In 1825 London was the main centre of speculation; but I am afraid that these companies have now their origin in other parts of the country. Reference has been made to a Liverpool paper. I fear that the place I represent [Manchester] can likewise furnish instances of schemes for objects that can never be beneficial to anyone, and on which the parties will only be throwing away their money. The fact is, the greater part of these companies are got up by speculators for the purpose of selling their shares. They bring up their shares to a premium, and then sell them, leaving the unfortunate purchasers, who are foolish enough to vest their money in them, to shift for themselves.

That, as Poulett Thomson remarked, the focal point of the boom was in Lancashire and that business in London was relatively unexcited, has already been mentioned in connection with brick production and with the finance of railway building.[1] The point will arise again when we come to consider the growth of joint-stock banking.

Apart from railways, banks and mines, probably the majority of the joint-stock companies formed during the mania were still-born, or survived only for a few years, and did not add conspicuously to the nation's capital stock. On the other hand, they were not all bubbles, and even the enterprises that failed were for a while responsible for investment expenditure which increased the national income in money terms—to say nothing of luxurious consumption expenditure on the part of rogues and knaves financed out of savings of widows and orphans, which we are given to understand was on a large scale! It was inevitable that a mania of this sort should be followed by a sharp setback, and the disappointment of the hopes of investors in the more blatantly foolish or fraudulent enterprises added to the gloom of 1837 and subsequent years.[2]

---

[1] See pp. 110, 115.
[2] The *Select Committee on Joint-stock Companies* (1844, VII, p. 4) divided the companies that failed into three classes: (*a*) *bona fide* but commercially foolish; (*b*) *bona fide* but with lax constitutions or negligent directors, or both, hence open to exploitation by fraudulent executives; (*c*) fraudulent from the outset, formed either with the object of driving the shares up to a premium or simply, in the extreme case, of enabling the promoters to abscond with the subscribed capital. It is to be remembered, of course, that Company Law was at this period in a very undeveloped state.

6. OTHER SECTORS OF THE ECONOMY

In the last three chapters we have been concerned almost entirely either with investment industries or else with industries that were undergoing rapid technical change and development. The latter category, by a relationship that is by no means entirely accidental, includes the leading export industries. What of those parts of the national economy that belonged to neither of these categories? Agriculture, of course, stands in a class by itself, and has already been briefly treated in Chapter IV. But there remain a whole host of other industries—boots and shoes, printing, tailoring and dressmaking and all the distributive and service trades, to name only a few—which between them probably gave employment to more people than those industries which figure most largely in the text-books of economic history. We have little direct evidence on how those engaged in these trades fared over the cycle. But two general considerations of a more or less *a priori* nature may here be mentioned.

In the first place, industries that produced neither exports nor capital goods must have been subject to smaller fluctuations on the demand side than most of those that have so far occupied our attention. It is evident that fluctuations in demand in consumer-good industries catering for the home market cannot have been so large proportionately as, for example, those experienced in railway building or in industries dependent on exports to the United States.

In the second place, industries which were less capitalistic and less technically progressive than those which we have discussed in the preceding chapters must have undergone relatively much less expansion of capacity during the boom. Indeed, in totally uncapitalistic occupations like domestic service, the concept of capacity or expansion of capacity is inapplicable. This involves two consequences: (1) The amount of investment carried out in the boom in areas largely dependent on industries of this description must have been relatively restricted; and a mild upswing naturally implied also a mild downswing. The moderate nature of the boom in London in 1836 was undoubtedly a case in point. (2) Industries which had not greatly expanded in the boom were not subjected to the burden of extra capacity in the recession and slump years which so depressed prices and profits in cotton and elsewhere. But if profits were on that account less depressed, for exactly the same reason production was less likely to continue to expand when demand ceased to grow or contracted. Not merely had capacity in such cases expanded less, but there was probably also less incentive to utilise fully such capacity as there was, since overheads were relatively light. So it is probable that, although in 1841–2 depression was felt to be most acute in the more progressive industries, output in those industries in 1841–2 bore a higher proportion to output in 1835–6 than did output in other parts of the economy.

That business was exceptionally depressed throughout the country in 1841 and 1842 is not to be doubted. From the spring of 1841 onwards trade reports became steadily gloomier and unemployment rose rapidly. Depression continued to deepen throughout the winter of 1841/2, and the spring of 1842 passed without any signs of the recovery in trade that was generally looked for at that season.[1]

[1] For the general picture of the state of trade in these years see *Circular to Bankers*, especially the issues of 9 April 1841, 14 May 1841, 2 July 1841, 26 November 1841, 29 April 1842, 17 June 1842, 9 September 1842.

The year 1842 was the trough of the depression and was marked by extensive civil disturbances. The intensity of the depression was demonstrated in debates in Parliament in July.[1] M.P.'s representing all parts of the country testified to the extent of the distress in their constituencies, and many experienced speakers described it as unparalleled by any previous depression within their recollection. Naturally the industrial districts of the north were hardest hit, but industry in the south of England did not escape; serious depression was said to prevail, for example, in towns in Devon and in the London book trade.[2] The unemployment figures quoted by some members bear more resemblance to those experienced in the 1930's than to the moderate percentages shown by the trade union records for the years after 1860. In Stockport there was in July 1842 50% unemployment; in Greenock, 60%; in Huddersfield, 33%. There were 20,000 unemployed in Birmingham, and 12,000 in Newcastle-on-Tyne.[3] (The total population of both sexes aged 20 or over in these two towns was given in the 1841 census as 99,000 and 29,000 respectively.) The speakers who gave these figures claimed that they were based on careful inquiry and were not at all exaggerated. And as trade had been felt to be generally unprosperous since 1839 or even in some cases since 1837, the unusual prolongation of the depression was scarcely less commented on than its intensity.

[1] *Hansard's Parliamentary Debates* (3rd series), LXIV, debates on Distress of the Country, in the House of Commons 1 and 8 July 1842 and in the House of Lords 11 July 1842.
[2] *Hansard's Parliamentary Debates, loc. cit.* col. 1200.
[3] *Ibid.* cols. 862, 1188.

CHAPTER XI

MONEY AND BANKING

1. INTRODUCTION

WE turn now to fluctuations in the sphere of money and banking. In the present chapter we shall not, save incidentally, attempt to assess the importance of monetary factors in the causation of the fluctuations in prices and activity that took place during the period. This is a matter upon which it is not easy to obtain any very conclusive evidence, and it will be more convenient to postpone discussion of it till the next chapter. At present our main concern is to consider the ways in which the supply of money altered in response to fluctuations in the foreign exchanges and in the general state of trade, and to study the part played by different banking institutions.

The plan of this chapter will be as follows. We shall consider first the Bank of England. Since the relation between the foreign exchanges and the state of the money market was a very close one, it will be necessary to pay special attention to the policy of the Bank with regard to the international bullion movements whose causes were discussed in Chapter VII. After pointing out the dependence of the market rate of discount on the level of the Bank's reserves, as revealed by the statistics, and the surprisingly small extent to which the rate of discount appears to have been affected by the general state of trade (save in so far as changes in the latter were associated with changes in the Bank's reserves), we shall then go on to discuss the part played by other banks. It will be necessary here first to demonstrate the relative unimportance of the country note issue as a factor in economic fluctuations in the period, despite the great amount of attention given to it by contemporaries. We shall then proceed to deal with the two most important topics, namely, the changes in the supply of bank money and money substitutes consequent upon, first, changes in discount rates resulting from international gold movements, and secondly, cyclical fluctuations in business. Since the formation of new joint-stock banks was very much a feature of the boom, the significance of this development will be considered under the latter of the two heads just mentioned.

2. THE BANK OF ENGLAND AND THE PALMER RULE

Analysis of the policy and actions of the Bank of England has figured very largely in the pages of all historians of business cycles in Britain from Tooke to the present day, and the same ground has in consequence been trodden over very many times. The dominant position occupied by the Bank makes it inevitable that a description of the part which it played should stand at the head of any account of fluctuations in the sphere of money and banking; but since much of this part of the history has been recited already by many authors and has so been worn threadbare, we shall endeavour here to treat it as briefly as possible.

From about 1832 until the passage of the Bank Charter Act of 1844, Bank of England spokesmen stated that the Bank's fundamental policy was guided by certain principles first enunciated by J. Horsley Palmer, then Governor of the Bank, before the House of Commons Committee on the Bank of England Charter in 1832. These principles subsequently became known as 'the principles of 1832' or the Palmer rule.[1]

The basic question which the Palmer rule was designed to answer was one which lay at the heart of the contemporary controversy between the Currency School and the Banking School. What action should the Bank take to safeguard its reserve during periods when it was tending to fall in consequence of an unfavourable state of the foreign exchanges? It was discovered soon after 1832 that this was not the only matter of principle which had to be decided in carrying on the business of the Bank; there were other problems for which the rule of 1832 made no explicit provision. But the question stated remained the crucial one.

The Palmer rule may be regarded as representing in some respects a compromise between Currency School and Banking School tenets. A few words on the chief issues which separated these two schools of thought will therefore here be appropriate.[2]

The Currency School included several different shades of opinion; but there was agreement amongst its members that the objective was to make paper money behave in exactly the same way as a purely metallic currency would have done. It was with this in view that Lord Overstone and others recommended the division of the Bank into an Issue Department and a Banking Department, as effected by the Act of 1844. Before the division was made formal in 1844, Currency School writers argued that the Bank should treat the two parts of its business as entirely distinct. As they saw it, it was purely for reasons of convenience that the same form of money was not always used in domestic as in foreign trade; the function of the Bank in its note-issuing capacity was simply to change the one form into the other—gold into notes or vice versa—as required by the public. Giving notes for gold was regarded as an operation not different in essence from giving gold bars in return for sovereigns. The Bank's job was to give gold certificates to those who found them more convenient to use than gold, and the gold so acquired was to be held against the certificates. Gold held in excess of that amount was to be considered to have been acquired by the quite different process of customers depositing money at the Bank—i.e. to have been received by the Bank in its banking, as distinct from its note-issuing, capacity.

[1] For Palmer's own exposition of his doctrine, see *Committee of Secrecy on the Bank of England Charter*, 1831–2, VI (henceforth cited as *1832*), QQ. 72–198; *Select Committee on Banks of Issue*, 1840, IV (henceforth cited as *1840*), QQ. 1142–6; and J. H. Palmer, *Causes and Consequences of the late Pressure on the Money Market* (1837). Cf. also T. E. Gregory, *The Westminster Bank* (1936), II, pp. 162–7; J. Viner, *Studies in the Theory of International Trade* (1937), pp. 224–9; E. V. Morgan, *Theory and Practice of Central Banking, 1797–1913* (1943), pp. 100–19; Sir John Clapham, *The Bank of England* (1944), II, pp. 162–4; J. K. Horsefield, 'The opinions of Horsley Palmer', *Economica* (1949), pp. 143–58. Most of our information on the details of the Bank's operations during the period derives from Tooke and from the evidence of Palmer and G. W. Norman, another Director of the Bank, before the Committee of 1840.

[2] For fuller modern treatments of the currency and banking controversy, the reader may be referred to Viner, pp. 218–89; Morgan, pp. 120–42; T. E. Gregory, Introduction to 1928 reprint of Tooke and Newmarch's *History of Prices*; E. Wood, *English Theories of Central Banking Control, 1819–1858* (1939); L. W. Mints, *A History of Banking Theory in Great Britain and the United States* (1945), pp. 74–124. Cf. also pp. 97–8 above.

This gold, equivalent to 'notes in the Banking Department' after 1844, was what the Bank was entitled to use as the basis of lending operations analogous to those of a commercial bank.

In its simplest form, the idea was that the solvency of the Issue Department was to be maintained automatically by 100% coverage of notes in circulation. But in practice this was always subject to serious qualification. After 1844 the admission of a Fiduciary Issue destroyed the principle by which convertibility was automatically guaranteed in this way; and before 1844 there was always a fiduciary issue in effect, for the bullion reserve was never as high as the circulation. In order, therefore, to ensure the convertibility of the note issue, a new idea had to be introduced, quite distinct from the automatic convertibility supposed to be achieved in the ideal case of the currency behaving exactly 'as if metallic'. This idea was that the reduction in the quantity of money brought about as the notes were withdrawn from circulation and exchanged into bullion for export would, by lowering commodity prices, remove the cause of adverse exchanges, so that the exchange of notes for gold would cease before the point of danger was reached.

For perfect consistency, the Currency School doctrine should have been that the solvency of the Banking Department, or of the Bank in its banking capacity, was to be ensured by the same means as the solvency of any other bank, viz. by preserving sufficient liquidity in its assets. In practice, however, it was conceded that the circumstances most likely to cause a drain on the Bank's reserves—namely, adverse foreign exchanges—were rather different from those most likely to lead to a run on other banks, and that the rise in discount rates brought about by a moderate curtailment of the Bank's securities would in itself normally be sufficient to halt a drain on the Banking Department's reserves. Had this not been the case, the reserve ratio required by the Banking Department would have had to be not far from the 100% laid down (in principle) for the Issue Department, on account of the much greater vulnerability of the Bank compared with other banks.

The Banking School was a less homogeneous group than the Currency School, and in matters of central bank policy it is not easy to formulate a body of doctrine that would have been accepted by all members of the School. The basic contention common to Tooke, Gilbart, Fullarton and other leading members of the Banking School was that the relationship between bank lending and the state of the foreign exchanges was a good deal less close than Currency School writers supposed. It was denied that high prices and adverse exchanges were particularly to be associated with an excessively high note circulation (as was implied by the Currency School argument that a reduction in the circulation would rectify the exchanges), and it was maintained that a restriction of the Bank of England's lending was neither necessary nor efficacious as the means of correcting a tendency to export of bullion. As a rule, it was claimed, an adverse balance of payments was due to special causes like bad harvests, and would therefore presently correct itself without any need for special action by the banking system. All that was required of a central bank was that it should hold an adequate reserve to be able to deal with such contingencies. The idea that it was appropriate to attempt to restrict the circulation in order to correct a drain was totally rejected, as imposing hardship on the mercantile community in return for no gain. Criticism of the Currency School notion that the note circulation was of prime importance in determining prices and hence the state of the exchanges was reinforced by pointing out the fallacy involved by the sharp distinction drawn by the Currency School between notes and bank deposits, the latter being supposed by Currency School writers to be not part of the circulating medium but merely 'means of economising the circulation'.

These, then, were the positions occupied by the two opposing schools. The Palmer rule may, as has been suggested, be regarded as a compromise between them, although in fundamentals it was rather closer to the Currency School.

The Palmer rule has often been stated, both at the time and subsequently, in such a way as to involve an arithmetical absurdity. It has been supposed that it was laid down that the Bank's securities should be held constant *and* equal to roughly two-thirds of its total assets. This plainly involved a contradiction if the amount of the bullion reserve was subject to alteration.[1] The proper statement of the rule does not involve this difficulty. What the rule really required was that at what were called 'times of full currency', when the reserve was at a maximum and the exchanges such as to cause neither import nor export of specie, the securities should be equal to two-thirds of the liabilities; and that *thereafter* the securities should be held constant, whatever happened to the bullion. The two-thirds provision was merely a technical matter, a general guide to the Bank of the sort of level to be aimed at. It was the constancy of the securities in face of gold movements that was the crucial part of the doctrine.

How did this compare with the precepts of Lord Overstone and the other Currency School writers? According to them, the main task of the Bank of England in its capacity as custodian of the nation's reserves was to ensure that the currency, composed as it was partly of gold and silver coin and partly of paper, should be made to behave in face of a drain exactly as it would have done had it been exclusively metallic. The amount of money in circulation, they argued, ought in the event of a drain to fall by the value of the specie exported. This would lead to internal deflation and so to rectification of the exchanges. To some extent the desired result was likely to come about automatically, for Bank of England notes would be paid into the Bank by parties wishing to obtain gold for exportation, and so would pass out of circulation. If the fall in the Bank's circulation brought about in this way were fully equal to the fall in its bullion reserve, the total quantity of money would have fallen to the required extent and no further action by the Bank would be necessary beyond making sure that Bank Rate did not fall below the market rate of discount so as to lead to an increase in the Bank's securities. No actual reduction of the securities was considered by the Currency School to be necessary if the circulation of its own accord fell to the full extent of the fall in the bullion; and as far as this case was concerned, the policies laid down by the Palmer rule and the Currency School were therefore identical. But it was commonly found in practice that a drain of gold from the Bank fell at least as heavily on its deposits as on its circulation, and that the automatic fall in the circulation was accordingly less than the fall in the reserve. To Currency School authors, deposits did not rank as money or currency, and in such a case they accordingly recommended that the Bank should reduce its securities until the circulation had fallen by the full amount of

[1] Cf. Clapham, II, p. 174; Gregory, *Westminster Bank*, II, p. 166.

the specie lost. The Palmer rule, on the other hand, did not discriminate between the treatment accorded to drains that fell on the deposits and drains that fell on the circulation; in either case the securities should be held constant so that the Bank's aggregate liabilities fell by no more and no less than its bullion reserve.

By this rule the passivity with respect to the securities which was prescribed by the Currency School for meeting drains which fell on the circulation was extended to cover also drains on the deposits. According to the Currency School, the reduction in the circulation in the former case imposed a sufficiently powerful upward pressure on discount rates to check the drain without there being any need for the Bank to push deflation further by curtailing its security holding. The theoretical basis for the Palmer rule was evidently the supposition that a decline in the Bank's deposits in itself effected the same reduction in the supply of funds in the money market as was produced by a decline in the circulation.

Here Palmer was taking a leaf from the Banking School book, for a leading doctrine of Banking School authors was that notes and deposits were fundamentally identical. The question at issue between the Palmer rule and the precepts of monetary orthodoxy as represented by the Currency School really resolved itself into a question of fact. (It must be admitted that in Palmer's own exposition this point does not stand out very clearly.) Were the deposits at the Bank 'active' in the sense that a reduction in them led to a reduction in the supply of funds in the market even in the absence of any change in the amount of the Bank's securities? The question does not of course relate to all the deposits at the Bank but only to those—reckoned to be between a quarter and a third of all private deposits at the Bank—which were liable to be exchanged for specie when the exchanges were unfavourable. The most important category of deposits of this description were the London bankers' deposits, but some of the deposits classed as 'other' in the Bank's returns—presumably the deposits of bill-brokers and other financial houses—were also liable to sudden reduction in times of drain.[1] Now, bankers' deposits at the Bank were not 'active' in the sense of being regularly switched from one account to another, for at this date balances at the Clearing House were settled in notes, not, as later, by cheques upon the Bank.[2] But there is every reason to suppose that they were active in the sense that they formed part of bankers' reserves, so that if a banker's balance at the Bank fell he was obliged to take steps to contract his liabilities. Those who maintained the fundamental identity of notes and deposits were fond of pointing out in this connection that before 1825 London bankers used to hold in notes the reserves which ten years later they had become accustomed as a matter of convenience to keep on deposit at the Bank.[3] Whether bankers regarded their deposits at the Bank as in all respects identical with cash—a question discussed *ad nauseam* in the literature[4]—was not really relevant, so long as a reduction in either necessitated a roughly equal reduction in aggregate liabilities. As there seems no reason to doubt that this was the case, the Palmer rule may be held to be vindicated once its fundamental premises are conceded. The policy of keeping

---

[1] *1840*, QQ. 1553–63 (Palmer).
[2] J. W. Gilbart, *Practical Treatise on Banking* (*Collected Works*, vol. II) (1865), pp. 394–401.
[3] Cf. *1840*, QQ. 3094–5 (questions put to S. J. Loyd by J. Hume).
[4] See, for example, the examination of S. J. Loyd (Lord Overstone) before the Select Committee of 1840, QQ. 3092–192.

the securities constant was well calculated to ensure that rises or falls in the Bank's bullion were associated with easing or tightening respectively of credit conditions in the London money market, though of course if the Bank had taken upon itself to reinforce the consequences of gold movements by reducing its securities in periods of drain and increasing them in periods of reflux, the effect would have been still more pronounced.

So much for the principle; what of its execution?

The criticisms levelled against the Bank of England in the 1830's were not confined to the charge that the principles underlying its policy were fallacious. It was also commonly argued—and the argument has been repeated by many

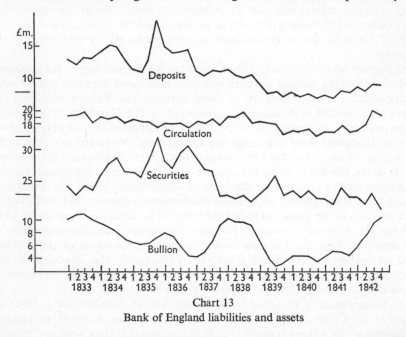

Chart 13

Bank of England liabilities and assets

modern authors—that the Bank did not even adhere to the principles which it purported to follow. This charge and Palmer's reply to it must next be considered.

A glance at Chart 13[1] will immediately demonstrate that if the cornerstone of the Bank's policy was really the maintenance of the securities at a constant level, then the charge of inconsistency between theory and practice must indeed be upheld, at least as relates to the earlier years of the period. But the defence put up by Palmer of why the securities were allowed to fluctuate in this way was more reasonable than has commonly been made out.

From the analytical point of view, the departures from the policy of constant securities can best be considered under three heads. Discussion of these will provide us with an opportunity to recount briefly certain of the more noteworthy episodes of the period in the monetary sphere as they affected the Bank of England.

[1] For the figures on which the charts in this chapter are based see Tables 31 and 32 at the end of the chapter.

(1) Currency School writers, whose doctrine was based on the importance of the distinction between the banking and the note-issuing functions of the Bank, commonly criticised the rule of keeping the securities constant as unsuitable for the conduct of a banking, as distinct from a note-issuing, institution. The amount of notes uncovered by bullion—in the terminology of the Act of 1844, the securities in the Issue Department—should, it was argued, indeed be held constant, but it was unreasonable to expect any bank to keep its securities constant if its deposits varied. In response to this argument, Palmer introduced a new distinction, which had admittedly not been contemplated in 1832, between changes in the deposits resulting from gold drains, and changes of a 'special' nature. By the latter was meant changes in the deposits resulting from variations in the balances of the Bank's customers such as the Government and the East India company, which by their nature were likely to be accompanied by variations in the opposite direction of deposits held by other banks. The securities should be held constant in face of changes in the deposits resulting from gold drains, Palmer argued, but changes of a 'special' character *should* be allowed to affect the securities. For example, during the 'shuttings', the periods of the year when government balances at the Bank were abnormally high in anticipation of the quarterly dividend payments on the national debt, there would have been acute and unnecessary stringency in the money market had the Bank kept its securities constant, since the extra funds in the hands of the Bank represented a subtraction from the balances normally held and used by commercial banks. Accordingly, it was the practice of the Bank at those times of year to make advances on approved security at what it reckoned to be the market rate of interest, instead of at the official Bank Rate. This system was instituted in 1829.[1]

The quarterly loans during the shuttings were commonly welcomed by the mercantile community, and the principle did not come in for any serious criticism. The explanation advanced by the Bank in justification of the inflated level of its securities between 1834 and 1837 was less generally approved, but the principle involved was essentially the same.

During these years, deposits at the Bank were subject to abnormal increases on three accounts.[2] (*a*) A loan of £15 million was floated for the government by Rothschilds in 1835 to compensate West Indian slave-owners under the Emancipation Act of the previous year. Subscriptions to the loan were to be paid into the Bank of England, where they were to accumulate in the Public Deposits until the compensation should actually be paid. The government offered a premium for prompt subscription to the loan, and in order to enable the public to take advantage of this, the Bank issued an offer to make advances on stock at $3\frac{1}{2}\%$ immediately the loan was contracted for. Advances were available on the special terms continuously from 5 August 1835 until 15 April 1836, during which time many subscribers paid their money into the Bank and then borrowed the same amount out again. The accumulation of the compensation money in the Public Deposits at the Bank reached its maximum of £8·5 million in November 1835. (*b*) In consequence of the recent abolition of its monopoly in the China trade, the East India Company was engaged in the years after 1833 in realising

<hr>

[1] Clapham, II, p. 137; W. T. C. King, *History of the London Discount Market* (1936), pp. 84–6.
[2] For the details, see Palmer's evidence, *1840*, QQ. 1142–1271, and Clapham, II, pp. 147–8.

some parts of its assets. The Company paid the money into the Bank in the Bank's own notes, and these were then lent out by the Bank at the market rate of interest to bill brokers and to Rothschilds. The East India Company's balance reached its maximum at £4·7 million in January 1837. (c) Between February and October 1834 there was also an exceptional accumulation, amounting to £3 million, of Savings Bank funds deposited with the Bank of England.

Palmer claimed that if securities acquired with the special deposits were excluded from the calculation, the amount of the securities held by the Bank during the years 1834–6 remained roughly constant at about £23 million, apart from two occasions when it was temporarily swollen by an unusual excess of government deficiency bills.[1] Seasonal and other such disturbances make it difficult to check this contention accurately from the Bank's published accounts, but there is no doubt that at least the most striking of the fluctuations in the securities during the period were to be explained in the way that Palmer suggested.

The general principle adopted by the Bank with regard to these deposits appears reasonable enough. Unlike bankers' deposits at the Bank, the deposits of the government and of the East India Company could on no reckoning be held to be 'active'; the piling up of these balances in the Bank would undoubtedly have led to stringency in the money market if the Bank had not taken offsetting measures. It could of course be argued—as it was argued by Tooke and others— that the Bank *should* have brought about financial tightness in 1835 and early 1836 by withholding the special deposits from use; but quite apart from the fact that the Bank was obliged to pay interest on the East India Company's balances, for the Bank to have deliberately brought about a rise in interest rates at a time when the exchanges were actually favourable, merely on the grounds that they might subsequently become unfavourable, would have been to go well beyond its avowed policy, or indeed that recommended by Currency School principles.

(2) The second reason for departing from the policy of constant securities was of a rather different character. Already during the Bank Restriction period, the distinction had come to be recognised between external drains, which required the Bank to engage in a contraction of credit, and internal drains owing to failure of confidence, which in contrast called for free lending by the Bank to banks and other houses which might be illiquid but were not insolvent. In accordance with this principle, the Bank had lent very generously during the crisis of 1825. Similarly, under the Palmer régime the policy of constant securities was not applied on occasions of internal drain. In 1837 there was no panic like that of twelve years earlier, but the Bank's securities were for a while swollen by loans undertaken in order to mitigate internal discredit.

The only occasion during the period when there was any substantial internal drain of gold from the Bank was in 1836–7. The first signs of trouble in the autumn of 1836 came from Ireland. The growth of other joint-stock banks to challenge the monopoly of the Bank of Ireland had been accompanied by much bitterness between the new banks and the old one, as well as between the new banks themselves; and to this was added a more than adequate share of the banking malpractices then current. A drain of gold from London to Ireland became felt in September, as rumours began to circulate of impending sus-

[1] *Causes and Consequences*, p. 21.

172

pensions amongst the Irish banks; gold was needed, because it was not clear whether the Act of 1833 making Bank of England notes legal tender applied to Ireland. In October some abatement in the drain took place;[1] at the beginning of November it resumed again with increased intensity, and on the 14th the Agricultural and Commercial Bank suspended payments. It was said that another bank, the National, was saved from a similar necessity only because Daniel O'Connell was on its board and brought political pressure to bear to secure assistance from the Bank of Ireland.[2] The difficulties of the Agricultural and Commercial arose fundamentally out of the illiquidity of its assets, three-quarters of which consisted at the time of its suspension of 'bills on hand', bills of small traders and farmers, the bank having had little connection with manufacturing industry. Sufficient of these bills had been realised to enable the bank to resume payments in September 1837; it failed finally in June 1840. But though its business may have been fundamentally unsound, the immediate cause of its first suspension lay in the hostility of the Bank of Ireland and the Provincial Bank of Ireland, which had collected large quantities of its notes and presented them for payment. A similar attack had been made in 1835, but on the second occasion the pressure on the London money market resulting from the recent external drain prevented the bank from being able to raise enough funds to resist.[3]

In Britain liquidity preference was evidently already increasing in October 1836, for the drain of gold from the Bank continued despite the improvement in the exchanges and the temporary intermission in the Irish troubles. The external drain, by causing stringency in the money market, had contributed to the internal one. With discredit growing and prices falling, difficulties began to be felt by those commercial banks in England whose policy during the boom had been particularly reckless. In November the first request for assistance was received from the Northern and Central Bank, one of the recently formed joint-stock banks in Lancashire.[4] At the end of the year, Esdaile's, a London banking house, was found to be shaken, and though not unsound required temporary assistance to tide it over its difficulties. Finally, throughout the first half of 1837, the Bank was extending assistance to the 'three W's' in the vain hope that they might thereby be enabled to carry through without suspending.[5] It is arguable that in this latter instance the Bank's judgement was at fault, and that it would have been better to have left these houses to their fate. But the general principle of the Bank's conduct was on none of these occasions objectionable.

(3) The increase in the securities held by the Bank in 1839 was perhaps the most fundamental departure from the principles of 1832. Palmer's defence was quite simple. The drain of that year was due in the main to corn imports and to impairment of foreigners' confidence in the ability of the Bank to maintain cash payments. If the Bank had held its securities constant and reduced its liabilities to the full extent of the (very great) fall in the bullion, it would have precipitated a financial crisis and caused widespread distress while contributing little to the

---

[1] F. G. Hall, *The Bank of Ireland 1783–1946* (1949), pp. 161–3.
[2] *Circular to Bankers*, 30 November 1838.
[3] The fullest account of the bank's history up to 1837 is in S. E. Thomas, *The Rise and Growth of Joint Stock Banking* (1934), pp. 270–81.
[4] Thomas, pp. 281–94; Clapham, II, pp. 154–6.
[5] Clapham, II, pp. 157–9, and pp. 58–9 above.

correction of the drain. Indeed, as far as the flight of 'hot money' was concerned, such a policy might easily have aggravated it. No doubt the discount rate could have been raised so high as to prevent importation of corn, but the procurement of the French Loan[1] was a preferable solution to reducing the nation to starvation. 'The principle of 1832', said Palmer, 'had always reference to ordinary circumstances, and I do not consider that the year 1839 was of that character.'[2]

Both the conception and the execution of the Bank's policy in the 1830's have been severely judged by historians of monetary thought and monetary institutions. Professor Jacob Viner, for example, has written: 'The adoption of the Palmer rule was a flagrant error, and the rule was repeatedly violated in such a manner as to make things worse instead of better.'[3] If the argument of the previous pages is correct, this view is quite lacking in foundation. The policy adopted was a consistent one, not very far removed indeed from the tenets of monetary orthodoxy, and its underlying principles were seriously departed from on only one occasion, namely, in 1839, and then for good reason. All in all there is no ground for disbelieving that the policy of the Bank ensured that international gold movements were accompanied by the appropriate expansion or contraction of domestic credit. This view will receive further support later in this chapter when we discuss the extremely close correlation that prevailed throughout the period between the market rate of discount and the level of the Bank's reserve.

It is not suggested, of course, that the Bank's conduct of its affairs was perfect. One might question its fundamental premises, and argue, as did Gilbart and other members of the Banking School, that the whole idea of establishing a relation between the bullion reserve and the discount rate was mistaken. Even without challenging its fundamental assumptions, there is no denying that the Palmer rule did not absolve the Bank from the need to exercise its discretion in a number of matters, and that errors were therefore liable to occur. An error might be made, for example, in deciding what rate of interest to charge on the advances during the shuttings, if the market rate were currently in a state of flux. Similarly, no rule of thumb enabled the Bank to distinguish a seasonal or other temporary movement from one whose roots were more deep seated. On these and such-like grounds the Bank's policy was sometimes open to criticism.

There was also one more persistent fault in its policy. When the Bank's discounts showed a tendency to rise which it was desired to check, the obvious thing to do was to raise the Bank Rate. Under the Palmer régime this was apparently regarded as an expedient to be avoided if possible, unless a jolt to confidence was felt to be specially desirable. Instead, the Bank preferred to offset the rise in discounts by the sale of Exchequer bills or other securities. In practice, arbitrage between the Exchequer bill market and the discount market was evidently imperfect, for it was almost always found that the sale of Exchequer bills did not suffice to check the increasing volume of bills presented to the Bank for discount, and that the Bank Rate had therefore ultimately to be raised after all. There was consequently on a number of occasions (e.g. the second quarter of

---

[1] See Chapter VII.   [2] *1840*, Q. 1426.
[3] *Studies in the Theory of International Trade*, p. 255. A similar view is expressed by T. E. Gregory, *Select Statutes, Documents and Reports relating to British Banking, 1832–1928* (1929), I, pp. xvii–xix.

1836) a delay between the efflux of bullion and the transmission of stringency to the discount market, which naturally attracted criticism. But whether the elimination of this delay would really have made much difference to the course of events on the occasions in question may well be doubted.[1]

3. The Bank's Reserve and the Market Rate of Discount

A comparison of Chart 16 (p. 185) with Chart 13 will immediately demonstrate how close was the inverse relationship throughout the period between the discount rate and the state of the Bank of England's reserve. This is brought out still more clearly by means of a scatter diagram (Chart 14a). As has already been suggested, the closeness of this relationship goes a long way towards refuting the charge that the Bank's policy failed in its avowed object of relating the price of accommodation to the behaviour of the foreign exchanges.

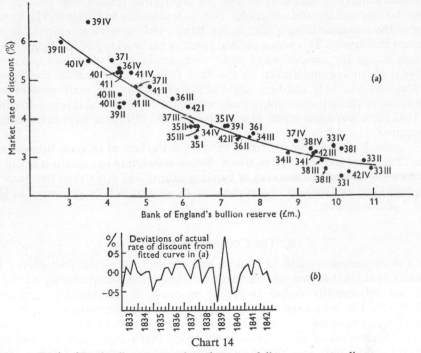

Chart 14

Bank of England's reserve and market rate of discount: scatter diagram

No less striking than the closeness of the correlation is the absence of any regular pattern among the deviations occurring between the actual rate of discount and those indicated by the fitted regression curve. One would naturally expect that for any given level of the Bank's reserve, the discount rate would be higher the more active the state of trade; to use Keynesian terms, in the boom when incomes are high, the quantity of money required for effecting transactions[2]

[1] This last point is further briefly discussed below, p. 187, n. 2.
[2] In Keynesian terms, M_1.

is correspondingly high, and so, *ceteris paribus*, should be the rate of interest. The scatter diagram does not reveal anything of this sort. There is in it no particular tendency for points corresponding to periods of active trade to lie above the regression curve, nor for points corresponding to slump periods to fall below it. To take one extreme example: two quarters more contrasted with respect to the level of activity than the second quarter of 1836 and the second quarter of 1842 can scarcely be imagined; yet in each the same Bank reserve (£7·4 million) was accompanied by the same average discount rate (3·5%). Deviations of the actual rate of discount in each quarter from those indicated by the regression curve are plotted in Chart 14*b*. These deviations are erratic and have no apparent relationship to the general state of trade.

This would not be particularly surprising if the variations in the level of the Bank's bullion reserve were themselves mainly due to variations in the currency needs of the country brought about by business fluctuations. Were that the case, it would scarcely be necessary to look for any further relationship between the discount rate and the state of trade. But, as was shown in Chapter VII, hardly any of the movements occurring in the Bank's reserve were actually to be explained in this way. This was a natural result of the working of the Palmer rule, which, except for periods when panic threatened, in principle prevented the amount of lending undertaken by the Bank from being responsive to business fluctuations. In 1838 the very slight efflux of gold in the early months was attributed to the improvement of trade within the country, and it is possible that in 1842 there was some reflux of a similar nature. But these were unimportant exceptions.

Something of a paradox therefore remains in the lack of relation between the rate of discount and the state of trade. Before attempting to explain it it will be necessary to discuss the working of banking institutions other than the Bank of England. The explanation of the paradox mentioned will be discussed in §§ 6 and 7 of this chapter.

4. THE COUNTRY NOTE-ISSUE

Both in contemporary and in modern writers, analysis of the part played by country banks in the economic fluctuation of this period has commonly started— and not infrequently ended—with the question of the country note-issue (Chart 15). The note-issue was the subject of the Parliamentary inquiries of 1840–1 which have been so extensively used as a source-book by historians, and it was the control of the note-issue to which Peel's legislation of 1844 was primarily addressed. It is therefore important to emphasise the relative unimportance of the country circulation and the extremely limited nature of the conclusions than can be gleaned from study of the statistics relating to it.

It will be useful to start with a brief survey of the media in which different types of transactions were commonly settled in this period.[1]

(1) Since 1829, the circulation of notes of denomination lower than £5 had been illegal in England, and in the 1830's and 1840's coin vastly preponderated in hand-to-hand circulation and in the payment of wages in all parts of England,

[1] The following paragraphs have reference only to England; in Scotland the state of affairs was different.

both London and the provinces.[1] The amount of sovereigns in circulation was generally agreed to exceed by a substantial margin that of Bank of England notes and country bank-notes added together, and the value of the silver coin circulating was also not negligible.[2]

(2) In the 1820's, circulation of Bank of England notes had been largely confined to London, and to a less extent Lancashire. In the next decade their use was being extended through the agency of the newly established Bank of England branches, but their circulation in the provinces probably remained considerably smaller in total than their circulation in London.[3] Bank of England notes were used in hand-to-hand transactions of the larger sort, and in

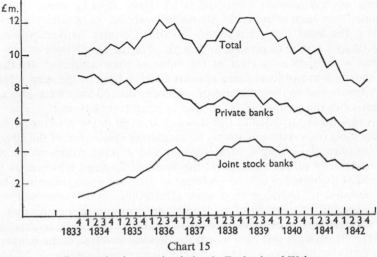

Chart 15

Country bank note circulation in England and Wales

the payments of the substantial, though dwindling, class of small traders who did not keep a bank account. Another important use can be inferred from the pronounced relation between the seasonal fluctuations of the Bank's circulation and those of tax receipts and government dividend disbursements.[4]

(3) Large wholesale transactions, and many smaller payments as well, were normally settled either by cheque or by a bill of exchange, which the recipient could discount or pay into his bank account.[5] In an earlier period the circulation of endorsed and reissued bills of exchange had been very common. In the

---

[1] 'Every gentleman here knows that nine-tenths of what is paid in the shops is paid in gold and silver', V. Stuckey, before *Select Committee on Banks of Issue* 1841 (1st session), v (henceforth referred to as *1841*), Q. 459. Cf. also *1832*, QQ. 1300–8 (W. Beckett): *1841*, Q. 149 (H. W. Hobhouse.)

[2] The best authenticated estimates are in Tooke, VI, pp. 696–711. Rather lower estimates were made by V. Stuckey before the *Select Committee on Joint Stock Banks*, 1836, IX, Q. 1401, (henceforth referred to as *1836*; thus also *Select Committee on Joint Stock Banks*, 1837, XIV, referred to as *1837*, and *Select Committee on Joint Stock Banks*, 1837–8, VII, referred to as *1838*).

[3] Cf. Gregory, *Westminster Bank*, I, p. 27.

[4] Gilbart, *Practical Treatise*, pp. 377–80.

[5] *1832*, QQ. 1424 (W. Beckett); 5328–33 (H. Burgess): *1840*, QQ. 567–76 (R. Cobden).

1830's it was becoming less so, especially in the case of smaller bills; but the practice had not disappeared, as we shall see presently.

(4) The circulation of notes other than those of the Bank of England was in the main confined to rural districts. In London, no private bank had issued notes for very many years. H. W. Hobhouse, a banker at Bath and chairman of the Committee of Private Bankers, estimated in 1841 that less than a tenth of private bank circulation at that time was to be found in industrial districts.[1] In such areas—the West Riding of Yorkshire being to some extent an exception— cash needs were met by coin and Bank of England notes.

Even in agricultural areas, the use of cheques was becoming more and more customary, and the type of transaction in which private notes were still used was becoming correspondingly restricted.[2] 'A great railway speculation', said Hobhouse, 'has been going on in my neighbourhood for several years without increasing the local paper circulation at all.' Country bankers valued their circulation as a source of prestige and as an advertisement,[3] but even so, few of them had a circulation as great as the value of their deposits.[4] By the early 1840's the main use of local notes appears to have been in the corn markets of country towns and in the purchase of livestock, though they were also used to a fair extent in the payment of rents and in retail transactions.[5]

Many reasons contributed to this downward trend in the country circulation. Probably most important was simply an increasing realisation of the advantages and economies of keeping a bank account and making payments by cheque. Deliberate policy played some part: the Bank of England frowned on private issue, and at its branches offered preferential discount arrangements to bankers who consented to abandon their own circulation. Also significant was the speeding-up and cheapening of transport and communications brought about by the railways and, of especial interests to banks, by the postal reforms of 1840 and 1841.[6] Note-issue was only worth the expense involved if the banker could be confident that his notes would stay in circulation for some time and so provide him with a source of funds. For this reason a banker would not normally choose to pay out his notes to a customer whose intention was known to be to make a remittance away from the district.[7] Outside a fairly limited radius, a bank's notes would not be generally acceptable; anyone receiving them would pay them into his own bank, which would then remit them for payment to the issuer or his London agent. No bank, of course, would ever reissue the notes of another bank in competition with it. One of the main reasons why private note-issue survived longest in rural areas was that in larger towns notes stayed out too short a time; in a country district there were fewer banks in competition and it

---

[1] *1841*, QQ. 13–17, 296.
[2] *1832*, Q. 978 (V. Stuckey): *1841*, QQ. 149, 178–80 (H. W. Hobhouse).
[3] *1832*, QQ. 1174 (V. Stuckey); 1559–63 (C. S. Forster).
[4] See passages cited by Morgan, *Central Banking*, p. 12.
[5] Tooke, III, p. 275, IV, p. 163; *1841*, Q. 456 (V. Stuckey).
[6] J. W. Gilbart, *Laws of the Currency* (*Collected Works*, vol. IV), p. 394. On the cost and inconvenience of postage to bankers before 1840, cf. L. H. Grindon, *Manchester Banks and Bankers* (1877), pp. 172–4.
[7] *1841*, QQ. 31, 145 (H. W. Hobhouse), and many other passages. Cf. G. Rae, *The Country Banker* (1885), p. 151: 'You would not give your own notes...to any one who, you have reason to suspect, would straightway cut them in halves and dispatch them by the first post as a remittance to London or somewhere else.'

took longer for notes to be remitted for payment.[1] But the improvement in the postal system meant that even banks in rural districts found their notes returning quickly, and so became less anxious to issue.

It was almost universally agreed amongst country bankers that in the matter of their circulation their part was entirely a passive one, and this doctrine came to occupy a central place in the writings of Tooke, Gilbart and other Banking School theorists. What determined the amount of the country circulation, it was explained, was the local volume of transactions of the type for which country notes were currently in use.[2] The time of year when a country banker's circulation was at its highest—as also his deposits—was after the harvest, when farmers were in funds. When a farmer was paid by cheque or a bill or in the notes of some other bank for his crops or for his livestock, he would take the proceeds to his own bank and obtain local notes in exchange.[3] Thus the country circulation was largely dependent on the condition of the agricultural interest. Observe, for example, in Chart 15, the steep rise at the end of 1838 and the beginning of 1839 when agricultural prices were abnormally high.[4] On the other hand, more general fluctuations in prices and credit left a certain mark as well; the boom of 1836 had ramifications even in remote rural areas, and so some rise in the country circulation took place. But in that case too, so the bankers maintained, their part was a passive one; their circulation rose simply in consequence of the rise in the volume of transactions.

This contention was open to the obvious objection that a banker could increase his circulation by more generous lending. In answer the bankers explained that their circulation depended little on their lending policy. Loans to farmers to tide over the months before the harvest, which were an important part of the business of bankers in agricultural counties, were admittedly made in local notes. But the amounts granted of this type of loan were not dependent on the general state of trade, and in any case notes issued in this way as a rule were quickly paid away and so stayed in circulation a relatively short time. Advances or discounts for industrial or commercial purposes were rarely made in local notes, because the banker knew that if they were the notes would be returned almost immediately.[5]

It was conceded by the more intelligent bank spokesmen that if *some* banks expanded their circulation by increasing their discounts, other banks would find that their own circulation automatically rose in consequence of the rise in in-

[1] *1832*, QQ. 3372–4 (S. J. Loyd): *1836*, QQ. 1161–4, 1263 (J. Gibbins). H. W. Hobhouse estimated that the notes of his bank stayed out between two and three weeks (*1841*, Q. 379). In Scotland, notes stayed out only about ten or eleven days, because the practice of keeping a bank account was so much more general than in England (*1841*, QQ. 1726–7 (A. Blair)).

[2] Cf. the utterances of country bankers collected together and quoted by S. J. Loyd, *1840*, Q. 2801.

[3] *1841*, QQ. 487–500 (V. Stuckey); Gilbart, *Practical Treatise*, pp. 466–8; *Laws of the Currency*, pp. 397–9.

[4] For the country as a whole, the increase in farmers' incomes in 1838 was probably not great (see p. 29) on account of the diminution of quantity sold; but in the south of England, where the circulation of country notes was greatest (Scotland being excluded from the figures given in Chart 15), the harvest was a good deal better than in the north and in Scotland. Similarly, in 1839 agricultural prices were lower than in 1838 by only a moderate degree; there was, however, a poorer yield in southern countries than in the previous year, which explains the fall in country circulation. Cf. Tooke, III, pp. 11–12, 16.

[5] *1832*, QQ. 972–5 (V. Stuckey); 1389, 1400 (W. Beckett); *1841*, QQ. 416, 418 (H. W. Hobhouse); 487–500 (V. Stuckey); 751 (W. Rodwell).

comes in the localities they served, and that this process would have cumulative force.[1] This had happened to a large extent in 1825, when country banks had issued notes and 'bankers' bills' (post-dated notes) in great abundance.[2] But in 1836 it was not prominent. There was certainly a great expansion of bank credit, but the expansion did not, save in exceptional instances, take the form of increased circulation, for it did not originate in districts or from transactions in which country notes were current. Such increase in circulation as did occur was predominantly passive, as the bankers claimed it to be.

Enough has now been said to demonstrate the extremely limited value of the statistics of the country circulation as an index of the fluctuation in the amount of bank money. For the most part, all that is measured by these figures is the volume of transaction of a particular type—and that subject to alteration in the course of the period—in certain particular districts. Interpreted in their proper light the figures are not, indeed, lacking in interest. But the practice common at the time of taking the note circulation as an index of the state of bank credit throughout the country was a result of the evolution of monetary controversies since their origin in the Bank Restriction period rather than of any close study of contemporary banking realities.[3]

5. THE EFFECT OF DISCOUNT-RATE MOVEMENTS ON THE BANKING SYSTEM

Section 2 of this chapter was devoted to demonstrating that the policy of the Bank of England was such as one would expect on *a priori* grounds to have ensured a fair correspondence between the state of the Bank's bullion reserve (as governed principally by the foreign exchanges) and the discount rate; and in § 3 it was found that such a correspondence did in fact obtain. We must now go on to consider the consequences for the total supply of credit within the country that ensued when gold was leaving the country and discount rates were rising. In particular, we must consider the ways in which the rise in discount rates brought into activity money and money substitutes to fill the gap caused by the contraction of the metallic base of the nation's currency in such circumstances. The responsiveness of the supply of credit to changes in the general level of business activity (as distinct from its responsiveness to interest rate movements) will be dealt with later, in §§ 6 and 7.

According to conventional banking theory, the effect of an adverse balance of payments is automatically to reduce banks' reserves, since they will have to draw on their balances at the central bank or on their reserves of currency notes in order to obtain from the central bank the gold that will be called for by their customers. This result will be intensified if the central bank reduces its holding of securities, but even if it does not do this, commercial banks will still have to reduce their lending unless they are willing to allow a fall in the ratio of their reserves to their liabilities.

The evidence of the country bankers before the Parliamentary Committees of 1832, 1836–8 and 1840–1 does not suggest that they were aware of any regular

---

[1] Cf. Wood, *Theories of Central Banking*, pp. 38–9.
[2] *1832*, Q. 1641 (J. P. Wilkins); Q. 4398 (J. B. Smith).
[3] For a good statement of this point, see Morgan, Chapter VI.

law of this sort.[1] Some of them did acknowledge incidentally that their liabilities often tended to fall when the Bank of England's liabilities fell, but the relationship does not seem to have been in the forefront of their minds, and many of those who did mention it were thinking, not of an automatic reduction in liabilities consequent upon their customers' expenditure exceeding their receipts, but rather of the deliberate withdrawal of funds by depositors who wished to avail themselves of the enhanced rate of discount in London. Country bankers knew from experience that seasons of pressure in London were usually followed by a deflation of prices which reacted adversely on the incomes and bank balances of their customers, but this relationship was subject to an appreciable delay and was not automatic. Many bankers, it is true, stated that they might become more cautious in extending loans and discounts to their customers if the foreign exchanges were markedly unfavourable, but the reason assigned was usually either the fear that a panic was imminent or else, if they practised re-discounting, that they would have difficulty in rediscounting their bills in London. Automatic reduction in country bank reserves in periods of drain was not commonly emphasised.

The reason for this departure from the normal modern picture of the working of a banking system can only be surmised. Most probably the answer lay in the nature of the forces operating on the balance of payments. We have seen in Chapter VII the importance of capital movements, especially short-term capital movements, in this connection. If an adverse balance of payments were the result of an increase in the number of foreign bills discounted in London, the greater part of the impact would be felt by bankers in London. Country bankers would not be entirely unaffected, since they would normally themselves have taken up some of the foreign bills through a bill broker. But the greater part of the total amount of funds used in the London discount market were London funds,[2] and probably the proportion of London funds used in the discount of foreign bills was still higher. Where long-term foreign securities were concerned, country bankers might also be relatively unaffected if the purchase of them were mainly a Stock Exchange speculation (as with the Spanish and other such bonds in 1833–5), or if there were a substantial delay between the acquisition of the bonds by merchant bankers and their disposal to investors throughout the country (as was often the case with United States bonds[3]). It is worth noting that in 1839, when an adverse balance of trade was undoubtedly largely responsible for the drain of gold from the Bank of England, there is more talk of gold being remitted from the country to London than on other occasions when the exchanges were unfavourable;[4] furthermore, the efflux of gold was on this occasion alone accompanied by an appreciable reduction in the Bank of England's circulation. It is therefore possible that in 1839 the adverse exchanges did directly cause some diminution in country bank reserves, which was not made up till 1842. But there is no reason to believe that the diminution was of great amount.

[1] Among the passages bearing on the question may be cited: *1832*, QQ. 1019–32 (V. Stuckey); 3577–8 (S. Gurney); *1836*, QQ. 1291–1311 (J. Gibbins); *1841*, QQ. 94–5 (H. W. Hobhouse); 460–9, 500–1, 528–9 (V. Stuckey); 832 (W. Rodwell); 1565–74 (P. M. James); 1645–7 (I. C. Wright); 1879–1900 (A. Blair); 2068–71, 2274–5 (P. W. Kennedy). Cf. also Gilbart, *Practical Treatise*, pp. 88, 121.   [2] See below.   [3] See p. 65.
[4] *1841*, QQ. 376 (H. W. Hobhouse); 781–3 (W. Rodwell).

It follows that the way in which country bankers were affected by fluctuation in the exchanges was predominantly through movements of the market rate of discount in London. We must now turn our attention to the implications of this.

Some words are necessary first on the structure of the London bill market and its relations with country banks. Some interesting statistical estimates relating to the bill market in the late 1840's were made by William Newmarch[1]. There is no reason to doubt that ten years earlier the proportional orders of magnitude were roughly the same. Newmarch estimated that in normal years the total volume of bills under discount at any one time (excluding bills held till maturity and never discounted) was approximately £100 million. Of this amount about one-sixth were foreign bills and about £22 million local inland bills discounted in the district where they were drawn without the intermediacy of the London market. Of the £78 million used in the discount of bills in London, £30 million were reckoned to be funds of country banks and the remaining £48 million the funds of London banks (including the Bank of England), bill dealers and insurance companies.[2] The £52 million of country bank funds used in the discount of local and London bills together comprised about two-fifths of total country bank resources.

The London discount houses were the agencies through which surplus funds of country banks found use in London. Banks in agricultural areas particularly tended to have surplus funds, since local demand for accommodation did not as a rule suffice to absorb all their resources. All country banks employed a London bank as agent to pay their drafts, receive their credits, and perform the other functions of a 'correspondent' bank, and some country banks kept their surplus funds with their London agent on deposit account. But the older City banks did not allow interest on the deposit accounts of their country connections, and even the London and Westminster, which did, allowed none on current accounts.[3] Most country bankers, therefore, found it a more flexible and advantageous system to employ their surplus funds in discounting bills of exchange procured for them through the agency of the discount houses.

London bankers were themselves large purchasers of bills, but many of them were already beginning to hold some of their earning assets in the still more liquid form of call loans to discount houses. This practice assisted the latter to become to some extent themselves dealers in bills as principals. They obtained the bills which they discounted or passed on to country banks either direct from merchants in the country or in London—bills drawn on retailers in favour of their wholesale suppliers formed a large part of those in circulation—or else from banks in industrial districts, amongst whom rediscount of bills discounted for customers was a growing practice.[4]

[1] *History of Prices*, VI, pp. 584–93; *Statistical Journal* (1851), XIV, pp. 143–83.
[2] Of total banking funds in use in London (including also funds used for purposes other than bill discounting), Newmarch estimated that City and West End bankers provided 40%, insurance companies, etc., 7%, Bank of England 20%, country banks 21%.
[3] For a full account of the relations between the London and Westminster and its country connections, see Gregory, I, pp. 236–53.
[4] On the structure of the London discount market during this period see King, *History of London Discount Market*, Chapters II and III. A somewhat similar organisation existed on a much smaller scale in big towns in the provinces. Stuckey stated that his bank procured most of the bills it discounted in Bristol, and P. M. James said that the Birmingham Banking Company had arrangements with some bankers in the surrounding country by which it took their surplus cash and gave them bills (*1836*, Q. 780; *1841*, Q. 641).

When the exchanges became unfavourable, London bankers and bill dealers would find their reserves dwindling and would take steps to reduce their purchase of bills, so bringing about a rise in the market rate of discount. It will be argued in a moment that in this period banks did not adhere to any rigid reserve ratio, and this was no doubt true of London banks as well as country banks; but there were obviously limits below which reserves could not be allowed to fall, and in any case a rise in discount rates would have to take place before a reduction in reserve ratios could become attractive. The rise in discount rates would tend to increase discounting at the Bank of England, and if the Bank wished to hold its securities constant, the Bank Rate would also presently have to be raised. These rises in the Bank Rate and in the market rate of discount in London would then have repercussions throughout the system. The nature of these repercussions is what we must now consider.

One immediate consequence of a rise in discount rates was to mobilise previously unemployed funds in London. Idle balances both at the Bank of England (for the Bank's private deposits were substantial) and at other London banks were transformed into active balances and helped to relieve the stringency.[1] Similarly, individuals in the country would send to London cash which they formerly lent out locally, or, more likely, which they formerly had on deposit with country banks.[2] Merchants and other borrowers in the country who in times of monetary ease were accustomed to send their bills direct to London bill brokers to be discounted took them instead to their local bankers when London rates rose, or else sought accommodation from their bankers in some other form, since local lending rates moved more slowly and to a less extent than rates in London.[3]

In consequence, the excess demand for accommodation in London was partly met by the mobilisation of idle funds, and partly transferred by a process of arbitrage to provincial districts. Country bankers experienced an increased local demand for accommodation, and at the same time found themselves able to earn higher rates by discounting London bills procured for them by the brokers. In most parts of the country, bankers' local lending does not appear to have been much reduced by the higher rates available in London. Interest rates charged to borrowers on non-negotiable security, especially, in agricultural districts, to farmers, were kept at a fairly high conventional level at all times, and many bankers apparently in any case considered it a duty to provide the accommodation that farmers needed.[4] The amount of bills drawn by farmers would depend on the value of their produce; only in exceptional circumstances would a banker refuse to discount for farmers the bills which they had received.[5] For rediscounting banks in industrial areas, the question of lending more in London did not arise, since they were net borrowers from the London market, not net lenders. In Scotland, however, it was stated by one witness that the amount of loans granted locally was affected to an important extent by the rates earnable in London.[6]

---

[1] Gilbart, *Practical Treatise*, p. 88; idem, *An Enquiry into the Causes of the Pressure on the Money Market during the year 1839* (*Collected Works*, vol. IV), pp. 268, 270.
[2] *1841*, QQ. 633, 637–8 (V. Stuckey); Q. 1883 (A. Blair).
[3] Gilbart, *Practical Treatise*, p. 88.
[4] *1832*, Q. 1014 (Stuckey): *1841*, QQ. 264 (H. W. Hobhouse); 460–9 (V. Stuckey).
[5] Gilbart, *History and Principles of Banking* (*Collected Works*, Vol. IV), p. 114.
[6] *1841*, QQ. 2040–1, 2087–9 (P. W. Kennedy). Contrast, however, *1841*, QQ. 1899–1900 (A. Blair).

The effect of a rise in the market rate of discount on the *total* amount of lending undertaken by country banks, that is to say, on the amount of local loans plus the amount of London Bills discounted, depended on the extent to which the rise in discount rates proceeded. At times when discount rates were very low, bankers found difficulty in securing worthwhile uses for their funds, and their reserves tended to pile up.[1] A moderate rise in rates would in such times cause them to increase their lending and reduce their reserve ratios. But if the rise in rates went so far as to threaten a crisis, they would immediately take steps to increase their liquidity. The matter was well summed up by Gilbart:

> When money is abundant, a banker will lock up with more money than he wants, because he cannot employ his funds. When money is so scarce as to betoken a pressure, he will also lock up strong so as to be prepared for any emergency.[2]

In our period there was no real crisis corresponding to those of 1825 or 1866, but in 1839 it appeared that one might develop in London when the Bank of England intimated that it might have to cease rediscounting for the discount houses.[3] This no doubt explains why the discount rate was higher during the last quarter of 1839 than during the third quarter, notwithstanding that the average level of the Bank of England's reserve was higher in the fourth quarter (cf. Chart 14a). On the other hand, there was no approach to a panic in most country districts. H. W. Hobhouse said that in 1839 when panic prevailed in London, 'we knew nothing of it in the country'.[4] Vincent Stuckey stated that in 1839 his bank had been able to lend very extensively, with great profit to itself, and that they had not been too particular about the type of security provided.[5]

All in all, it appears that most bankers were willing enough to reduce their reserve ratios if the interest rates available offered sufficient incentive. It emerges very clearly from the testimony of country bankers that they did not think in terms of a fixed or even a normal ratio of cash reserves to liabilities.[6] Almost all those questioned on the matter insisted that no hard and fast rule could be laid down, and that everything depended on the circumstances. A typically flexible policy was that stated by Stuckey: 'Whenever I find our reserve below £30,000 I then always begin to replenish; when I find it above £50,000 I think it is fair to send it away.' Some bankers spoke of their balances with their London agents as part of their reserves; others did not. Often they spoke indifferently of cash, bills of exchange and government securities as comprising their reserve. The distinction between what could nowadays be called the first-line and the second-line reserve was very blurred; in some circumstances bills of exchange might be more readily convertible into cash than balances with a London agent.

There can be little doubt that the variability of bankers' reserve ratios and the flexibility of bank credit which it involved were largely the result of the extreme liquidity of bills of exchange. Bills of exchange were the main means of providing working capital to industry, and, as will be seen presently, their use to finance the

---

[1] Cf. *1836*, QQ. 639–44 (J. Amery).   [2] *Practical Treatise*, p. 68.
[3] *Select Committee on Bank Acts*, 1857 (2nd session), x, Part II, Q. 5194 (D. B. Chapman).
[4] *1841*, Q. 155.
[5] Some of the loans were on the security of railway companies' property (*1841*, Q. 634).
[6] *1832*, QQ. 5559–61 (H. Burgess); *1836*, QQ. 992–6, 1247 (J. Gibbins); 2848 (D. Robertson); *1837*, QQ. 2336–7 (D. Robertson); *1841*, QQ. 115–20 (H. W. Hobhouse); 583 (V. Stuckey); 717 (W. Rodwell); 1543–4 (P. M. James); 1600 (I. C. Wright); 2105–9 (P. W. Kennedy).

creation of fixed capital was by no means uncommon. And it was the rate of interest on bills of exchange which was first and most powerfully affected by drains and inflows of bullion arising out of foreign exchange fluctuations. Since bankers regarded good-quality bills as scarcely inferior to cash (save in times of panic), it is not surprising that the supply of finance to industry was endowed with considerable elasticity.

An interesting light on a rather different consequence of the system of bill finance is cast by the estimates of the volume of bills of exchange created in each quarter which were made by Newmarch on the basis of stamp-duty figures (see Chart 16). As Newmarch pointed out, when the market rate of discount was high, the volume of bills created tended to increase. Of course, the discount

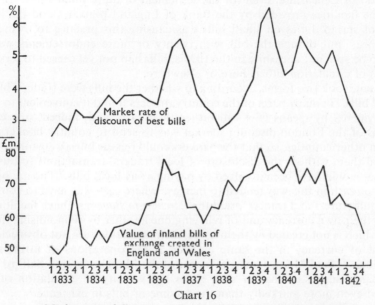

Chart 16

Market rate of discount and value of bills of exchange created

rate was not the only influence governing the quantity of bills drawn; it was also largely affected by the general state of trade. But the effect of movements in the discount rate is quite pronounced, especially on occasions when the rate was high. Observe, for example, the sharp rise in the volume of bills in the third quarter of 1836, when the most intensive phase of the boom was past but interest rates had only just begun to rise. Noteworthy too is the high volume of bills in 1840 and 1841, when trade was mediocre or worse.

There appear to have been several reasons to account for this relationship. In the first place, bankers and others preferred, when money was scarce, to receive tangible and negotiable security for loans which in normal times they would have been content to make by way of an advance.[1] In the second place, in many lines of trade a conventional discount was allowed for cash. As a rule wealthy

[1] *Select Committee on Bank Acts*, 1857 (2nd session), x, Part II, QQ. 1426, 1520–5 (W. Newmarch).

185

firms would pay cash and take the discount. But if the market rate on bills rose above the conventional discount, it would be more profitable to pay in a bill.[1] Bills issued for either of these reasons did not as such serve either to aggravate or to mitigate the tendency to stringency in the money market which had called them into existence. They may, however, have been useful as a means of bringing into activity funds that would not have been advanced on less negotiable security.

But there is also evidence that when money was dear bills became more acceptable in the settlement of transactions in a way which rendered them actually a substitute for cash. It is well known that up till the 1820's, bills of exchange bearing numerous endorsements formed a predominant part of the circulation of Lancashire, even for the settlement of quite small sums.[2] By the 1830's the facilities provided by the Bank of England branches and the heavy burden of stamp duties on small bills was causing this practice to dwindle in importance. But though the bill with twenty or more endorsements was no longer to be seen in Lancashire in the 1830's, bills had not yet ceased to serve the purposes of circulation either there or elsewhere.

The usage took two forms, according to whether the bills were traders' bills or bankers' bills. In many parts of the country, traders found it convenient to settle their payments by means of a bill rather than cash, and, indeed, one of the functions of the London discount market was to send to country bankers bills drawn in other counties, so that the bankers could reissue bills to customers who requested them without the disclosure of local traders' transactions to business rivals that would have been involved by paying away local bills.[3] The use of bills in place of cash in this way tended to increase where cash was hard to come by. 'As manufacturers and traders', said the *Circular to Bankers*, 'have facilities for creating their own currency and of relieving one another by economising the use of that which is not created by themselves, their operations are not obstructed by the want of currency in the same manner as the operations of farmers and graziers are.'[4] Paul Moon James, manager of the Manchester and Salford Joint Stock Bank, suggested that in such times the velocity of circulation of bills increased even more markedly than the volume of bills in existence.[5]

It was also a common practice in many parts of the country, including Lancashire—though perhaps in the 1830's somewhat less common than it had earlier been—for a bank to pay away to its customers, instead of cash, bills bearing its endorsement or bills at dates varying from 21 days to 3 months payable at the bank or its London agent. Many of these bankers' bills so issued might circulate till maturity. Sometimes a bank would simply exchange bills of its own for bills of the same échéance brought to it by customers, charging a commission instead of discount.[6] 'The banker puts out his own paper that will circulate for other paper that will not circulate', said J. C. Dyer, a director of the

---

[1] Gilbart, *Enquiry*, p. 269; *History and Principles*, p. 139.

[2] See T. S. Ashton, 'The Bill of Exchange and private banks in Lancashire, 1790–1830', *Economic History Review* (1945), pp. 25–35.

[3] Newmarch, *Statistical Journal* (1851), p. 163. Cf. *1832*, QQ. 1424 (W. Beckett); 5328–33 (H. Burgess); *1836*, Q. 1983 (General Austin).

[4] *Circular to Bankers*, 17 June 1831.   [5] *1841*, QQ. 1504–5.

[6] *1832*, QQ. 4122, 4128, 4274–90 (J. C. Dyer); 4361–2, 4373–8 (J. B. Smith): *1836*, QQ. 673 675 (J. Amery); 1854 (W. G. Cassels); *1840*, QQ. 375 (J. B. Smith); 547–76 (R. Cobden).

joint-stock Bank of Manchester. This practice was naturally more resorted to at times when discount rates were high. 'I believe it is a matter of notoriety', said Gilbart, 'that at Manchester the banks draw a great number of bills in times of pressure.' In London, he added, this would not be done by banks, though more bills would be issued by traders: 'the number of trade bills in seasons of pressure is greater in proportion to the business.'[1] Both traders' and bankers' bills thus served as substitutes for cash when cash was scarce.

The upshot of the preceding discussion is that the supply of means of effecting payments was fairly readily expansible in response to rises in discount rates. When discount rates rose, idle cash in the hands of bankers and others was mobilised, and increased resort was had to methods of payment which dispensed with cash. In view of the variety of ways in which a rise in discount rates thus stimulated an increase in the supply of money and money substitutes, the burden of proof would appear to be on those who would seek to maintain that on occasions when the Bank of England's reserve was depleted by export of bullion, the rise in the rate of discount restored equilibrium by restricting the demand rather than by increasing the supply of loanable funds.

That is not to say, however, that variations in the discount rate caused by fluctuations in the foreign exchanges had no effect whatsoever on the state of trade. Most of the principal fluctuations in investment that occurred during the period can, it is true, be fairly readily explained without reference to the state of the money market; but it is difficult to believe that in such a year as 1839 the extreme tightness of credit did not have some effect in curtailing marginal investment projects and in discouraging unduly high holdings of stocks. More important was the easing of credit brought about by the reflux of bullion in 1835. The extent to which this actually reduced the cost of loans was not, indeed, very great. But there is good reason to suppose that the cheapening of credit just at the moment when the boom was gathering pace had a disproportionate psychological effect. As was argued in Chapter X, the fall in discount rates in 1836 provides a plausible explanation of the timing, at least, of the 'mania' which characterised the last phases of the upswing; and this 'mania' had in its turn further repercussions in the monetary sphere by encouraging the formation of joint-stock banks—of which more anon.[2]

---

[1] *1841*, QQ. 1222–3. Cf. also *1840*, QQ. 1128–9 (G. F. Muntz).

[2] The question may be asked to what extent faults in the policy of the Bank of England were to be held responsible for the fall in the discount rate and its effect in encouraging the mania. It was pointed out by many observers at the time that the market rate of discount fell in the second quarter of 1836, notwithstanding that the inflow of bullion had by then given way to a drain; and this was with some show of reason attributed to the Bank's tardiness in raising Bank Rate. (See Clapham, *Bank of England*, II, pp. 149–53; above, pp. 174–5.) On the other hand, it is to be noted that, presumably also as a result of the Bank's policy, a similar delay had elapsed between the beginning of the inflow of bullion in 1835 and the fall in the market rate of discount: in the last quarter of 1835 the Bank's reserve increased considerably, but the statistics show no change in the market rate of discount till March 1836. Therefore although it is possible that speedier responsiveness on the part of the Bank might have imposed some check on the mania in May and June of 1836, it would also have caused the fall in discount rates to have started earlier, and its effect might thus well have been not to prevent or moderate the mania, but simply to make it occur a few months earlier.

6. THE LONG-TERM RATE OF INTEREST

So far in this chapter, our attention has been concentrated mainly on the behaviour of the market rate of discount on bills of exchange, and on the consequences of movements in this rate. Nothing has so far been said about the
long-term rate of interest as measured by the yield on consols. It is to be
emphasised, therefore, that when it was said just now that the supply of means of
effecting payments was fairly responsive to changes in interest rates, the relationship referred to was not liquidity-preference in the strict Keynesian sense.
The implication of the Keynesian system would appear to be that a rise in
interest rates leads to an increase in the supply of active money by causing a
reduction in the amount of cash (M_2) held for the speculative motive.[1] The
changes in the capital value of bonds which bring about this result do not, of
course, occur unless there is a change in the long-term rate of interest. Changes
in discount rates do not as such affect capital values to any appreciable degree.

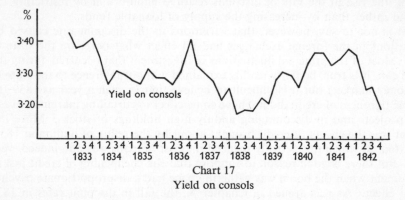

Chart 17
Yield on consols

Was the phenomenon of liquidity-preference in the Keynesian sense, or anything like it, present in our period? Were movements in the yield on consols and
similar securities important in determining the supply of active money? The
answer is probably that they had some importance, but not a very great one.
After 1834 the amplitude of the fluctuations in the yield on consols was very
small (see Chart 17), the difference between the highest and lowest *prices* being
scarcely more than about 8%. It is unlikely that movements of this extent had
any great influence on the relative preference of bankers for government bonds
and cash. Most bankers in this period regarded government securities, if they
held them, as forming part of their reserve, to be realised if necessary (or more
frequently borrowed upon) in seasons of pressure, but otherwise to comprise
a relatively stable proportion of their assets.[2] Speculation in the funds for the
purpose of making capital gains was not considered at all respectable banking
practice, nor was this one of the charges brought against the newly formed
joint-stock banks; their sins were of a different character. On the other hand, it is
rather more probable that individuals' cash holdings varied in response to

[1] Cf. J. M. Keynes, *General Theory of Employment Interest and Money* (1936), pp. 166–74.
[2] *1836*, QQ. 2399–2400 (S. Martin); 1445–85 (V. Stuckey); 1926–9 (J. W. Gilbart); *1841*,
QQ. 1967–76 (A. Blair).

changes in the yield on bonds more or less along the lines depicted by Keynesian theory. In periods of acute pressure, one of the means by which extra cash was called into service was by the low price of the funds which resulted when bankers and others were forced to sell out.[1] But in comparison with the effects of the much larger movements in the discount rate, this was probably of subsidiary importance.

Much the same may be said of the influence of movements in the long-term rate of interest on the cost of finance for industrial borrowers. This influence was indirect and of limited extent. The main sources of loan capital to industry were by the discount of bills and by advances from banks. The rate of interest charged on advances was determined partly with reference to the London discount rate, and partly by convention—not by the yield on consols.[2] The state of the bond market did, it is true, affect the willingness of investors to buy foreign stocks and the issues of domestic joint-stock companies, and the rising prices of the funds around 1833 no doubt contributed to the recovery for this reason. But then, as later in the period, such movements as occurred in the yield on government stock are probably best regarded as no more than symptoms of the general state of credit; they did not in themselves exert any great effect on the supply of finance to industry.

The relation between the fluctuations in the discount rate and the yield on consols presents certain points of note which may here be briefly considered in parentheses. The relation between the two was fairly close, and it seems not improbable that bankers gave more attention to the relative advantages of holding their second-line reserves in bills as against bonds than they did in weighing up the relative advantages of bonds and cash.[3] The relationship was not, however, invariable, nor did it exactly take the form of the two rates of interest regularly moving in the same direction.

From the crisis of 1825 until 1830, both the (short-term) rate and the (long-term) yield were on the whole falling, and the rate was below the yield. In 1831, certain forces combined to cause an efflux of bullion, and the rate rose. The yield also rose and, rather surprisingly, its rise was of such an extent that it remained above the rate. In 1832 both fell, but the yield remained above the rate, and not till 1833 did it fall back to its 1830 level. The reasons for the sharpness in the rise of the yield in 1831 and its fairly slow fall in the two following years can only be guessed. A very large conversion operation was carried out in 1830, and it is possible that this had a disruptive effect on markets.[4] Probably more important was the effect of the political uncertainties arising out of the Reform Bill controversy in increasing liquidity preference in 1831–2.

In the next few years more normal relations between the yield and the rate returned. It is interesting to note that although the yield rose in sympathy with the rate at the end of 1836, the rise in the yield was of shorter duration, and there

---

[1] Gilbart, *Practical Treatise*, p. 88.
[2] Cf. *1841*, QQ. 127 (H. W. Hobhouse); 1639–42 (I. C. Wright); 2119 (P. W. Kennedy); Appendix, p. 306. Rae, *The Country Banker*, p. 136; Gregory, *Westminster Bank*, I, pp. 28–30. See also p. 183 above.
[3] Gilbart, *Practical Treatise*, pp. 68–75.
[4] For details of the conversion, see J. R. McCulloch, *Taxation and the Funding System* (1852), p. 461; S. Buxton, *Finance and Politics* (1888), I, p. 127; E. L. Hargreaves, *The National Debt* (1930), p. 161.

was already a substantial falling back in the first quarter of 1837, the quarter in which the rate reached its peak. This may perhaps be interpreted as the result of bankers deciding that no real panic was in prospect, and that it was not worth while selling out government securities if a capital loss was thereby involved.[1]

The relative movements of yield and rate in the years 1839–41 are also worthy of note. During these three years the rate was high but tending to fall, whereas the yield was tending to rise. This may be held to give support to a theory of the relationship between yield and rate advanced with considerable plausibility by T. T. Williams in 1912 but subsequently somewhat neglected.[2] Williams held that a rise in the yield was to be expected whenever the rate *exceeded* the yield (irrespective of whether the rate itself was rising or falling), and similarly that the yield tended to fall whenever it exceeded the rate (as in 1833). The logical basis of the idea is that the rate is the independent variable, determined principally by factors other than the behaviour of the yield, and that owners of capital tend to move from bills to bonds and vice versa according to which of the two is currently giving the higher return. As far as our period is concerned, this hypothesis, while not entirely satisfactory, certainly seems to fit the facts better than the hypothesis that rises or falls in the rate tended to be associated with rises or falls respectively in the yield.[3]

7. The Responsiveness of the Supply of Credit to Fluctuations in the Level of Activity

It was shown earlier in this chapter that movements in the market rate of discount in our period can to a very large extent be explained with reference to movements in the Bank of England's bullion reserve; and attention was drawn (pp. 175–6) to the paradox that changes in the general state of trade, which might have been expected to carry with them corresponding changes in the amount of money balances required for transaction purposes, appear to have had no regular effect on the rate of discount, except in so far as they were associated with fluctuations in the foreign exchanges and in the Bank's reserve. In fact, there was a rough inverse correlation between the state of trade and the level of the Bank's reserve, so that the chart of the market rate of discount does bear a certain resemblance to the course of general business fluctuations. But

[1] Compare Stuckey's statement (*1832*, Q. 1014) that when his bank found it necessary to reduce its liabilities, 'we generally resort *in the first instance* to the sale of government securities' (italics added).

[2] T. T. Williams, 'The rate of discount and the price of consols', *Statistical Journal* (1912), LXXV, pp. 380–400, 653–8. Williams's view was discussed and in large measure accepted by F. Lavington, 'Short and long rates of interest', *Economica* (1924), pp. 291–303.

[3] The two years between the third quarter of 1834 and the second quarter of 1836 are the part of our period in which the relative movements of yield and rate are most difficult to reconcile with the Williams rule. During this time the rate regularly exceeded the yield by between $\frac{1}{4}$ and $\frac{1}{2}\%$, but the yield showed no tendency to rise. If it were legitimate to modify the Williams hypothesis to allow a certain *normal* excess of rate over yield, this would be explained; but what economists have usually supposed is the opposite, that on the average the yield exceeds the rate by a certain margin in order to compensate for the greater risk of holding bonds. One may, however, call attention to the fact that, for whatever reason, the rate did exceed the yield for much of the middle part of the nineteenth century. For the statistics, see Williams, *loc. cit.*, and, for the earlier years, the sources cited below (p. 201). Cf. also J. R. Hicks, 'Mr Hawtrey on Bank Rate and the long term rate of interest', *Manchester School* (1939), pp. 28–9.

the state of trade does not appear to have exerted any independent influence on the discount rate; it is found that for any given level of the Bank's reserve the discount rate tended to be much the same, irrespective of whether trade was prosperous or depressed. It follows that the idle money and money substitutes brought into circulation as a result of rises in interest rates, by the means described in the two preceding sections of this chapter, served merely to fill the gap created by the efflux of bullion, and did not as such serve to provide the extra cash required in consequence of more active trade. Fluctuations in the state of trade seem in general to have brought about the requisite changes in the money supply without any change in the discount rate being involved. We must now proceed to consider the means by which this result was achieved.

In speaking as we did above (p. 184) of the variability of banks' reserve ratios, it is not to be supposed that this variability was a function of interest rates—or at least of quoted interest rates—alone. In times of prosperity banks would receive more numerous requests of a credit-worthy or supposedly credit-worthy nature for advances. Since advances on non-negotiable security commonly carried a high and relatively rigid interest rate, this implied that the banks were put in a position to earn a higher return on their resources, even though neither the discount rate nor the rate on advances had been altered. An improvement in the state of trade was for this reason likely to induce bankers to expand their lending just as a rise in the quoted rate of interest might do, even if no such rise took place.

In a similar way business men who in times when trade was slack could not find use for all their resources in their own concerns, and did not wish to suffer the illiquidity and risk involved in the purchase of bonds, would leave their money on deposit account at their banker's, earning a low interest rate, and transfer it to current account when trade became more active and the working capital required in their businesses increased. Such a transfer from deposit account to current account might, if it proceeded beyond a certain point, tend to induce the banker to keep a higher ratio of reserves against deposits, but it would not necessarily do so if the banker's reserve was ample in the first place.

The working of the 'confidence' factor tended to produce the same result. By this is meant not merely that in good times bankers were wont to share to an irrational degree the optimism of their business customers, although this was no doubt the case.[1] In good times the public would be willing to receive bank money in payment; but when trade was bad, and failures were taking place amongst banks as well as amongst other firms, all but the most solid banks would come under suspicion. The public would become more insistent on payment in cash; bankers' liabilities would fall, and a higher ratio of cash would have to be held in reserve against those that remained. 'Failures affecting localities have the same effect on private and joint-stock banks as adverse exchanges. . . on the Bank of England', wrote the *Circular to Bankers* in its issue of 26 November 1841, when the depression was moving towards its trough. The publicity given by the Parliamentary inquiries into the banking system was alleged by bank spokesmen to have enhanced the volatility of the public confidence.

[1] Cf. Lord Overstone, *Tracts* (1857), pp. 31–3.

Considerations of this type go some way towards explaining the paradox that movements in the state of trade do not as such appear to have had any regular effect on interest rates. In good times the demand for money would be stronger, but banks would be in a better position and more willing to meet it, even if rates of interest did not alter.

The tendency for the supply of bank credit to be responsive to the state of trade for these reasons probably applied fairly generally in trade-cycle history until banks' reserve ratios became more standardised, and fear of bank failures relatively a thing of the past. But in the 1830's there was a special factor tending to enlarge the supply of credit during the years when trade was expanding, which greatly strengthened the tendency referred to. This was the growth of joint-stock banks, to which we now turn.

8. A SPECIAL CASE OF RESPONSIVENESS: JOINT-STOCK BANK FORMATION

The timing and development of joint-stock bank formation in the 1830's was in many respects similar to that of the railway boom in the same period, and consideration of it raises some similar questions to those discussed in Chapter VIII. As may be seen from Table 30, there was steady but unspectacular development of joint-stock banks from 1829 to 1835, and then a sudden leap forward in 1836. This was followed immediately by a tailing away, although the stream of new bank formations did not quite dwindle to nothing till 1844.[1] A similar pattern is to be found in the figures of the number of private banks absorbed by amalgamation with joint-stock banks, save that in this instance the figures remain fairly high in the early 1840's—presumably as the result of the absorption of banks whose position was being embarrassed by the depression.

The prominence of bank formation in the boom of the 1830's was largely the result of the recent legislation which for the first time rendered joint-stock banks legal. The many failures of private banks after the crisis of 1825 brought general acceptance to the idea that the English banking system would be strengthened by following the Scottish example and abandoning the existing prohibition of banking firms with more than six partners. Accordingly, the Banking Copartnerships Act of 1826 (7 Geo. IV, c. 46) permitted the formation of banking firms with any number of partners with unlimited liability outside a radius of 65 miles from London. A certain number of joint-stock banks were set up in the next few years, but, the pace of expansion did not become really fast until the 1830's. The speeding up after 1833 has commonly been explained as the result of the clauses affecting joint-stock banks in the Bank Charter Act of 1833 (3 & 4 Will. IV, c. 98). This Act contained a clause (the 'Declaratory Clause') stating that nothing in existing legislation was to be held to prohibit the formation of banks of more than six partners in London so long as they did not issue notes. The passage of the Act of 1833 was immediately followed by the formation of the London and Westminster, whose sponsors had in fact been largely instru-

[1] The pattern of events in Scotland, where joint-stock banks were no novelty, was rather different; there the period of most active formation of new banks was 1838–40, especially 1838 (A. W. Kerr, *History of Banking in Scotland* (1884), pp. 164–7; C. W. Boase, *A Century of Banking in Dundee* (1867), pp. 402–13).

mental in securing the insertion of the Declaratory Clause.[1] Other London joint-stock banks soon followed.

As in the case of railways, the number of joint-stock banking companies formed in the 'mania' of 1836 equalled or surpassed the number of those established in all the preceding years. Also, as with railways, the proportion of bubble companies was inevitably higher among the flotations of the mania period than among the flotations of the earlier years.

Table 30. *Joint-stock bank formations and amalgamations*

Year	(1) No. of joint-stock banks established in England and Wales	(2) No. of private banks absorbed by amalgamation with joint-stock banks*
1826	3	3
1827	3	—
1828	—	1
1829	7	3
1830	1	—
1831	7	1
1832	7	2
1833	10	2
1834	11	6
1835	9	5
1836	59	26
1837	5	3
1838	1	1
1839	6	2
1840	6	5
1841	2	3
1842	2	6
1843	2	7

* Excluding 17 amalgamations taking place between 1826 and 1843 of which the precise date is not known.

Sources: (1) S. E. Thomas, *The Rise and Growth of Joint Stock Banking* (1934), Appendix M; (2) J. Sykes, *Amalgamation Movement in English Banking* (1926), p. 4. Particulars given by different authorities of the number of banks formed in each year are not perfectly consistent.

There is no particular difficulty in explaining why joint-stock banks should have been among the main objects of the mania of 1835–6, especially since the fall in discount rates in the first half of 1836 had particular importance for banking institutions. Joint-stock banks were an innovation, and those already in operation had paid good dividends. Their success was not to any great extent the result of the advantages of large-scale and regional balance which ultimately were to give them their supremacy over private banks, since these advantages were as yet relatively little utilised; rather it was due simply to their greater enterprise and readiness to experiment. Moreover, the joint-stock principle greatly facilitated entry to the banking business, making it possible for newcomers to challenge the position of established banks to an extent that would otherwise have been impossible.

[1] Gregory, *Westminster Bank*, Chapters II and III; Clapham, *Bank of England*, II, pp. 128–30. The fullest account of the details of early legislation affecting joint stock banks is in S. E. Thomas, *op. cit.*

193

The sudden expansion of 1835–6 is therefore not difficult to understand. It is perhaps rather more debatable just why the rate of expansion speeded up earlier in the 1830's. The legislation of 1833 was of crucial importance to the London joint-stock banks, but its effect on country joint-stock banks was limited to the removal of certain minor disabilities relating to the drawing of bills, which had in any case been largely a dead letter;[1] and it was in the country, especially in Lancashire, that joint-stock bank formation thereafter became most active. To some extent, it is true, the number of banks established in a given year imperfectly indicates the amount of activity currently in hand in bank promotion, since there were sometimes substantial delays between the original planning of a new bank and its first opening for business. The National Provincial, for example, did not open till 1833, though the first meeting of its founders had taken place in 1830.[2] But this was rather exceptional, and in most cases the delay was not more than a year—much shorter, for obvious reasons, than the delays involved in railway flotation. There is no doubt, therefore, that there was a great quickening of public interest in joint-stock bank formation around 1833. How much of this was due to the publicity given to banking questions by the inquiry of 1832 and the legislation of 1833, and how much to a general improvement in the state of trade and confidence throughout the country must be a matter of conjecture.

The means by which the establishment of new joint-stock banks led to an increase in the total supply of credit were, in the main, twofold: in the first place, they attracted deposits from people who had formerly kept no bank account; and in the second place, even where the deposits attracted by the new banks were not new deposits but had formerly been lodged with a private banker, the effect was still expansionist, for the new banks in general utilised their resources more fully and kept lower cash ratios than the old ones.

The joint-stock banks attracted deposits from people who had formerly had no banker by canvassing for custom—a purpose for which the numerous proprietary of a joint-stock bank gave it a powerful advantage—in a manner which private bankers would have thought undignified, and in particular by catering for the needs of the small depositor. Successful and old-established private bankers, both in London and in the provinces, were generally reluctant to accept small unsteady accounts. By the late 1820's Jones Loyds, for example, were refusing to accept any new accounts 'except of the highest class'. The joint-stock banks, in contrast, welcomed small accounts and paid interest on them.[3]

By catering for small accounts the joint-stock banks managed to obtain a good deal of business without encroaching on the preserves of private bankers. But naturally this did not make up the whole of their custom, and at least in the provinces most of the joint-stock banks' deposits probably belonged at first to former customers of private banks.[4] Those who had bought shares in a new joint-stock bank naturally transferred their deposits to it unless their tie with

---

[1] *1832*, QQ. 951–52 (V. Stuckey); 4126–27 (J. C. Dyer); 5280 (H. Burgess).
[2] H. Withers, *National Provincial Bank 1833 to 1933* (1933), pp. 31–2.
[3] Grindon, *Manchester Banks*, pp. 36–7; Gilbart, *Practical Treatise*, pp. 664–5; Gregory, *Westminster Bank*, I, pp. 110–12.
[4] *1841*, QQ. 777 (P. M. James); 1942, 2131 (General Austin). Contrast the statement of Alderman Salomons quoted in Gregory, II, pp. 198–9.

their old bank was very strong. Shareholders were apparently an important source of business, and the evidence before the Select Committees of 1836–8 is full of allusions to the anxiety of joint-stock banks to secure a *numerous* body of proprietors. Many joint-stock banks when they first set up followed the policy of securing business and good-will ready made by absorbing an existing private bank by amalgamation. A few of the new banks, especially the National Provincial, deliberately set out to absorb a large number of private banks in order to secure the advantages of widely spread branches and avoid dependence on local business.[1] In this way the number of private banks in existence fell by over a hundred in the ten years following 1833,[2] and many accounts were transferred direct from private to joint-stock banks. In addition, many deposits were drawn away from private banks simply by competition. This competition apparently most often took the form not so much of offering higher interest on deposits—though this was sometimes done—as of offering to depositors extremely generous terms on which they might overdraw their accounts or have their bills discounted.[3] Competition of this sort, though effective, was naturally risky, and some private bankers were of the opinion that the joint-stock banks actually did them a service by taking away their worst accounts.[4] On the other hand, joint-stock bank representatives argued that it was perfectly legitimate for them to take greater risks than private bankers were willing to do, since their capital resources were greater.[5]

It was natural that the joint-stock banks should be more anxious than private bankers to use their resources to the full and to avoid keeping a higher reserve than was absolutely necessary. They had had to struggle to secure a footing, and the biggest and most profitable accounts—those of large landowners—mostly remained in the hands of private banks. There is little doubt that by the 1830's many of the more successful private bankers had ceased to exert themselves very energetically to maximise their profits. Both country bankers and those London bankers whose happy life was portrayed by Bagehot in a celebrated passage in *Lombard Street* were commonly men of very substantial private means; indeed, their credit as bankers to some extent depended on this being known to be the case. Such men would not be likely to strain after every penny of profit at the cost of having to scrutinise the credentials of some questionable borrower or of having to organise the establishment of a new branch in a small but growing industrial centre. 'Were the profit of a private banker, in proportion to the amount of capital employed,' said Gilbart, 'to be reduced to the average rate of profit of joint-stock banks, he would soon think of retiring from business.'[6] The private banker had a position to lose; the joint-stock banks had a position to make.

Note-issue was not prominent among the means employed by joint-stock bankers to enlarge their business. Joint-stock banks normally took over the

---

[1] *1836*, Q. 2510 (S. Gurney); Gilbart, *Practical Treatise*, pp. 174–5; Sykes, pp. 9–13.
[2] *Accounts and Papers*, 1843, LII, p. 9.
[3] The payment of interest on deposit account by the London and Westminster and other London joint stock banks was a departure from the former practice of London banks, but private banks in the country had always allowed interest. Cf. Gregory, I, pp. 28–30, 110–15 and *1836*, Q. 2263 (J. Harding). The importance of competition by bidding up deposit rates appears to be somewhat exaggerated by King (*History of London Discount Market*, pp. 39–40).
[4] *1836*, Q. 2298 (S. Martin).   [5] *1836*, QQ. 764–5 (P. M. James).
[6] *History and Principles*, p. 9.

circulation of private banks when they amalgamated with them, and in consequence of this aggregate joint-stock bank circulation rose steadily up till 1836.[1] But instances of joint-stock banks pursuing a deliberate policy of pushing their circulation as a prime source of capital were relatively rare. The most active centre of joint-stock bank formation, especially in the year 1836, was in Lancashire, and there local notes were never viewed with favour. The Bank of Manchester, for example, one of the earliest of the joint-stock banks (established 1829), for a while issued notes, but its circulation was not found to be generally acceptable and was abandoned in 1841.[2] There were exceptions: the Northern and Central, one of the banks assisted by the Bank of England in 1837, issued notes in plenty and endeavoured to keep them in circulation by establishing branches over a wide area.[3] But note-issue was not the main part of the business of the representative joint-stock bank.

The most commented-on practice of joint-stock banks, and that in respect of which they differed most markedly from the private banks, was their extensive rediscounting of bills discounted for customers. Private banks had occasionally resorted to rediscount, but it was not a normal part of their business. The newly established joint-stock banks in industrial districts regularly rediscounted and so were enabled to take up from customers far more bills than their own resources would have permitted. Many of them kept very low cash reserves and relied on further rediscount to supply them with extra cash should they require it. The endorsement of a joint-stock bank, with its many shareholders and unlimited liability, rendered bills acceptable in the London market even if the parties on whom they were drawn were quite unknown to the bill dealers.

The practice of rediscounting was not in itself objectionable, and was indeed the natural consequence of localised banking and of the contrast between the capital needs of rural and industrial districts. The strictures passed on rediscounting as such by bankers who happened themselves to be in a position to dispense with it can only be considered rather foolish. But the system was obviously liable to abuse. Many joint-stock banks assumed contingent liability on rediscounted bills vastly out of proportion to their own resources, and were rendered helpless at times when rediscount became difficult or impossible. It was this that was the immediate cause of the failure of the Northern and Central, for the refusal of the Bank of England in 1836 to discount bills bearing the endorsement of any joint-stock bank *of issue* made such bills unpopular in the London market unless their soundness was unquestionable. Another common and dangerous practice was the use of bills to finance the creation of fixed capital, these bills being periodically renewed and rediscounted in London. In Lancashire and the north-east this was apparently very often done.[4]

Rediscounting did not as such increase the supply of bank money—save in so far as it led banks to keep lower reserves—since, of course, rediscounted bills were not financed by the banks that rediscounted them. It was often said that

[1] Cf. *1841*, Q. 936 (J. W. Gilbart).
[2] Grindon, p. 242.
[3] The affairs of the Northern and Central were exhaustively investigated by the Committee on Joint Stock Banks of 1836–8. See evidence of W. G. Cassels, T. Evans, J. R. Lyle, H. Moult and T. Broadbent, *passim*; also Grindon, pp. 265–71, and Thomas, *Rise of Joint Stock Banking* pp. 281–94.
[4] Gilbart, *Practical Treatise*, pp. 34–5, 175–6.

rediscount was the most important means by which joint-stock banks increased the supply of credit,[1] but no increase would have been forthcoming had banks in London and rural areas not been willing to take up the bills; had they not been willing, it is doubtful whether the joint-stock bank boom would have proceeded nearly as far as it did.[2] The part played by the rediscounting joint-stock banks was to enable loans to be made to local manufacturers and traders on security that was acceptable in other parts of the country. It is true that the boom in joint-stock bank formation was not confined to borrowing counties; large numbers of new banks were also set up in agricultural districts, and these provided new channels through which rural funds could be brought to industrial districts.[3] But it was in the borrowing counties that the bulk of the new banks were set up. It therefore requires to be explained how it was that sufficient extra *funds* were forthcoming to render rediscount practicable on so large a scale in 1835–6.

Contemporary observers supposed the reason to lie in the relative ease of credit generally, particularly the fall in the discount rate in the earlier part of 1836.[4] This in turn they attributed to the improvidence of the Bank of England; but we have seen earlier in this chapter that the Bank's policy at this time, though perhaps erring a little on the side of tardiness, was not essentially different from that which it followed during the rest of the period, and that the fall in the discount rate is to be viewed rather as the natural result of the influx of bullion that followed the improvement of the foreign exchanges in May 1835. Leaving this question aside, however, what effect did the fall in discount rates have upon the facility of rediscounting, and hence upon the growth of joint-stock banks that relied on rediscounting? The answer is apparently that the effect, though not inconsiderable, was largely psychological. It was not simply a case of the increased supply of bills coming into the market being discounted by the extra funds available as the result of the bullion influx, for had that been so the influx in question would have been accompanied by less fall in the discount rate than took place on occasions when there was a similar influx but no comparable increase in the supply of bills—and the figures do not support this, at least not to more than a slight degree. The explanation is perhaps rather to be found in the general willingness of commercial banks to increase their lending in good times, especially on so liquid a security as bills of exchange, so long as they did not fear that the boom had gone so far as to threaten a crisis. Now the absence of any tendency to credit stringency in 1835, followed by the actual fall in the discount rate in 1836, both helped foster the 'mania' in business at large and hence the general level of prosperity and confidence amongst bankers and their customers, and also, more important, provided bankers with the assurance they needed that a crisis was not impending. Hence it was that bankers in lending districts were willing to increase their holdings of bills and enable the joint-stock banks to finance their activities by rediscounting to an unparalleled extent. The importance of the institution of rediscounting in facilitating this elasticity of credit supply in

[1] Thus *1836*, QQ. 2426–40 (S. Martin); *1840*, Q. 546 (R. Cobden).
[2] Cf. *1836*, QQ. 836–44 (H. Moult).
[3] Compare the list of joint-stock banks in Thomas, Appendix M, and *1836*, evidence of R. Gilbart, T. Nimmo, J. Harding and S. Martin.
[4] Cf. *1841*, QQ. 1032–34 (J. W. Gilbart).

response to the increase in business activity was that banks possessing a surplus of funds over local needs would not have been willing to expand their lending to the same extent as they did had they not been able to do so by means of taking up liquid and supposedly credit-worthy bills bearing the endorsement of the joint-stock banks that had rediscounted them.

The joint-stock banks played a large part in the finance of the boom, particularly in Lancashire, and provided industry with fixed and working capital alike. Insufficiently secured loans to manufacturers, especially for the creation of fixed capital, were the most common of the many unsound banking practices which accompanied the early development of joint-stock banks. It was estimated that nine-tenths of the losses of banking capital in Manchester between 1833 and 1842 arose from this cause.[1] Even the London and Westminster, whose lending policy was for the most part very conservative, made extensive loans to railway companies, which it had cause to regret.[2] That the rapid proliferation of new banks should have been accompanied by much bad banking was inevitable; inevitable too, perhaps, was that more publicity should be given to the banks that failed than to those that were conducted on sound principles from the start. Trafficking in shares, excessive loans to shareholders and bank directors, and outright fraud figure largely in the annals. The early joint-stock banks had considerable difficulty in obtaining the services of officers who were both competent and honest, and their directors were often inexperienced and exercised too little supervision over the business. The importance of the difficulty of obtaining qualified bank officers was no doubt the reason why the Committees of 1836-8 devoted what at first sight appears to be so disproportionate an amount of their attention to the means of control exercised by banks over branches remote from the head office.[3]

To sum up: there can be no doubt that the growth of joint-stock banking was of prime importance in providing funds to finance the expansion of trade in the years up to 1836, and in particular in the year 1836 itself. The recovery of trade in 1838-40 was not accompanied by any great further development of the banking system, but despite the shocks sustained in 1837 most of the banks formed in the earlier years were still then in existence, and doubtless many of those inaugurated in 1836 took a few years before coming into full operation. When trade began to deteriorate again after 1840, bank failures became more numerous and surviving banks had to practise retrenchment in order to safeguard their positions, with the result that, despite the fall in the money value of transactions, discount rates were not particularly low in relation to the level of the Bank of England's reserve.

The part played by the joint-stock banks was more than just the passive one of providing industry with the extra funds called for by an expansion in trade which had origins outside the monetary sphere. There is plenty of evidence that the joint-stock banks actually intensified the boom by relaxing security requirements and pressing loans on their customers in an attempt to increase their business. In this way the supply of credit, so far from imposing a brake on the growth of

[1] Grindon, p. 280.
[2] Gregory, *Westminster Bank*, I, pp. 266–7.
[3] The managerial difficulties encountered by the early joint-stock banks are well described by Gilbart, *Practical Treatise*, pp. 174–91, and Thomas, pp. 294–6.

activity, actually acted as a destabiliser.[1] The formation of joint-stock banks served to transmit the boom to regions of the country which had previously been unaffected by it, and to intensify the boom in regions where it was already under way. Likewise, when recession came and banks were compelled to restrict their

Table 31. *Bank of England liabilities and assets (in £ million)*

Year	Circulation	Deposits	Securities	Bullion
1833: I	19·3	12·8	24·3	10·1
II	19·3	12·1	22·8	10·7
III	19·8	13·1	24·2	10·9
IV	18·2	13·1	23·6	9·9
1834: I	19·1	14·0	26·0	9·4
II	18·9	15·1	27·6	8·7
III	19·1	14·8	28·7	7·7
IV	18·0	12·6	26·4	6·7
1835: I	18·6	11·3	26·3	6·3
II	18·3	11·0	25·7	6·2
III	18·2	13·2	27·9	6·3
IV	17·3	19·2	32·0	7·1
1836: I	18·1	14·8	27·9	7·8
II	17·9	13·8	27·1	7·4
III	18·1	14·1	29·4	5·7
IV	17·4	14·4	30·4	4·3
1837: I	18·4	11·2	28·8	4·1
II	18·2	10·4	26·9	4·7
III	18·9	11·1	26·6	6·3
IV	17·9	11·0	22·6	8·9
1838: I	19·0	11·3	22·8	10·1
II	19·0	10·4	22·4	9·7
III	19·7	10·0	22·8	9·6
IV	18·2	10·3	21·7	9·3
1839: I	18·4	9·0	23·0	7·1
II	18·1	7·6	23·9	4·3
III	18·0	7·8	25·9	2·8
IV	16·3	7·1	22·9	3·5
1840: I	16·8	7·7	23·5	4·3
II	16·9	7·1	22·4	4·4
III	17·2	7·4	23·4	4·3
IV	16·1	6·8	22·3	3·5
1841: I	16·5	7·1	22·3	4·3
II	16·6	6·8	21·5	5·1
III	17·6	8·0	23·8	4·8
IV	16·7	7·7	22·6	4·6
1842: I	16·9	8·6	22·5	6·1
II	17·8	8·1	21·3	7·4
III	19·9	9·0	23·1	9·4
IV	18·8	9·0	20·5	10·3

Source: official returns.

The discount rate did not, it is true, actually fall during the upswing of the cycle, except on occasions when the state of the foreign exchanges provided an explanation. But the quoted discount rate is the London rate on bills of the first quality, and this is not to be taken as necessarily representative of the terms on which accommodation was available throughout the country. The importance of the joint-stock banks lay largely in the loans they made to borrowers in the provinces on inferior security.

operations or to close down altogether, manufacturers who during the boom had relied on bank finance were liable to find themselves in difficulties even if their own businesses had not been affected by any great reduction in consumers' demand.[1]

9. CONCLUSIONS

We may now attempt to summarise and set in perspective the argument that has been developed in the course of this chapter.

The main determinant of the market rate of discount was the state of the foreign exchanges. The behaviour of the Bank of England, with one or two exceptions, was not such as to prevent fluctuations in its bullion reserve from bringing about their due effect on the supply of credit. When gold flowed out, the supply of funds in the London money market fell and discount rates rose. When this occurred, banks and individuals were induced by the extra opportunity of profit to reduce their holdings of idle cash, and increased resort was had to bills of exchange as means for the settlement of transactions. On account of this elasticity in the supply of credit, an adverse turn of the exchanges was not normally likely to occasion undue inconvenience to traders, and probably to most borrowers the cost of accommodation did not rise in proportion to the rise in the quoted rate of discount.

This does not mean that movements in the foreign exchanges and the fluctuations in the discount rate to which they gave rise were of no importance in the cyclical process. The effect of the level of interest rates on the more speculative types of business was probably substantial. The 'mania' of 1836 apparently owed more than a little to the reduction that took place in discount rates in the early months of the year, when business was already moving towards a peak.

Fluctuations in the volume of business activity and in the level of prices do not appear to have affected interest rates except in so far as they led to movements in the foreign exchanges. Fluctuations in the demand for cash for transactions purposes as such had little effect on the cost of accommodation. It is suggested that the reason for this was that the supply of credit tended for a variety of reasons to vary with the state of trade, independently of any changes that might take place in interest rates. In prosperous times banks were more willing to lend and businesses to make use of idle balances, the public was more willing to accept bank money, and, perhaps most important of all in the 1830's, new banks were formed which were anxious to undertake as much lending as possible. In the depression the flow of new banks ceased, failures and closures of existing banks were widespread, and confidence suffered a general weakening.[2]

---

[1] For an instance of this in 1837, see *Statistical Journal* (1838), I, p. 107 (on the Welsh flannel trade).

[2] It is interesting in this connection to compare the discovery of Lord Beveridge ('The trade cycle in Britain before 1850', *Oxford Economic Papers* (1940), pp. 92–4) that in the first half of the nineteenth century the 'Gibson paradox' (rising commodity prices being associated with falling bond prices) did not hold, and that the truth was in fact more nearly the reverse. This may be explained along the lines suggested in the last paragraph above. In later periods the confidence factor became less important, bank reserve ratios became more stable, and the banking system ceased to grow at the same rate; it is therefore not surprising to find that fluctuations in the level of activity then came to be most commonly accompanied by fluctuations in interest rates in the same direction, in a manner not to be observed earlier in the century.

Table 32. *Circulation of notes and of bills, market rate of discount and yield on consols*

Year	Note circulation in England and Wales (£m.)			Value of bills of exchange created in England and Wales (£m.)	Average market rate of discount of bills (%)	Yield on consols (%)
	Private banks	Joint-stock banks	Total			
1833: I	—	—	—	50·8	2·5	3·43
II	—	—	—	48·3	2·9	3·38
III	—	—	—	51·6	2·7	3·39
IV	8·8	1·3	10·2	68·1	3·3	3·41
1834: I	8·7	1·5	10·2	53·3	3·1	3·35
II	8·9	1·6	10·5	50·9	3·1	3·27
III	8·4	1·8	10·2	55·6	3·5	3·31
IV	8·5	2·1	10·7	51·8	3·8	3·30
1835: I	8·2	2·2	10·4	56·7	3·5	3·28
II	8·5	2·5	10·9	57·2	3·8	3·27
III	7·9	2·5	10·4	58·3	3·8	3·32
IV	8·3	2·8	11·1	57·4	3·8	3·29
1836: I	8·4	3·1	11·4	64·0	3·6	3·29
II	8·6	3·6	12·2	64·8	3·5	3·27
III	7·8	4·0	11·7	78·1	4·5	3·31
IV	7·8	4·3	12·0	73·4	5·3	3·34
1837: I	7·3	3·8	11·0	74·5	5·5	3·33
II	7·2	3·7	10·9	63·0	4·8	3·30
III	6·7	3·4	10·1	63·1	3·8	3·28
IV	7·0	3·8	10·9	58·1	3·4	3·22
1838: I	7·0	3·9	10·9	63·5	3·2	3·26
II	7·4	4·4	11·7	62·9	2·7	3·18
III	7·1	4·3	11·4	71·8	2·9	3·19
IV	7·6	4·6	12·2	68·2	3·2	3·19
1839: I	7·6	4·6	12·3	72·9	3·8	3·23
II	7·6	4·7	12·3	74·0	4·3	3·21
III	6·9	4·2	11·1	82·0	6·0	3·28
IV	7·3	4·2	11·4	74·7	6·5	3·31
1840: I	6·9	3·9	10·8	76·8	5·2	3·30
II	7·0	4·1	11·1	73·6	4·4	3·26
III	6·4	3·6	10·0	79·3	4·6	3·33
IV	6·6	3·8	10·4	70·7	5·6	3·37
1841: I	6·3	3·6	10·0	75·5	5·2	3·37
II	6·4	3·8	10·3	70·4	4·8	3·33
III	5·8	3·3	9·1	76·4	4·6	3·35
IV	6·1	3·4	9·5	64·1	5·2	3·38
1842: I	5·3	3·0	8·3	67·9	4·3	3·36
II	5·3	3·0	8·3	63·8	3·5	3·25
III	5·1	2·8	7·9	62·5	3·1	3·26
IV	5·3	3·1	8·4	55·2	2·6	3·19

— Not available.

Sources: Note circulation, official returns. Bill circulation, Tooke and Newmarch, *History of Prices*, VI, pp. 584–92, corrected (following N. J. Silberling, 'British prices and business cycles, 1779–1850', *Review of Economic Statistics* (1923), p. 258) for apparent error in the figure for 1841, II, where Newmarch gives 60·4. (This correction receives support from the stamp duty figures in *Accounts and Papers*, 1854, XXXIX, p. 290. Silberling also gives a different figure from Newmarch for 1833, IV, without comment or explanation; but although Newmarch's figure is certainly surprisingly high, it is not inconsistent with the stamp-duty figures (*ibid.* p. 288), and there seems insufficient reason for rejecting it.) Market rate of discount, Silberling, *loc. cit.* p. 257, derived from monthly figures in *Select Committee on the Bank Acts*, 1857 (2nd session), X, Part I, pp. 463–4. Yield on consols, from unpublished statistical material ancillary to A. D. Gayer, W. W. Rostow and A. J. Schwartz, *The Growth and Fluctuation of the British Economy, 1790–1850* (quoted by courtesy of the authors).

CHAPTER XII

THE PATTERN OF THE CYCLE

IT remains now to attempt a synthetic review of the period as a whole. We shall first go through the several phases of the cycle chronologically in order to analyse the nature and causes of the movements taking place during them, and we shall then pass on to some brief conclusions on the character of the cyclical process generally in the period. Conclusions arrived at in earlier chapters on causes influencing the course of fluctuations in particular sectors of the economy will not be recapitulated in detail.

1. THE RECOVERY, 1833–1834

The first phase to be analysed is the recovery which, following previous chroniclers, we have taken to begin in 1833.

Before asking what caused the recovery, we must first ask what the recovery was a recovery of. The need for caution on this point was made apparent in Chapter IX, where it was shown that in the cotton industry there was no question of a recovery in output in 1833, or indeed in any year between then and 1836, since output had been rising steadily ever since 1827 and did not grow any faster after 1833 than it had done before. The recovery in the cotton industry (which, such as it was, is to be dated from 1834 rather than 1833) was primarily a recovery in prices, profits and, above all, investment. Whether cotton was in this respect typical we lack the evidence to tell with any certainty. There is, however, no doubt that the volume of investment of almost all sorts turned upwards around 1833. This is borne out by the behaviour of the brick index, by the tonnage of new ships built, and by the evidence relating to railway building; it is borne out also by what we know of wool and a number of other manufacturing industries. It is clear, too, that by 1834 the level of profits generally throughout industry was felt to be more adequate than it had been for some years, and most prices were rising. That there was a general recovery around this date in investment, in prices and profits may thus be taken as certain.

Whether the cotton industry was exceptional amongst consumer goods' industries in lacking a similar increase in rate of growth of output is difficult to ascertain. On *a priori* grounds one would not necessarily expect that the behaviour of the cotton industry should be representative of that of consumer goods' industries generally, since the peculiar conditions that brought about the rise in output of cotton goods between 1827 and 1833 were unlikely to be paralleled in less capitalistic and less progressive industries. But none the less cotton may be rather less of an isolated instance than one might be disposed to imagine. To take one measure: the Official value (i.e. quantity) of exports, even when exports of cotton goods are deducted, increased its rate of growth very little in the years normally regarded as those of recovery.[1] Another measure, in

[1] Percentage rate of growth per annum of Official value of exports, excluding cotton goods, was 4·3 between 1825 and 1831, 5·1 from 1831 to 1836.

itself not decisive, of course, but still suggestive is the amount of coal shipped from the Vend area: this shows no increase in rate of growth in 1833 and 1834, though an increase is in evidence in 1835 and the following years.[1] Some similar results are to be gleaned from figures relating to the consumption of imports: consumption of sugar actually rose more rapidly in the latter half of the 1820's than it did in the earlier half of the 1830's. Though indecisive in themselves, such facts as these suggest some reason to doubt whether either consumption or production of consumer goods in real terms rose to any unusual extent in 1833 or 1834, though there is more evidence of a rise in 1835 and 1836.

The main variables, the recovery of which around 1833 we have to explain, are thus prices, profits and investment; with them presumably rose also the money value of the national income.

The delay that elapsed between 1825 and the return of what was considered to be a satisfactory state of trade was unusually prolonged in comparison with normal cyclical experience; there were minor revivals in 1827–8 and 1830–1, and on the latter occasion trade was for a while tolerably prosperous,[2] but these revivals were not long-lived, and in neither case does any substantial volume of investment appear to have been undertaken. One of the main reasons for this prolonged delay in the arrival of recovery was undoubtedly to be found in the predominance of high corn imports during the period. The price of wheat was consistently high, and in no year between 1824 and 1832 were wheat imports negligible. The worst harvests were in 1828, 1829 and 1830; for three years in succession the annual rate of expenditure on imported wheat exceeded £3½ million. The harvest of 1831 was somewhat better, but corn imports remained high. 1833 was the first full year when the harvest factor was entirely favourable.

As was seen in Chapter VII, the fall in expenditure on corn imports in 1833 was not offset to more than a relatively small degree by unfavourable developments in other items in the foreign trade balance, and the harvest improvement is no doubt to be regarded as the most important proximate cause for the revival that took place in 1833. But little further improvement on this score took place in 1834, and the net effect of foreign trade in the latter year, as measured by the movement of the 'income balance' (see Chapter VII) was unfavourable. The tendency for stocks of corn to accumulate in consequence of the continuing abundance of the harvest in 1834 and 1835 exerted some favourable influence on incomes, but it seems unlikely that this influence was of comparable importance to that which had been experienced from the reduction in expenditure on corn imports in 1833. In large part, therefore, the explanation of the rise in profits and investment in and after 1834 requires to be sought elsewhere than in the balance of foreign trade or the consequences of harvest fluctuations.

The main elements of the explanation have already been discussed in earlier pages, especially in Chapters VIII, IX and X. In broad outline they appear to be similar to the forces that are normally thought of in trade-cycle theory as contributing to the creation of a more favourable climate for investment when the

[1] Sweezy, *Monopoly and Competition in the English Coal Trade, 1550–1850* (1938), p. 160.
[2] *Circular to Bankers*, 20 August 1830, 7 January 1831, 27 May 1831. On the course of fluctuations before 1830, see W. Smart, *Economic Annals of the Nineteenth Century, 1821–1830* (1917).

slump has run its course. They had been in operation some years before 1833 in a smaller degree, but had not then led to full recovery, partly on account of the adverse harvest situation.

The first of these factors may be described as the gradual absorption or digestion of the investment carried out in the previous boom. The form which this process took in the cotton industry was analysed at length in Chapter IX. There the extra capacity was brought into use by increasing output and lowering prices, and although profits fell in the process, the extent to which they fell was limited by cost-reducing technical advances which entrepreneurs were driven to seek out, by the tendency for expansion within a firm—whether vertical or horizontal—to carry with it economies of scale, and by the fact that demand was not actually falling but was either rising slowly or else was fairly elastic (especially in the export market in northern Europe). As a result, surplus capacity was absorbed, and a state of affairs was gradually reached in which an increase in demand could elicit much more considerable investment expenditure than it would have done a few years earlier.

Somewhat similar processes were probably taking place in other manufacturing industries, as also in building and shipbuilding. In each of the latter industries, a large amount of capital had been brought into existence in recent years and time was required to absorb it. In each, moreover, it was likely that it would be gradually absorbed, even in the absence of a rise in the money value of the national income. Mere growth of population would tend to increase the demand for houseroom (accompanied, probably, by a reduction in demand for the products of less capitalistic industries), and the migration of rural dwellers to the towns had the same effect. Shipping and shipbuilding benefited from the rise in the volume of the country's foreign and coasting trades, which was being brought about by the continuing increase in production. It is possible also that, in both shipbuilding and house-building, investment had in some sectors of the market fallen so low as to fail to provide fully for replacement—a stage which was certainly not reached in cotton, and probably not in most branches of manufacturing industry.

A second category of forces favouring revival includes two events whose timing was of a largely fortuitous character. First of these was the beginning of work on the several railway schemes that were prompted by the example of the Liverpool and Manchester. By 1834, the rate of annual expenditure on railway building is estimated for the first time to have approached the £1 million mark. It was argued in Chapter VIII that this may be regarded as a non-cyclical phenomenon in the sense that the growth of railway-building activity (as distinct from railway promotion) in 1834–6 was the result not of current changes in the state of business but rather of the fillip given to railway projects by the opening of the Liverpool and Manchester Railway in 1830 on the one hand, and on the other hand of the long delays involved (for technical reasons) between the projection of the railways launched under the inspiration of the Liverpool and Manchester and the start of work on actual construction.

In a different sense, however, the first (pre-mania) phase of the railway promotion boom of the 1830's was not devoid of a cyclical element. By explaining it with reference to the example of the Liverpool and Manchester, and thus giving prominence to 'imitation', we are moving close to the Schumpeterian theory of the clustering of innovations.[1] The exact timing of the growth of railway promotion was, even on this reckoning, largely the result of fortuitous circumstances, in that the date when the Liverpool and Manchester opened was determined by the technical difficulties encountered in its construction. For this reason there is one important difference between the causal nexus suggested and that implied by Schumpeter's model, since in the latter the original innovating entrepreneur and his imitators both carry out their investment within the time-span of the same cyclical upswing; whereas, in the case at present under consideration, the gestation period of the original innovation was so long that imitation, instead of taking place in the same upswing, helped to inaugurate the following one. But the tendency for the inception of many new railway schemes to be grouped together as a result of the example of the Liverpool and Manchester did mean that railway building, even before the mania stage had been reached, did not proceed in the regular manner sometimes expected of innovatory investment, but instead contributed appreciably to fluctuations in the aggregate of investment expenditure.

Railways building did not yet in 1833 and 1834 contribute a great deal directly to the increase in effective demand. But the spectacle of these novel and ambitious new works being set under way exercised a favourable effect on confidence, a factor whose importance is not to be underrated. The effect on confidence was probably also of moment in connection with the second of the two fortuitous circumstances mentioned. This was the encouragement which was given to the development of joint-stock banks by the 'Declaratory Clause' of the Bank Charter Act of 1833. The growth of banking facilities helped to prevent the recovery in business from leading to any credit shortage, and in some cases it apparently played a still more active part, stimulating investment by the provision of finance on easy terms. The timing of the Act of 1833 was from the cyclical point of view entirely arbitrary, since it was determined by the date of expiration of the Bank of England's charter. But it was argued in Chapter XI that the Act of 1833 cannot be held entirely responsible for the increase in the number of new joint-stock banks formed, since only London banks were affected by the Declaratory Clause, and the growth of joint-stock banks after 1833 was at least equally rapid in the provinces. Moreover, although relatively little had been done for the first few years after the passage of the in some ways more important Act of 1826, activity in the sphere of bank promotion had been growing for some time before 1833. It seems, therefore, that legislation does not provide the whole explanation and that a general revival of business confidence must have been partly responsible for evoking increased interest in joint-stock banks in the early 1830's—and on this a little more requires to be said.

The process by which the course of time repairs the psychological damage created by a slump and crisis once some measure of stability has been attained is a commonplace of business-cycle literature, and was given particular attention by older writers.[2] The nature of the process can only be stated in very general terms with reference to the length of time elapsing since the last boom and crisis, the stabilisation of prices and the absence of any seriously inhibiting factors such as

[1] Cf. J. A. Schumpeter, *Business Cycles* (1939), Chapter III, especially pp. 99–101.
[2] Cf. A. C. Pigou, *Industrial Fluctuations* (1929), Chapters III–VII; F. Lavington, *The Trade Cycle* (1922), pp. 54–6; also Schumpeter, pp. 151–5.

harvest failures. It appears most likely that a psychological recovery of this sort played some independent part, if not a very large one, in the revival of investment and business generally in the early 1830's. The increasing interest in joint-stock banks just cited seems to require to be explained at least partly in these terms.

The same sort of thing no doubt took place in other sectors of the economy as well. In most cases the effect of the revival in confidence was naturally to encourage activity. But the improvement in confidence had one or two manifestations that tended in the opposite direction. Speculation in Spanish securities in 1834 and early 1835 contributed to the drain of bullion from the Bank of England which led to higher discount rates. Speculation in imported commodities in 1833 tended to depress business by lowering manufacturers' profit margins, in so far as industrial raw materials were involved, and by increasing consumers' expenditure on imports in money terms. This latter increase was admittedly balanced by an increase in exports to some of the countries the value of whose own exports had been enhanced by the rise in prices, but increased expenditure on imports from northern Europe, for example, did not stimulate exports to any great extent, and the net effect was unfavourable. In 1834 most of the import prices that had been driven up by speculation fell again, and pressure from this source ceased; but in the meanwhile it had been an impediment to trade, and in its absence business would have been more generally prosperous in 1833 than it was.

Summing up, then, on this first phase of the cycle, we may say that the factors contributing to the recovery included harvest improvement, progressive absorption of previous investment, development in the spheres of railway promotion and banking and also a more general revival of confidence. But it would be a mistake to exaggerate the extent of the recovery to which these factors had given rise by the end of 1834. Some of the factors quoted had already been operative to a lesser degree at an earlier date, when the state of trade was felt none the less to be dull, and in both 1833 and 1834 there were certain elements in the situation which were not favourable to prosperity. In consequence, some industries, like the iron industry, remained depressed, and the volume of investment, though rising, was as yet by no means high.

2. THE BOOM, 1835–1836

The second cyclical phase consists of the boom years 1835 and 1836, culminating in the 'mania' period of spring and early summer 1836.

During the first part of 1835 most of the favourable tendencies that had been in operation in the previous year continued without fundamental change. The same factors as had previously been encouraging investment in manufacturing and in construction continued to do so to an increasing extent, and the growth of investment led to a growth in income and demand. But before the year was very far advanced a new element entered into the situation. This was the development of boom conditions in the United States which succeeded the minor recession of 1834, and brought a tremendous increase in the demand for British exports. This in itself would have been sufficient to raise the level of activity in this country considerably above that which had prevailed in 1834.

But the improvement in the American trade was not the only new favourable feature in the situation. In May 1835 the foreign exchanges ceased to move unfavourably, and some of the gold that had flowed out in the last eighteen months began to return. The tendency that had been in evidence in 1833 and 1834 for discount rates to rise was accordingly arrested and then reversed at just the time when trade was in any case beginning to become especially active.

The improvement in the exchanges which was responsible for this was the result partly of the cessation of the Spanish security speculation and partly of a certain amount of dis-stocking of imports, the relative significance of the two factors being difficult to ascertain.[1] The drawing on stocks referred to helped to improve the overall balance of payments and so reduce the discount rate; but its direct effect on incomes through the 'income balance' and the foreign-trade multiplier was unfavourable. Consumers' expenditure on imports rose sharply as their prices were sent up; but since the volume of imports was relatively low, the purchasing power of overseas suppliers did not rise in proportion, and exports to certain of our leading foreign markets showed a tendency to sag. According to the calculations shown in Chapter VII, the favourable movement in the overall income balance in 1835 was not very great, notwithstanding the rise in exports to the United States. However, a large part of the rise in expenditure on imports in 1835 must evidently have been 'induced' by the rise in incomes, and there can be little doubt that if it were possible to isolate autonomous factors, the unfavourable effects of disinvestment in import inventories would be found to fall short by a considerable margin of the influence exerted in the opposite direction by the rise in exports to the United States and the other favourable items in the income balance. But none the less, the tendency to draw upon import stocks in 1835 exerted an unfavourable influence on incomes through the foreign-trade multiplier effect, in contrast to the favourable influence it exerted through the monetary effect.

In Chapter XI it was argued that the supply of money and money substitutes was endowed with considerable elasticity, and the conclusion was drawn that movements in discount rates within moderate dimensions were on that account unlikely as a rule to have any very great effect on trade. It might therefore be supposed that the favourable monetary effect of movements in the foreign balance in 1835–6 was only of minor significance. In fact, however, it is not certain that this was so. The actual extent of the fall in the discount rate was slight, but coming as it did at a critical stage of the boom it appears to have had an important psychological effect. The last stages of the boom, especially its culmination in the spring and early summer of 1836, were marked by a 'mania', a sudden excessive improvement in business confidence, of whose nature we shall speak further in a moment; and its timing strongly suggests that the fall in discount rates was at least the proximate cause. It was probably no more than a proximate cause; the stage had been set for the mania by the continuance of tolerably active and improving trade for several years and by the sudden fillip given by the American demand in 1835.

What is meant by saying that the final stages of the boom were characterised by a mania and that this mania was responsible for many of the features both of the boom and its aftermath? In brief, 'mania'—the term is borrowed from the writers of the day—may be described as a sudden rise in profit expectations and weakening of normal standards of business caution unjustified (or not fully

[1] See p. 92.

justified) by current changes in the objective rate of profit, and investment may be called 'maniacal' when so motivated. It is not suggested that all of the increase in investment expenditure that took place in 1835–6 was of this description; undoubtedly the objective rate of profit had already risen to a substantial extent by 1835 for reasons already discussed. But it does appear that the change in the tempo of business that took place in the autumn of 1835 and after requires to be explained largely in psychological terms. Of course, as the boom advanced, the rise in investment (whether the investment was 'maniacal' in origin or not) led to a rise in incomes which justified the investment *ex post* (at least temporarily) and also induced further investment by raising profit rates. Much investment, moreover, which was undertaken in a spirit of irrational optimism, and brought disappointing returns to those who had sunk their capital in it, none the less proved of the greatest social utility—railways providing the most obvious example. But it remained true that irrational optimism was largely responsible for the original motivation of the investment in question. To be more specific:

(1) The great crop of new railway projects appearing in the last phase of the boom could not be justified by objective changes in profit conditions, and the same was true of many of the other joint-stock flotations of the period in mining and other fields. Many of these projects admittedly did not lead to much investment until a somewhat later date, and so did not contribute directly to the increase in activity in 1835–6, but a long delay of this sort was not by any means universal.

(2) Bank formation is an item of rather special character. That many of the banks formed in 1836 were 'maniacal' in the sense defined, and that many existing banks expanded their operations very freely and incautiously in the boom, is not to be doubted. Actual expenditure by banks on bricks and mortar was not an important item, of course, but the easing of the supply of credit to industry was. This easing is not fully reflected in recorded figures of discount rates, since it largely took the form of relaxing security conditions. Probably this was the principal respect in which the effects of the mania extended to manufacturing industry, since the boom in joint-stock company flotation was chiefly confined to railways, finance and mining. Similarly, in retailing and wholesaling, instances are quoted of banks pressing loans on small traders. The mania was liable to affect the business expectations of manufacturers and traders themselves directly, and this too was probably not without its significance; but the supply of credit was probably more important as the means by which the general prosperity was conveyed to regions not much affected directly by the rise in exports to America or the other more outstanding features of the boom.

(3) The over-extension of operations by firms engaged in the finance of exports to the United States was another manifestation of the mania, as was the uncritical readiness with which their acceptances were received in the London discount market.[1] Had it not been for this, exports to the United States might have suffered a serious check.

---

[1] The purchase of long-term American bonds which also helped indirectly to finance the growth of exports to the American market can hardly be regarded as 'maniacal', since at the time of issue these bonds appeared sound enough, even on a sober appraisal, and they had been sold in large quantities for some while before the mania proper can be deemed to have started.

These were the chief manifestations of the mania. Speculation in commodities was not a form which the mania took to any great extent. There were, however, in 1836 substantial rises in prices brought about by the general increase in demand and by the need to replenish the stocks of imported goods which had been run down in 1835. The restocking which took place in 1836 led to an increase in the value of imports outstripping the increase in consumers' expenditure on imports, and as this in turn led to an expansion of exports, it had an inflationary effect which was the counterpart of the deflationary effect mentioned above that had arisen from the dis-stocking of 1835. This provided a further stimulus to business in 1836, and helped to account for the high tide of the boom being reached in that year. On the other hand, by giving Britain an adverse balance of trade *vis-à-vis* Europe it may have contributed in a minor degree to the adverse movement of the foreign exchanges which began in the second quarter of the year, and which was reflected a little later in a rise in discount rates.

To summarise the main features of the concluding phase of the upswing in 1835 and 1836: the same factors as had led to the cumulative growth of investment and incomes in 1833 and 1834 continued to operate with equal or greater force in 1835 and 1836. To these factors were added the consequences of the American boom and the unexpected easing of the credit position brought about by the influx of bullion in 1835 and early 1836. Finally, there took place a semi-pathological increase in confidence which carried the boom to new heights and accounted for the outstanding features of its concluding stages in the first half of 1836.

3. THE RECESSION, 1837

The next phase of the cycle to be discussed is the recession of 1837. A difficulty that arises before we endeavour to explain its causes is that a certain amount of doubt exists on just how serious and widespread the recession was. There were substantial falls in almost all prices and in both value and volume of exports, and a good many reports were heard of unemployment and distress in industrial districts.[1] But consumption of raw cotton and a number of other important commodities continued to rise scarcely less rapidly than in 1836; railway-building activity rose, and though brick production fell somewhat, it remained above the level of 1835 and continued to do so notwithstanding a further slight fall in 1838.

However, there is no denying that there was a recession of some sort. Equally certain is that it was in very large part attributable to the decline in exports to the United States, a decline to be explained principally with reference to causes on the American rather than on the British side. The industries that suffered most in 1837 were those that relied on the American market, and many of the other features of the recession can be traced back to the same source. But even apart from the American crash, some falling off from the high-water-mark of the early summer of 1836 was inevitable, and had indeed taken place well before the beginning of 1837. It is of the essence of speculative manias to be of short duration, and there is no need to look for very abstruse reasons to explain why the joint-stock company mania of 1836 came to a halt. It did not end spectacularly; already in July 1836 it was on the wane, but there was nothing in the way of a crisis till well into 1837.

[1] Cf. *Annual Register*, 1837, chronicle pp. 55–6.

Probably the proximate cause of the tailing away from the middle of 1836 onwards was the increasing stringency of credit, which was caused by the adverse balance of payments, just as the fall in discount rates had earlier helped to initiate the mania. The result was a sharp curtailment in the number of 'maniacal' new investment projects planned in the latter part of 1836, and a still further curtailment in 1837. The immediate effect on physical investment was probably not great, since most of the boom-time projects that were actually carried out were of such a character as to be stretched out in their actual execution for quite a time after they had been begun. But it required the passage of only a short space of time for the unsound or fraudulent nature of many of the projects to become clear, and when this happened, as it did progressively throughout 1837, the prejudicial effect on confidence was bound to be severe. The failure of the Anglo-American finance houses and the difficulties experienced by the Northern and Central Bank and the Agricultural and Commercial Bank of Ireland were prominent examples. The effect on confidence of these and other failures was the reason for the monetary stringency in the earlier part of 1837, since the foreign exchanges had ceased to be unfavourable before the end of 1836.

In one important category of investment, railway building, there was no fall in 1837, but instead a rise of moderate dimensions. There was also a rise in ship-building and probably also in investment in coalmining. But in investment in manufacturing industry there was clearly a decline, and in total this probably somewhat surpassed the increases in investment in the categories just mentioned. The decline in aggregate investment seems to have been accounted for principally by the collapse of the mania and its repercussions on confidence and credit and by the depressing effect of the decline in exports. There does not appear to be any evidence that either rising costs in the investment goods' industries or falling profit rates occasioned by the increase in capacity created by previous investment played any important part in initiating the recession. As far as the latter is concerned, much of the investment projected in the boom did not really bear fruit and lead to competitive pressure on profits till rather later. A certain amount of pressure may already have been felt in 1837, but there is little suggestion that it was this which first turned the boom into recession.

The violent recession in the United States, aggravated in its effects on British exports by the collapse of a large part of the financial mechanism by which Anglo-American trade had been organised and financed, was, as has been stated, the most important depressive influence in the British economy in 1837. But other items in the foreign-trade balance also had some significance. One of the subsidiary causes of the prosperity of 1836 had been the building up of stocks of imports, which, by increasing the purchasing power of certain of our overseas suppliers, had led to a greater proportional increase in British exports to them than in expenditure by British consumers on the imports in question. The building up of stocks in 1836 meant that some fall in the volume of imports would have been likely in 1837, even in the absence of any fall in demand. As it was, the fall in demand owing to the recession greatly strengthened this tendency, and the fall in the volume of imports was very drastic, inventory investment being replaced by a certain amount of inventory disinvestment. There was accordingly an adverse movement in the income balance *vis-à-vis* those foreign countries whose demand for our exports was dependent on the value of their exports to us. As against this, however, there was a favourable movement in the income balance *vis-à-vis* northern Europe; our exports to this area actually rose in value, as a result of the elasticity of demand for British exports which apparently prevailed there in response to falls in prices, and of the tendency for the level of activity in certain Continental countries to be still on the upgrade.

The figures given in Chapter VII show, as is to be expected, a substantial deterioration in the aggregate income balance in 1837. It was suggested, however, that the fall in the level of expenditure on imports in that year was not entirely due to the fall in incomes, and that the fall in import prices which largely accounted for it was partly explicable by the abnormally high prices reached in 1836 as a result of the need to rebuild stocks after they had been run down in 1835. In so far as this was so, one would expect the consequence to be a switch of consumers' spending away from imports towards home goods, off-setting in some measure the tendency for the demand for home goods to decline as a result of the fall in incomes. It is possible that there may here be found some part of the explanation of the remarkable rise in the value (as well as the volume) of cotton goods sold to home consumers in 1837. Shifts in income from export industries to industries catering for the home market may well have been an important feature of the transition from the boom of 1836 to the recession of 1837.

In any case, the fall in import prices was one of the factors that limited the severity of the recession. Others were the rise in railway building and the carry-over of investment projected in the boom. Most important of all as far as the maintenance of high output was concerned was the anxiety of entrepreneurs to use their capacity fully even in face of poor demand and at the cost of lower profit margins. To this point we shall recur.

4. UNEVEN RECOVERY, 1838–1840

The peculiarities of the years 1838–40 arise from the interaction of different rhythms in different sectors of the economy. The behaviour of the foreign-trade balance during these years was subject to the operation of a large number of complex factors which have been described in earlier chapters and need not here be recapitulated at length. Suffice it to say that in 1838 there was a natural rebound from the extreme violence of the recession that had affected our export trades in 1837. There was some revival in exports to the United States; disinvestment in import inventories, with its adverse effect on the income balance, ceased; and there was something of a boom in Belgium and France. At the same time merchants were still too cautious after the troubles they had suffered in 1836–7 for the rise in import prices to be anything other than very moderate.

Already before the end of 1838 the increase in corn imports consequent upon the harvest failure was beginning to cause a reversal in the trend of the income balance. It was preceded and accompanied by deflationary drawing on domestic stocks of corn to an extent which may have been substantial. The continued growth in corn imports was chiefly responsible for the very sharp adverse tendency in the income balance in 1839, although at the same time a number of other unfavourable factors were also at work, including an unexpected rise in several import prices owing to supply difficulties. The increase in exports was not a sufficient offset. The balance of payments had a seriously depressing effect on the level of activity in 1839, both by the operation of the foreign-trade multiplier and by raising interest rates. In 1840 corn imports were lower and a certain amount of relief was felt from a number of other sources as well; but even so the income balance remained a good deal less favourable than it had been in 1838, and the gold lost by the Bank of England in 1839 did not return in any quantity.

The level of domestic investment as a whole in 1838–40 was probably less than the level attained in 1835–6 by an appreciable margin, even though the gap was less than might have been expected. Railway building rose steeply in 1838 and remained high till 1840, with 1839 probably the peak year of the three. This was the delayed result of the mania of 1836, and constituted the chief inflationary element in the economy in the years 1838–40. The building and completion of railways brought with it some other types of investment as well; in such a region as County Durham the railways made possible the sinking of coal mines in locations which had previously lacked transport facilities. But as yet this creation of 'new economic space' (to use Schumpeter's term) was probably of significance in a few instances only. The main stimulus to demand provided by railway building was through the constructional expenditure itself.

In some branches of investment, expansion of capacity had not yet in 1836 gone so far as to exhaust profitable openings, and for them the recession of 1837 came, so to speak, prematurely. The most striking case in point is shipbuilding. Building in some regions, notably London, may perhaps also be taken as an example, since the boom in building in many parts of the country had not yet attained more than moderate dimensions by 1836; however, the rise in brick production between 1836 and 1840 was, in many areas, due less to this cause than to railway building.

In most branches of manufacturing industry the years 1838–40 witnessed a pronounced decline in the level of investment, though not yet its complete cessation. The general business recession of 1837 was, as has been explained, due in its origins to the fall in exports to America and the inevitable reaction from the mania period rather than to exhaustion of investment opportunities; but when the dust of 1837 had settled, it became clear that capital accumulation had proceeded to a point which involved severe competitive pressure on prices and profit margins, and in 1838–40 this pressure became the principal factor, and a very powerful one, in discouraging investment.

The reasons which led to the continuance of a certain amount of investment in manufacturing industry, notwithstanding the decline in profits, were in part similar to those that had brought about a continued growth of capacity in the cotton industry in the late 1820's. Factories required to be filled with machinery, and the pressure on profits made entrepreneurs anxious to seek out methods of reducing costs, even if they involved a certain amount of capital expenditure. In some cases, too, the length of the gestation period delayed the completion of investment projected during the boom till well beyond the end of 1837. But there was also more completely new investment than there had been in the late 1820's, and this may be taken to suggest that although older firms were not doing too well, the profit rate was still high enough to attract new capital to the construction of plant of the latest design. The principal reason for this was most probably that the high level of railway-building activity, together with a number of other favourable factors mentioned above, caused the national income to decline less than might have been expected after the boom had passed its peak. The effect of railway building was particularly prominent in the iron industry, where, despite complaints of falling profits, capacity continued to grow rapidly, especially in Scotland. In textiles, the effect of railway building was not as direct as in the iron industry, but the support afforded by railway building to the national income generally helped to prevent profit rates from falling to true depression levels.

If investment decisions are thought of as a function partly of the quantity of capital capacity in existence, and partly of the level of the national income,[1] we may say that although in textiles in 1838–40 the capacity factor was unfavourable as a result of investment undertaken during the boom, the national-income factor, especially in 1838, was more favourable than is commonly experienced in cyclical contractions, and the amount of new investment put in hand was therefore not altogether negligible. By contrast, in such industries as shipbuilding the relative smallness of the expansion in capacity achieved before 1836 was probably the more important factor in sustaining the level of investment in the ensuing years.

The difficulty of interpreting the cyclical pattern in 1838–40 is mainly the result of the conflicting movements of foreign trade and domestic investment. In aggregate, domestic investment probably fell in 1837 and recovered in 1838 with the growth of railway building; 1839 saw a further rise in railway building and probably in investment as a whole, leading to a level not enormously less than that of 1836. In 1840 there was a decline in some branches of investment, but others rose, and in all the decline does not seem to have been very great. But whereas domestic investment thus appears to have reached a peak in 1839 (albeit a peak not standing much higher than its neighbours), 1839 was much the worst year in our entire period as far as the foreign-trade balance was concerned; and it is difficult not to believe that the adverse tendency on the foreign trade side in 1839 made the aggregate level of effective demand lower than in either 1838 or 1840—quite apart from the reduction in the real value of output and consumption due to the harvest failure. The assignation of 1839 as a peak in business-cycle chronology thus appears to be an error, based, doubtless, on the movement of exports, which was unrepresentative, and on that of prices, which was the result of special causes mostly on the supply side and did not extend to the generality of British manufactures—as the movement of the value/volume ratio (i.e. price) of exports bears witness. The occurrence of a balance of payments crisis in 1839 may also have contributed to the year's having been identified as a 'minor peak', since such crises are commonly regarded as natural concomitants of inflationary situations.

Taking a general view of the three years 1838–40 together, investment, as has been said, was apparently lower than in 1835–6, if not by a very great margin, and the foreign trade position was much worse than in the former boom period when corn imports had been negligible and exports to America had been a good deal higher. Money incomes must therefore have been lower in total. But the

[1] Cf. M. Kalecki, *Essays in the Theory of Economic Fluctuations* (1939), pp. 116–49, and N. Kaldor, 'Mr Hicks on the trade cycle', *Economic Journal* (1951), pp. 837–41.

volume of industrial output was almost certainly considerably higher than in 1835–6, because of the great increase in capacity that had taken place in the meanwhile, and the anxiety of entrepreneurs to use that capacity to the full. So it was in practically all the industries discussed in Chapter IX and X. Industrial prices and profits were falling steadily, and this was, indeed, the main feature of the period; but it did not check the growth of output, and may even in some cases have accelerated it by giving entrepreneurs a stronger incentive to introduce more efficient methods of production.

This inelasticity of supply, which was stressed by contemporaries no less in this period than it had been eight or ten years earlier, possibly helped to stabilise money incomes as well as real incomes, in so far as it carried with it a redistribution of real income away from profit to wages—a redistribution that was much commented on and complained of by the entrepreneurial class, particularly in the cotton districts—and so brought about a reduction in the propensity to save. We have not in earlier chapters devoted any discussion to the possibility of changes in the propensity to save, since nothing can be said about it that is not conjectural to the highest degree. Whether the propensity to save was higher or lower in 1837–40 than it had been in the upswing phase is uncertain, since there were forces pulling in opposite directions. On the one hand, the fall in profits, as just observed, shifted the distribution of income in a direction favourable to high consumption, especially in comparison with the years 1835 and 1836 when profits were highest. On the other hand, the rise in the price of corn at the end of the 1830's involved a shift of real purchasing power from wage earners to farmers, and this operated in the opposite direction. Moreover, such investment as continued to take place after 1837 was probably more largely financed out of current savings than had been the case in the earlier years, when the banking boom was at its height and bank finance was most readily obtainable. The difficulty experienced by many railway companies in getting shareholders to pay up their calls once railway building really got under way suggests that many shareholders were obliged to make their contributions to railway finance in ways that involved curtailment of consumption; and the same may well have been true of cost-reducing investment undertaken in manufacturing industry in response to competitive pressure.

5. The Depression, 1841–1842

The severity and widespread nature of the depression in 1841–2 has stood out throughout previous chapters. The deterioration of trade in these years, which was accompanied by a decline in output even in those industries where it had continued to rise after 1837, was not due to foreign trade. Both the direct effect, as measured by the income balance, and the monetary effect, as measured by the overall balance of payments, moved favourably, especially in 1842. All the evidence goes to support the judgement expressed in the issue of the *Circular to Bankers* of 8 October 1841, that the principal cause of the trouble was 'the interruption in the internal exchanges of commodities...and not in the diminution of foreign trade.' Exports to the United States staged a minor recovery in 1841, and though they fell away badly in 1842, this was offset by a substantial increase in exports to northern Europe and by the favourable movement of the income balance *vis-à-vis* 'other' countries, brought about by the extensive, albeit doubtless largely unplanned, accumulation of import inventories in that year.

The deterioration in trade that took place in 1841–2 was primarily caused by the fall in domestic investment. Railway building contracted sharply, especially in 1842, as the lines under construction were progressively completed. Industries like coalmining and shipbuilding, whose expansion had not by 1836 gone so far as to preclude further development in 1837–40, now at last found that satiety had been reached. In manufacturing industry, although the peak in investment had been reached in 1836, the growth of capacity had by no means entirely ceased in 1837–40, and this led to still further competitive pressure on profits, until finally any large-scale new investment became out of the question. The increasing number of bankruptcies and bank failures caused confidence to be weakened, and there was scarcely any important sector of the economy where investment did not decline. The low value of capital equipment as security made banks extremely reluctant to lend to manufacturers,[1] and this—as in 1837–40, only more so—made it likely that an increasing proportion of whatever investment did take place would be financed in a way that involved a reduction in consumption. There is, moreover, reason to doubt whether there was in this depression the usual stabilising influence exerted in cyclical downswings by dis-saving undertaken in order to preserve accustomed consumption standards. Apparently, assets of working class families had, before the depression reached its acutest stage, already in many cases been heavily drawn upon as a result of the extremely high cost of living, so that by 1842 the means of dis-saving no longer existed.[2]

A detailed comparison of the depression of 1841–2 with other cyclical depressions experienced in the British economy does not fall within the scope of the present study. But discussion of the depression would be incomplete if no attempt were made to explain the reasons for its exceptional severity, a feature attested from a multitude of sources.

Our analysis has not revealed any one outstanding cause to which the severity of the depression may be attributed. But there are three factors to which the principal responsibility may perhaps be assigned.

The first and most indubitable is the harvest situation. The high prices of corn in the depression years and the large corn imports with which they were associated depressed the level of money incomes and reduced the purchasing power of such income as was still earned. (This, of course, is not inconsistent with the statement made above that the import factor did not explain the *deterioration* of conditions in 1841–2.) The prevalence of a high cost of living for several years in succession largely accounted for the exceptional intensity of the distress observed in the manufacturing districts. To distinguish between the various factors, long-term and short-term, which contributed to the high corn prices and imports of 1839–42 is not altogether easy, as was seen in Chapter IV; but the trade cycle itself did not on any reckoning play an important part in bringing them about, and this factor may therefore be deemed of an exogenous nature from the point of view of the cyclical process.

The second factor that may be held to have contributed to the severity of the slump is the severity of the depression in the United States at the same time. Here evidently there was mutual interaction; but an exceptionally acute

[1] *Circular to Bankers*, 29 July 1842.   [2] Cf. *Report on Stockport*, 1842, xxxv, pp. 219–21.

depression in the United States was to be expected in any case, in view of the violent and speculative character of the boom that had preceded it, a boom much surpassing in magnitude anything experienced in the American economy either in the 1820's or in the 1840's.

The importance of the third factor to be mentioned is more debatable than that of the two so far discussed; but it may well have been substantial. A feature of the depression years was the complaint that profits were being forced down to an unprecedented degree as a result of industrial capacity being excessive in relation to demand. The fall in profits depressed investment, and also at the same time led to the reduction in output and the unemployment of labour—results which did not necessarily follow to anything like the same extent from a merely moderate decline in profits—by lowering prices below the level of prime costs and by driving entrepreneurs to bankruptcy. Now the pressure on profits of excess capacity is, of course, a regular feature of cyclical depressions; but there was in the early 1840's a factor tending to make it particularly oppressive, namely, the continued expansion of capacity that took place in many industries between 1837 and 1840 after the peak of the boom had been passed.

The reasons for this continued expansion were discussed in the previous section. In so far as it was merely the result of the carry-over of work projected in 1836 or earlier, or of capacity having in some sectors been expanded to only a moderate extent by 1836, or in so far as it represented an effort on the part of entrepreneurs to meet competition by finding ways of increasing output and efficiency, it has no special significance in the present context. But it was suggested above that it was also in part due to the maintenance of the national income at a level that was rather unusually high for a recession phase, especially in 1838 before corn imports became heavy. The principal support of the national income in these years was railway building, and when, with the decline of railway building after 1840, this support was withdrawn and incomes at last fell really seriously, entrepreneurs in textiles and other industries found themselves burdened with capacity considerably greater than would have been the case if the full force of the depression had been met immediately after 1836. Hence the exceptionally severe pressure on profits.

If this view is correct, it provides a certain link between two of the peculiar features of this cycle, namely, its 'double-headedness' and the intensity of the depression in which it closed. If the railway building and the other expenditures which sustained income in 1838–40 had instead been carried out in 1835–6, the boom at that time would, of course, have been to that extent more violent than it was, and the stimulus to investment in manufacturing industry would have been likewise greater. Had that been so, the boom having been particularly powerful, we should have expected a correspondingly violent recession. But there are limits to the extent to which capacity in an industry can be increased in the space of one or two years, and it is extremely probable that the deferment of the peak of railway building till some time after 1836, by keeping effective demand at a tolerably high level for a considerable while after the boom had passed, caused the total expansion of capacity in manufacturing to be greater than it would have been if the peak in railway building had come in 1836. If so, the same factors as were responsible for the double-headedness of the cycle may be held to have contributed to the severity of the ultimate slump.

The three factors just mentioned are probably those to which the greatest weight should be attached. In addition there were, of course, other causes which may have had a share in causing the depression to be a particularly bad one. The folly of some of the investment undertaken in the boom; the instability of parts of the banking system; the unusually rapid increase in the young adult age group in the population—all these may have played some part in earning for this depression its especially bad reputation.

6. THE PATTERN OF THE CYCLE

If we regard the years 1837–42 as forming a single cyclical contraction phase, this phase must appear long, confused and heterogeneous. But in many respects it is really more readily understandable than the upswing phase which preceded it. The basic characteristic of the years of contraction was the progressive depression of profits and of the marginal efficiency of capital which was brought about in consequence of earlier decisions—partly 'maniacal' decisions—to expand capacity. But this basic tendency was overlaid by a number of complicating factors, in particular (1) the inevitable reaction in 1837 from the more extreme manifestations of the mania of 1836, (2) the effects of fluctuations in business in the United States, (3) the long gestation period of much of the investment projected when the boom was at its height, and (4) fluctuations in harvests and corn imports.

The first and second of these factors were together responsible for the suddenness of the deterioration in the climate of business in 1837, a deterioration which was in some respects more extreme than was justified by the underlying realities of the situation at that time, and which was in consequence followed shortly by a certain recovery. The second factor also contributed more generally to the unfavourable state of trade during the contraction phase, since exports to the United States did not nearly regain their 1835–6 level even in such relatively good years as 1839. The third of the factors mentioned, in conjunction with the fact that in a good many investment lines satiety had not yet been reached when the storm broke in 1837, meant that in some sectors of the economy investment remained high or even rising till 1840, and that there was thus a substantial delay between the turning point of 1836 and the advent of the depression in its full force. The fourth factor, harvests and corn imports, accounted for much of the gravity of the depression, and also for the unsatisfactory state of trade in 1839, a year when certain of the other relevant variables—railway building and exports to the United States—were relatively favourable.

These and other complications which have been discussed in earlier pages had a good deal of influence on the details and timing of the pattern of fluctuations between 1837 and 1842. But they did not conceal the fact that the basic cause of what seemed to entrepreneurs to be so unsatisfactory a state of trade was the pressure on profits of capacity built during the boom (or during the next few years as a result of decisions reached during the boom), and the consequent fall in the marginal efficiency of investment. The rise and fall of railway building involved some important special considerations, but fundamentally it conformed to the same pattern. The slump was the logical consequence of the boom.

It is not so easy to single out any one characteristic or dominant feature of the

217

boom. That there was a cumulative interaction of some sort between investment and income can hardly be doubted. But the upswing phase seems to have owed a good deal to a number of circumstances of an extraneous or even fortuitous character. An improvement in the harvest was what started it off. The further improvement in trade in 1835 was heavily dependent on the boom in the United States, and the increase in expenditure on railway building in that year and in 1836 was to be explained with reference to much earlier events, and not by the current relationship between demand and capacity, or anything of that sort. Finally, the concluding stages of the boom can hardly be explained without the supposition of a largely irrational improvement of expectations. In contrast, irrational pessimism does not seem to have played an important role in the recession. One is left with the impression that in this particular cycle the upswing was a less simple phenomenon than the downswing, although it so happened that the course of the downswing was interrupted and confused by a variety of complicating factors.

That we should find the upswing more difficult to explain than the downswing is from one point of view not altogether surprising. Students of the theory of the trade cycle—and this applies equally to modern and to older theoretical writers—have usually found it tolerably easy to explain how an upward movement in economic activity, especially in investment, is liable when once under way to proceed by its own momentum to a level higher than can be permanently maintained, with the result that a falling-off presently becomes inevitable. But in explaining how the upswing is originally initiated, economists have often been compelled to fall back on general references of a not entirely satisfactory character to the long-run forces making for economic progress. In our present case, the difficulty is not confined to the initiation of the upswing, since, even after its earliest stages were passed, the upswing appears to have required to be sustained to an appreciable degree by extraneous forces. The two questions, why was there an upward movement to start with, and why did it go to lengths which made a recession inevitable, are thus not entirely distinct, though they are distinct in some respects.[1] We have not been able to give any single answer to these two related questions; all we have been able to do is to recite a number of separate factors, the relative importance of which is open to debate. If this is considered unsatisfactory, it may perhaps be taken as an indication that the theory of economic progress is as yet in a less advanced state than the theory of economic fluctuations.

So much for the pattern of the cycle looked at from the point of view of effective demand. In some respects this pattern conforms to the now most widely accepted type of theoretical model, namely, that based on the interaction of the multiplier and acceleration principle or some analogous formulation; in other not less important respects it does not. It will have been observed that, with regard to some of the latter, reference to Schumpeter's theory has proved illuminating, though it would not be true to say that our general approach has been on Schumpeterian lines.

Several allusions have been made in the last few pages to the effect of fluctuations in the United States on the course of the cycle in Britain. How should we

[1] The mania, for example, is much more relevant in answer to the latter question than it is in answer to the former one.

sum up the nature of the interaction between the two economies in the cyclical process? It was argued in Chapter V that the origins of fluctuations in the United States were fundamentally of an internal character, and lay particularly in the spheres of banking and land speculation. Economic relations with Britain had some effect on the course and character of the fluctuations undergone, and probably increased their severity to some degree, but they were not the prime cause. The reverse relationship was more important. Fluctuations in the United States undoubtedly both increased the amplitude of the cycle in Britain and had an important bearing on its timing. The American demand played a very large part in raising incomes in 1835–6 and so in creating an atmosphere favourable to the carrying out of domestic investment, 'maniacal' and other. In the absence of the rise in exports to the United States in these years, it is likely that the boom would have been delayed and would have been somewhat different in character. The advent of sharp recession in 1837 was also largely attributable to the American connection.[1]

But that does not mean that the cycle in Britain was fundamentally an 'imported' phenomenon and a reflection of the cycle in America. The mainstay of the British cycle was domestic investment, even though the behaviour of that investment was materially affected by fluctuations in the foreign balance, and there can be little doubt that, in the absence of the stimulus received from the American boom, the partly psychological cumulative interaction of income and investment would none the less in due course—perhaps when construction of the railways projected at the beginning of the 1830's got properly under way—have led to a peak from which a falling away would have been inevitable. Fluctuations in exports to the United States increased to a substantial extent the amplitude of fluctuations in *aggregate income* in Britain, but whether in their absence fluctuations in *domestic investment* would have been very much milder—as distinct from having a different timing—is much more difficult to say.

The most outstanding difference between the picture that has emerged of fluctuations in the British economy in our period and that which we should have been led to expect from customary views of the trade cycle is in relation to the volume of output (and the level of employment, which generally moved with it). Investment appears to have reached its peak in 1836, and between then and 1840 prices and profits were falling in most sectors of the economy; yet in the cotton industry, above all, and also in coal, iron and possibly the woollen and worsted industries, output continued to rise till 1840, the rise in the cotton industry (apart from the abnormal year 1839) being scarcely less rapid than it had been before 1836. For a variety of reasons previously discussed, capacity did not cease to expand after 1836, and despite low prices entrepreneurs were anxious to use their capacity to the full or even to find ways of spreading their overheads by increasing their output still further. The resulting short-period inelasticity or negative elasticity of supply, which was so marked a feature of the period, may perhaps be attributed in part to the marriage of ownership and control which was as yet almost invariable in manufacturing industry, as well as to the re-

[1] The partial recovery in and after 1838 appears to have been primarily due in both countries to domestic rather than to internationally transmitted causes, though there was a similarity between the course of events in the two inasmuch as there were sectors of each economy in which investment had not yet reached the point of satiety when the initial sharp recession came in 1837.

latively high elasticity of demand facing the representative manufacturing firm. It was not till 1841 that the growth of output was decisively reversed, as the level of demand fell more steeply, and entrepreneurs who had been carrying on at a loss came to the end of their financial resources, or decided that prices had fallen so low that complete stoppage represented the most economic policy. Other entrepreneurs, as in the iron and coal industries, came together to restrict output by concerted action. When this stage was reached, output fell, though usually remaining well above its pre-1836 level, and employment fell still more steeply, as a result of cost-reducing innovations which continued to be carried out under the stimulus of threatening loss.

In the constructional industries, and in investment generally, the situation was, of course, quite different, and output seems to have followed a good deal more closely than in consumer goods' industries the pattern of fluctuations in demand, as determined in the case of investment industries by profits prevailing or expected at the time when the relevant investment decisions were taken. Whether for rational or irrational reasons, the volume of investment does not seem to have been much affected by the cost of capital goods; moreover, in the constructional industries reductions in real costs were not so readily effected as in factory industries, and the incentive to spread overheads by maintaining or increasing output was not present to the same degree. There were therefore not the same obstacles to a fall in output once the boom had passed its peak.

7. THE TREND OF REAL WAGES

We have not in previous chapters devoted much attention to movements of wage rates, because they do not reflect very prominently the fluctuations with which we have been mainly concerned. A brief account of the movements shown in the available series on money wage rates and the cost of living may, however, shed some light on the characteristics of the period as a whole, and may be compared with the movements just discussed in the volume of output.

The principal data are shown in Table 33. The authorities from whose calculations the figures on money wage rates are derived emphasise the conjectural nature of many of their results, especially as applied to single years taken in isolation; but the figures may none the less be taken as a fair indication of the broad trends over the period.

The year-to-year movements occurring in the individual series are many of them not easy to explain. We should not expect to find much cyclical movement in the cost of living, on account of the preponderant importance of food prices, and hence of harvest variations, in determining its fluctuations. But cyclical movement is also relatively absent from the money wage-rate series. Wages of operatives in cotton factories is the only series which shows a fairly clear-cut relationship with fluctuations in business activity. In the other series whatever relationship there may have been was evidently much obscured by frictions and lags. The rise of wage rates in agriculture between 1836 and 1839 probably reflected the rise in the prices of agricultural produce during that period. The relatively high rates of wages in engineering and shipbuilding in the years 1840–2 were no doubt connected with the late arrival of the cyclical peak in railway building and shipbuilding. Several of the series—for example, those for agri-

Table 33. *Money wage rates and the cost of living*

Year	(1) Agricultural labourers in England and Wales (1892=100)	(2) Printers (compositors) (1891=100)	(3) Operatives in cotton factories (d. per week)	(4) Cotton hand-loom weavers (d. per week)	(5) Builders (U.K. average) (1900=100)	(6) Engineers (1900=100)	(7) Shipbuilders (1900=100)	(8) London artisans (1900=100)	(9) Tucker's cost-of-living index (1835=100)	(10) Silberling's cost-of-living index (1835=100)
1830	74	78*	115	75	53†	88‡	88‡	65·3	107	109
1831	76	78*	114	72	53	88‡	88‡	63·3	113	112
1832	78	78*	114	72	53	88‡	88‡	63·2	111	110
1833	79	78	114	72	53	88‡	88‡	63·5	106	108
1834	77	78	115	84	53	91	91	62·3	102	103
1835	74	78	116	75	53	91	91	61·3	100	100
1836	75	81	117	75	54	91	91	61·2	105	112
1837	76	81	117	75	55	91	91	61·2	111	112
1838	78	81	116	75	56	91	91	61·2	112	119
1839	80	83	112	75	57	91	91	61·2	120	124
1840	80	83	112	75	57	95	91	61·2	114	122
1841	80	83	113	75	57	95	92	61·6	118	117
1842	80	83	113	75	57	92	92	61·6	103	107

* Average 1822–32. † Average 1822–32. ‡ Average 1827–33.

Sources: (1) A. L. Bowley, *Statistical Journal* (1899), LXII, p. 563; (2) Bowley, *Statistical Journal* (1899), LXII, p. 709; (3) and (4), G. H. Wood, *Wages in the Cotton Trade* (1910), p. 127; (5) Bowley, *Statistical Journal* (1901), LXIV, p. 112; (6) and (7) Bowley and Wood, *Statistical Journal* (1906), LXIX, p. 190; (8) and (9) R. S. Tucker, 'Real wages of artisans in London, 1729–1935', *Journal of the American Statistical Association* (1936), p. 79; (10) N. J. Silberling, 'British prices and business cycles, 1779–1850', *Review of Economic Statistics* (1923), p. 235.

cultural labourers, hand-loom weavers and possibly London artisans—show the effects of the upsurge of trade unionism which culminated with the formation of the Grand National Consolidated Trades Union in 1834 and its subsequent collapse.[1]

But if no striking generalisations can be made about the year-to-year movements of wage rates, the trend characteristic is more readily discernible. A comparison of the course of money wage rates with that of the cost of living shows clearly that this was not a good period for real wages. Comparing the average of 1830–2 with the average of 1840–2, we find that two important series, London artisans and operatives in cotton factories, show an actual decline in real wages; in agriculture the rise in money wage rates scarcely did more than keep pace with the rise in the cost of living; while even in the series for builders, where the rise was greatest, the rate of increase of real wages was barely $\frac{1}{2}\%$ per annum. There was no doubt a certain shift of population from low-paid to high-paid occupations which caused the average earnings of those in full work to rise rather more than the figures in Table 33 would suggest; but the general impression remains that the extent to which the standard of living of the working class improved during the period was small—even if no account is taken of housing conditions, which are not reflected in the real wage figures, and which were notoriously a black spot in this phase of Britain's economic evolution.

In view of the strong upward trend of industrial output, this comparative stagnation of real wages may appear rather surprising. But it must be borne in mind that industrial products accounted for only a small proportion of working-class expenditure, and production of food was not increasing at nearly the same pace. The growing inability of British agriculture to provide for the needs of the population save in years of exceptionally good harvests, coupled with the restrictions imposed by the Corn Laws on the importation of supplies from abroad, kept the cost of living high. Probably there would have been pressure on the food supply even if there had been free trade in corn, since cheap foreign corn was not available in great abundance in bad harvest years; but the rapid increase in corn imports that followed the repeal of the Corn Laws supports the conclusion, suggested by *a priori* reasoning, that the operation of the Corn Laws did contribute in some measure to bringing the prophecies of Malthus nearer to fulfilment than would otherwise have been the case. It may be added that the much-complained-of tendency for competition from immigrant Irishmen to keep down the rate of pay for unskilled work was really another manifestation of pressure of population on the means of subsistence, migration causing Ireland's Malthusian problem to spill over into Great Britain.

But if inadequate food supply was one reason for the relative failure of real wages to rise, the nature of much of both the foreign and the domestic investment that was carried out during the period was also such as not to bring a great deal of benefit to real wages in Britain, at least in the short period. Capital export, consisting mainly of the purchase of United States securities, contributed relatively little to the immediate cheapening of imports, with the important exception of one commodity, cotton; and more than half of the cotton imported was in any case exported in the form of yarn or cloth. Similarly, much of the investment carried out in manufacturing industry at home was concentrated in

[1] See S. and B. Webb, *History of Trade Unionism* (1920 edition), pp. 113–79.

cotton textiles and other industries selling a large proportion of their output abroad, so that a substantial part of the benefit went to the foreign consumer and was reflected in an adverse tendency in Britain's terms of trade over the period.[1] This deterioration in the terms of trade did not necessarily mean that an hour of British labour was being exchanged for a diminishing quantity of foreign goods; but it did mean that the benefit obtained from investment expenditure which increased the productivity of labour in British industry accrued in some measure to the foreigner instead of bringing benefit to the country where the investment was undertaken. Much of the investment in manufacturing industry, moreover, was of a labour-saving character, and not all the labour displaced could be readily transferred to other employment. Outside manufacturing, railway building was the outstanding domestic investment line. Its long-run effect on the economic structure and the standard of living in Great Britain can hardly be over-estimated. But in the early 1840's this effect was still mostly in the future, for, with a few exceptions such as in the coal industry, the shifts in industrial location and reductions in real costs that were made possible by railway transport had scarcely yet had time to be realised.

8. THE PERVASIVENESS OF THE CYCLE

A question which it is natural to ask before concluding is to what extent the fluctuations that have been the subject of this study may be regarded as having pervaded the entire economy, and to what extent they were restricted to particular regions and industries.

In this connection, comparison may be made both between the experience of individual industries which were subject to fluctuations of significant amplitude, and between the experience of these industries considered as a group and that of other sectors of the economy where the impact of fluctuations in activity was less direct and less important. As far as the former comparison is concerned, it is evident that there was, especially in the years 1837–40, a good deal of divergence between the timing of fluctuations in different industries, and hence in the timing of fluctuations in income and activity in regions dependent on them. The peak of prosperity for the textile industries came in 1836, for the coal industry in 1838, for shipbuilding in 1839–40, and a still more striking discrepancy is to be found between the behaviour of the indices of brick production for different parts of the country. It appears that changes in the level of aggregate income were not a sufficiently powerful influence to be able consistently to keep different industries in step with one another, although in years of extremes of prosperity or depression, like 1836 and 1842, a fair degree of uniformity was attained. At other times, conditions peculiar to the individual industry or region were paramount in determining the extent of its prosperity.

But what of those parts of the economy that were not directly affected at all by fluctuations in exports and in investment? We should be in danger of exaggerating the importance of the fluctuations that have been described in the foregoing pages if we did not always bear in mind the preponderant importance of agriculture and its ancillary industries in most English counties at this date. To large

[1] Cf. W. W. Rostow, 'The historical analysis of the terms of trade', *Economic History Review* (1951), pp. 53–76.

classes of the population, perhaps to the majority, economic well-being varied more with the state of the harvest and the price of corn than with the fluctuations that have occupied the greater part of our attention. We should not place so much stress on the effects of harvest fluctuations on aggregate money income and effective demand as to forget their much more obvious and important effects on *real* incomes, and also their effects on the distribution of incomes. The benefits derived by farmers from bad harvests were probably less in our period than they had been at an earlier date, but a rise in the price of corn would still normally betoken a redistribution of income, sometimes a considerable one, in favour of farmers at the expense both of town dwellers and of agricultural labourers. Moreover, cyclical fluctuations themselves often involved important shifts in income from one sector of the economy to another, as was suggested on p. 211 with reference to 1837. Likewise the labour employed in the railway building which was the principal support of investment after 1838 was of a totally different character from the labour employed in most of the investment lines that preponderated in 1835–6. The imperfect synchronisation of fluctuations as between industries and as between home and export markets, in conjunction with the high proportion of the population dependent on an industry where output and prices were governed more by the weather than by the level of demand, meant that changes in the distribution of income between social classes and between industry groups were a feature of short-period fluctuations scarcely less important than changes in the aggregate of incomes.

On the other hand, we should not underrate the pervasiveness of the fluctuations we have described. The prosperity of 1836 and the depression at the end of the period seem in particular to have been pretty general throughout the country. There were a variety of ways in which a district not directly interested either in exports or in industries where investment was particularly active might none the less be affected by the fluctuations proceeding elsewhere. Many small towns in rural districts had one or two manufacturing industries catering for a widespread market. The rate of flow of labourers from country to town was governed by the employment opportunities in industry, and when these opportunities were poor the pressure of population on the land was felt more acutely. The construction of railways had an influence over a very wide area. Finally, even entirely agricultural regions were affected by the boom in joint-stock bank formation, and it appears that local traders were often induced to expand their operations by the free availability of bank finance during the boom. This last link may well have been the most important of all.

INDEX